CW00554166

AN UNCERTAIN VOYAGE

Also by the author:

No Memorial

The Power to Silence
A History of Punishment in Britain

A House in Bow Street
Crime and the Magistracy London 1740-1881

The English Bastille
A History of Newgate Gaol and Prison Conditions in Britain
1188-1902

The Rule of Law in Britain
From the Roman Occupation to the Present Day

For the Sake of Example
Capital Courts-Martial 1914-1920

Military Intervention in Britain
From the Gordon Riots to the Gibraltar Incident

The Devil to Pay
The Mutiny of the Connaught Rangers, India, July 1920

Shell-Shock
A History of the changing attitudes to War Neurosis

AN UNCERTAIN VOYAGE

By

ANTHONY BABINGTON

AN AUTOBIOGRAPHY

Barry Rose Law Publishers Ltd

ISBN 1 902681 18 5

Correction:
We regret the spelling of A.V.E.J. Mindham has been incorrectly spelt at pp.382 and 383.

Published by
Barry Rose Law Publishers Ltd
Little London
Chichester
West Sussex

"Commend me to them;
And tell them that, to ease them of their griefs,
Their fears of hostile strokes, their aches, losses,
Their pangs of love, with other incident throes
That nature's fragile vessel doth sustain
In life's uncertain voyage, I will some kindness
do them."

William Shakespeare
Timon of Athens, Act 5, Scene 2

CONTENTS

1944

It was as though I was swimming under water - deep water - and struggling desperately to reach the surface. I could feel the weight bearing down on top of me; there was a loud drumming in my ears, an immense pain and an increasing sense of helplessness.

Then the pressure was easing and suddenly I broke the surface. I was lying in bed in a small room which seemed to be full of nurses, and a man in a white coat was bending over me. "It's all over now," he said. "It was a wonderful operation and they got all the shrapnel out of your head. When you come round properly you'll find that you're unable to speak and unable to move your right arm or your right leg, but don't be alarmed - we know all about it."

I was too weak and too weary to collect my thoughts so I closed my eyes and fell asleep immediately.

When I woke up again the first thing I noticed was that my head was encased in bandages, some of which were joined under my chin. It appeared to be night-time as the lights were on and there was a black-out board across the window. I gradually took in my surroundings. The room was bare of furniture except for a narrow bed, a bedside locker, a cupboard and several upright wooden chairs. Two young nurses in the uniform of VADs were fiddling with a contraption which looked like an oxygen cylinder. Presently they both came up to the bed and one of them said to the other, "Now that he's conscious we'd better take his temperature." She shook a thermometer and pushed it under my tongue. I could not feel it there and I heard the glass casing snap. This threw the nurses into a panic. They hurriedly removed the broken ends of the thermometer and dabbed the inside of my mouth with cotton-wool. They were still doing this when I dropped off to sleep.

The next time I woke up it was daylight and the black-out board had been removed from the window. An attractive dark-haired VAD was busy tidying the bedside locker. She noticed that my eyes were open and she said cheerfully, "That's good, you're awake. Colonel Calvert is on his way round to see you with the Ward Sister. He's the surgeon who operated on you yesterday. I expect you're wondering where you are? Well, you're back in England, safe and sound in hospital. We're going to look after you here and make you better."

At that moment the door opened and the Sister came in accompanied by a small man with greying hair and a pleasant, kindly face. When they were standing by the bed the Sister told him that I had arrived the previous day without any documents. "We only know his rank, his name and his regiment," she said, "so we can't notify his next-of-kin where he is." The surgeon asked me to indicate if I would be able to write down my home address with my left hand, and I nodded affirmatively. I felt certain that I could do it since my brain was functioning quite clearly. He placed a pencil in my hand and the Sister held a pad on the bedclothes. I knew exactly what I intended to write, but I was dismayed to find myself drawing a series of short, very crooked lines. The surgeon shook his head. "No, it's no use," he said. "We'll have to wait until his papers catch up with him."

From then on I spent most of my time sleeping fitfully. Whenever I woke there was usually a tube connected to my left upper arm and a nurse would be sitting by my bedside recording my blood-pressure on a chart. Doctors visited me frequently. They often held up a finger in front of my face and told me to follow it with my eyes as they moved it from side to side. I had a perpetual headache, far more severe than any I had ever had in the past, for which I was given periodic pain-killing injections. Sometimes I felt so ill and in such discomfort that I wondered whether I should keep on trying to stay alive.

The VADs who were looking after me were eager to help in every way possible. They were marvellous at interpreting my feeble sign-language and they invariably knew what I wanted. When I cupped my hand and raised it to my mouth they would immediately produce a drink. When I pointed to my genitals they would fetch a urine bottle. When I clapped my hand on my forehead they knew that my headache had become unbearable and they would hurry away for a syringe. They had to feed me, as I was lying immobile on my back. A nurse would sit on my bed and would transfer the food from a plate to my mouth. I had to drink from a cup with a long, narrow spout; this was extremely awkward because the fluid would often pour out, almost chocking me.

An orderly came in every day to shave me. I found it an odd sensation as my face seemed to be divided by a vertical line above and below my nose. On the left side of this demarcation I had normal feeling: on the right side I could feel nothing at all.

I awoke one morning feeling slightly better. The Night Sister came to see me on her early round and she stood by my bed for several minutes studying my charts. Then she said, "You're over the worst now and you should be out of danger. You'll have to be very patient because you have a long and difficult time ahead of you. The doctors think you might get back a little movement in your right side - in the leg, at any rate. But I'm afraid they think it unlikely that you'll ever be able to speak again."

She put a hand on my forehead and went on quietly, "You must make up your mind that it's not going to get you down. At your age I'm sure you'll still have a lot to live for."

After she had gone I began to appreciate the awful reality of what had happened to me. I was completely dumb and there was a strong possibility that I might never recover the use of my right arm and leg. At the age of 24 my life had wholly disintegrated. The pleasures and excitements, the hopes and the dreams were all ended. I had become a helpless cripple, even deprived of the ability of speaking to those around me.

The future seemed too awful to contemplate. And then I started to think of the past.

PART I

THE PRELUDE

CHAPTER 1

In 1927 I was sent as a boarder to St Anselms, a prep school in Surrey, and one of the first lessons I learnt there was that the population of Britain was divided unalterably into two distinct and distant categories. First, there were "people like ourselves," a small, select minority; and secondly, there were the surrounding hordes of "brickies or brickbats," who vastly differed from us in accents, habits, manners, and outlook. I had no doubt in my own mind that I ranked as a non-brickbat; at least the other boys at St Anselms seemed to accept me as such, although they regarded my credentials as being somewhat dubious when they discovered I had been born in the south of Ireland.

In fact, my family had originally come from the north of England where for many generations, as far as I am aware, they had led respectable and unexceptional lives, until the discovery of the Babington Conspiracy in the reign of Elizabeth I. The instigator of this, my namesake Anthony Babington, was the owner of a large estate at Dethick in Derbyshire. During his boyhood he had served as a page to Mary Queen of Scots while she was imprisoned in Sheffield under the care of the Earl of Shrewsbury. The young Anthony had formed a passionate devotion for the captive queen and had become an ardent supporter of her cause. Later on, in 1580, he came to London at the age of 19 to study law at Lincoln's Inn, but he soon gave up his intention of being called to the Bar, preferring the fashionable life of the capital where, according to the *Dictionary of National Biography*, "his wealth, his cultivated intelligence, his charm of manner, and his handsome features secured him a good reception at court." Although his family were Anglicans he had been secretly received into the Church of Rome, and in the course of his social activities he had come across a number of other Catholic youths who regarded Elizabeth as an usurper, and who had pledged their allegiance to Mary. As a result of discussions amongst a few of them, and with the active encouragement of the Jesuit priesthood in France and Spain, the Babington conspiracy evolved. At the end of 1585 Mary, still in captivity, was moved to Chartley Hall, an isolated, moated manor house in Staffordshire belonging to the Earl of Essex. While she was there she kept in regular contact with the conspirators, letters from them being concealed in the bungholes of casks of ale delivered to the manor by a local brewer. Her replies were returned in the bungholes of the empty casks. By July 1586 the plans were sufficiently advanced for Anthony to set them out in full in a letter to Mary. There was to be a national rising throughout England, coinciding with an invasion by a French Army. "Six noble gentlemen" would undertake the "tragical" task of assassinating Queen Elizabeth, and Mary, having been rescued from Chartley Hall, would be installed in her rightful position on the English throne. Mary assented to the ·scheme making several suggestions for its improvement.

Unfortunately for the conspirators, the whole of the correspondence passing in and out of Chartley Hall in the ale-casks was being intercepted and read by agents employed by Sir Francis Walsingham, Queen Elizabeth's Secretary of State. Early in August 1586 Anthony Babington, the other five "noble gentlemen," and a Jesuit priest, who was acting as an intermediary with the French Government, were all seized and imprisoned in the Tower. After being subjected to many hours of interrogation and torture they were tried by a special commission and sentenced to death. The method of execution for high treason was particularly barbaric, though it could be tempered by the clemency of the executioner. On this occasion, however, an order had gone out from the Privy Council that no mercy was to be shown. The condemned prisoners were dragged on hurdles to a scaffold in St Giles's Fields, around which a massive crowd of spectators had assembled. Each of the youthful conspirators, when his turn came to die, was left hanging for a short time and was cut down while he was still fully conscious. He was then ripped open, disembowelled, and castrated. Finally, in accordance with the prescribed ritual, his body was decapitated and hacked into quarters.

Following the discovery of the conspiracy and the execution of the culprits it is probable that Anthony Babington's close relations were tarnished with dishonour and shame. I have seen an old family tree which shows that around this time two Babington brothers decided to settle in Ireland, one of them going to County Londonderry in the north and the other, my immediate ancestor, to County Cork in the south. Apparently they left England as voluntary emigrants rather than as enforced exiles. The sombre shadow of disgrace cannot have overhung the family for many years as early in the reign of James I one of the northern Irish Babingtons was appointed Bishop of Londonderry.

The southern branch of the family seem to have taken their place in the carefree, hedonistic fellowship of the Anglo-Irish gentry, now referred to as the Protestant Ascendancy. The occupations of successive generations of

3

my male ancestors, as recorded on the family tree, were predictable enough. The majority were lawyers, usually barristers who practised on the Munster Circuit. Some of the rest were clergymen, others were doctors, and quite a few held commissions in the navy or the army. The occupational patterns of the Londonderry Babingtons was very similar, but it is doubtful whether there was very much intermingling between the kinsmen from the north and the south because of the distance involved. Probably their principal meeting-place was Trinity College, Dublin, the great Protestant University of Ireland, which was attended by most of the men from both branches.

My paternal grandfather was a solicitor. At some stage in his career he had become Crown Solicitor for Cork, a fairly lucrative appointment peculiar to Ireland which entailed, in addition to his private practice, the handling of all government legal business in the county. His wife came from Bristol; she was by all accounts, a cold imperious lady who had dominated him completely. They divided their time between two homes, a town house in the outskirts of Cork City, and a country residence on the beautiful wooded slopes overlooking the entrance to Queenstown (now called Cobh) harbour. I do not remember either of them. They only existed for me as dimly-defined historical figures, and from the faded images of brown-tinted photographs. They had two children, both sons. The elder, Sydney, read law at Trinity College, Dublin, and qualified as a barrister; the younger, Oscar, my father, departed from family traditions and graduated at Trinity College in civil engineering. Sydney, a popular, convivial extrovert with a magnificent

4

tenor voice, was inflicted with a serious alcohol problem. He practised for a short time on the Munster Circuit and died very young from what was described as "constitutional debility," but was doubtless due to excessive drinking.

My father had always had an urge to travel abroad and directly he came down from Trinity he applied for and obtained a civil engineering appointment in India, on a project which was expected to last for about five years. Before he left Ireland he married my mother, a member of an impecunious Anglo-Irish family from the west of County Cork, whose principal distinction was that in their less indigent days they had helped to found one of the best known hunts in Munster. My mother had two brothers and a sister older than herself, and a younger sister May, who was her closest companion throughout her early life. I never knew very much about her father, except that he had spent several years in serving as a soldier in the army of Garibaldi, the Italian patriot, and that after he returned to Ireland he had never had a settled occupation. He had died while his children were still very young. At the time of her marriage my mother and her favourite sister May had recently completed their education at a school in France, arranged and paid for by their eldest brother. From their photos, and from what I have been told about them, they were both attractive and vivacious girls. They became engaged at about the same time, May's fiancé being a young doctor from a County Cork family who had just entered the Indian Medical Service. By a fortunate coincidence his first appointment was to be in Assam, a province in the extreme north-east of India where my parents were going to live.

My mother and father learnt to love India and to respect the Indian people, although it must have been difficult to assimilate their culture and their outlook firsthand as there had been little or no intermingling at that time between the British Raj and the local inhabitants. During my childhood I often heard my mother speaking about the enchanted years of her early married life in Assam, and I grew up with visions of the grandeur and mystical enchantment of the Himalayas towering into the clouds; the impenetrable jungles, and the isolated villages ringed by groves of bamboo and fruit trees. Listening to her reminiscences I could hear the calls of the wild animals during the night-time, and I could visualise the limitless expanses of the rice-fields in the valley of the Brahmaputra.

In their homes, the British Raj were surrounded by large numbers of servants, ranging from those who performed the lowest duties to the trusted household attendants. It was customary for the male employees to wear the family crests of their masters pinned on their turbans in the form of ornamental clasps. I still keep, as a memento of former times, one of the gilt crested badges which were worn by my father's staff. After my parents had been in Assam for less than a year they acquired an additional employee, an ayah, when my brother Arnold was born. They remained in India for the full five years of my father's engagement as his periods of leave were insufficient for them to make the long journey home, and when they eventually returned to Ireland their excitement was tempered by the sadness of leaving a country which had given them so much happiness. They both wanted to travel again, and it was not long before my father applied for and obtained a three-year contract to work for the Central Argentine Railway which was about to embark on an extensive programme of reconstruction and development. At the time she sailed for Argentina my mother was pregnant again and her second child, my sister Noreen, was born at a hospital in Buenos Aires.

The manner of life in Argentina appealed to my parents from the start. The easy informality and the warmth and kindness of the people were reminiscent of the ambience in which they had both grown up in the south of Ireland. It was fortunate for them that they were good linguists and learnt Spanish very quickly, as a number of their new acquaintances could speak little or no English. At the conclusion of my father's contract he obtained further employment in Argentina, this time with a government-sponsored company working on the construction of a large dam in the central province of Cordoba. Before the new job commenced my parents were able to fit in a brief visit to Cork. They had decided to send Arnold, then aged seven, as a boarder to a prep school in the north of Ireland, and to leave him in the care of his parental grandparents. Noreen, who was only two, accompanied them back to Argentina, where they had rented a ranch-house in an isolated region close to the site of the dam. Cordoba in those days was open, undeveloped, and sparsely populated. Their house was surrounded by vast prairies, mostly used for rearing cattle, and pampa grasslands dwarfed by lofty mountains. My mother told me that neither she nor my father had felt lonely or cut off while they were living there; indeed, they had enjoyed the stillness and the solitary beauty of the landscape which was all around them. Their time in Cordoba passed very quickly. They had ample opportunities for riding and playing tennis, their favourite forms of exercise, or, in their moments of relaxation, for reading the masses of books they had brought with them from Ireland. The engineering staff at the dam formed their own small international community, in which they were joined by the ranchers with homes in the vicinity and there was a continual round of social activity.

When the First World War broke out in August 1914 the dam was less than half completed but the British and German engineers, who were the mainstay of the project, applied for immediate release from their contracts so that they could return to their own countries and enlist. The company refused their requests and made it clear that they intended to invoke the aid of the Argentinean authorities in preventing any of them from leaving Cordoba before the engineering work on the dam was finished. As most of the men were accompanied by their wives, and often by their children as well, they had little alternative other than to remain. And so, the British and German engineers continued to work together as colleagues and to live side-by-side in Cordoba while their compatriots were shelling, shooting, and bayoneting each other on the battlefields in Europe.

The early expectations that the war would be short were soon dispelled as the opposing armies on the Western Front became deadlocked in the sterile immobility of trench warfare. By the summer of 1915 the military situation of the Allies had deteriorated considerably. There was stalemate in the west, the Russian armies were disintegrating in the east, the Austrians were over-running northern Italy, and the invasion of Gallipoli was proving to be a costly failure. While these events were occurring the British and German engineers at Cordoba were becoming increasingly anxious to return home. After holding a joint meeting they made another application for release from their contracts, and once more their request was refused. They then gave notice that at the end of another month they would all refuse to do any further work on the dam. Faced with this threat the company accepted their demand. When the month had expired they were permitted to leave Cordoba without hindrance and to go their various ways.

My parents and Noreen travelled by train to Buenos Aires and after staying at a hotel there for a few weeks they managed to obtain a cabin on a liner which was preparing to join a transatlantic convoy in New York harbour. Noreen remembered the excitement of the voyage home, but she had been too young to comprehend the constant danger from the lurking German U-boats. She was one of the very few children on board, and both the adult passengers and the crew made a great fuss of her. My mother and father never left her by herself day or night, and to her considerable delight she was allowed to stay up to dinner with them every evening. Eventually the convoy put in at Sierra Leone in West Africa for a brief stop before setting out on the final lap of its journey to Southampton, which was completed without mishap.

As soon as he had settled my mother and Noreen at his parents' home in Cork, my father returned to England and enlisted in the Royal Marines. Having nominally passed through the ranks he was commissioned a 2nd Lieutenant at the end of his basic training. I know almost nothing about his experiences while he was on active service, except that he spent most of his time at sea, apart from a spell of duty with the Royal Naval Division on the Western Front. He was fortunate enough to come through the war unscathed and finished with the rank of captain. From time to time he had managed to spend short periods of leave in Cork and my younger sister Eve had been born in 1918, a few months before the Armistice was signed.

My father was demobilised in 1919 and soon afterwards he obtained an appointment as engineering consultant on the staff of General Birdwood, who had recently taken over the command of the Northern Army in India. Birdwood had persuaded the authorities to sanction the construction of a roadway and a chain of fortifications across the Khyber Pass on the North-West Frontier. This pass was the most northerly as well as being the most strategically important of the passes between Afghanistan and the Punjab. It wound for 33 miles through steep, rugged mountains and was persistently harassed by hostile tribesmen. It was agreed that my father was to retain his civilian status, although for administrative reasons he was granted the honorary rank of full colonel. He was advised that during the initial stages of the project he would virtually be living under active service conditions, but that later on it would be possible for him to be joined by his wife and family.

He managed to delay his departure from Ireland until after I was born on April 4, 1920.

CHAPTER 2

My father commenced his new appointment during the early part of 1920, at the height of the "Troubles" in Ireland, when the IRA was waging a bitter guerrilla campaign against the British military garrison and the Royal Irish Constabulary. It was around this time that Lloyd George's coalition government at Westminster began to employ the infamous Black and Tans in an effort to out-terrorise the terrorists. This force, though nominally a branch of the civil police, was virtually autonomous, behaved in an undisciplined, brutal, and oppressive manner from the outset of their service. Repeated atrocities were perpetrated by both sides and the whole of Ireland was in a state of upheaval.

After my father's departure my mother stayed on at the home of her parents-in-law in Cork. It was an anxious time for her, as the IRA regarded all the Anglo-Irish families as being their natural enemies and as legitimate targets for attack. Sometimes the danger came from quite a different quarter. One evening when my mother's brother Richard was returning home from a party, he was chased round the streets of Cork City by a group of drunken Black and Tans who wanted to detain him as a suspect. He had no difficulty in out-pacing them since he was something of an athlete, and he eventually escaped over a high wall amid a hail of revolver bullets. This experience made him extremely angry as he had only recently been demobilised after serving as a junior officer in a Scottish Regiment on the Western Front.

My father remained on the North-West Frontier for about a year before being moved back to continue his work on the Khyber Pass project from General Birdwood's headquarters at Rawalpindi. He rented a house on the outskirts of the ancient city and arranged for my mother to join him there with Eve and me, bringing an Irish nanny with her to look after us. The two elder children were to stay in the UK. Arnold was already at Portora, the Public School in the north of Ireland, and Noreen was sent to Cheltenham Ladies College. They were both entrusted to the care of their grandparents in Cork. It was by no means unusual, in the days before the development of air travel, for the more affluent British parents who were living in distant countries overseas to leave their children at schools in Britain, and to be separated from them completely for periods of as much as three or four years.

My first positive memories of my childhood are of friendly Indian servants in turbans, or playing in a garden with Eve and a terrier puppy, and of being bitten by a pet mongoose which I had probably teased. I have been told that we remained in the same house until I was four years old, when General Birdwood transferred his headquarters and the whole of his staff to the hill station of Muree, which is almost 8,000 feet above sea level and has a much cooler and far less enervating climate than the intense dry heat of Rawalpindi. After spending about six months in Muree my mother's health started to be affected by the height and my parents decided, with some reluctance, that it would be best for her to return to the UK with her two children. It was then 1924 and my father expected that his work in the Khyber Pass would only take another year or two to complete. Having spent most of their married life abroad both my parents wanted to settle down in their own home in Ireland or England. Their remaining ties with Ireland had lessened considerably. The passage of time, and the altered circumstances, had distanced them from the life of their native country. Old friends and close relations had scattered, and my father's parents had died within a few months of each other during the previous year. The Troubles were now ended and County Cork had become a part of the Irish Free State, a self-governing Dominion within the British Empire. Amidst a new and understandable surge of nationalism, the future standing of the Anglo-Irish minority was in question. My parents therefore decided that their home should be in the south of England. Madge, my mother's elder sister, was living in Devon at the time and offered to find her a furnished house there as temporary accommodation.

During the following year General Birdwood was appointed Commander-in-Chief of all the military forces in India, and was subsequently promoted to the rank of Field Marshal. In reorganising his General Staff he offered my father a permanent position as his civil engineering adviser for the entire fortification system of the North-West Frontier. It must have been a very tempting offer, but my father declined to accept it. His parents had left him a comfortable inheritance and, although he was only 43, he had made up his mind to retire from full-time employment. An additional reason for his decision may have been his awareness that he was gradually succumbing to the illness which had afflicted so many members of his family in the past, and he was desperately hoping that a total change of environment would bring about an improvement in his condition. As far as I know, he sought no assistance or advice. Like most sufferers in the early stages of alcoholism he was probably reluctant to disclose the nature of his problem and his own solitary struggle to overcome it. One of my principal regrets has always been that I never had an opportunity of knowing him until the last few anguished years of his life. It was then too late for us to establish any form of meaningful relationship with each other. I heard afterwards that in his day he had been a delightful companion and extremely popular - a man of great kindness with an infinite charm. This portrayal filled me with great sadness when I realised what might have been if the course of fate had been different.

After my father had returned from India we moved from Devon to a hotel at Ventnor in the Isle of Wight, and we remained there until he bought Kenley Court, which was to be our family home for the next seven years. It was a large, rambling three-storied house with about 10 acres of grounds, consisting of flower gardens, lawns, fields, and orchards. It was approached by a neglected, uneven cul-de-sac called Firs Road. Kenley in those days was an unspoilt Surrey village adjacent to an RAF airfield, used principally for the training of fighter-pilots. At first we had a resident staff of four, which was quite a normal number for a sizable country residence in the 1920s. There were an Indian married couple, the husband being the cook and his wife the housekeeper, an Irish maid, and an English chauffeur. Their sitting-room was in the kitchen area, connected by a back staircase with the second floor where they all had their bedrooms. We also had two gardeners, both local men who came to work every day. The family's bedrooms were on the first floor, separated from the back staircase by a green baize-covered door which was always kept closed. After a while my parents engaged a governess for Eve and me, a formidable French lady, known by everyone in the household as "Mademoiselle". She gave us lessons at the dining-room table every morning and soon had us speaking fluent French.

Arnold had wanted to join the Royal Navy, but he had failed a medical test because of a temporary vision defect. However, he had been accepted as a cadet in the Merchant Service and when we moved to Kenley he was undergoing a course in the training ship HMS *Conway*. Noreen was uncertain what she would like to do when she left Cheltenham. She was exceptionally attractive and talked vaguely of becoming an actress. Her housemistress joined with my parents in seeking to persuade her that if she wanted to take up a career her aspirations should be more realistic.

I think it was at the instigation of Arnold and Noreen that a hard tennis court was laid out at Kenley Court soon after we had arrived there. At any rate, they both made frequent use of it when spending their holidays at home.

To the best of my knowledge my father never played tennis on our new court, and he soon gave up his visits to the golf club he had joined in the vicinity of Kenley. He had planned to spend part of his time breeding dogs on a small scale, and he wanted to obtain a consultancy in London where he could utilise his considerable experience as a civil engineer. For a short time he was very enthusiastic about the dog-breeding scheme. A set of kennels and a fenced-off enclosure were erected in a field near the house, and one afternoon he returned home in the car with two thoroughbred fox-terriers, a male and a bitch. But his interest did not last for long. As soon as the first litter of puppies was born he gave them all away and sold the bitch. From then on neither the kennels nor the enclosure were ever used again. My father was at that time becoming increasingly preoccupied with a commercial venture in which he had become involved both professionally and financially. As a result of a proposal he had seen in the personal columns of a national newspaper, he had become associated with a group of men who were endeavouring to trade a newly-invented device for reducing the petrol consumption of motor vehicles. They had set up a company and my father, as well as being a director, had been appointed the technical adviser, in spite of the fact that he had no expertise in mechanical engineering. Since the others were without funds it had been agreed that he would be responsible for financing the company until it began to balance its books. Several people advised him that the petrol-saving invention should not be put on the market before it had been adequately tested, but he would not listen to them. He was also receiving ominous warnings with regard to the honesty of Michael Byrne, his agent in Cork, who had been looking after his Irish affairs since he had gone to India at the start of the Khyber Pass project. For several years Byrne had been arousing comment because of his extravagant life-style, and his lavish spending on himself and his family.

I do not recall when Eve and I found out about our father's secret drinking habits. I rather think it had been a progressive awareness rather than a sudden discovery. We accepted it as we accepted all the other incomprehensible and distressful happenings in life, like head-colds, bilious attacks, and unfair scoldings. None of the grown-ups ever spoke about it in our hearing, but no overt attempts were ever made to conceal it from us. We guessed that most of his drinking took place behind the closed door of his study, on the ground floor of the house in an extension alongside the seldom-used billiard room. On the whole, the routine of our home life continued as though everything was normal, but there were occasions when this was impossible. One Sunday at lunchtime we had all sat down at the table and were waiting for our father to join us before we began eating. He eventually emerged from his study and when he attempted to carve the joint at a side-table his hand was so unsteady he could not control the knife. My mother, who had been watching him closely, sent for the Indian cook to take over the carving, and my father wandered unsteadily out of the dining-room saying he still had some work to do. He never reappeared during the whole of the meal. His condition used to vary from day to day, and sometimes from hour to hour, but his periods of complete sobriety became increasingly infrequent. There was an occasion a few days before our second or third Christmas at Kenley Court when he said that he would help Eve and me to decorate the house. We were both overjoyed as we were very fond of him and it was a long time since we had seen his mood so jovial and relaxed. After we had been working together for about an hour, he suddenly told us that he would have to break off to write some urgent business letters. He promised to rejoin us as soon as he had finished. When he came back he had changed into a different person. He tried several times to mount a small set of steps with an armful of streamers and holly, but he was swaying about so precariously he was obliged to abandon the attempt. Without saying another word he returned to his study, closing the door behind him and leaving the two of us, our exuberance vanished, to carry on disconsolately by ourselves.

When I was seven and Eve was nine our parents decided to dispense with the services of Mademoiselle and to send us both to boarding schools. We were to start at the beginning of the summer term, Eve at a school in Seaford on the Sussex coast and I at St Anselms, not far from where we lived. On my first day I was taken there by my mother and father and the three of us saw Mr Campbell, the headmaster, in his private sitting-room. Andrew Campbell was a stern, humourless Scotsman in his early forties. He had opened St Anselms a few years after the end of the First World War, with accommodation for about 50 boys. It had soon acquired a reputation for its excellent teaching standards, particularly in the classics, and its proficiency at competitive games. Campbell's own house, where he lived with his wife and their eight-year-old daughter, adjoined the School buildings, so that during term-time he was always close at hand to supervise the activities of his pupils, and - what he considered of greater importance - to mould the development of their characters. I retain a mental picture of him standing in front of a class, tall, erect and unsmiling, with his legs slightly apart and his hands clasped behind his back. He is wearing a brown plus-fours suit, such as he wore habitually, with a pervasive tweedy smell which I have associated with him ever since. His manner towards his pupils was aloof and censorious. He tried persistently to instil them with a sense of shame because of their mental inadequacy, the defects in their personal qualities, and their lack of manly virtue.

The attribute of manliness was all-important in the eyes of Andrew Campbell and he expounded about it at length in the interview with my parents on my first day at St Anselms. Every boy in the school was taught to box, he said, and they were encouraged to settle their differences "with the gloves on" in the gymnasium under the direction of one of the seniors. Much of the curriculum was devoted to physical training and organised team games. Hardiness was cultivated by long walks and cross-country runs in all weathers; in addition, there was a compulsory early morning dip in the school swimming pool on all but the coldest days for every boy who had passed the one-length swimming test. He touched lightly on the maintenance of discipline at the school, mentioning that he only used the cane when he considered it to be absolutely necessary, but without disclosing his view that even the most trivial act of misconduct frequently justified a flogging. I listened with a sense of increasing gloom to his description of the bleak regime he imposed on his pupils. He then turned to a different subject and asked my parents if I had been entered yet for a public school. They replied that I had not. In that case it must be done without delay, said Campbell, as the best public schools had very long waiting-lists. He emphasised that he liked his boys to go to schools which would develop their highest qualities, and he suggested that he should discuss the matter again with my father at the end of the term, when he had had an opportunity of assessing my potentialities.

At that time I had been an avid reader of *The Magnet*. Every week I used to follow assiduously the adventures of Harry Wharton, Bob Cherry, and the other members of the Famous Five. I had firmly believed that what occurred at the mythical Greyfriars was typical of the happenings at most of the prep and public schools in Britain, so I was prepared for some unpleasant experiences during my early days at St Anselms. On my first evening in the junior dormitory my forebodings came to pass. Immediately after the lights had been switched off I was informed by the others that every new boy at the school had to climb out at one end of the large window, walk along the parapet outside, and re-enter at the other end. I could do it right away, they said, or I could wait until it became darker; but in either case if I was seen from below I would have to pretend that the exploit had been my own idea. It was a tall window , about 12 feet in width, with its lower end some three feet above the level of the floor. There were casement openings at each end, separated by an expanse of glass in a fixed frame. I chose to go through with my ordeal straight away. Before I began, the other boys gathered round me with words of well-intended advice. I must avoid looking down, they told me, otherwise I might feel giddy as the dormitory was on the second floor and outside there was a sheer drop down to a gravelled driveway. The best method was to walk sideways, facing into the dormitory. I must take it slowly and avoid an inclination to rush. There were plenty of good hand-holds if I selected them carefully. Having given me all the guidance they thought I required, they led me to one of the open casement windows. I realised that the whole of my future standing at St Anselms was now in the balance. I summoned up my courage, mounted the window-ledge, and stepped out into the night. The parapet seemed extremely narrow. My eyes strayed fleetingly to the ground below, half-hidden by darkness. I had always had a bad head for heights. I felt myself swaying precariously and I hesitated for a moment, wondering if I could go through with it. By an effort of will, I turned round cautiously so that the front of my body was towards the window. I pressed myself tightly against it and clutched desperately at the wooden frames. I was vaguely aware of a row of upturned faces on the other side of the glass. Then I commenced to edge my way nervously along the parapet until was midway between the casements. This was the point of no return, the most hazardous position of all. In a moment of panic I stood still quivering, almost sobbing with fear. I forced myself to move again. As I came closer to the open window, my final haven, I impulsively quickened my speed and hauled myself over the intervening space. In my frenzied haste to get off the parapet I nearly lost my balance, but I retained it sufficiently to end up lying on the floor of the dormitory. The others eagerly inquired how I had felt. It had not been too bad, I lied, not nearly as bad as I had expected. Back in my bed I had lain awake, still terrified by the recollection of the perils through which I had passed.

The following morning I had a presentiment that my initiation was not yet complete. After breakfast my class was given some history book to read and we were told to sit quietly at our desks while the form-master went off to attend a staff meeting. We had been seated in silence for a while when a boy called Rabidge came over to me and asked if it was true that all the people in Ireland lived in pigsties. I responded with some equally puerile and equally insulting comment about the English, as I felt that I was expected to do. The next moment, in accordance with the prescribed procedure, we were locked together in ritualistic combat. We fought our way to the open part of the classroom in front of the desks, and we stood there face-to-face punching one another unscientifically. We varied this periodically by wrestling on the floor, then regaining our feet and renewing the interchange of blows with renewed vigour. The rest of the class, forgetful of the admonition to silence, grouped around us in a circle, cheering on their favourite contestant. The clamour terminated abruptly and I was aware that they were all scampering back to their desks. Rabidge and I broke off our fight and stood side-by-side, panting, bloody, and dishevelled. Mr Campbell eyed us from the doorway.

"How disgraceful!" he exclaimed. "I could hear the noise from the far end of the corridor. Which of you started this?"

"I did, Sir," said Rabidge. "It was nothing to do with Babington."

Mr. Campbell turned to me. "Is that right?"

I had read *The Magnet* long enough to have assimilated the Greyfriars culture. I tried to react as Harry Wharton or any member of the Famous Five would have done. "No, Sir," I told him, "It was me who began it."

"That's not true," Rabidge protested. "I hit him because he was a new boy and I wanted to see if he'd fight back."

"Very well," said Mr Campbell. "It's plain that neither of you is going to tell me what really happened so I'll have to punish you both."

He ordered us to report to his study at 12 o'clock which, as I discovered later, was his usual time for administering the "swish." It was to be the first flogging I had ever received. I can still recall the agony of those four strokes, and the feeling each time the cane descended that it was cutting savagely into my flesh. Andrew Campbell was merciless when he was punishing his pupils, however young they happened to be. There was a general belief at St Anselms that he enjoyed inflicting pain. After he had flogged us both, first Rabidge and then me, he ordered us to shake hands with each other and to promise him that our quarrel would be forgotten. In fact we had no quarrel and there was no enmity between us; a short while later we were to become the closest friends. In the dormitory that evening, in accordance with custom, we proudly displayed the weals on our backsides to satisfy the morbid interest of our fellows.

CHAPTER 3

I managed to adjust myself fairly quickly to the regime at St Anselms, although I constantly missed the easeful, pampered way of life at Kenley Court. Andrew Campbell imposed on his pupils a form of strictly disciplined austerity. Comforts were kept to a minimum, and food was adequate but frugal. He provided an ideal preparation for those who were destined in later years to administer the less civilised outposts of the British Empire.

Every morning began, during the summer term, with "cold plunge". At six o'clock Mr Campbell, fully dressed, would bang loudly on the school gong, whereupon all the boys who had passed the elementary swimming test would run downstairs to the hall in their dressing-gowns and bedroom slippers. Campbell would then lead them to the open-air swimming pool, about 300 yards from the main school building, where they would strip off their pyjamas, dive naked into the deep end, swim a length, and climb out with chattering teeth to rush for the cover of the changing room. I had been taught to swim by my mother's sister Madge during various holidays in the south of Ireland, so I had passed my test without difficulty during my first few weeks at St Anselms. As I was accustomed to the chilly waters of the Atlantic Ocean, the rigours of cold plunge on a frosty May morning did not daunt me overmuch.

Andrew Campbell's predominance at St Anselms was absolute and his rules of conduct were inflexible. He even sought to control the habitual functions of our bodies. After breakfast every day we had to sit at our desks in the main schoolroom for an hour, working on our own. As soon as this period of private study began the first four boys on a prescribed list would slip away to the lavatories. As each one returned to the schoolroom the next boy on the list would go out in his turn. Anyone who had registered no results on three successive days was supposed to apply to the matron for a laxative, which usually consisted of either syrup of figs or the hated castor oil. These obligatory retirements were seldom utilised for their intended purpose; instead, they were regarded as a welcome break from the tedium of enforced concentration and, by some, as an opportunity for smoking a furtive cigarette in the sheltered privacy of a locked closet. On Saturdays and Sundays the rigid timetables were suspended and pupils' bowels were permitted to operate in accordance with the ordinary dictates of nature.

Classes lasted for the whole of the morning, six days a week, and the afternoons were devoted to organised games. I enjoyed the lessons, particularly the periods of English which was taught in the junior form by a master with the ability to impart to his pupils some of his own love of literature. He had served as a young officer on the Western Front and discussed with us the respective merits of the Great War poets. I remember him telling us that the spirit of the battlefield emerged far more truthfully from the writings of Wilfred Owen, Siegfried Sassoon, and Edmund Blunden, than from the idealistic fantasies of Rupert Brooke. I liked the history lessons too, but only if the master brought the past to life, rather than presenting it as a prosaic inventory of kings, queens, campaigns, and victories. Latin was compulsory and appeared frequently in our syllabus; Greek was optional and very few boys were taking it. Even in those days many people were beginning to doubt the advantages of a comprehensive classical education in the circumstances of the modern world.

I realised during my early days at St Anselms that it might be inadvisable for a new boy to exhibit too much enthusiasm for learning before proving himself on the games field, lest he be branded as a "swot". Swots were treated with universal disdain. Their lack of interest in sport was contemptible: their studiousness, an affront. We had only one swot at the school who was at all popular, and he was regarded as a special case. Minden was small for his age and tubby, with a round face and thick spectacles. He had two claims to fame. The first was that he was in the process of writing a novel, an adventure story, and he used to read out the latest instalments to an attentive audience in our dormitory every evening before lights-out. The second of his distinctions was more venturesome. He had created a false impression among the staff that he was a habitual sleep-walker, and he used this as a cover to permit him to move stealthily around the school building on nocturnal expeditions. Sometimes he would go down to the kitchen and return to the dormitory with a selection of cakes and biscuits, which he would then share with the rest of us. On other occasions he would listen outside the door of the masters' sitting-room when they were having an after-dinner conference on school affairs, and he would later regale us with what he had overheard. If he was unlucky enough to meet any of the staff he would put on his sleep-walking act to good effect and be led back to his bed. The fact that he was wearing his spectacles never seemed to arouse any suspicion.

Not to be outdone by Minden, I started writing poetry, or, rather, rhyming doggerel, which I also read to our dormitory companions in the evenings. The general opinion was that Minden's talent greatly exceeded mine because he was capable of producing a far larger output of words than I could ever manage with my single page poems. Nevertheless, I was immensely grateful for the kudos I achieved by becoming recognised as the junior school poet laureate of St Anselms.

The most important member of the staff in the eyes of the boys was Sergeant-Major Jakes, the physical training instructor, who visited the school three or four times a week to teach us boxing and gymnastics. A word of praise or reproach from him carried twice as much weight as it would have done if it had come from the lips of a master, as Jakes was for us the epitome of perfect manhood. He was employed by a number of other prep schools in the surrounding area and he enjoyed telling us how well or how badly our standard of progress compared with theirs. He was considerably elated once because a pupil of his at another school had knocked out his opponent in a boxing contest. We heard of this singular feat with a mixture of incredulity and admiration. It opened up new horizons for us. We were informed by Jakes that the boy who had delivered the blow, and the one on whom it had landed, had received equal acclaim from their fellows. In our boxing lessons from then on we punched each other harder than we had ever done before in the hope of landing a knock-out and achieving a similar renown both for ourselves and for the school.

I was a weekly boarder which meant that during term-time I usually went home at weekends. My parents' chauffeur would call to collect me on Saturday afternoons after games were finished, and I would have over 24 blissful hours at Kenley Court before being driven back to school on Sunday evenings. Although I was never unhappy there these moments of return were tinged with depression. They were associated in my mind with the bells of a local church which were always tolling for Evensong when the car was entering the school gates. In the years that follow, whenever I hear church bells pervading upon the stillness of a Sunday evening it afflicts me momentarily with a spasm of melancholy.

Sundays were the most unpopular days of the week for the boys who had to remain at St Anselms , as Mr Campbell was an uncompromising puritan who believed that the Sabbath should be devoted entirely to religious observance, biblical study, and cheerless, non-competitive exercise. Apart from Matins in the parish church, the day was divided between long walks in crocodile and protracted periods of silent Bible-reading. In Mr Campbell's view any horseplay or boisterous conduct profaned the Sabbath and was deserving of severe punishment. In consequence, the caning session on a Monday was often an extra busy one. Some of the boys had devised a scheme for relieving the boredom of the Sunday reading periods. They used to cut out the pages of magazines, adjust them to the right size, and insert them into their Bibles. If the master on duty came anywhere near their desks it was quite easy to conceal the illicit text with only a minimal chance of detection.

I usually arrived back at school on Sundays in time for the evening reading session. I had done so on one occasion, during my second term, when Andrew Campbell himself was the presiding master. After about half-an-hour I had become so engrossed in a disguised magazine article that I had not noticed him standing directly behind me. Suddenly he had reached over my shoulder, seized up the Bible from the desk in front of me, and shaken out the false pages on the floor. Then he had replaced the Bible and strolled away without saying a word. The following morning I had met him on the stairs on my way down to breakfast and apart from a cold "good morning" he had not spoken to me. I was beginning to think, hopefully, that he might intend to overlook the matter. Perhaps he was aware, I thought, that most of the other boys were doing exactly the same thing as I had done. At the end of the after-breakfast period of preparation, when the last of his pupils had returned from their visits to the lavatories, he mounted the dais and announced, "We have in our midst an anti-Christ, someone who defiles the Holy Book." He paused to let the fearful revelation sink in, then fixing his eyes on me and raising his voice he said, "Stand on the table, Babington, where everyone can see you before I take you upstairs for a flogging." Obediently, but with a faltering step, I went up to the dais and mounted the table beside which he was standing. He left me there for three or four minutes before he led me out of the room. After we had gone, as I discovered later, the other boys engaged in a spirited argument about how many strokes I would receive, the lowest estimate being four and the highest, because I had committed an act of sacrilege, being a prediction of eight. When I came back sore and shaken, they were avid to know which of them had been right. I was so aggrieved by their callousness I felt tempted to exaggerate wildly and claim I had withstood a record flogging of 10 strokes, but I remembered that my lie would become apparent when they examined my weals in the dormitory that evening. I therefore told them the truth, that Mr Campbell had given me a total of six, each of which had been harder than I had ever received from him before.

I often invited my special friends to come to Kenley Court for Sunday lunch, and my parents would send the car to collect them from the school after they had attended church service in the morning. My mother told me that if I wished I could have them for the whole weekend, but I was reluctant to do so as I was afraid they might see my father in one of his off-spells, and did not want his condition known to the other boys. Rabidge, who lived very close to the school, was a weekly boarder too, and took someone home with him nearly every weekend. During my first term he asked me to spend a Saturday night at his house because it would be his ninth birthday on the Sunday and he was having a party in the afternoon. We set off to walk there after we had finished playing cricket, both of us carrying our pyjamas and our sponge bags in our satchels. While we were taking a short cut along a narrow track flanked by tall hedgerows we became aware of six bricky boys from the nearby council school coming towards us. When they were about 25 yards away they stopped abruptly and spread out in a line, completely blocking our path. We would have liked to turn back as they were obviously looking for trouble, but we felt in honour bound to carry on, even though at a slackened pace. It was a "Charge of the Light Brigade" situation. In desperation, I suggested to Rabidge we should tell the brickies that if they really wanted a fight it would be a lot fairer for only two of them to take part in it, but he assured me it would be no use as you could not expect any sportsmanship from brickbats; they would not have tried to ambush us at all, he said, unless they were in a majority of three to one.

I kept my final card to the very end. When we were within 10 yards of their cordon I prayed that, even then, we might be saved by a miracle. I was amazed by the speed of the response, for at that very moment a police sergeant on a bicycle, appearing from nowhere, came riding up behind us. "What's going on here?" he inquired. We told him that we were going to Rabidge's home for the weekend and the council school boys were blocking our way. "All right," he said, "You can follow me, but if you give them any lip while we're passing I'll let them sort you out." He rode slowly just ahead of us and the brickbats parted to let him through. We strutted behind him, feeling very pleased with ourselves, and aware of the hostile scowls directed at us by the erstwhile ambushers. A few yards the other side of them the sergeant stopped, telling us he would stay there for a few minutes to make sure we were not followed, and advising us to run off as quickly as possible. We needed no encouragement to do so. When we were at a safe distance from the brickies we paused for breath and Rabidge exclaimed, "What a stroke of luck, that policeman turning up." Because I did not want to seem boastful I refrained from telling him it had not been luck at all; it had been nothing less than a miracle - a miracle for which I myself was indirectly responsible.

At St Anselms in the summer we played cricket. During the Christmas term every boy, no matter how young, played rugby football, and in the shorter Easter term we changed to soccer. The school had regular fixtures at all three games against other prep schools in Surrey and the neighbouring counties. Although Mr Campbell had been to a soccer playing public school he made no secret of his preference for rugger, as a more manly game, and he used to take parties of his pupils to watch the international matches at Twickenham. We always went to one of the open, seatless stands, where we remained in a group with him and some other of our masters in the centre. On one occasion, when England were playing Ireland, some young men immediately in front of us had a fairly large Irish Free State flag on a pole which they began to wave as soon as the game commenced, and they continued doing so in spite of a storm of protests from the people behind them, whose view of the field was being obstructed. There were repeated shouts of, "Put down that flag." The man who was holding it shouted back, "The Irish flag comes down for no one." An angry spectator edged up behind him, seized the pole from his grasp, and broke it in half across his knee. The Irishman attempted to recover the flag, a struggle developed and they started to exchange punches. People all round were calling on them to break it up and others intervened to drag the combatants apart. By this time the Englishman had a black eye, and blood was streaming from the Irishman's nose. They were persuaded to discontinue their fight and they exchanged addresses for the purpose of renewing it on another occasion. I was immensely shocked by the entire episode as I had not realised before that grown-up men could behave in such a childish manner. Britain, I decided, must still be a very violent and disorderly place despite what we were told at school about it being one of the most civilised countries in the whole world.

I can only recall attending one first-class cricket match during my time at St Anselms. Surrey were playing against a combined counties 11 in a one-day exhibition game at Purley, a few miles away, and Mr Campbell cancelled all lessons and took the whole school to watch. We were told it would be a wonderful chance for us to see the legendary Jack Hobbs at the crease. Unfortunately, he was clean-bowled in taking his third delivery, but most of us managed to get his autograph. The day was chiefly memorable for me on account of the sardine sandwiches and Cornish pasties we were given with our picnic lunch.

Our boxing contests were held annually during the last week of the winter term. They took place on the same afternoon as the Christmas tea party, to which mothers, fathers, and close relatives were invited. Having gorged ourselves with cakes, jellies, and ice-cream we all sat down together to sing carols about peace, fellowship, and goodwill, accompanied by one of the masters on a piano. Then the boys hurried off to change into cotton vests and trunks and, in front of their anxious parents, proceeded to belt each other around a boxing ring. The whole occasion was typical of Andrew Campbell's inspired insensitivity.

Fortunately for me, reading was not condemned as a "sissy" pastime by my new companions, and discussions on books were quite in order. Someone put me on to G.A. Henty's adventure novels which I read one after another with great enjoyment. The senior assistant master asked the boys in the junior dormitory if they would like him to read to them every evening before the lights were put out. We all welcomed his suggestion. The books he chose were lusty tales of heroism, endurance, and chivalry, probably intended to have a beneficial influence on our youthful minds. He started with Anthony Hope's *Rupert of Hentzau* and then continued with its sequel, *The Prisoner of Zenda*. I found them both exciting enough but the fictional illusion for me was incomplete, as the State of Ruritania remained mythological throughout, and never achieved a credible reality. On the other hand, A. E. W. Mason's *The Four Feathers*, which he read to us next, made a deep impression on me. I had already made up my mind that, like Harry Feversham, I had been born a natural coward, though I was sure would have lacked his ability to redeem his reputation. In my most horrific fantasies I imagined myself standing in a battle-line with swarms of screaming Dervishes bearing down on me waving large curved swords. And every time one of our masters spoke to us about his experiences on the Western Front, going over the top in a hail of machine-gun bullets or crawling into No Man's Land on a night raiding party, I became more and more convinced of my own yellow streak, for I knew that I would never have the courage to do such things. I foresaw my future years as abounding in white feathers.

I confided my apprehensions to Rabidge, who admitted that he had once had similar terrors himself. However, his father had told him that the Great War had been the last big war the British would ever fight; from now on the League of Nations would ensure that all disputes between countries were settled peaceably. As far as Dervishes were concerned, Rabidge felt pretty sure that campaigns against them were only carried out by soldiers of the regular army. We would have nothing to worry about, he said, because our valour on the battlefield would never be put to the test.

CHAPTER 4

In due course the atmosphere at St Anselms lost its strangeness and I was accepted by my fellow-pupils as a member of their small community. Time passed very quickly, following an inexorable pattern. Term after term, senior boys departed to their public schools and more juniors arrived in their places to be put through a similar initiation to my own. And in the meanwhile, I was progressing up through successive forms and passing through successive phases of my development.

After a few years I started to play for the school at rugby football, soccer, and cricket. This was not an especially meritorious achievement because after the swots and the juniors had been excluded there only remained a comparatively small number of boys out of which the teams could be selected. I enjoyed both the thrill and the kudos of representing my school. Each time we boarded the coach for an away fixture I felt a sense of adventure, as though we were setting out on a valorous expedition, carrying the St Anselms flag into hostile territories. We knew that we would be engaging our opponents before a crowd of their own supporters who would be inspiring them to renewed efforts and willing our defeat. After the matches we were always treated with friendliness and hospitality. On one occasion we played another Surrey school and we were told that a member of their team was a Greek prince. I found myself sitting next to him at tea and somewhat to my surprise he was natural, chatty, and charming. It was disappointing in a way, as he was more like a typical English schoolboy than a royal prince of a foreign country. Even so, he must have had made quite an impression on me because years later, when he became engaged to Princess Elizabeth, I immediately recognised his photograph in the papers.

Eve was as happy at her boarding school as I was at mine. During the holidays we used to swop our experiences. We were seeing less and less of our father, and the occasions were becoming increasingly rare when he seemed to be sober and normal. Once or twice a week he would be driven up to London for meetings with his business colleagues, and when he returned home in the evening he would usually go straight to his study. When I was nine Michael Byrne, his agent in Ireland, committed suicide by shooting himself in the temple with a revolver. My father hurried over to Cork, to find his Irish affairs in a state of chaos. The Babington Estate was deeply in debt. Houses had been allowed to fall into disrepair, rents had only been collected spasmodically, and bills had remained unpaid. Even worse, for years Byrne had been an inveterate gambler, though an unsuccessful one, and had covered his losses by embezzlement, forgery, and fraud at my father's expense. He had died a pauper.

At the end of the following year my father contracted double pneumonia. When Eve and I came home for the Christmas holidays, a sick room had been set up for him on the first floor, where nurses in spotless white uniforms looked after him by day and by night. This was before the time of antibiotic drugs and little could be done for him as his powers of resistance had been totally undermined by his continual heavy drinking. There was little gaiety at Kenley Court that Christmas and no decorations were put up. The house was hushed in an ominous silence; the doctor came in once or twice a day; adults held whispered conversations in the corridors; and home had ceased to be home any more. One morning Noreen, who was then 20, asked Eve and me to come for a walk with her in the garden. As we were strolling through the orchard she said quietly, "You both know that Daddy is very ill - and when people are very ill they sometimes die." Eve started to cry and I noticed that Noreen was crying too. "Do you mean he's already dead?" I asked. "No," she replied. "He's still alive, but he had a very bad night and he's terribly weak." A short while later we were passing the house and we saw our mother standing in a downstairs window. She was obviously in a state of deep distress, wiping her eyes with a handkerchief. When were closer she beckoned Noreen to come inside. Noreen went in, telling us to wait for her on the path. After a few minutes she returned and put an arm around each of us. "I want you both to be very brave," she said. "What I was warning you about has happened. Daddy has just died."

It was the first time I had come into contact with death. I found it frightening and unfathomable. The realisation that we would never see our father or speak to him again; the very concept of non-existence. Arnold had left the Merchant Navy by then and he was miles away from us, rubber-planting in the Federated Malay States. We never saw him or spoke to him either, but that was altogether different. He still existed. He wrote letters home and sent us birthday and Christmas presents. We knew that one day Arnold would be coming back, but Daddy was never going to return. Although we had been told that he would for ever be in heaven, I found eternity as difficult to understand as extinction.

Eve and I had been allowed to see our father once more for a couple of minutes, standing at the door of his sick-room. I was surprised that lying there in the clean-sheeted bed he did not appear to be dead but merely sleeping. He looked younger than usual, and far more tranquil than I had ever seen him in the past. I would have liked to stay with him a bit longer, but we were told by the nurse that now we had said "good-bye" to him we should come away, and she closed the door behind us. It was considered that we were too young to attend the funeral. We were watching from a window when the undertaker's men arrived, solemn and black-coated, with a horse-drawn hearse. We heard the hammering as the lid of the coffin was fastened down with a callous and terrible finality, and we saw it positioned in the hearse. Then my mother, Noreen, the members of the staff, and a few family friends emerged from the house and entered a line of waiting cars. After the cortège had driven away Kenley Court seemed very still, very sad, and very empty.

Like the majority of the boys at St Anselms I had never encountered the hardships of economic reality. We knew that our parents were well-off and that our essential needs were always provided. It had not occurred to me that my father's death could possibly interfere with the well-settled continuity of my life at school, and could destroy my little world of certainties. But this was to be. When his affairs had been sifted by his executors it had become apparent that my father had been heading for bankruptcy. He had poured out thousands of pounds on the development of the petrol-saving device, but to no avail as it had proved to be a total failure and all further research on it had now been abandoned. The company which had been formed to commercialise the project was then in the throes of liquidation, with no remaining assets and numerous liabilities. As for the Babington Estate in County Cork, it would only remain solvent if most of the larger houses were sold off in the immediate future.

My mother was warned that she was going to be left with an extremely small income and she was advised to reduce the standard to which we had been living in every way possible. Within a few months of my father's death all the staff at Kenley Court were given notice, the car was sold, and the house was put on the market. Eve was taken away from her boarding school in Sussex at the end of the Easter term and was sent to a day school within walking distance from home, but when my mother attempted to remove me from St Anselms, Andrew Campbell was horrified and insisted that she should discuss the matter with him before reaching such an irrevocable decision. At their subsequent interview he told her that my whole future would be blighted if I had to leave at the age of 10. To give me a reasonable chance to succeed in life I would have to stay there until I was 13, and then go on to the leading public school for which my name had been entered. He said she would have to raise the money somehow, for instance by gifts and loans from her richer relatives, or by selling her jewellery and family heirlooms. How she funded my education was a matter for her, but funded it must be. She replied that she thought it might just be possible to keep me at St Anselms for another two or three years, but she could see no prospect of my being able to go on to an expensive public school, so she thought it would be more realistic to remove my name from the waiting list.

Kenley Court was proving extremely difficult to sell, as the market for big houses was abysmal in 1930. The Great Depression had set in during the previous year and it was a time of disappearing export markets, mounting unemployment, and general economic stagnation. In the meanwhile, my mother was endeavouring to cope with the daily problems of running our excessively large home single-handed. It was an occupation of which she had had no previous experience, as she had married and gone to live in India immediately after she had left her French school, and from that time forward my parents had always been able to employ a staff of domestic servants. Now, suddenly, she was confronted with the responsibility for looking after a fatherless family, at the same time as she was trying to teach herself the basic elements of cooking and household management. Kenley Court was like a millstone round her neck and eventually, because the property market was showing no signs of improvement, she was obliged to sell the house for a ridiculously low price. It remained a private residence for a few years more and was then converted into five self-contained flats.

When we moved out of Kenley Court my mother rented a small, semi-detached house in Purley, a few miles away. It was modern, jerry-built, and entirely lacking in character. The front garden was mainly tiled and was flanked by two low hedges; with a gravel path leading from the pavement gate to the front door. The garden at the back, entirely overlooked from both sides, consisted of a lawn about 20 yards long surrounded by narrow flower-beds. Escape from our adjoining neighbours was impossible even inside the house, as the partition wall was so thin that the sound of their radio and their voices continuously intruded on our privacy. Purley was sufficiently close to St Anselms for me to remain a weekly boarder. I used to travel between the school and my new home by bus, always sitting on the upper deck as far forward as possible. In those days the upper decks of buses were open to the elements; the seats were not upholstered, and if it rained the passengers had to cover themselves as best they could with pieces of tarpaulin attached to the backs of the seats in front of theirs. These short journeys, which cost a penny each, were among the chief pleasures of my school-week. The rush of air as we gathered speed; the enhanced impressions of height and movement; and the sublime sense of detachment as I hung precariously over the side of the accelerating vehicle.

I do not believe that my mother gave any serious thought to Mr Campbell's suggestion that she should finance my continued education with donations or loans from her relations. The most she did was to ask some of them for their advice. Her bachelor brother Dick, who lived in the vicinity of Cork city and spent most of his time on the golf course, was more interested in sporting than academic attainments. He claimed that he had never passed an exam in his life, and he had no regrets about it. Any youthful distinction he had achieved had been as an oarsman and by playing rugger for Munster. Uncle Dick's solution for my future was that I should leave school at the earliest age possible and should then enlist as a private in the regular army with a view to obtaining a commission through the ranks. This proposal did not appeal to me at all, partly because I had no wish to be a "gentleman-ranker", and partly because I realised that my secret cowardice, known only to Rabidge, would effectively preclude me from a military career. My mother also discussed my future with my Uncle Willie, the widower of her favourite sister May. When he had retired from the Indian Medical Service, with the rank of lieutenant-colonel, he had opened a private nursing home in the presidency of Madras, where he was reputed to have practised hypnotism as a cure for mental illness. It was easy to believe that this was true as his eyes were rigid and penetrating whenever he looked straight at you. We used to play chess together on his visits to Kenley Court, and I always avoided meeting his gaze in case he hypnotised me into making bad moves. Uncle Willie advised my mother to take me from St Anselms immediately and to send me to the local council school, where he was sure I would receive a perfectly adequate education. I was very shocked when I heard of his suggestion as the boys in that school, apart from being extremely bricky, were our sworn enemies, and if I had been transferred there from St Anselms there was a likelihood that I would be torn to pieces.

The next few years at St Anselms were marred for me by the embarrassment of poverty. School uniform was a perpetual worry. I knew my mother was encountering the greatest difficulty in making ends meet and was very reluctant to ask her for the things really needed. The other boys had their clothes replaced directly they had outgrown them, or at the first signs of wear and tear, whereas some of my garments were too small for me and others were patched and darned. I recall my feeling of bitter humiliation on one occasion when one of the juniors fell over in the schoolroom, ripping his shorts across the back, and heard someone say laughingly, "You'll look just like Babington now." Another mortifying experience with regard to clothing happened to me at regular intervals throughout the summer term. We used to have a special blazer for boys who were playing, or who had played, in the school cricket eleven, and although I was a permanent member of the side, I did not have one because I had not told my mother anything about them. Whenever we had a match the matron would borrow a blazer for me from someone who was out of the team that day, and I would have to wear it whether it fitted me or not.

During the summer term my indigence in comparison with my companions was also apparent when it came to permissible outings from school. Mr Campbell encouraged parents to take their sons to the floodlight tattoo at Aldershot and the Royal Tournament at Olympia - doubtless for their masculinity and for the triumphal inspiration of martial glory. Sometimes I was the only person in my dormitory who had not been to one or both of these pageants, and I had to listen to an excited discussion among the others about the displays which they had just seen.

Andrew Campbell had sent my mother details of the

"acceptable" public schools which took day-boys as well as boarders, but the fees charged by all of them were beyond the reach of her income. I was relieved when she told me this, as I had no wish to go to another school at which I would suffer the perpetual embarrassment of being surrounded by boys with wealthy parents.

My mother had then consulted a firm of educational specialists in London and had told them that she would be willing to move to any locality in England provided it contained a good school to which she could afford to send me.

They immediately recommended Reading School, a minor Public School, which, they said, was inexpensive and had an excellent reputation both for teaching and for sport. She accepted their advice and notified Andrew Campbell accordingly.

Reading School had originated during the twelfth century as the teaching establishment of Reading Abbey. It had been refounded by Henry VII as a grammar school and had continued as such until early in the twentieth century when it was elected to the Headmasters' Conference, thus being converted into a Public School. In the 1930s it had had three boarding-houses, but by far the majority of pupils had been day-boys.

My mother had never been to Reading before, nor did she know anyone who lived there. During the Easter holidays, with the help of a local estate agent, she had managed to find a three-bedroom house just outside the town, close to the neighbouring village of Shinfield. It was a detached property with a small garden and an open parkland on the opposite side of the road. What was all-important was that the rent was fairly low. Reading School and the school which Eve was going to attend were both on the Shinfield side of Reading and would be within easy walking distance of our new home.

It was arranged that I would start at Reading School in the autumn. Five other boys were leaving St Anselms that summer, and during our final term they talked continuously about the famous Public Schools to which they would be going, comparing their traditions, their customs, and their reputations. I had the feeling that all of them were joining a closed fraternity from which I would be everlastingly excluded. The six of us were inattentive to our lessons that term because we were thinking of the days that lay ahead of us. The summer months were perfect - warm and dry. After supper we would wander into the playing fields, often overhung with an evening haze, and would sprawl in a circle on the close-cropped grass planning the futures we had devised for ourselves. My own dreams were altogether fanciful. I had given up the idea of becoming a civil engineer like my father; I had decided instead to follow so many of my forbears and to become a barrister. This was by no means the full extent of my ambition. I also wanted to write successful poetry, novels and plays, and I hoped to be capped for Ireland at rugger. Possibly I would be able to find time to stand for Parliament, but I had not yet made up my mind which party I would belong to, as my political affiliations were so far undetermined. I kept these aspirations to myself for they were far too precious to be shared with my friends; they were too fragile to face the hazards of reality, and too personal for subjection to laughter and derision.

A week before we broke up we had found out that the masters were going to hold an evening meeting to discuss what they were going to say about us in our summer term reports. We persuaded Minden to go out on one of his spurious sleep-walking expeditions in order to listen to their conversation outside the door of their sitting-room. He was away for more than half-an-hour and when he returned to the dormitory he told us that he had heard them talking about the future prospects of the boys who were about to leave. Minden repeated what had been said about all of them except me. I asked him if my name had been mentioned and he replied that he had not heard it, but sometimes they were speaking so quietly that they had been inaudible, even though his ear was pressed against the door.

Next morning, Minden sat next to me at breakfast. After all the others had left the table he turned to me and said, "I told you a lie last night. I heard them talking about you quite a lot. They were saying how sorry for you they were because your mother was now so hard up."

He added dramatically, "Poor Babington! When you leave here you'll be entering a world of brickbats."

CHAPTER 5

During the four years we spent at Reading my mother succeeded in keeping within her meagre income, but often with considerable difficulty. Although we never went short of food, clothing, or any of the basic necessities of normal living, we could seldom afford even the most modest extravagances. My mother did not discuss her impecuniosity with Eve and me; nor did she dwell upon the financial constraints which were essential in order to balance her budget. But we accepted the obvious. We knew, without being told, that in the period ahead of us all expenditure would have to be reduced to an absolute minimum. There would be no summer holidays by the sea and few family outings or expeditions. I do not recall that we were ever saddened by the change in our fortunes. In fact we adjusted to our new economic circumstances so easily and readily that when our radio and refrigerator from the Kenley Court days gave out we realised they would not be replaced, and we learnt to manage without them. Our life-style at home was simple and frugal but was always contented.

We had barely settled into the house at Reading when Eve and I had to start at our new schools. As I left home on the first morning of the term I wondered if there would be any unpleasant initiation ordeals like there had been at St Anselms. I had been told that there were just over 500 pupils at Reading School, 100 of whom were boarders, and that approximately a third of the day-boys were "free-placers" whose fees were paid in full by the local authority. On my arrival I deposited my satchel and cap, and made my way to the crowded quadrangle where all the other boys seemed to be grouped amongst their friends. For 5 or 10 minutes I stood by myself, isolated and self-conscious, longing for someone to talk to me. Eventually another boy about my own age, with a friendly smile and an agreeable manner, came up to me and asked if I was a "new-bug". When I said that I was, he offered to show me where to go and what to do until I had been allocated to my form. I gladly accepted his kindness. Presently we were all summoned to the main hall above the cloisters, known as "Big School", where the masters were already seated in a single line of chairs on the dais, with the Head standing in front of them. It was the first time I had seen Mr G.H. Keeton, who had been Headmaster ever since 1914. I formed an impression of a stocky, middle-aged man with heavy horn-rimmed spectacles, who never seemed to relax his serious, worried expression. Keeton was a brilliant classical scholar and was also a former English rugby international; he was feared and respected by both the boys and by the staff. When we had formed up facing the dais someone played an introductory chord on a piano and we all sang the school song, commencing with the lines:

Eight hundred years and more have passed
Since Reading School was founded.

Pride in the longevity of the school was manifested again in the second verse:

The noble voices of the past
Are clearly to us calling;

Examples of such men as they,
Prevent the weaker falling.

After Mr Keeton had congratulated all the boys who had won scholarships and exhibitions to various universities, he read out the form lists for the coming school year, and then dismissed us to our class-rooms.

I returned home in the afternoon feeling thankful that there were, apparently, no unofficial ritualistic torments for new boys at Reading School. However, on my second day, after the last lesson, when went to the locker-room to collect my cap a boy, who I had been told was a known bully, was standing by the peg where I had hung it. I noticed that about a dozen other boys were standing around expectantly to see what was going to take place. As I reached up for my cap the bully seized my arm and swung me round towards him. Then he accused me of using his peg and told me that I must apologise for my cheek. I replied that the pegs had no names on them and I had not known that they belonged to anyone in particular. That was no excuse, he said. He had "bagged" this peg for the whole term, and as a new boy I should have made sure it was still free before I had hung my cap on it. "Are you going to apologise or not?" he asked. He had pulled me out into the open part of the locker room beside the washing-basins, and the spectators, whose numbers were growing, had formed themselves into a circle around us. I realised at once that the reserved peg was only a sham, a devised pretext. His real purpose was to test me out, to see whether I would fight him or submit. He let go of me and backed away with his fists raised. He was bigger than I was and strongly built.

"Well?" he inquired.

It was a similar situation to the one which had faced me with the window-ledge in the dormitory on my first night at St Anselms. I knew that if I refused his challenge I would reveal myself as a funk, a stigma which would be attached to me for the rest of my time at the school.

"I've done nothing wrong," I told him. "I'm not going to apologise."

There was a murmur of anticipation among the onlookers.

"Very well," he said. "You've asked for it."

He rushed at me swinging in punches from both sides and leaving himself completely uncovered in front. In that split second I saw that he had never been taught how to box. I hit him as hard as I could between the eyes with my left fist, and on the side of the jaw with my right. The shock of the blows, together with his own momentum caused him to lose his balance and to fall heavily on the stone floor. He tried to regain his feet, but subsided into a sitting position with a dazed look on his face and blood trickling from the centre of his forehead. I stood for an instant, tense and uncertain, wondering what he would do next, and hoping that the fight was over. Then a more senior boy stepped between us and, placing an arm across my chest, said authoritatively, "Break it up. He's had enough." I was only too thankful to grab my cap and go. As I left the locker-room I saw the bully leaning over a basin, with one of his friends cleaning up his face. They both ignored me.

It did not take very long for me to get to know, and to

like, the majority of the other boys in my form. There was a different approach to lessons than there had been at St Anselms, a greater keenness and urgency to learn, probably because most of my classmates came from the less privileged sections of society. On the whole, the masters were pleasant to us and were good teachers. English and history gave me the most enjoyment out of the lessons in our syllabus: mathematics and science gave me the least. I continued to take Latin, and for my modern language chose French.

Games were compulsory on three afternoons every week, and during the winter all boys who were not excused on medical grounds had to play rugby football. Early in the term, trial matches took place and those who showed any ability were picked out for special divisions according to their age groups. To my intense relief I was chosen for the under-14 special division. I was also given a place as full-back in my House junior team, a junior for this purpose being any boy below the age of 15. Day-pupils were assigned to Houses according to where they lived. If their homes were in the east side of the town or a short way beyond its eastern fringes, they went to East House. Likewise, if their homes were to the west side they were put in West House. If they lived outside the immediate vicinity of Reading they became members of County House. Although there were three separate boarding houses they were treated as a single entity for competitive events at the school and their House was known collectively as "Boarders". Owing to the geographical position of Shinfield I was placed in West House.

My first match in the inter-House championship for junior 15s was refereed by the games master, Mr Gwyn Francis, popularly known as "Fanny", who had been a well-known Welsh rugby international. When I was leaving the field after the game had finished, he called me over and asked me if I had ever thought of playing in the forwards rather than at full back. "The trouble for you will be that we have another boy at the school, a little older than you, who is an outstanding full back. I'm sure you won't want to be a permanent second-fiddle to him." I thanked him for his advice and as I turned to walk away he said, "By the way, I was most impressed with your play. If you become a forward I'm pretty certain you'll be playing for the school in a few years time." I was thrilled by his words, but disappointed nonetheless as I had set my heart on playing at full back for Ireland.

My sister Noreen was living in a flat in London. She had worked for several years as a private secretary in a government office before being taken on by the Duchess of Atholl as her social secretary. The Duchess, who was then about 60, had been the first woman MP to be elected for a Scottish constituency. Subsequently she had devoted herself to what were classified as "public activities," and she had become an ardent and persistent campaigner against the menace of Fascism. As her social secretary Noreen lived an interesting and enjoyable life, sometimes working at the Duchess's London house and sometimes at her estate in the Scottish Highlands. My brother Arnold had not been so fortunate. The British company which owned the rubber plantations he was managing in the Federated Malay States had succumbed to the Great Depression and had gone into liquidation. Arnold realised that he had little or no chance of finding another job as a planter in Malaya for the moment, as the general slump was hitting the rubber industry particularly hard and most of the estates were reducing their staffs. So he returned to England, jobless at a time of massive and mounting unemployment. He arrived home during my first term at Reading School, and although he moved into bed and breakfast accommodation in London, he came down to Shinfield for most weekends and he was always willing to give me advice whenever I asked him for it.

One of the matters troubling me was whether or not I should join the school OTC, the Officers Training Corps. Membership was not compulsory, but most boys belonged to "the Corps" unless they or their parents had conscientious or other objections to it. Even though I did not consider myself a pacifist, I had formed an intense dislike of militarism in all its aspects, and I had no desire to spend my time learning parade-ground drill, fieldcraft, or infantry tactics. I consulted Arnold about it and he had no doubt that I ought to join. He was quite certain that we would be involved in a war within the next few years, and that the more men who had already received a basic military training, the better we would be able to survive the initial battles. By the autumn of 1933 we were under no illusions as to what was taking place inside Germany. We read every day in the newspapers about the ruthlessness of the Nazi party, the liquidation of their political opponents, the concentration camps, and the brutal persecution of the Jews.

All of this seemed very far away from us, as distances in those days appeared to be much greater and few people travelled abroad. There were other features of Nazi policy, however, which were more proximate and were far more menacing. We saw photos of German youths, uniformed, tough and unsmiling, on courses of pre-military training. We heard rumours that Germany was secretly re-arming and was adjusting her economy to the requirements of warfare. And in news programmes at the cinema we watched the demented fury of Adolf Hitler as he ranted and raged about the necessity for German expansion, before massed audiences of chanting robots. During the month of October, Germany withdrew from the Disarmament Conference at Geneva and left the League of Nations. After that I reluctantly joined the OTC.

The Corps paraded once a week after lessons were over. I recall the discomfort of the thick, rough khaki uniform the first time I wore it, and the difficulty of adjusting the calf-length puttees so that they fitted smoothly without any folds. Once a term we had a field-day when we were transported to the open countryside by coach to enact a mock battle. The highlight of the year was the annual camp which always took place during the summer holidays. Several OTC camps were organised by the army every August in different parts of England, at each of which detachments from various schools were grouped together, living under canvas for a week's intensive training. Unless a boy had attended at least one camp he was not permitted to enter his name for Certificate "A". This was usually taken at the age of 16 or 17 and consisted of a written examination and a practical test. If you had passed you were supposed to be qualified to receive an immediate temporary commission in the army in the event of a general mobilisation. Most of us had joined the OTC for the primary purpose of being in possession of Certificate "A" if Britain should become involved in another war.

At the beginning of my first summer term at Reading, Fanny asked me if I had played cricket for St Anselms . I replied that I had been one of the opening pace bowlers in the school side and I had batted half-way down the batting order. "In that case," he said, "we'll probably put you in the under-15 special division. We always have a need for all-rounders." A few days later my name was listed with a dozen or so other juniors for a trial in the nets at the end of the afternoon classes. To my disappointment Fanny was not there. The trial was conducted by the housemaster of one of the boarding houses, a very tall, gaunt clergyman with whom I had never come in contact. He stood alongside the nets making notes on all of our performances and told us afterwards we would hear in due course which of us had been selected for the special division. In the changing-room another boy informed me that he had managed to glance at the master's notes. He had seen against my name, "Batting: N.G." and "Bowling: N.G." He suggested that N.G. might be an abbreviation for the comment "Not good," but it was apparent to me that it might equally well stand for "No Good". In consequence, I was not at all surprised to learn that I had not been numbered among the chosen few. When I next met Fanny he said, "I'm sorry to see you didn't make it. It was obviously one of your off-days. Don't lose heart, though, there'll be further opportunities later on."

After I had had two or three games in the division to which I was allocated I realised that I would have no chance of getting another trial for the special division. The standard of play was deplorably low, nobody watched us or examined the results, and the participants did not take the matches seriously, only wishing to get them over as quickly as possible. I felt that this was definitely not for me so I decided to abandon cricket for good and to take up rowing instead. Reading was in its infancy as a rowing school at that time and did not compete in any regattas or other inter-school events, although the training facilities were excellent as the boathouse was situated on a long broad stretch of the Thames. Each of the Houses was allowed to have a limited number of oarsmen, and at the end of the summer term representative House fours competed against each other for the rowing championship over a course about a mile long. The West House captain of rowing told me I would probably have to wait a year for acceptance as he had already reached his permitted quota. He said I had the right build for an oarsman and he would like to get me in as soon as possible, but in the meanwhile I would have to go on playing every week in my cricketing division.

I was enjoying my school days a great deal and taking part in a number of different activities. I became a keen member of the Debating Society, I acted in the annual school plays, and I took part in sketches, most of which I had written myself, in nearly all the school concerts. I was still a voracious reader, concentrating mainly on 19th and early 20th century novelists such as Dickens, Galsworthy,

Trollope, and Thackeray. My ambitions had remained undiminished and I told all my friends that I was going to be a barrister, without considering seriously how this could ever come about. As a preliminary it would be essential for me to go to a university and to take a degree. In those days most undergraduates were privately financed, but my mother would have been in no position to pay my fees and nobody else was likely to do so. The only alternative was a scholarship or an exhibition. These were few in number and competition for them was intense. I knew I was too idle to undertake the amount of extra work which would be necessary before I became a serious candidate. Besides, you needed money to start at the Bar. It was common knowledge that most newly called barristers were lucky if they could even cover their professional expenses during their first few years in practice. So I went on pretending to myself and refusing to face reality.

Sometimes it seemed that our futures would probably be denied to us, and that to plan for the years ahead was to indulge in idle fantasy. Month after month Hitler was proclaiming his "New Order", based upon the supremacy of the German Master Race. When in the spring of 1935 he announced the introduction of military conscription in Germany, in flagrant violation of the Treaty of Versailles, we felt as though the iron hand of destiny was tightening its relentless hold around us.

That summer Uncle Dick wrote to my mother offering to pay for a month's holiday for the three of us in the south of Ireland. In his moments of generosity he was apt to do things in style. Not only did he book us accommodation at a hotel on the coast of County Cork, but he sent her three first-class tickets for the journey, and a cheque to cover our incidental expenses en route. It was a great thrill for Eve and me to travel on the evening express from Paddington to Fishguard, to dine in the restaurant-car, to make the night crossing in single cabins on the boat, and to sail slowly into Cork harbour in the early morning sunlight. Uncle Dick sent his car, driven by his gardener, to meet us at the quayside. We were taken to his house in Sundays Well where his housekeeper had prepared a huge breakfast for us, before the gardener drove us down to our hotel. We were still on holiday in Ireland when Noreen became engaged. Her fiancé Norman Parkes, was a fairly successful London barrister who had recently received a great deal of publicity by defending a young army lieutenant on a charge of spying for Germany, in what had become known as "The Officer in the Tower" case. Directly he had heard the news, Uncle Dick told my mother that he wanted Noreen to have the sort of wedding her father would have wished for her, and that he would be happy to pay the entire cost.

The marriage took place the following autumn in the picturesque village of Mayfield in Sussex, where friends of Norman's had lent their large country house for the reception. Uncle Dick gave Noreen away, Eve was her chief bridesmaid, and Arnold and I were ushers. After spending their honeymoon in Austria and Italy, Noreen and Norman moved into a flat in Westminster. At that time Norman was still a stranger to Noreen's family and we found him a difficult person to get to know because he was shy and reserved, as well as being extremely formal. But he thawed on acquaintanceship. We soon found that behind his withdrawn manner he was both kindly and thoughtful, and he had a dry, but puckish sense of humour. In the early days of their married life they had an excellent living-in Swiss maid at the flat, who used to help Noreen with the cooking. Even when they were dining at home by themselves Norman liked to change into a dinner jacket in the evening.

After my sixteenth birthday Noreen and Norman decided that the time had come for me to abandon my airy-fairy notions and to start thinking seriously about my career, so they asked me to come to dinner with them and to spend the night at their flat. During the evening Norman asked me bluntly, "How long do you intend to stay at school and what are you going to do when you leave?" I told him I was determined to become a barrister. I had recently inherited a small legacy from an aunt of my father's which would be sufficient to cover my entrance fees on becoming a student at an Inn of Court, and also the payments involved when I was eventually called to the Bar. He inquired what plans I had made about going to a university and whether I had investigated the possibility of getting a scholarship or an exhibition. I replied that I would not expect my mother to keep me for an extra three years on her meagre income. I intended to leave school in a year's time, to get a part-time job and to maintain myself while I was taking a degree. "Let's be practical," Norman said. "What sort of part-time work are you going to do?" When I told him I would like to become a journalist he said that a couple of men who had been at Oxford with him were now in Fleet Street and he would ask them how I should make a start.

My last year at Reading School was full, carefree, and personally eventful. I had passed School Certificate with the necessary number of credits to gain me exemption from matriculation, so I was put into the lower sixth form along with other boys commencing a two-year course of study for Higher Certificate. As I did not intend to sit for this exam, I was able to enjoy the lessons without feeling myself under any pressure or strain. Furthermore, I could devote a large amount of time to other activities like the dramatic and debating societies, and to writing and acting in sketches at the periodic school concerts. Rugby football continued to be one of my principal interests; I played for the school side as a forward, usually in the centre of the back row. We were extremely successful that winter, remaining unbeaten throughout, with the result that no less than eight of us were invited to take part in the final trial for the Berkshire Public Schools team. I still disliked the OTC. I had attended the annual camp in Yorkshire during the previous summer holidays, which had increased my aversion to military life and had left me with a deep impression of the subservient anonymity of the private soldier's existence. However, my 10 days at camp had made it possible for me to take and to pass Certificate "A". After that, I had no further interest in the Corps and I evaded the parades as often as I was able to do so.

I was now a House Prefect and I felt it my duty to set an example to the younger members of the house by entering for the school boxing championships. I was graded a middleweight. My first two contests were comparatively easy, but I lost my bout in the semi-finals to an Australian boy who eventually won the weight. During the last round he landed a punch on the side of my jaw which momentarily dazed me and caused bells to ring in my head. If he had realised my condition he could have finished the fight with another blow, but fortunately for me he did not press home his attack and he allowed me to recover. Afterwards the physical training sergeant-major said to me, "That was a good scrap - your left against his right. I put him marginally ahead of you on points." I had vowed to myself that I would never box again, and I kept to my vow. Boxing had never appealed to me as a sport. I derived no enjoyment out of hitting my opponent and I disliked it intensely when he hit me. St Anselms had obviously failed to indoctrinate me with a sufficiently manly approach to life.

All through 1936 the war clouds were continuing to gather over Europe. In March, Hitler had ordered his troops to reoccupy the previously demilitarised Rhineland. In July, civil war had broken out in Spain and Germany had sent the specially-recruited Condor Legion to fight with General Franco's rebels. In October, Mussolini and Hitler had agreed on their respective spheres of expansion and had formed the Rome-Berlin Axis to support each other in further acts of aggression.

Reading School had just decided to take up competitive rowing, modestly at first, with a representative four rather than an eight, which would be entered for various junior events at down-Thames regattas during the summer term. I was delighted to be chosen for a place in the provisional school boat, rowing at two. One of our Old Boys, a keen member of Reading Rowing Club, had offered to coach us, and since all the crew were living locally, we had trained nearly every evening during the Easter holidays. Although we did not gain any trophies at regattas that year, we were successful in winning a number of preliminary heats and on several occasions we were only narrowly defeated in the final race of our event. One of the most exhilarating experiences in rowing is to come up from behind to overtake the rival crew - seeing the bow of their boat, then the oarsmen one after another, and lastly their cox, as you pull ahead in a flurry of blades and spray. Every regatta was an adventure for me. The carnival gaiety of the atmosphere. The friendliness and camaraderie of the contestants. The blazers of the men and the bright-coloured frocks of the ladies in the stands. The undulating strains of a brass band, partly heard amid the clamour and the cheering. The excitement of the finals in the fading light of the evening. This was for me a taste of the drama of living.

One of Norman's journalist friends had recently become the Chief Press Officer at a Government Ministry, and a few weeks before the end of the term he invited me to lunch with him at the National Liberal Club with a view to giving me his advice on my career. It was the first occasion on which I had been into any London club and I was expecting an atmosphere of warmth and conviviality: instead, I found the setting rather awesome; the subdued voices in the dining room, the long deserted passages, and the numerous portraits of grim-expressioned Victorian or Edwardian statesmen. My host, who was helpful, though brisk and plain-spoken, told me that Norman had discussed my future with him and had lent him some of my manuscripts to read. "They're not without promise," he said, "and they show you have a definite bent for writing." He did not know, he went on, whether or not it would be possible for me to combine journalism with reading for the Bar, but that was a problem I would have to sort out for myself. Obviously I would need a job which allowed me the maximum amount of time for studying - for instance, working on a weekly or a Sunday newspaper. However, before I did anything else I must try to get the best training and the best qualifications for myself as a reporter. He recommended that I should write to Donald Spendlove, the News Editor of the Press Association, inquiring if there were any vacancies on his staff of telephonists. He knew Spendlove very well and he would put in a good word for me. Telephonists, he explained, accompanied reporters on assignments and phoned their copy to the sub-editors for them. It was an excellent way of learning the trade, and a way in which several of the top journalists in Fleet Street had begun their careers. "In your letter to Mr Spendlove," he said, "tell him the basic details about yourself, age, education, exams passed etc. - and about your interest in writing. Mention that you got a junior county cap at rugger, but keep quiet about the fact that you write poetry. It might give the wrong impression." As I left the National Liberal Club, my excitement was tempered by a dread, founded on my own imagination, that telephonists would be obliged to wear a uniform. Although I expected to start in my employment at the very bottom, I thoroughly disliked the prospect of being dressed up as a messenger boy.

My interview at the Press Association took place during the following week. I was seen in a small office by a member of the News Room's staff who told me that a telephonist was regarded as a trainee-reporter, and in consequence the pay was extremely low. Occasionally they were promoted to the reporting staff of the Press Association, but normally they stayed for a couple of years and then obtained jobs on national or provincial newspapers. There was a vacancy for a telephonist at that moment, he said, and if I still wanted to apply, the News Editor would be willing to offer it to me. I told him I considered myself unbelievably lucky to be given this opportunity, and we settled then and there that I would start work directly I had broken up at school.

To my intense relief he never suggested that I should go to a clothing room to be fitted for my uniform.

CHAPTER 6

The Press Association, generally known as the PA, was the largest news agency in Britain, supplying its services to all the national and to most of the provincial papers in the country. It only dealt with news which emanated at home, foreign news being covered by Reuters, an associated company. Apart from its own reporting staff in London, the PA had a network of reporters on local papers all over England, Wales, and Scotland, who could act as its agents in the event of any interesting story breaking suddenly in their area.

When I joined the PA in the early autumn of 1937 the agency was occupying temporary premises in St Bride Street, a turning off Ludgate Circus, while its new offices, to be shared with Reuters, were being completed in Fleet Street. The St Bride Street building was utterly inadequate for the size of the staff and the scope of their activities. The News Room was on the first floor. Donald Spendlove, the News Editor, sat at a large table opposite "Tommy" Tomlinson, the Diarist, who was responsible for the daily allocation of jobs to reporters and telephonists. Also seated at the table were a senior editorial assistant and the chief telephonist. Elizabeth, the News Editor's secretary, had her desk in a corner behind Mr Tomlinson. A connecting door led into the overcrowded reporters' room, which they shared with the telephonists. The sub-editors and all the other departments were upstairs, crammed into the second and third floors. Somewhere up there, too, was the office of Henry Martin, the Editor-in-Chief. I never saw the inside of it, nor did I ever find out exactly where it was located.

On my first morning I was shown into the News Room

where Mr Spendlove shook me by the hand and told the chief telephonist, Peter Hoare, to look after me. Peter took me back to the reporters' room, and introduced me to some of the other telephonists, of whom there were about a dozen in all. He showed me the notice board on which every morning he put up a list of duties for the day, after he had received his instructions from Mr Tomlinson. For the whole of that week, he said, I would be going around with another telephonist and learning the job. During my second week I would be expected to perform my duties on my own. Then he suggested we should go down for a coffee at the ABC cafe next door, which I gathered that the reporters and telephonists tended to treat as a Press Association canteen, and frequently visited for a moment of relaxation before they started the day's work. There were few opportunities for tranquillity in the rackety atmosphere of the reporters' room. I remember it as being constantly hazy under a pall of cigarette smoke; and the dissonance of chattering voices, telephones ringing, the pervasive rattling of typewriters, and the continual bustle as people came and people went. There was the same sense of urgency in the News Room. Incessant phone calls; half-finished cups of coffee; ash-trays full of smouldering stubs; accumulating piles of copy on the centre table; and the door to the reporters' room perpetually opening and closing. Bewildering as it was for the new arrival, I realised that this was the environment of the newspaper world.

Most of the telephonists worked from 9:30 in the morning until about 5:30 in the afternoon, though a few were on the early turn, and one of them had to come in late in the afternoon and remain on duty until midnight. The Press Association normally covered all the newsworthy trials at the Old Bailey, London Sessions in Newington Causeway, and Middlesex Sessions off Parliament Square, and I used to spend a good deal of my time sitting in the press galleries at these courts, slipping out periodically to phone a batch of copy for one of the reporters. I was also sent to Magistrates' and Coroners' Courts, and every now and then to cases being tried outside London. All this stimulated my interest in the law and I watched with fascination the adroit manner in which experienced barristers conducted their cases. Although the courts occupied a large part of the telephonists' regular routine, countless other assignments were listed on our notice board, such as meetings, conferences, and conventions. Sometimes we accompanied reporters to demonstrations or disturbances, and on two occasions I stood amongst a silent crowd at dawn outside the gates of Wandsworth Prison while a convicted murderer was being hanged.

The most unpopular duty we had to fulfil was the phoning of after-dinner speeches. The telephonist would turn up in the middle of the evening at the hotel, restaurant, or other venue where the function was taking place, and he would send in a message to the PA reporter at the press table to say he had arrived. Then followed a long tedious wait in some sort of ante-room, while the speeches were being made. I used to think that there could be few sounds more hollow and more irritating than laughter at an unheard joke, or applause for an unseen speaker. Eventually the reporter would emerge, immaculately turned out in a dinner jacket, and hand over his copy to be phoned to the sub-editors. The only recompense for the boring evenings was that we could claim overtime for them, and our salaries were so small that we were continuously on the lookout for ways in which to augment them. A more welcome duty was to be sent off accompanying a reporter on an assignment which necessitated spending one or more nights at a hotel. These trips were known as "out of towns" and were eagerly sought after, because the daily maintenance allowance enabled a telephonist to live quite comfortably and still make a profit. Reporters and telephonists were equally dishonest when filling in their claims for expenses. It was a recognised practice that you found out the most expensive way of getting to a place and claimed accordingly. If possible, you travelled by a cheaper route. Fictitious taxi rides were not at all unknown, and telephonists habitually falsified the number of calls they had made from public call boxes whilst phoning their copy. Donald Spendlove, who had to check all our claim-forms before passing them to the cashiers' department, was fairly tolerant with regard to the chicaneries of his staff, provided they were not carried to excess. From time to time someone would be summoned to the News Room and would find Spendlove sitting at the table frowning slightly with a form in his hand. He would point to an item with his pencil and say quietly, "I couldn't possibly pass this. You'd better take it away and make out a new one."

Telephonists received a basic wage of a guinea a week, equivalent to one pound and five pence in decimalised coinage. Junior reporters on the Press Association at that time started at a salary of eight pounds a week. I think that all the telephonists were living at home, and presumably all were contributing towards their keep, but in spite of the smallness of our pay our lives were never dominated by financial constraints. The paperback Penguin publications kept us well supplied with good literature and an organisation called the Privilege Ticket Register enabled us to obtain seats at West End theatres for considerably less than normal cost. Apart from the weekends, we had very little free time, as most of our evenings were occupied with phoning after-dinner speeches or attending shorthand courses. We did not spend much money on lunches. If we happened to be back from a morning assignment we usually went down to the ABC tearoom for a cheap snack, and once in a while a group of us would go along to the Strand Palace where they served a two-course meal for one shilling and sixpence, less than 10 pence in the coinage of today.

When we left Reading my mother decided to move to London, and she had rented a comfortable five-room flat on the first floor of a block in Prince of Wales Drive, directly overlooking the trees and the foliage of Battersea Park. Eve had obtained a job with a firm of interior decorators in Oxford Street. Before employing her they had asked to see some of her paintings and specimen designs.

Fortunately they had liked what she showed them and they had taken her on as a trainee-assistant. My mother had always placed a high value on the preservation of close family ties, and often on a Sunday Arnold would come over from his flat in Pimlico, or Noreen and Norman from theirs at Westminster, to join us for our midday meal. Arnold's affairs had taken a turn for the better. After progressing through various ascending grades in his company he was now the assistant director of personnel. As for Norman, his practice at the Bar was steadily increasing and he had become the head of a small set of chambers at Dr Johnson's Building. I met all the other members of the set, two of whom I found particularly interesting. The first was Norman's closest friend, Conolly Gage, a man of immense charm from Northern Ireland. The other, equally charming, was a young Welshman called Elwyn Jones, who had an ambition to become a Member of Parliament. He was an ardent Socialist and he had just written a condemnatory study of fascism in Britain which had been published by The Left Book Club. Years later he was to become a very popular and much respected Lord Chancellor.

At the Press Association we were working a five-and-half-day week, like most other non-manual employees in Britain during the 1930s. On Saturday mornings the mood in the reporters' room was quite different from other days, with everyone in casual clothing, a prevalent sense of lightheartedness, and a total absence of the customary activity. It used to seem almost as if the weekend holiday had already begun. There was a rule that if a telephonist was not out on a job he was allowed to leave at half-past twelve, and I had joined the London Irish rugger club at the beginning of the season after I had been assured by Mr Tomlinson that he would always get me away in good time for Saturday afternoon matches, provided they were taking place in the vicinity of London. I would usually have time for a coffee and a sandwich in the ABC before I hurried to the station to meet up with the other members of the team, as we were notified in advance which train we were going to catch. From then on, Fleet Street and the Press Association would fade from my mind and my thoughts were filled with the match ahead of us. The pattern was always the same. The muted joviality of the journey; the walk to the ground; the nervous anticipation of the changing-room; and the ecstatic moment, like an instant of liberation, when we doubled together on to the field in a cluster of green jerseys, to the cheers of our supporters on the touch-line. There followed the game itself. The physical abandonment to the contest. The total commitment to winning, and the thrills of fluctuating fortunes right up to the final whistle. Afterwards, muddy and bruised, both teams would pile into a shallow, communal bath-tub in an easy fellowship of steam, perspiration, and tranquillity. The home side always provided a huge tea-meal after the match, served by a group of wives, girl-friends, sisters, and other female adherents of their club. In the evening there would be drinking and singing in the bar and, usually, an impromptu dance to the music of a gramophone or piano.

The chief telephonist at the Press Association was even worse off financially than the other telephonists as he could not supplement his income with expenses or with out-of-towns, but he was able to allocate himself a certain number of evening duties phoning after-dinner speeches at the ordinary overtime rate. Although our low rate of pay sufficed for our own modest needs, we all suffered, nevertheless, from a certain amount of social embarrassment because most of our friends and acquaintances in other occupations were obviously better off than we were. Moreover, they seemed to imagine that our type of employment must carry a far higher salary than was actually the case. I found it especially frustrating that I could not afford to take out some of the incredibly attractive girls that I was meeting. I could have made a clean breast of my financial position and suggested that we should each pay a proportion of the cost, but such a course would have been utterly abhorrent to the male chauvinist sentiments of my generation. It was preferable to pretend that we were kept so busy in the evenings and at weekends that we never knew in advance whether or not we would be free for a private assignation. I was constantly falling in and out of love, and Eve used to chide me on the fickle nature of my passions.

The dreaded prospect of another European war was never far from our minds. In February 1938 Anthony Eden, the Foreign Secretary, resigned as a protest against the British Government's continued appeasement of the fascist dictators, Hitler and Mussolini. A month later the German Army invaded Austria. Winston Churchill warned the House of Commons that Europe was confronted with "A programme of aggression, nicely calculated and timed, unfolding stage by stage." He said that we, and all the other free nations, would be left with the choice of either submitting like Austria had done or taking effective measures while time remained.

At that time I considered myself to be an ardent Irish Nationalist. I do not think I talked much about Irish politics but I may have done so from time to time on Saturday evenings with my friends at the London Irish Rugger Club. At any rate, as soon as my first season with the club had ended another member, a man about 10 years older than me, invited me to meet him for lunch in a pub near Fleet Street. During the course of the meal he told me that he had become involved in the formation of a new society called the Anti-Partition of Ireland League, the object of which would be to campaign by peaceful and lawful means for the abolition of the border between the Irish Free State and Northern Ireland, and for the reunification of the whole country into a single independent state. They were anxious to gain the support of as many Anglo-Irish Protestants as possible, and he asked me if I would like to become a member. I replied that before I decided whether or not to join the League I wanted to attend one of its meetings in order to satisfy myself that it was genuinely committed to the use of non-violent and lawful methods. He said he approved of my cautious approach and he would contact me again in the near future.

I received an invitation to the inaugural meeting of the London branch of the Anti-Partition of Ireland League. It was held in a small hall in a back street in Clapham. At one end, a large Irish Free State tricolour was draped across an entire wall. In front of the flag the committee was seated at a table facing the audience, which consisted of some 30 to 40 men and women of all ages. The lighting was dim, and before the proceedings commenced the atmosphere was quite conspiratorial, people speaking to their neighbours in hushed voices. I heard two priests in the row behind me commenting approvingly that it was reminiscent of the clandestine Sinn Fein meetings in "occupied Ireland" during the Troubled Times. Most of the speeches were in a low key and gave an impression that very little thought had been given to the function and the immediate programme of the League. The only constructive proposal put forward by the newly-elected president was that members should write repeatedly to their MPs and their local papers reiterating the contention that there would be no peace and prosperity in Ireland until the partition of the country was ended. At the conclusion of the meeting I decided to join the League and I paid my first year's subscription. I do not remember hearing from them again.

Some of the most notable staging-points in our formative years are unplanned, unheralded, and unsought, so that they seem, in retrospect, to be predetermined stepping-stones in our progression to maturity. Soon after my eighteenth birthday, one of my school friends called Frank Shaw invited me to spend the weekend at his parents' house in Goring-on-Thames. He told me that two young Germans, a brother and sister from Hamburg, would also be staying and he wanted my help in entertaining them. They were the children of a business acquaintance of his father's, said Frank, and he warned me that the whole of their family were fervent Nazis. I arrived at the Shaws' house in time for lunch on the Saturday and was introduced to the German guests, Otto, who was 21, and Helga, aged 19. Although it was only the last week in May the weather was unusually mild with clear unclouded skies, and the four of us spent the whole afternoon swimming and sunbathing at a Thames-side lido near Goring. Otto and Helga, who both typified the Nazi concept of the Nordic master-race - tall, blond, and athletic - had recently returned from a strenuous hiking expedition in the Black Forest, organised by the Hitler Youth movement. As I had expected of them, they were strong swimmers and graceful divers and I had the impression that they enjoyed showing off their proficiency. Neither Frank nor I found them a particularly easy pair to entertain. Although their English was fluent, Otto was arrogant, tight-lipped and uncommunicative: his sister confined herself to polite replies and never originated a topic of conversation herself. Once, while the two of them were swimming, Frank inquired, "Well, what do you make of the ravishing Helga?" I told him truthfully that I found her difficult to assess. Her face and features were undoubtedly attractive, though marred by her stolidity of expression; her body was nicely proportioned, bronzed and shapely. But in spite of her physical attributes she was lacking, for me at any rate, in the evocative, indefinable endowment of sex-appeal. Frank said his reaction to her was the same as mine. That evening the Shaws had invited a number of their younger friends to supper, and we all packed in around a narrow table on their patio. Otto was seated facing me. He had drunk too much, as I had too, and during the meal we became involved in a heated argument in which he was trying to defend the German invasion of Austria and the persecution of the Jews. I remember saying furiously that Hitler had made a national cult of brutality and aggression, and his equally vigorous retort that Chamberlain had made a national cult of decadence. Before I could say anything more Helga, who was seated beside me, laid a restraining hand on my arm, and Mrs Shaw intervened from the head of the table, "Now then, you two! We're here to enjoy ourselves, so let's have no more political arguments."

I went up to my room before the party had ended because I felt tired, slightly drunk, and heartily ashamed of my outburst to a fellow-guest in the Shaws' house. I had just climbed into bed when there was a soft tap on the door. I said "Come in," and to my surprise Helga entered and closed the door behind her. "I've come to apologise for my brother's behaviour," she explained. "He shouldn't have accused you of being decadent. But you're equally to blame for riling him about the Führer. We think different from you about these matters and we'll never change our views."

She had advanced to the centre of the room. Suddenly she asked, "Tony, have you any Jewish blood?" I told her that as far as I knew I had none.

"Good," she said. "I didn't come here to talk about your quarrel with my brother. I came for a different purpose." As she spoke she was unbuttoning her blouse with one hand and loosening her skirt with the other. "I like you," she went on, "and you made me realise at supper how much you wanted me - the pressure of your body against mine."

With a ridiculous sense of modesty I averted my eyes from her as she was undressing. When I glanced at her again she was standing with her back to me, completely naked, methodically folding her clothes on a chair. She asked me in a matter-of-fact tone if I had ever made love to a girl before. Instinctively I wanted to claim that I had, but I knew that the truth would soon become apparent, so I admitted that this was to be the first time. "Everybody must start once," she commented.

She turned round and started to walk briskly towards the bed. I had no idea what posture should be adopted by the male in such circumstances so I threw aside the blankets and sheet, and lay back waiting for her.

And then the smothering carnal embrace and the subsidence of the mattress as her weight on it was added to mine.

After it was over I reflected that the experience had been exciting enough, but I wondered whether the act of love was always so unromantic and so clinical.

CHAPTER 7

I had made up my mind that I would continue as a telephonist on the staff of the Press Association for about two years. I planned to join an Inn of Court as a student in the summer of 1939 and to start looking for a new job during the following autumn. As soon as I became a reporter on a weekly newspaper I would enrol at a university and commence my law studies. I told Mr Spendlove and Mr Tomlinson my intentions and they were both very helpful, promising to assist me in every way they could.

The PA employed a certain number of reporters on "space", which meant that they were not members of the regular staff, but only worked on a part-time basis as and when they were required. I became quite friendly with one of them, David Birch, and from time to time I acted for him as his telephonist. David was in the middle twenties. A short while previously he had resigned his job as a reporter on a national Sunday newspaper because he wanted to earn his living as a freelance journalist. "It was probably a crazy idea," he said to me once when we were lunching together, "but we're two of a kind, you and me. It was no more crazy than the course you've set for yourself." He had gone on to inquire what progress I was making with my writing, and I told him that whereas I managed to place an occasional article with a paper or magazine I was having no success in selling my short stories. He advised me to try to interest a good literary agent in my work. "They study the markets and they know where to send your stuff," he said. "You don't have to pay them a fee. They take a set commission on anything they sell for you." David was a prolific writer who seemed to have no difficulty in getting his articles published, so I was delighted when he offered to give me an introduction to his own firm of agents. He arranged for the woman who handled his work to see a selection of my manuscripts, and when she read them she wrote to me saying that in her opinion the quality of my work was saleable and her firm would like to act for me. From then on I used to send her everything I wrote and though she managed to place most of my articles, she never succeeded in selling any of my short stories.

My work as a telephonist left me very little time for writing except at weekends, and during the winter, when I was playing rugger every Saturday, it meant that I only had Sundays completely free. I had decided not to join a rowing club while I was working for the Press Association owing to the difficulty of making myself available for mid-week training and for Saturday regattas. During the summer of 1938 I took up tennis, partly because I enjoyed the game and partly to keep myself fit for my next season with the London Irish. I used to play regularly with a group of friends, sometimes singles and sometimes foursomes, at the public courts in Battersea Park. Towards the end of July that year the chief telephonist was promoted to fill a vacancy on the PA reporting staff, and Donald Spendlove offered me his job. At first I was delighted, but when I thought it over I began to doubt if I would be wise to accept. It would be another year before I began to look for a job and I realised that I still had a great deal more to learn by watching how able and seasoned reporters carried out their work. Although experience in the News Room would undoubtedly broaden my knowledge of the editorial process, it would teach me very little of the skills I was so anxious to acquire. I told Mr Spendlove exactly how I felt about the matter and he agreed that what I had said was true. As a result, he appointed two of us as joint chief telephonists, alternating at weekly intervals, so that each of us could spend half of his time in the News Room and the other half going about with the reporters.

One of my principal responsibilities in the News Room was to draw up the list of assignments for the telephonists, under the supervision of Mr Tomlinson, and if necessary to decide who would be sent on an "out-of-town". The chief telephonist had numerous other duties, some of them routine and some of them *ad hoc*. For instance, every day at noon he was required to ascertain the price of gold on the London bullion market and to try to make an interesting news item out of it if there had been an exceptional rise or fall compared with the previous value. Another of his responsibilities was to find out from the War Office if the results of any courts martial had been promulgated, and whenever a promulgated case had an interesting twist, to write a few paragraphs about it. If we were very busy Donald Spendlove used to give me quite a lot of news items to write up for provincial papers.

It was extremely exciting to be working at the nerve-centre of the largest news agency in Britain. There, in that small, overcrowded room we were in continual contact with reporters who were covering all the principal stories of the day, and we were constantly receiving dramatic news flashes concerned with contemporary events; sometimes I took them myself if the calls were put through on my telephone.

In those days, whenever we made plans for the long-term future we always qualified them in our minds with the proviso "if there's not a war." That was the extent to which the looming menace of Nazi Germany overclouded our lives. Having absorbed Austria into his Greater Reich, Hitler had turned his attentions to Czechoslovakia, with its large German-speaking minority living in the Sudetenland. In February 1938, Leon Blum, the French Premier, made a categorical announcement that if Germany were to invade the Sudetenland, France would honour her treaty obligations to protect the Czechs from aggression. Although Britain was bound by no similar commitment to defend the Czechoslovak borders, it was inconceivable that if France was forced to intervene we would not do so too.

During the spring, negotiations commenced between the Czech Government and the leader of the Sudeten Nazis, which were conducted in the face of a growing campaign of intimidation by the Germans and proved entirely unproductive. In an effort to avert the impending catastrophe the British Prime Minister, Neville Chamberlain, sent Lord Runciman on a mission to Prague as an "independent mediator", with the object of persuading the two sides to agree on a compromise solution. Runciman could achieve nothing and he returned to England after two weeks of abortive talks. With the approach of autumn the situation remained deadlocked. Early in September Hitler delivered his most vitriolic attack yet upon Czechoslovakia, and the following day the Sudetenlanders abandoned any further attempts to settle the matter peaceably.

I was then 18, so I had reached the minimum age of enlistment in the armed forces. I had thought long and hard about my position. I detested Nazism and everything for which it stood, but like so many others in my generation, who had grown up in the lingering shadows of Passchendaele and the Somme, I was well aware of the pitiless and imbecile futility of the battlefield. Nevertheless, I recognised the concept of a just war, and had no doubt about the moral propriety under the existing circumstances of defending the Czechs against a German invasion of their soil. I therefore made up my mind that should Britain become involved in the conflict I would volunteer for service with the army.

On September 15, Chamberlain, on his own initiative, had flown to Munich for private consultations with Hitler with regard to the crisis. He returned to London two days later to inform the Cabinet of his view that the Czechs must be persuaded to cede the whole of Sudetenland to Germany as the only way of preventing a German invasion. The Cabinet agreed with his opinions, and it was also shared by the French. The Czech Government was then notified of an Anglo-French proposal that all the areas in their country containing over 50 per cent of German inhabitants should be handed over to Germany. It was made clear that unless they accepted this advice, they would receive no assistance from either France or Britain if the Germans invaded their country. I was in the News Room that week and I remember Donald Spendlove remarking that this had been one of the most shameful events in recent British history.

When the Czech Government received what virtually amounted to an Anglo-French ultimatum, they immediately resigned and were replaced by a non-party administration which, bereft of support from any quarter, was compelled to agree to the terms proposed. Having been instrumental in procuring what he perceived as a lasting solution to the impasse, Chamberlain flew back to Germany for more discussions, only to be informed by Hitler that the Anglo-French plan did not go far enough to satisfy his demands. He returned to England on September 24, after two days of fruitless negotiations, to tell the Cabinet of the failure of his mission. At that moment if looked as though war was inevitable. The Czechs had ordered a full, and the French a partial mobilisation, and Hitler had issued a final warning to the Czechoslovak Government that if they did not agree by 2 p.m. on September 28 to the outright cession of the whole of the Sudeten territories to Germany, he would take them over by force on October 1. The day before the German ultimatum expired Neville Chamberlain broadcast a message to the nation in which he said that although he regarded war as a nightmare he was still convinced that if any country tried to dominate the world by armed might it would have to be resisted. The government disclosed a short while later that orders had been issued by the Admiralty for the immediate mobilisation of the Fleet.

The British people dispassionately prepared themselves for war. There were no cheering crowds, no flag-waving, no apparent militancy, and no manifestations of patriotic fervour. There was only a settled resignation and a sense of grim foreboding. We all carried on with our normal lives, but against an abnormal background in which gas-masks were being distributed and leaflets being circulated directing us about black-out precautions. It was anticipated that during the initial phases of the forthcoming conflict the enemy bombers would inflict a terrible devastation on English cities, with wholesale casualties, and that London would become one of the principal targets. On the day after Chamberlain's broadcast I walked through Battersea Park on my way home from work, and I saw the teams of volunteers digging long, narrow trenches across the grass-covered spaces in a pitifully inadequate attempt to provide air-raid shelters for local inhabitants. A few antiquated anti-aircraft guns had been positioned alongside the river, and squads of young soldiers in shirt-sleeves were erecting bell-tents nearby. I stood there watching for several minutes, finding it difficult to believe that all this was really happening.

I had made up my mind to send in my notice to the Press Association and to join the army as soon as we declared war on Germany. I did not know exactly how a person enlisted, whether it was by application to the War Office or to a Regimental Depot, but I assumed that there would be some sort of official guidance when the time came. I half remembered reading that during the Great War, or it might have been the Boer War, there had been special enlistment booths at which attractive girls were continuously at hand to give a hug and a kiss to every man who volunteered for service. I asked Mr Tomlinson about it and he said that nothing so pleasurable had happened to him when he had joined up in 1916 - he had merely received his call-up papers through the post, telling him when and where to report. On the afternoon of September 28 the atmosphere in the News Room was tense and unusually quiet as we awaited the expiry of Hitler's ultimatum. Two o'clock passed and it was clear that the Czechoslovak Government had refused to comply with the German terms. In the vacuum of information which followed, every time a telephone rang we were expecting to hear that Germany had started to invade the Sudetenland. Then came the dramatic message that Hitler had invited Chamberlain, Daladier, and Mussolini to meet him in Munich immediately in order to re-examine the situation. Chamberlain had just announced in the House of Commons that he had accepted the invitation and was preparing to make a final effort to prevent the outbreak of war.

The Munich meeting, to which the Czechs had not been invited, began at noon the next day and continued until the morning of September 30. The four leaders concluded by drawing up a joint memorandum setting out their view that the whole of the Sudetenland should be taken over by Germany within a period of 10 days, and that an international Commission should settle the new frontiers between Germany and Czechoslovakia. Before he left Munich, Chamberlain had a private meeting with Hitler at which they both put their signatures to a draft declaration pledging themselves to resolve any future disputes between their two countries by the method of consultation, and affirming their determination to work together for the peace of Europe.

On his return to England Neville Chamberlain was accorded a hero's welcome. The mood of relief and rejoicing was universal. The onset of a slaughterous war had suddenly been averted; the oppressive gloom of recent days was miraculously dispelled. People felt that they could revert again to their ordinary lives, with their jobs, their families, and their friends. They could revive once more their desires and their dreams for the years which lay ahead of them. Chamberlain flew back from Munich to Heston where a number of his Cabinet colleagues were waiting to greet and congratulate him. Then he set out on a triumphal drive to London. All the available Press Association reporters were positioned at various places along the route which the Prime Minister and his entourage would be following on their way to London, to describe the reception he received as he passed by. However, Donald Spendlove considered that his coverage of the occasion was still inadequate and he decided to send out a few senior telephonists as additional observers. He told us that he did not expect us to describe the crowd scenes as the sub-editors would be inundated with similar accounts. He only wanted us to report any dramatic or unusual incidents we happened to witness. I was instructed to stand in Victoria Street opposite the Army and Navy Stores. By the time I arrived the crowds were about 10 lines deep on either side on the road so I squeezed myself in between two girls on the top step of a shop, telling everyone round me that I represented the Press Association and it was essential that I should get a good view. While we were still waiting I became aware of a party of about a dozen young men a short distance away from me, all wearing the black pullovers which had been adopted as their uniform by the British Union of Fascists. As

I watched they started to give the Nazi salute and unfurled a canvas banner on which was written:

HITLER IS OUR ALLY.
NOW LET'S DRIVE OUT THE JEWS.

There were shouts of indignation from people all round and a number of men began moving in a hostile manner towards the fascists, who turned to face them with their fists raised. "There's going to be a punch-up," one of the girls beside me exclaimed approvingly. I felt so angry at the provocative behaviour of the men in black that I completely forgot I was on duty as reporter, and I made up my mind that if an attempt was made to pull down the banner I would join in.

Before any fighting had started two police constables appeared on the scene. They immediately approached the group, confiscated the banner and arrested both of the men who were bearing it aloft. I noticed that another constable remained in the vicinity until the procession had passed. Later on I telephoned a brief account of the occurrence to the PA. That was my first personal experience of outside reporting.

Minutes before Chamberlain drove past, seated in the back of a limousine with the Foreign Secretary, the Earl of Halifax, at his side, his approach was heralded by tremendous outburst of cheering from the direction of Victoria Station. When his car appeared the crowd became quite hysterical. The noise was deafening. People screamed, shouted, and waved their arms above their heads. Women were jumping up and down: men throwing their hats in the air. I had never before witnessed such an eruption of mass emotionalism. I read afterwards that Chamberlain had been given a similar jubilant reception all the way to Downing Street, where he had stood in the windows of Number 10 to acknowledge the continuing acclamations. He had proclaimed to those assembled outside that he had returned from Germany bringing "peace with honour", and that he believed he had secured for the British nation "peace in our time". In a three-day debate on the Munich agreement in the House of Commons during the following week Winston Churchill had declared that the reality of the situation was that Britain had sustained a total and unmitigated defeat.

At my age it was easy for me to feel optimistic now that the threat of war had been removed. My career appeared to be progressing in accordance with my plans, and I would soon be in a position to start applying for a job as a reporter. For the moment I was perfectly happy. Naturally I would have liked to have had a higher salary, but my financial position was to some extent alleviated by the fact that my literary agents were now selling my articles with regularity and were providing me with a second source of income. This enabled me to enter more fully into the social activities of my friends, and I could afford every now and then to take a girl to a film, a play, or to dinner at some fairly modest restaurant in Soho. I was constantly falling in and out of love to an extent that made me a little ashamed of my inconstancy. Sometimes my ardent, though transitory devotion, met with a favourable response: sometimes it was wholly unrequited. As for rugby football, I had begun my second season with the London Irish and I believed I was playing a bit better than I had done during the previous year, owing to the fact that I was growing accustomed to the more aggressive style which contrasts the club from the schoolboy game. I felt that I had every reason to think that life was good.

CHAPTER 8

Hitler had promised Neville Chamberlain during their private discussion in the autumn that the Sudetenland was his last territorial demand in Europe, and most of us had trusted the Prime Minister's assurance that the Munich Agreement had indeed secured us "peace for our time." This sanguine mood, encouraged by Government Ministers, had persisted for the whole winter. Early in the New Year Sir Samuel Hoare, the Home Secretary, had stated in a public speech that, with the new spirit of co-operation between the major European powers, Britain was about to enter a Golden Age in which the living standards of the people would rise to levels never experienced before.

On March 14, 1939 the euphoria had abruptly ended and our wishful visions of the years ahead had vanished into oblivion. During the early hours of the morning on that day, the German Army had stormed across the Western frontiers of Czechoslovakia and marched into Prague. At the same time, Germany's Hungarian allies, operating in close complicity, had invaded from the east. The Czechs were powerless to resist, and the occupation of their country had been completed within 24 hours without a shot being fired. Hitler had announced at once that Czechoslovakia was now incorporated into the Reich as a German Protectorate.

We knew then that Hitler had lied in denying his aggressive intentions in Europe, and that Chamberlain had been deceived. We knew that in the absence of a miracle a major war, in which we would be one of the principal protagonists, was now inevitable. Even before the subjugation of Czechoslovakia the Germans had started to voice their claims to the Free City of Danzig, and the Polish

Corridor to the sea. On the last day of March Chamberlain informed the House of Commons that if Germany took any action which clearly threatened Polish independence both Britain and France would be compelled to lend Poland all the support within their power. About the same time he announced in Parliament that Britain would be doubling the territorial army. The spring of 1939 was filled with rumour and apprehension. At the beginning of April the Italians, the junior partners in the Rome-Berlin Axis, invaded Albania. A few weeks later Hitler repudiated the German non-aggression pact with Poland and the Anglo-German naval agreement. On April 27 the British Government had announced the introduction of compulsory military service for all men of 20.

The first militia men, as the conscripts were to be called, would have to register in June and they would be called-up in July for a period of six months. The process was to be repeated in subsequent years. I was just 19 at the time and my own age-group would become eligible for call-up in the summer of 1940, when I was hoping to be studying law at a university. I decided to inquire if it would be possible for me to defer my military service until after I had qualified, or else to register with the first militia men in spite of my age. I typed out a statement giving the reasons for my application and I went round to the War Office in Whitehall. I was politely received by an orderly who asked me to sit in a waiting-room while he found out if there was anyone available to see me. He returned half-an-hour later and told me that one of the staff captains dealing with conscription would try to answer my questions. I was shown into a small office in which the captain, in civilian clothing, was sitting behind a desk. He motioned me to a chair and said amiably, "It's nice of you to offer yourself for call-up a year too soon, but I don't think they'd ever wear it. Your best bet's to try to get your service deferred until you've finished your university training." He went on to tell me that the information they had received so far about the operation of the compulsory military training scheme had been extremely sketchy, but he was certain that there would be special provisions regarding students and trainees. He offered to make a note of my name and address, and to send me a copy of the relevant regulations as soon as they were issued. As I was getting up to leave he glanced down at my typewritten statement, which was lying on the desk in front of him, and said, "I didn't notice this before - you were born in County Cork." I pointed out that at the time of my birth the Irish Free State had not yet come into being. "It makes no difference," he said, "Anyone who was born in Ireland - even in the North of Ireland - will not be eligible for conscription. I can tell you that for certain. So you won't have to worry about getting your call-up deferred after all."

The following week I wrote a letter to the War Office saying that, as most of my contemporaries were going to be called up for six months military service and I myself was ineligible for conscription, I would like to be allowed, in due course, to register as a "voluntary militiaman". After a long delay the War Office replied, telling me that what I had proposed would not be possible, but suggesting that if I wished to make a contribution to the military preparedness of the country there was no reason why I should not enlist in the territorial army. I discussed the matter with Arnold and Norman. Both of them agreed that since I did not wish to avoid the military service which was being imposed to my contemporaries the best course for me to take would be to follow this advice.

I wanted to join an Irish infantry regiment, so the obvious choice was the London Irish Rifles, the territorial unit of the Royal Ulster Rifles. I went along one afternoon to their depot at the Duke of York's headquarters in King's Road, Chelsea. I found it crowded with would-be recruits, as on the previous day the government had announced that men who were already serving in the territorial army would be exempted from being called-up as militia men. After I had given my particulars at the recruitment desk I was told to join the long line of people waiting outside the doctor's room to be medically examined. I took my place behind a lanky, spotty-faced youth, and I gradually progressed forward until was standing at the head of the queue. Then the door opened and the spotty-faced youth came out, adjusting his tie with one hand and beckoning to me with the other. "O.K. Chum," he said, "It's all yours." And lowering his voice he muttered confidentially, "The Doc's an Irishman and he's half-pissed."

When I walked into the room the doctor, a portly middle-aged man in shirt-sleeves was sitting on a table, swinging his legs back and forth violently and singing to himself. He broke off when I entered and told me, in a rich Dublin brogue, to strip to the waist. When I had done so he came over to me and I could distinctly smell the alcohol on his breath. I was wearing a London Irish Rugger Club tie that day and he obviously recognised it, as he picked it up from the chair on which I had laid my clothes and commented, "If you're fit enough to play for that gang of cut-throats you'll be fit enough for anything. All the same, now that you're stripped off I'd better listen to your heart." He held his stethoscope on my chest for a moment and then removed it. "You'll do for the fray," he said. "You can get yourself dressed and send in my next victim." While I was putting on my clothes he sat at the table filling in a form. That was the entirety of my medical examination before I joined the territorial army.

As soon as I had been passed fit by the doctor I was sent to another room to be sworn in. I was then told to join a group of about 30 other recruits in a yard at the back of the building. Presently a sergeant appeared, who ordered us to fall in in two ranks, and kept us standing to attention while he addressed us. The regiment, he said, was in the process of forming a second battalion to which we would all be posted. He told us the date and time of our first evening parade and warned us not to be absent or to arrive late for it. Uniforms were scarce at the moment but it was hoped they would be available in the near future, and until they were issued we would parade in our civilian clothes. It would be advisable for us to start toughening ourselves up right away for the compulsory camp in the summer, because we would be living like real soldiers for a fortnight, under army discipline, and it was going to make or break us. He asked if we had any questions, and when no one spoke he gave us the order to dismiss.

We were issued with our uniforms a few weeks later -

a suit of battle-dress, a pair of boots, a steel helmet, and a caubeen, the distinctive head-dress of the London Irish Rifles, which consisted of a kind of khaki bonnet surmounted by a green-feathered hackle. Each of us also drew a set of webbing equipment, complete with scabbard and bayonet. Most of the time on our early parades was spent on the square. As we were a rifle Regiment the words-of-command, the arms-drill, and the foot-drill, were slightly different to those I had been taught in the OTC at school, but the variations were easy to learn. Sometimes we went round to Chelsea Barracks to be drilled by a sergeant-major from the Irish Guards. When we graduated to fieldcraft and tactics I had the feeling that the training in the British Army, as far as the infantry was concerned, had virtually stood still since the Armistice in 1918, and that 21 years later it was basically attuned to the trenches on the Western Front.

Many people doubted whether Adolf Hitler, even at that stage, was convinced that Britain had either the ability or the will to go to war in support of Polish independence. It was well known that the German Foreign Secretary, von Ribbentrop, who had been German Ambassador in London until 1938, was of the opinion that the British nation was decadent and degenerate. Probably von Ribbentrop and others had attached undue significance to the Oxford Union resolution, passed by a substantial majority in 1933, that "this House will under no circumstances fight for King and Country." And far more recently, the fact that the Labour party, with the support of the Liberals, had bitterly opposed the introduction of conscription and had tabled a motion of "No Confidence" in the government for its abandonment of the principle of voluntary enlistment. I had myself stood at the roadside in Battersea watching a long procession of demonstrators, interspaced with brass bands, marching towards Hyde Park to take part in an anti-conscription protest meeting. They were carrying banners denoting that they represented various branches of the Labour, Independent Labour, and Communist Parties, and were chanting in unison, "Down with the call-up! We won't serve!"

As the summer advanced the rumours of German war preparations and the militant outbursts of German political leaders increased. Nevertheless, I decided to pursue my plans on the assumption that we would remain at peace. At the beginning of July I joined the Middle Temple as a student. After my great-aunt's executors had advanced me the necessary money from my legacy, I filled in the entrance forms and took them to the Treasury in Middle Temple Lane. My papers were processed by the Deputy Under-Treasurer who asked me if I was related to my namesake, a Lord Justice in the Northern Ireland Court of Appeal, who was an Honorary Bencher of their Inn. I replied that we were cousins and although we had never met, he and my father had been at Trinity College, Dublin together. "In that case," the Deputy Under-Treasurer said, "you are doubly welcome to the Middle Temple." He had invited me to come back during the Long Vacation when he would be less busy and he could show me round the Hall and the Library.

I would like to have started reading for my degree at London University in the autumn, at the commencement of the academic year, but it was impossible to arrange anything until I had obtained a part-time job. Out of the first few letters I sent to newspapers, the only favourable reply I received came from a Liverpool daily, arranging for me to see their London editor. I took some of my published articles to show him, and he appeared to look at them with a certain amount of interest. He handed them back and remarked, "You have an obvious bent for feature-writing. I would be happy to offer you a job, but I can't see how we would fit you in." He went on to tell me that the paper only kept a very small staff in London, and that everyone was employed on a full-time basis. He needed reporters who would be ready to go anywhere at any time, and it would cause the utmost difficulty if I was trying to combine my work for the paper with my studies for a degree. The only possibility, he said, was that they might be able to engage me as an occasional writer for their London Diary. He would give the matter further thought and would write to me if he was able to come up with anything.

I suspended my efforts to find a suitable job soon afterwards, on the advice of Donald Spendlove. One evening we had happened to be leaving the News Room at the same time after we had both finished work, and he suggested that we should walk to Blackfriars station together as he wanted to have a word with me in private. The Press Association and Reuters had moved into their new shared premises by then and as soon as we had left the building and were walking along Fleet Street he asked me about my interview at the London office of the Liverpool paper. I told him exactly what had happened, and he said thoughtfully, "I'm afraid that's what you're going to be up against whenever you apply to national or provincial papers." He told me that if I had intended to make a career as a journalist, the PA would have offered me a job as a junior reporter within the next few months. As it was, he was investigating the possibility of their taking me on as one of their regular "space" reporters. "We would have to fit in your hours of work with your commitments as a student," he said. "For instance you could do your reporting solely at the weekends during your term-time at the university, and work normally during the vacations." He warned me that it might prove difficult to persuade the management to agree to the idea - he had already broached it with the Editor-in-Chief, whose reaction had been decidedly unenthusiastic. However, Mr Spendlove continued, if I liked the sound of his proposal he would try to arrange it for me, and I need not approach any more papers about a job unless he was unsuccessful. I replied that this would be the perfect solution for me, and I found it hard to thank him adequately for trying to bring it about. Before we parted company at the entrance to the station he asked me not to mention our discussion to anyone else at the PA because, until the matter was decided, the fewer people who knew about it the better.

At some time during that summer I was going to spend a fortnight's holiday in France with Denis McCarthy, a fellow member of the London Irish Rugby Club with whom I had become very friendly during the previous season when we had played together regularly. Denis was a few years older than I and had just qualified as a solicitor. At first we had intended to go away by ourselves, but later he had asked whether I would mind if his fiancée, Jill, came too and brought one of her girl-friends with her. They would pay for themselves, he said, and for all our common expenses we would "go dutch". I told him I would have no objections at all; in fact I would welcome the idea. I had always liked Jill, who was working at the time as a model with a London agency. I knew her quite well because she had often come to watch our matches, and had stayed on afterwards for the evening parties in the pavilion.

The three of us had met in a pub for a preliminary discussion. Denis offered to look after all the booking arrangements, and Jill said that as soon as she had fixed up the fourth member of the party we could all have dinner together at her flat and decide which part of France we wanted to visit. She intended to approach one of her old school-friends, who was then a dancer in the chorus of a successful West End musical, but was probably going to terminate her contract in the summer. The next day Denis rang me in the News Room to tell me that Jill's friend Jacky was leaving the cast of the musical at the end of July and was very keen to come on the trip with us. "Jill and I are delighted," he said, "and you will be too when you meet her. She's extremely attractive and tremendous fun. You'll probably fall madly in love with her - most men do."

I met Jacky for the first time at Jill's flat on a Sunday evening. I was already there when she arrived, and as she entered the sitting-room my immediate impression was of a fairly tall girl with short light-brown hair, wearing a loose fitting black pullover, which did nothing to conceal the perfection of her figure, and grey corduroy slacks. Jill was preparing dinner in the kitchen, and after he had introduced us, Denis put his arms round Jacky's waist and said to me, "What did I tell you? Isn't she adorable? It's a pity she's not in a skirt tonight. She has the most lovely legs you've ever seen."

Jacky freed herself from him and retorted, "I have to totally expose my legs on six days every week to gratify all the lechers like you in the audience, Denis. On the Sabbath I always put them into retreat."

Jacky was not beautiful but, as Denis had said, she was immensely attractive, and it was exciting to think she was coming with us. I realised during the course of the evening that she was also an interesting and lively companion. I was puzzled by the way in which she combined a cynical worldliness with a youthful freshness and vivacity. I commented on this to Jill afterwards and she told me that Jacky was an orphan and had had a very unhappy childhood. She had severed her links with her adoptive parents as soon as she left school, and had "knocked around" for a while before becoming a chorus girl.

After dinner that evening Denis had produced a selection of maps and brochures which he had obtained from travel agents. Having discussed a number of different possibilities we eventually agreed that we would spend a week in Paris and then go on to Nice. As we all wanted to keep down the cost of the holiday, the girls said they would share a double-room at the hotels, and Denis suggested to me that he and I should also share a room. We had a slight difficulty with regard to dates. Jill had a fashion-show early in September, I had my TA Camp in August, and Denis, who was a pilot in the Air Auxiliary Force, had his annual training in July. Finally, we decided that the best time for all of us would be immediately I returned from camp at the end of August.

After that, we met together on several further occasions to discuss our plans over a drink or a meal. It was seldom easy to find a time which would be convenient to all four of us, as when Jill, Denis, and I were free on a weekday evening, Jacky would be at the theatre, and her Sundays seemed to be almost fully occupied with her own social activities. Even when we met her she was usually in a rush to get away to another engagement. I felt increasingly disconcerted because I was not getting to know her any better. She persisted in treating me as an acquaintance rather than a friend, and the distance between us never seemed to lessen. I suppose, in truth, I was vexed that she took such little notice of me.

The day before I went to camp Donald Spendlove spoke to me again about my being made a space-reporter on the staff of the Press Association. He said that the idea had been accepted in principle, and it only remained to work out the details. "You'll be away for about a month," he continued, "and I hope to be able to put a definite proposition to you immediately on your return."

Our camp was situated on a desolate plain in Yorkshire, miles from the nearest town. I thoroughly disliked my initiation into the life of a soldier, not because of the spartan routine - I was young enough and fit enough to contend with that - but because of the complete lack of privacy. It was very difficult, if not impossible, to be alone at any time during the day or the night. We slept eight to a bell-tent, lying side-by-side, our palliasses almost touching, with our heads by the canvas verge and our feet round the centre-pole. Some men kept their socks on all night and the stench was putrid. Reveille sounded at six o'clock and we were given half-an-hour's physical training before breakfast. Every day was hard and long. We drilled and marched endlessly; we went out on field exercises and night operations; we dug trenches and filled them in again. For our evening recreation, we plied ourselves with beer in the canteen or took part in an impromptu sing-song in the camp theatre.

The day before we finished our period in camp we heard with incredulity that Molotov and von Ribbentrop, the Foreign Secretaries of Russia and Germany, had signed a Non-Aggression Pact in Moscow, and that the British Government had re-affirmed our commitment to defend Polish independence. There were rumours that Britain was going to mobilise a number of reservists, but to our immense relief we struck camp the following morning and were put on a special train for London. The national newspapers that day were full of the new crisis, most of the leader-writers being in agreement that the Russians had now granted Hitler a licence to commence another war. When I arrived home I found an urgent message awaiting me to contact Denis without delay. I rang him immediately and he told me he had just been called-up. He was then in the process of getting his things together as he had to report to a depot in Norfolk in the evening. He had already been in touch with the travel agents to cancel his own and Jill's bookings, because she did not want to go without him, but if the emergency was over in a few days they would come to France and join us.

"The travel agents were very good about it," he said. "They even returned our deposits. I've cancelled the hotel bookings for one of the double rooms and kept on the other."

"You might have talked to Jacky first," I commented. "She'll be furious about it."

"It was her idea," he replied. "She thought it would be the most practical and most economical solution under the circumstances - apart from other considerations." After a pause he added, "I can't imagine what she sees in you. In this life the most undeserving bastards seem to get all the luck."

Eve and I had arranged to give a joint cocktail party in the flat that evening, and we had each invited a few of our friends to stay on for a meal afterwards. I had intended my own supper guests to include my travelling companions, and all three had accepted. However, Denis had told me during our telephone conversation that he would not have time to come to Battersea, even for a quick drink, before catching his train to Norfolk. I was wondering how Jacky would behave towards me in light of the new development in our relationship. In fact, I was amazed at the change in her attitude. From the moment she arrived she treated me as though we were very close friends who had been going out together for months past.

While Eve and I were washing-up together after the party, she remarked suddenly, "I suppose you fancy yourself as a great man-of-the-world now, slipping off to Paris with a chorus-girl? Jacky has told me all about your latest plans."

"It wasn't planned," I remarked, "It's merely the way in which things have worked out."

"How convenient for both of you!" she said caustically. "Are you in love with her?"

I replied that I found Jacky immensely attractive. "Oh yes she is," Eve agreed, "in a sexy sort of way."

She then started to lecture me on the need for taking precautions. I would look pretty stupid if Jacky landed me with a baby. Had I thought of that? What would I do if it happened? Would I marry her or would I prefer to make payments on a weekly paternity order? I knew very well that I could not afford to do either, she said.

I told Eve coldly that I was perfectly capable of managing my own affairs. She retorted that she sometimes doubted if I really was, and she considered it her duty as my sister to try to prevent me from behaving like an idiot. After we had continued to wash up in silence for a few more minutes she remarked, as though to herself, "I wonder why it is that immature youths make such fools of themselves about girls with large bosoms?"

The day after Jacky and I reached Paris we had read in the French papers that Britain and Poland had signed a treaty of mutual assistance. France was already in the process of calling-up various classes of reservists, and almost daily waiters and other male members of the staff at our hotel had to leave hurriedly to report for duty. Several people asked Jacky how it was that a young, fit man of military age like me could be on holiday with his girl-friend while his country was on the verge of war. When she informed them that I was a soldier in the territorial army they were even more surprised that I had not yet been mobilised.

Jacky used to tell everybody that I was a Fleet Street reporter and she was an actress, but she was intentionally vague about both of us and she never went into more detail. I knew that her great dream was to be a film star. She had only left the chorus-line of the West End musical during the previous month because she intended to go to Hollywood in the autumn in the hope of picking up a few small parts to start off her acting career. "If I'm unsuccessful," she said cheerfully, "I can always find work as a strip-tease dancer in a Los Angeles night club. I'm fortunate enough to have all the necessary endowments for the job."

Just after the start of our holiday Jacky had suggested that we should pool our French currency, and that I should take charge of all the financial arrangements as she wanted to forget about money for a fortnight. Neither of us had been to Paris before and we were determined not to waste a minute of our time there. We filled our days with sight-seeing and visits to art galleries; in the evenings, we relaxed, dining cheaply at modest restaurants in Montmartre and remaining at our table until well after midnight. I had fallen deeply in love with her and was so idyllically happy that thoughts of Hitler, Poland, and the Danzig Corridor had receded from my mind. Then, one morning before we left the hotel after breakfast, I had received a telegram from Arnold urging me to return home immediately. Advance parties of all territorial units had just been called-up, he said, and it was expected that the whole of the territorial army would be mobilised at any moment.

"Absolute rubbish!" Jacky exclaimed, when I gave her the telegram to read. "If the army wanted you to be in England they'd have told you so." She handed it back and looked at me imploringly. "Please don't go back," she said. "I don't want this to end yet. I'm enjoying it too much."

I felt that I could not ignore Arnold's telegram completely, and eventually Jacky agreed with me. We decided to move forthwith to some place closer to the Channel Ports, so that I could get back quickly if I was called-up. A girl in the Paris office of our travel agents told us that it would be possible to change our previous arrangements without any difficulty as all the resorts were so empty because of the crisis. Our booking at the hotel in Nice could be transferred, at a similar rate, to a hotel in Le Touquet which was owned by the same proprietors, and we could go there as soon as we pleased. I sent Arnold a telegram letting him know our change of address and telling him that I could be in London in a matter of hours if the TA were mobilised.

Le Touquet was inert, gloomy, and deserted. On our first full day there we went for a walk along the desolate esplanade before having lunch, and we stopped for a drink at an open-air restaurant at which we were the only customers. A lugubrious young man was crooning into a microphone to the accompaniment of a piano:

Every time it rains, it rains
Pennies from heaven.
Don't you know each cloud contains
Pennies from heaven.

We listened in silence, sipping our absinths, and then Jacky said suddenly, "I can't stand it here - the whole place is so mournful. Let's go back to Paris."

I told her I felt the same as she did about Le Touquet, but I did not think we should act too precipitately. After further discussion we agreed that we would stay on for a day or two longer before deciding if we wanted to move again.

The following morning I was woken up by a woman wailing and sobbing outside our bedroom door. I saw that Jacky was awake too and I told her that I was going out to investigate, but she said it would be better if she did it herself. She slung a negligé across her shoulders and disappeared, bare-footed, into the passage. She returned about 10 minutes later, looking serious and despondent. She threw off her negligé and climbed back into bed without speaking.

"What was the trouble?" I asked.

"It was one of the chamber-maids," she replied. "The Manager's looking after her now. She'd just been told that the Germans invaded Poland at dawn this morning. She kept on blubbering, "Nous sommes fini! Nous sommes fini!"

"It's probably another one of these wild rumours," I commented.

Jacky shook her head. "Unfortunately it's the truth. The

Manager heard it on the radio from Paris. The bastards have bombed Warsaw already."

"If it's really true, we'll have to leave right away," I said. "As soon as we're dressed and packed we'll get a taxi to Boulogne."

A moment later, while I was sitting on the side of the bed reaching for my slippers, Jacky leant across behind me and encircled my neck with her arms. "Why this great hurry?" she inquired. "It's still terribly early and I'm bloody sure the British Army can manage without you until this evening."

In the outcome we caught a boat which left Boulogne around midday. It was far less crowded than I had expected. Jacky and I remained on deck until we had sailed out of the harbour and then went down to the bar. I was about to get drinks when a man standing beside me noticed my TA badge and insisted on buying them for me.

"We owe it to you," he said. "After all, you'll probably be in the front-line trenches this time next week." He was with a blowzy, red-haired woman whom he described as his girlfriend. After introducing us to her, he nudged me and winked. "We've been in France for a few days," he explained, "playing the same parlour games as the two of you have been up to. C'est la vie!"

Jacky and I remained with them in the bar throughout the crossing. During this time the redhead barely uttered a word and her male companion seldom stopped talking. He told us at the outset that although he was only 32 and perfectly fit, he would not be allowed to join up because he was in a reserved occupation connected with aircraft production. He kept on repeating how eager he was to enlist and how much he envied me for being able to serve in the forces. He greatly embarrassed me by standing round after round and refusing to let me buy a single drink. "You don't realise how honoured I feel to be doing this," he said. "Chaps like you are the nation's heroes. We'll be relying on you lot for our survival." By the time we were entering Folkestone Harbour all four of us were rather drunk. We said goodbye to them before we disembarked and the last time we saw them they were walking very unsteadily towards the Customs Hall on the quayside.

On the train from Folkestone to London Jacky and I sat very close to each other holding hands. We were both feeling sad, pensive, and sentimental. From time to time we passed clusters of barrage balloons floating inertly over the fields and the buildings, trailing ropes to the ground below them. In the distance they looked squat and humorously-shaped like children's inflated toys. However, they formed a constant reminder of the imminence of war.

When we were walking through the platform barrier at Victoria a Police Officer approached me and advised me to report to my unit without delay as the territorial army had been mobilised during the morning. I parted from Jacky on the station concourse. After our protracted farewell embrace she wiped a tear from her eye, turned, and headed for the steps which led to the Underground. I took a taxi to the Duke of York headquarters, where I was instructed to report back in uniform with all my kit by nine o'clock that evening. I was advised to get a meal first as the cookhouse would not be operating until the following morning.

My mother and Eve had supper with me before I returned to the Duke of York's headquarters. Although we tried to be cheerful we could not pretend that it was a happy occasion, and we all knew that it was the last meal we would be taking together in the flat for the foreseeable future. Mother was going away next day to stay with friends in the country, as everyone who did not have an essential reason for remaining in London was being urged to leave if they could possibly do so. Eve would probably be moving out too. Her employers had contingency plans, if war broke out, to evacuate their West End offices and move out to temporary premises in a provincial town.

I decided to walk to the Depot rather than to catch a bus from Battersea to Sloane Square, because I wanted to be alone with my thoughts. It was the first night of the black-out. The street lamps were unlit and no illumination was visible from the windows of shops and houses. There were few pedestrians on the pavements and the vehicles which passed me were driven with nervous incertitude, due to the unfamiliar darkness of the roads.

I stopped for a few minutes on Chelsea Bridge, looking down at the scarcely discernible river below me, and fought to overcome the depression which had overwhelmed me. I did not want to be a soldier and I had no wish to fight a war. I wanted to get back to my ordinary life, back to my career, and back to my family, my friends, and my home. I had a feeling that the past had now been totally ended and that nothing would ever be the same again. Wherever I turned my mind I seemed to be confronted by the mournful spectre of finality.

I humped my pack on to my shoulders and set off again into the night. I remember thinking that walking alone down a silent street in the black-out gave you the impression that the inhabitants on either side of it were purposely turning their backs on you.

CHAPTER 9

Most of the battalion had already reported by the time I arrived at the Duke of York's headquarters. We hung about in a shed for another hour before the members of my platoon were ordered to fall in with all their kit in the yard outside. When we had formed up we were addressed by our platoon commander, a young 2nd Lieutenant of about my own age, who told us we were going to be billeted at an empty house nearby. Reveille would be at 6 a.m. next morning and would be followed by 30 minutes physical training in the roadway in front of our billet. We would then be marched to headquarters for breakfast, and to be given our orders for the day. He said he regretted that we would have to spend the night without blankets or palliasses as these were not available for the moment, but he reminded us that we were now on active service and we must be prepared to rough it. The platoon sergeant told us later that the company officers were "roughing it" at a posh hotel in Sloane Square.

The house in which we were billeted was in a fashionable terrace, overlooking a garden-square. It was completely devoid of furniture, carpets, and curtains, but our advance party had put bulbs in all the light sockets and had suspended black-out blinds over every window. The sergeant allocated us our rooms and decided how many recumbent men each of them would accommodate. We took off our boots and slept in our clothing on the bare floor-boards, pillowing our heads on our rolled-up battle-dress blouses. In the morning, close on 30 of us had to wash and shave in cold water under three running taps, two in the bathrooms and one in the kitchen.

Even then, we were all hoping that the Germans would pay heed to the British ultimatum which had been delivered to them on the previous day. The news from Poland was that the Poles were fighting gallantly and desperately in the face of the massive German onslaught, but already they were proving no match for the invaders and were falling back in every sector of the front. The British and French Governments still appeared to be looking on irresolutely.

We drilled throughout the day - in the morning, under our own NCOs at the Duke of York headquarters and in the afternoon under Irish Guards NCOs at Chelsea Barracks. On one occasion we were being watched by our own company commander and during a 10-minute break he called me over to reprimand me for not reporting to the regiment as soon as the territorial army had been mobilised.

"It was irresponsible and selfish of you to remain in France while the crisis was deepening," he said. "I was called up last week myself and I had to forfeit my own continental holiday." I replied, somewhat tactlessly, that even if I had been able to report on the previous morning I would have been sent away again as nothing had been ready for us. "Your behaviour was irresponsible," he repeated, "and the fact that we weren't quite ready for you has absolutely nothing to do with the matter."

That evening everyone in the company, apart from those on guard duty, was allowed out on pass until midnight, or more precisely, until the army's customary deadline of "2359 hours". The sergeant-major had informed us that the company commander would prefer us all to clear off for a few hours rather than to spend the evening lazing around in our room. Immediately the afternoon parade had finished I had rung Jacky's flat from a public telephone box in the hope that she would be able to meet me for a meal, but as there was no reply I went out instead with three of my friends from the platoon. We had two simple objects in our minds - we wanted to escape from the barren discomfort of our billet, and we wanted to get ourselves thoroughly drunk.

In spite of the fact that Britain had mobilised, men in uniform were still quite a rarity in London and we were treated with extreme cordiality wherever we went. In several pubs we were provided with drinks by complete strangers who would not allow us to buy any for them in return. At some stage we were joined by an amicable corporal from the Irish Guards, a reservist stationed at Chelsea Barracks. He had told us that he regarded the London Irish Rifles as his regimental blood-brothers, and that since he had an extensive knowledge of the pubs in the area he would like to come along with us and to act as our guide. According to the corporal, whenever a group of Irish Guardsmen went out drinking they always decided how much money they wanted to spend and each of them paid his share to the member of the party who was going to act as their banker. We agreed that it seemed an eminently sensible idea and we also concurred with the corporal's proposal that, as he was our senior both in age and in rank, he should be our banker for the remainder of the evening.

At closing-time we were in a pub in Sloane Street, all feeling very hungry. The corporal told us that his cousin owned a restaurant just round the corner, and that if we went there with him we would get a meal at a greatly reduced price - we might even get it for nothing. He suggested we had another whip-round, in case we had to pay, and having received our contributions he went on ahead to make the necessary arrangements. When we arrived at the restaurant there was no sign of the corporal, so we found the proprietor and asked him if he knew where his cousin had gone. Having heard our story, he commented that he was a New Zealander and had no relations in the Irish Guards.

"I'm afraid you chaps have been taken for a ride," he said. "You've fallen for one of the oldest con-tricks in the world." As we were about to leave he asked us if we had any money left. We replied that we had very little and certainly could not afford to eat at a restaurant like his. He then invited us to sit down at a table and to place our orders. "I hate people being ripped off," he said, "and I'm not going to let you finish your evening without having a good meal under your belts. This will be on the house."

We returned to our billet just before 2359 hours to spend another night on the bare boards. As it turned out, we were not issued with any blankets for another three days and we did not draw our palliasses until the following week.

The next day, September 3, the British Government delivered a final ultimatum to Hitler at 9 a.m., expiring at 11 a.m. It was made known that the Prime Minister would address the nation on the radio at 11.15 a.m. My platoon spent the initial part of the morning being drilled by our sergeant and by our platoon commander. As the time for the crucial broadcast approached we were formed up on the roadway outside our billet. One of the neighbours placed his wireless beside an open ground floor window and turned up the volume for our benefit. Then we heard Neville Chamberlain's voice, grave and sorrowful, telling us that the Germans had ignored the ultimatum and that our countries were already at war. His brief announcement ended. There was no exaltation, no martial music, and no patriotic song. The neighbour switched off his radio and closed the window again.

We had scarcely resumed our drilling when the air-raid sirens erupted in the strident, undulating wail, which was to become so familiar in the years ahead. The platoon commander seemed totally nonplussed by the situation. He wanted the sergeant to send a runner to company headquarters to find if we should break off the parade and take cover. The sergeant, a Great War veteran, told him that by the time the runner had returned with directions the German bombers would probably be overhead.

"If you want any of the platoon to stay alive, Sir," he said despairingly, "we'd better get them down to the basement in our billet bloody quickly." To our intense relief the officer heeded the sergeant's forthright advice and after we had huddled in the basement for about 10 minutes the sirens sounded the "all clear". In fact, the warning had been a false alarm.

For the next few days numerous rumours were circulating about the future of the battalion. Sometimes we were being sent to Northern Ireland to complete our training; sometimes we were about to go to France, half-trained, to join the British Expeditionary Force;

sometimes we would sail in a short while for the Middle or Far East. I was friendly with our company clerk who told me, in confidence, that all these reports were incorrect. He had seen a memorandum in the company commander's private file to the effect that our division was not scheduled for foreign service until the spring of 1940. In the immediate future the battalion would be carrying out guard duties on "vulnerable points" in the Home Counties. Reinforcement drafts were to be sent to the 1st Battalion of the Royal Ulster Rifles in India and to their 2nd Battalion in France. Another contingent was being posted to the Regimental Depot in Northern Ireland. This would principally consist of public school boys with cert. "A", who would be attached to a potential officer's squad. He said that the three platoon commanders had already submitted their recommendations for the potential officer's squad, and my name was included in the list for my platoon.

During the first few weeks of the war evening passes were given out liberally in the battalion. It was realised, no doubt, how much our morale would suffer if we were compelled to spend much free time in comfortless, unfurnished, and unheated billets. Nobody was living at the Battersea flat for the moment and I went there frequently with my friends from the platoon to shave in hot water and to take a bath. Sometimes we were allowed to have overnight passes, expiring at 0659 hours, and we were able to enjoy the added luxury of a night in bed. It was difficult to go out for the evening without spending money, and most of us were extremely hard up as we were existing entirely on our army pay. A few of the lucky ones were having their pay made up to the level of their pre-war wages by their peace time employers, but they were a very small minority.

In the middle of September a list of men who would form the detachment for the regimental depot in Northern Ireland was posted on the company notice-board. To my surprise my name was not included. I asked the company clerk if he knew the reason, and he told me, again in strict confidence, that the company commander had removed my name with those of two others from the Depot party list, and he had transferred us to the proposed reinforcement draft for the battalion of the Royal Ulster Rifles in France. "Perhaps the three of you were specially selected," he suggested consolingly. "The draft originally consisted mostly of reservists and other old sweats. He might have wanted to add a little young blood to give it a better balance." I soon became accustomed to the fact that a man in the forces during a war generally becomes an automaton. He does what others decide he should do and he goes where others think fit to send him.

After two weeks of valiant resistance the Polish Army and Air Force had been virtually destroyed. It was then that, in accordance with a secret agreement between Hitler and Stalin, the Russian armies invaded Poland's thinly manned eastern frontier and continued their advance until they had linked-up with their German allies. By the end of September the Poles had been completely subjugated and their entire country had been partitioned between the two merciless dictators. It was obvious that the full might of the German forces could now be turned on Britain and France. There was a common belief among British people at that time that the pattern of warfare on the Western Front would be resumed from the point where it had terminated in 1918. The weapons, of course, had become more sophisticated and prepared defensive positions were less assailable, but most of us still visualised a battlefront with mud-spattered soldiers crouched in their trenches, barbed wire entanglements, continuous shelling and sniping, night patrols, bayonet charges, and enormous casualties.

I told Norman and Arnold that I was expecting to be drafted to the British Expeditionary Force, but I did not disclose the fact to my mother or my sisters as I wanted to spare them from worry for as long as possible. Norman had been called up from the reserved list and was now serving as a major in the Judge Advocate General's Office in London. He had insisted on Noreen going off to stay in the country with their six-month-old daughter Miranda, and for the moment he was living by himself in their Westminster flat. On the outbreak of war Arnold, who was then 33, had tried to volunteer for aircrew duties in Bomber Command, but he had been rejected on the ground that he was too old. However, in view of his experience of navigation while he had been in the merchant service he was advised to apply for the RAF Air Sea Rescue branch. He did so, and he had been notified that he would be granted an immediate commission after completing a course of training which would probably commence in about four month's time.

Arnold had just become engaged and he was planning to get married in November, shortly before commencing his service in the RAF. He was very keen that I should be his best man, and when he and Helen, his fiancée, learnt of my impending departure for France they decided to arrange their wedding a month earlier than they had intended so as to increase the chance of my still being in England.

The reinforcement draft which was going to the 1st Battalion of the Royal Ulster Rifles sailed for India at the end of September. There was no definite news about when our contingent would leave for France, but some of us believed that we might not be needed until the 2nd Battalion began to suffer casualties. Our territorial army company commander had been posted to the Depot and had been replaced by a fiery, extrovert reservist. Captain Lacey looked every inch a soldier with his bristling moustache, his erect, stocky figure, and his faultless turn-out. He had been decorated with the Military Cross in the Great War and he had been wounded twice on the Western Front. From the moment he took over the company he had sought to instil us with his own aggressive spirit, his frenzied hatred of the Germans and his veneration of the naked bayonet. I could never make up my mind if his temperamental excesses derived from the fact that he was constantly acting a part or were simply due to the fact that he was slightly deranged. He would start our daily parades with an hour's bayonet fighting, over which he officiated himself. One of his favourite forms of training was what he called "the mad minute course." This consisted of a series of rows of straw-filled sacks hanging upright from wooden frames shaped like goal-posts. We had to charge at them from a distance of about 50 yards and to drive our bayonets into as many sacks as possible, before Captain Lacey blew a blast on his whistle to indicate that the "mad minute" had ended. He used to stand beside the frames, shouting excitedly, "Kill the buggers! Kill! Kill! Kill!" One of his favourite sayings was that we must feel no more compunction about slaughtering Germans than we felt about crushing beetles underfoot.

To Captain Lacey's annoyance our training programme was temporarily suspended when the company was detached from the battalion for a month to carry out guard duties on "vulnerable points". Our three platoons had to operate independently in widely separated localities. Mine was sent to protect the railway bridge over the River Thames at Staines against possible acts of sabotage by enemy agents. We were billeted in a pavilion on the water's edge, which was completely bare except for our bedding and a long trestle-table on which we ate our meals. The sergeant had his own room at one end. Our food for the day was deposited in hot containers every morning by the company cooks, and was usually dried-up and tasteless by the time it was served to us for lunch. We complained about this to the platoon commander, but he said he could do nothing about it. He was staying at a hotel about a mile away from the pavilion and apart from his brief daily inspections we seldom saw him at all.

Our platoon had been divided into two groups which alternated on a 24 hour tour of duty. We had to provide sentries for both ends of the bridge and to patrol the area generally. The remainder of the guard was on stand-by in the pavilion in case of an emergency. I had been promoted to the rank of Lance-Corporal, and during my period of duty I had to walk across the bridge fairly frequently, either to visit the sentries on the far side or to take out their reliefs. The space between the outer edge of the railway tracks and the sides of the bridge was quite narrow and it was an intimidating experience to flatten oneself against the parapet while an express train went hurtling past.

After we had been in Staines for a couple of weeks my platoon was moved to a new assignment, guarding an RAF headquarters in a large, private house in Buckinghamshire. We were billeted at a school-hall in a neighbouring village, and once again we were divided into two separate guards which alternated on a 24 hour tour of duty. The guard-room was a bell-tent at the main gates by the side of a two-mile drive leading up to the front of the house. Winter came early that year, intruding on the closing months of autumn with cloud-laden skies, bleak winds, and periodic frosts. The bell-tent was inadequately warmed by an old-fashioned smelly paraffin stove, which occasionally erupted into flames and had to be quickly extinguished with buckets of water before it set the canvas alight. The guard commander had few moments to relax as, apart from posting sentries and continually sending out roving patrols, he had to check and approve the passes of everyone entering or leaving the premises, even if they happened to be very senior officers. I preferred this new duty to guarding the bridge at Staines, and the other corporals shared my feelings. We enjoyed having more work to do and being entrusted with greater responsibility.

The guard commander had to report to the RAF duty officer at midnight in the deserted Officers' Mess to hand him a record of all the people who had visited the headquarters during the day. I found that the duty officers invariably invited me to sit down in comfort, and gave me a stiff whisky to drink while they were examining my lists. After this brief interlude of civilised living, I was always reluctant to return to the atmosphere of the draughty bell-tent, with the stench of paraffin, the upright wooden chair, the bare trestle table, and the unshaded calor-gas lamp. The final hours of darkness before the first light of dawn were usually the coldest and the longest.

I applied for 48 hours leave to be best man at Arnold's wedding and this was granted. When I went to company headquarters to collect my pass Captain Lacey said he would like to see me in his office. He told me that he had received very good reports about me from the RAF and he had decided to make me a full corporal. I was delighted to hear I was going to be promoted, both for the pride of wearing a second stripe on my sleeve, and for the more mercenary reason that I would receive a higher rate of pay.

"You'll keep your new rank when you go on draft to the Royal Ulster Rifles," he added, "but I must give you a warning. You'll be serving with regular soldiers who've never taken orders from a territorial NCO before. In all likelihood someone will start taking the piss out of you. As soon as that happens, ask him to come round the corner and put up his fists. Even if he gives you a good hiding you'll win respect for your attitude; on the other hand, if you give him a good hiding your reputation in the battalion will be made. I've soldiered for many years with the RUR; I know how their minds work."

He started to write out my pass and without looking up he continued, "I'm very envious of you, I wish I was going on the draft myself."

Although I had applied for 48 hours leave, Captain Lacey granted me a pass for 72 hours. As he handed it to me he said, "You know, corporal, the two most gratifying experiences a man can have are screwing a virgin and bayoneting a Hun."

"I've never done either, Sir," I admitted.

"Then you can look forward to both," he said "I commend them to you."

Arnold had been married in a village in Sussex where Helen's mother had an old-world cottage. It was a happy occasion, but tinged with sadness as most of the younger men there were either in the Forces already or were expecting to be called-up for service. In a way the gaiety and celebration had about them the character of make-believe. Pretence was easy because life in the English countryside had, so far, been very little affected by the war. There had been no bombing raids on neighbouring towns; there were few apparent shortages, and there had been almost no casualty lists containing the names of relatives and friends. It was as though for one brief moment we were luxuriating in the after-glow of a world which had ceased to exist. In the evening we had a family party at the hotel where some of us were spending the night. My mother was there; so were Eve, Noreen, Norman, and several cousins whom we saw very rarely. When we drank a toast to the future we were all conscious, I think, of the adversities which might lie ahead of us in the months and the years to come.

The next morning I went up to London. Jacky had written to me suggesting we should have dinner together for the last time before she sailed for New York during the following week. We had not met since our return from France as she had had a dancing engagement at a music-hall theatre in the north of England, but we had kept in touch by letters and telephone calls, and I was excited at the thought of seeing her again. We went to a cinema in the afternoon, dined at a restaurant in Soho, and spent the night together at the Battersea flat. Both of us had accepted by then that our brief affair had only been of an ephemeral nature. We agreed to accept the fact philosophically and to remain what she described as "close and cuddly friends". After she had gone to America we gradually lost contact, and a couple of years later I heard she had married a middle-aged producer in Hollywood. I saw her once in a film, playing a small part as a London prostitute. Eve saw it too and remarked that, although she had not thought much of Jacky's acting ability, she considered that the casting had been really excellent.

What became known as the "phony war" continued for the whole of that winter. The Luftwaffe confined itself to reconnaissance flights over Britain and the RAF retaliated with leaflet raids on Germany. The huge French and German Armies confronting each other on the Western Front remained immobile and passive in their defensive positions. The BEF officially described as being "somewhere in France", was still deployed in a non-active role to the south of Lille and spent its time either in training or in strengthening the protective lines along the Franco-Belgian border.

Popular songs usually reflect the prevailing moods of a period. During those months we had the absurd and bombastic "We're going to hang out the washing on the Siegfried Line," treating warfare as a jovial game at which the British were pre-eminent. After the debacle of Dunkirk the Germans used the tune in a propaganda film as a derisive accompaniment to scenes showing British soldiers, haggard and dazed at the moment of surrender, stumbling towards their captors with their hands above their heads.

I infinitely preferred "Somewhere in France," both for the melody and the simple sentiment of the lyric:

"When she's talking, she's talking to no one but you.
She's proud - oh so proud - of the things you will do.
Every beat of her heart is somewhere.
Somewhere in France with you."

I liked too, "We'll meet again", as it epitomised the sadness and yearning of every wartime parting - those partings which were now becoming such a central feature in the lives of so many of us.

CHAPTER 10

The months I spent in the 2nd Battalion of the Royal Ulster Rifles were among the happiest of my entire army service, mainly because they taught me the true significance of the word "comradeship". Nearly all the officers and men in the battalion were regulars or mobilised reservists, mostly coming from Northern Ireland but with a sizeable proportion from the Irish Free State. The majority had campaigned in Palestine and on the North-West Frontier during the immediate pre-war years, and so they had already undergone the frightening experience of advancing under hostile fire.

The London Irish draft consisted of five Corporals and 60 Riflemen. On the morning after our arrival we were spoken to by our new CO, Lieut-Colonel Fergus Knox, who had watched us drilling for half-an-hour beforehand. He told us sadly that we looked more like a band of willing cowboys than a squad of trained soldiers. He had decided, he said, that before he allowed us to join the companies to which we had been posted we would have to undergo a week of intensive drilling under the regimental sergeant-major. From that day forward we were always known throughout the battalion as the "cowboy" contingent.

The 2nd Royal Ulster Rifles had been sent to France directly after the outbreak of war as part of the highly-trained 3rd division, which was commanded by General Bernard Montgomery, at a time when his name was scarcely known to the British public. The RURs formed one of the three battalions in the 9th infantry Brigade, under the command of the immensely popular Brigadier Brian Horrocks, who was also destined to achieve military renown during the next few years. Monty was feared, respected, and trusted by his men. He was, at the same time, a natural leader and a great showman. He seemed to realise that it was essential for him to imprint his individuality on the whole of his division, and he did this by sending periodic messages to be read out to his troops, by allowing them to see him as often as possible, and by presenting himself as being "something of a character" with his unconventional habits in regard to dress. Even his code of stringent discipline, which permeated down through the ranks, had about it a personal quality. Brian Horrocks was quite a different type, though his men held him in equal esteem and had as great a confidence in his leadership. He was affable and unpretentious, and liked to wander round our billets chatting casually with us. Because he was an effortless communicator, he was unusually aware of any rumours or speculations circulating among the troops in his Brigade.

At first I wondered if I would ever be wholly accepted in the Royal Ulster Rifles, or if I would be regarded perpetually as a part-time territorial soldier. As soon as I was posted to a company I tried to lose my London Irish identity. I wanted to be one of them, and not an imposition from outside. I was relieved to find that they viewed my arrival with quizzical interest rather than with any semblance of hostility. The other two corporals in my platoon were friendly and helpful from the start. They were both in their upper twenties and both were "old sweats" in the regiment. In spite of the difference in our ages and our backgrounds I had soon established a fairly close relationship with them, and the three of us often went out together for the evening when we were all off duty. One of them was a Dubliner, with the nickname "Pug". He had enlisted as a boy-soldier at the age of 16 when he had been almost illiterate, and he told me once that the army had given him his self-respect as well as teaching him to read. Pug had become a good boxer and had been a semi-finalist as a middle-weight in the last army championship to be held before the war. The other, an equally interesting character, was generally known as "Fitz" and came from Belfast. During the time he was serving in India he had begun to take an interest in Victorian literature, and he could talk quite knowledgeably about the novels of such authors as Dickens, Trollope, Tolstoy, and Thackeray. Pug and Fitz used to tease me incessantly, but never unkindly, about my lack of worldly experience, and what they always referred to as my "feather-bedded upbringing".

A few weeks after I had joined the battalion my company had to provide the regimental quarter guard. This was a 24 hour duty at battalion headquarters, which was then in a disused casino. The guardroom was a nissen hut at the gates, about 50 yards from the building. The day before I was due to start, Pug was tipped off by one of his friends in another company that some of the prisoners in the guardroom were planning to break out forcibly while the sergeant of the guard was away having supper. "They think it will be a push-over with you in charge," Pug said. He told me that three of the men then in custody were really bad and dangerous characters who had been in-and-out of trouble since the day they had joined the battalion. They were all awaiting courts martial, two of them for assaulting

NCOs and the other for disobedience. He advised me to keep my wits about me, and to have my bayonet handy at my side, all the time the sergeant was away. "They'll stop at nothing to escape," he warned, "because they know they're heading for bloody great sentences at their trials." The regimental quarter guard was composed of a sergeant, a corporal, and eight riflemen. It commenced its duties at 6 p.m. on one day and continued until 6 p.m. on the next. Two sentries were mounted at the gates and the other members were on "stand-by" in the guardroom, ready to turn out at a moment's notice. Late in the evening the sergeant handed over to me while he went away for half-an-hour to the Sergeants' Mess. When he had gone I looked around the nissen hut wondering what form the attempted breakout would take. There were eight prisoners all told, but most of them were being detained for relatively minor offences. The three awaiting court-martial were seated on the floor in a group playing cards. I noticed them glancing at me and I thought they were exchanging whispers. Three of the guard were lying on blankets just inside the door, with their eyes closed. Two others were reading newspapers and one was writing a letter. It was quite obvious that if the would-be escapers were to make a sudden dash for it, they would be outside the hut before anyone but myself had fully realised what was happening. However, there was nothing I could do except to watch and to wait. After a few minutes one of the card-players stood up and walked to the table at which I was sitting.

"Corporal," he said, "Is it true that you were a lawyer in civvy-street?"

"I was a law student," I replied, thinking of my status at the Middle Temple.

"Then you know all about self-defence?" he asked. "I'm going to rely on it at my court-martial and I'd like you to explain to me what I have to prove."

During the time I had worked for the Press Association I had been in court on several occasions when Judges were directing jurors about the legal principles of self-defence, so I was able to tell him the law on the subject fairly accurately. While we were talking the other two card-players broke off their game and strolled across to listen. The three of them were standing close together on the far side of my table and I wondered whether, by pre-arrangement, they were forming up for their attempted breakout. To my immense relief I noticed that all the available members of the guard were now alert and were paying close attention to the movements of the prisoners.

Very soon the three men were all consulting me about their forthcoming courts martial and what possible defences would be open to them. We were still discussing their various cases when the sergeant returned from his supper. He immediately ordered them to go back to their own end of the guardroom, and when they had done so he reprimanded me for allowing more than one prisoner at a time to approach the table. "Those buggers are bloody ruffians," he said. "If you gave them half an opportunity, they'd bash your brains in - and they'd think nothing of it."

Pug heard later that the three had abandoned their planned escape because they did not want to land me in any trouble after I had been so helpful with their defences. I hoped this rumour was true, as it was the first occasion on which I had given legal advice to prisoners before their impending trials and it was personally gratifying to think that they might have been satisfied with my guidance.

I was very impressed by the efficiency of the regular army officers and NCOs in the battalion, and by their diligence in looking after their men. We were billeted in empty, unfurnished houses on the outskirts of a small town, but we spent a great deal of our time taking part in field-training schemes, mostly on a divisional level, which lasted for anything between a few days and a week. During these exercises we would be continuously fighting mock-battles - marching, digging, attacking, defending, raiding, and patrolling. We had to snatch an hour or two of sleep, lying on the ground without cover, in our rare interludes of inactivity. To add to the rigours, there would be long phases when eating and smoking were forbidden, because Monty, like a modern Cromwell, seemed to believe that self-denial formed an essential foundation for a soldier's capability and resolution. When the scheme had ended we would spend the best part of a day on the long and weary return march to the town where we had our billets, thankful to be going back to the infinite luxury of nights indoors with blankets, palliasses, and warmth.

Even when we were not on field exercises our programme of training continued without respite, but we had time for sport and recreation as well. I played rugger for the battalion and the brigade. Both teams consisted mainly of officers, and although the matches were keenly contested the standard was fairly mediocre. Soccer aroused far more enthusiasm among the Other Ranks. An inter-company competition was taking place in the battalion when the cowboy contingent arrived, and the results of the games were followed with keen interest. I took part in a trial, and much to my surprise I was chosen to play at centre-half in the company side. I received far more credit for this from the men in my platoon than I was given for representing the brigade at rugger. Pug had urged me to enter my name for the divisional boxing championship and he offered to give a little private coaching, but I adamantly refused to do so.

It was not long before I had become used to the customs, the attitudes and the regimental pride of the battalion. The prospect of going into action together in the near future strengthened our sense of camaraderie, and I think that the other members of my platoon soon ceased to regard me as a migrant from a different social order. They used to tell me a great deal about the lives of the British troops in pre-war India. What had troubled them far more than the extreme heat of the plains had been the protracted absence from home and the total segregation from the company of women. There were the brothels, of course, in the prohibited districts, but few men would choose to visit them for fear of infection with a dreaded venereal disease. There was also, for those who were inclined, a man in nearly every company who was willing to indulge in homosexual practices for payment. But most of the troops remained celibate, preserving the slender hope that they might meet a British girl of the appropriate social class who was living in India or was out on a visit there to relatives or friends. And so, the soldiers continued to be bored, brave, obedient, quarrelsome, sexually frustrated, frequently drunk, and only longing for the day when the troopship would be carrying them out of Bombay at the end of their period of foreign service. Listening to their reminiscences, I wondered sometimes if the conditions they described had altered very much from the time of Rudyard Kipling.

Pug, Fitz, and I used to go out drinking two or more times a week, depending on how many evenings we could afford on our pay as corporals. Sometimes we would agree to separate in order to pick up girls, and when this happened we would shamelessly recount our amorous exploits, our success or our failures, to the other two on the following morning.

"Let's have all the f---ing fun we can," Pug said crudely. "This time next week we might all be f--- ing dead." Apart from the occasional visit from an ENSA concert party the battalion was unable to organise any evening entertainment for us as the whole division was on continual stand-by duty in case of a sudden German attack.

I was summoned to see the company commander one morning after I had been with the 2nd Royal Ulster Rifles for about three months. He told me that our platoon sergeant was being transferred to the battalion orderly-room."I've considered very carefully who to put in his place," he said, "and the company sergeant-major and I both agree that you're the most suitable person. Your promotion to the rank of lance-sergeant will be coming through in today's Part Two Orders." I was dumbfounded as this was something that I had never expected, but I thanked him and returned to my billet. My first thought was how Pug and Fitz would receive the news, as in my opinion they had every reason to be annoyed at being overtaken by a territorial NCO. I found an opportunity to inform them before the order was posted on the company notice-board. They both appeared to be pleased rather than angry, and invited me to join them in a celebratory drink in the canteen as soon as parades were finished for the day. My concern remained as to how my promotion would be viewed by the company as a whole.

The celebratory drink in the canteen with Pug and Fitz lasted far into the evening. We walked back together to our billet and went up to the room which we shared with a lance-corporal. Immediately I entered I saw three bottles of beer lying side-by-side on my palliasse and a piece of white cardboard stuck on the wall above it, on which was written:

GOOD OLD COUNTY CORK!
BEST WISHES FROM THE PLATOON.

That was one of the proudest moments of my life.

The following morning I had my first breakfast in the sergeants' Mess. We sat at long wooden tables, laid with earthenware crockery, and were waited on by orderlies. I could hardly believe that at the end of the meal I would not be standing in a queue to dip my tin plate and my eating utensils into a tub of lukewarm, grimy washing-up water. The Mess was presided over by the regimental sergeant-major who ruled it with a rod of iron. When he welcomed me as a new member he told me he had never imagined the day would come when they would be joined by a non-regular NCO, and he added somewhat ruefully, "I suppose we'll have to get used to this sort of thing, now there's a war on."

I was not left for long to settle into my duties as a platoon sergeant before I was temporarily detached from the company to join a patrol group which was being formed to carry out a special operation. There were about 20 of us under the command of Captain Tighe-Wood, a very popular officer whom I had met before as a fellow-member of the battalion rugby team. He told me that the CO had allowed him to select any NCO or man he wanted for the group.

"Part of the reason why I chose you as my sergeant," he said, "was that you're supposed to be a good map-reader, and the little job we'll be doing involves a lot of cross-country movement by night." He had been given no information as to where or when it would take place. All he knew was that we would be covering a distance of some 20 miles at a fast pace, attacking a building, and heading back to base as quickly as possible. The whole operation was to be carried out under the cover of darkness.

For the next few weeks the patrol group went out on a training exercise every night. Hour after hour Captain Tighe-Wood used to lead us in loose formation over a cross-country route at a gruelling pace. When we were close to our objective we would halt, and I had to go forward with half-a-dozen men and two Bren light machine-guns to take up position on the flank of the building we were about to attack. At a prearranged time, my party would open fire with blank ammunition to cover the rest of the group while they were making a frontal assault. They would let us know the attack was over by sending up a flare. On that signal it was my responsibility to get the covering party back to our own lines as speedily as I could, without trying to join up again with the main body of the patrol.

One morning we were on the grenade range when we were visited by Brigadier Horrocks. He watched us practising for a while and then asked us to gather round him as he wanted to speak to us. He was relaxed and informal as always. He wished us good luck and congratulated us on how well we were acquitting ourselves on our nightly exercises. Finally, he thanked us all for volunteering for the assignment.

I said to Captain Tighe-Wood afterwards, "It's the first time any of us knew we were volunteers, Sir."

"Then it was my mistake," he replied cheerfully. "I must have forgotten to tell you."

As happened so often during the war, at a moment when we were mentally and physically prepared for the operation it was called off. We were never told why. Tighe-Wood broke the news to us with obvious regret. He said, with a glance in my direction, that if a similar opportunity occurred in the future, he hoped that we would all volunteer for it again.

I returned to my company and to my own platoon just in time to take part in a divisional exercise which lasted for a whole week. A few days after it finished I was called off a morning drill parade and ordered to report immediately to the commanding officer at battalion headquarters. Lieut-Colonel Knox saw me in his room. He was sitting at a table with an untidy pile of papers spread out in front of him when I was shown in, and he laid aside the document he was reading and said, "I've decided to put you up for a commission. I wanted to tell you personally, though your company commander knows all about it. There's a selection board sitting at divisional HQ next week and you'll be appearing before them. I have no doubt whatever that you'll be successful." He brushed aside my thanks and added, "I hope you'll come to this battalion as an officer, you'd always be welcome. By the time you're commissioned we'll probably be in the thick of it."

The Selection Board, consisting of a lieutenant-colonel, a major, and a captain, sat for a day at divisional headquarters. There were about 20 candidates for commissions, mostly from infantry regiments. We queued up in a single line outside the door of the room and were admitted individually for our brief interviews. When it came to my turn I entered, saluted, and remained standing rigidly to attention while the members of the Board studied my appearance. After a moment's silence the colonel said, "You may stand-at-ease, sergeant. We've read a good report about you from your commanding officer and there are just one or two additional matters on which we'd like to satisfy ourselves. I will start the ball rolling myself." I was conscious of three pair of eyes fixed on me as he proceeded to the inevitable question. "What school did you go to?" I told him and there was a pause while they noted down my reply. Then the major took over. "What games do you play?" he asked. I wondered if I should enumerate all the games I had ever played, but I decided that, since I was being assessed for my ability to become an officer and a gentleman, I could not go far wrong if I confined myself to only mentioning rugby football. The captain seemed to take an immediate interest; he wanted to know if I had belonged to any rugger club before I joined the army, and what was my usual position on the field. The colonel interrupted the discussion by inquiring about my father's service in the Great War; in particular whether he had held a commission or not.

Next came what was obviously the climactic moment of the whole interview. Having glanced at his watch, the colonel leant forward in his chair and speaking slowly and deliberately, said "I want you to think carefully before you answer this one. What do you consider to be the most important quality a junior officer should possess?" Without hesitation I replied, "The ability to look after his men." He looked surprised. "That's an interesting choice," he commented. "Nearly everybody so far has come up with 'courage', 'bravery', 'audaciousness' - a rose by any other name, etc. We have nothing more to ask you. You'll be notified of our decision in due course."

The first indication I was given of the successful outcome of my interview was my posting a few weeks later to an officer-cadet training unit in the Malvern hills. Before I reported there I was told to remove the chevrons from my sleeves because, although I would continue to be paid as lance-sergeant throughout the course, officer-cadets wore no insignia of rank other than white bands around their caps.

The OCTU was in a new hutted camp a short distance from Malvern. The cadets lived in comparative comfort, sleeping eight to a room in two-tier bunks. All my new companions had been in potential-officer squads at their regimental depots for the whole, or almost the whole, of the time they had been in the army. This fulfilled the requirement that they were being "commissioned through the ranks" but it meant that they knew very little about the organisation and the functioning of a battalion in the field. It is doubtful, too, if the segregated circumstances of their ranker-service had taught them very much regarding the character and philosophy of the ordinary infantry soldier.

The eight people in my room managed to get on very well together from the start, which was fortunate as we had to live in close proximity for several months. We had come from an assortment of peace-time occupations. There were two bank clerks, a Lloyds underwriter, a shop assistant, an accountant, a veterinary surgeon, and a wealthy young man who had worked in his family's linen business. Two of my room-mates in particular stand out in my memory. The first is George, one of the bank clerks. He was slightly older than the rest of us and was the only one of us who was married. He had a shy, reserved manner, a kindly disposition, and an equable temperament. He seldom went out in the evening, preferring to stay in the camp reading a book or writing to his wife. The second person I remember very clearly is Christopher, the underwriter, who had graduated at Oxford University just before the war. There was nothing he enjoyed so much as an impromptu disputation, and he would frequently make an inordinately contentious statement merely in the hope of stimulating an argument. He had an immensely powerful physique and I was told that he might well have gained a rugger blue if his sight had not been so bad. He played in the second row for the OCTU rugby team, and as I packed down behind him, as a wing forward, he made me promise that whenever a scrum broke up I would face him in the direction of the ball.

I was disappointed with the training we received at the OCTU because it taught me little that I had not learnt already. The bulk of our time was spent being drilled on the parade-ground or listening to detailed explanations about the mechanism and the characteristics of the ordinary infantry weapons. The only really interesting lectures were given by a Colonel Crookenden, a veteran with two rows of medal ribbons, who taught us infantry tactics. He had dropped his official rank on rejoining the army and was serving on the OCTU staff as a captain, but he was always known as "colonel". Our company commander and our platoon commander, neither of whom impressed us much, were both pre-war territorial officers. The former had been an assistant master at public school and seemed to be more concerned with our suitability for admission to an Officers' Mess than with our aptitude for leading soldiers into battle. The member of the staff who was most closely in contact with us was our platoon sergeant-instructor, a regular army NCO with 12 years' experience. Although smart, efficient, and soldierly, he was an utter rogue, with a propensity for borrowing money from his cadets, which he never repaid. It was rumoured that if you subsidised him sufficiently he would be sure to give you a good report at the end of the course. He never asked me for a "loan" and I never offered to make him one.

On our free evenings most of the cadets who had any of their pay still unspent went out drinking in the town. Three of us used to frequent a small, congenial public house well away from the beaten track, and we soon became involved with a hard-drinking, loose-living group of civilians who had made it their regular meeting place. The men were all working in the vicinity; some were expecting to be called-up in the none-too-distant future and some had well-paid reserved occupations. As regards the women, they were either local inhabitants or fairly recent evacuees from urban districts liable to air-raids. Several belonged to a newly emergent genus - a product of the times. Their husbands were in the forces, serving overseas, and they were lonely, bored, sexually-deprived, and constrained by moral precept to indefinite celibacy. Probably most of them had started to visit bars and drinking clubs merely in search of companionship, but inevitably they formed friendships with the men they met, and sooner or later these relationships usually became physical. In consequence, they were generally regarded as good-time girls and propitious pick-ups; or more crudely as "enthusiastic amateurs".

After the pub had closed our group would often carry on drinking at private houses or, if the evening was fine, we sometimes packed a few cars with rugs, torches, sandwiches, and bottles and went off for a late-night picnic in the Malvern Hills. When there was a dance in the neighbourhood which was open to the public we frequently went to it, especially at weekends. I was living above my pay as a lance-sergeant, and I found myself rapidly getting through the small amount of money I had managed to save before the war.

Towards the end of our course at OCTU we had to fill in forms stating in which regiments we would like to be commissioned. We were told that the guards and the cavalry preferred their junior officers to have private incomes, and that they would not accept anyone without interviewing him first. Most of the cadets chose the regiments in which they were already serving, but I was reluctant to do this myself since there was no certainty that I would be sent back to the 2nd Battalion of the Royal Ulster Rifles and I did not want to end up in one of the territorial battalions. In addition, two of the cadets, particular friends of mine, were both in the Royal Sussex Regiment and were constantly trying to persuade me to go along with them. They felt quite certain it would not matter, from the point of view of my application, that I had no affiliations whatsoever with the county of Sussex. In the end I fell in with their proposal. When the official list of War Office postings went up on the company notice-board I found that I was going to be commissioned in the Dorset Regiment.

Our final few weeks at OCTU were pervaded by an end-of-the-last-term-at-school atmosphere. We were allowed time off to arrange our officers' uniforms. Several of the large firms of men's outfitters from London had taken single-room premises in Malvern which were regularly visited by their representatives. I went to one of them, and always made an appointment for midday so that I could meet someone for lunch in the town after my fitting.

On the last evening of the course we had a farewell dance in our recreation room, and afterwards I went on to a party at the house of one of my civilian friends. I slept out that night, returning to the camp an hour before reveille. The corporal in charge of the guardroom said he would have to charge me for being absent without a pass, despite the fact that I was leaving the OCTU that morning. He started to write out a charge-sheet and I noticed that he was describing me in it as "Officer-Cadet Babington". I pointed out to him, courteously I hope, that ever since midnight I had been a 2nd Lieutenant. The corporal grinned and started to tear up the sheet. "If you're already an officer, Sir, I can't charge you," he said, "but can I be one of the first people to congratulate you, and can I suggest that you now go straight to your room and get yourself properly turned-out with your correct badges of rank." We shook hands and I hurried away, thankful to have avoided a last-minute reprimand from my company commander.

After breakfast we travelled by train to London; a hundred-or-so newly commissioned subalterns in brand-new uniforms, all of us self-consciously aware of the solitary pip on each of our shoulders. We had been granted seven days leave before reporting to our depots or battalions. I had been hoping to be posted to the 1st Dorsets, part of a regular army brigade defending Malta, but I was being sent to a territorial battalion stationed on the coast of Kent, which had suddenly become the British forward line of battle.

The "Phoney War" had ended in the spring of 1940. In April, Hitler's armies had overrun Denmark and Norway. In May, they had invaded Holland and Belgium as a preliminary to a massive attack on France. Then had followed the evacuation of the BEF from Dunkirk with the loss of most of its tanks, artillery and other heavy equipment, and the capitulation of the French to the all-conquering German forces. In July, the Italian dictator Mussolini, concluding that the fighting was all but over, had entered the conflict ingloriously on the side of the supposed victors, a move which was described by Winston Churchill as a "rush for the spoils". By mid-summer the Germans were concentrating a huge invasion force on the northern coast of France, facing across the narrow waters of the English Channel. Britain was now at bay, with her back to the wall.

My new battalion belonged to a territorial division, ill-equipped and only half-trained, which was manning a section of the shore to the north of Dover. The open Kentish countryside behind us had been strewn with obstacles to impede an air-borne landing. The placid green fields were blemished with concrete pillboxes and lacerated with the fissures of anti-tank ditches. Our duty, I was told, was to hold up the enemy until the reserve formations, which were desperately short both of armour and armour-piercing weapons, could mount a counter-attack. Despite the vulnerability of our position the men in the battalion seemed in good heart as they waited stoically for the impending onslaught.

The exigencies of war were encroaching on the lives of many of the families in Britain, including my own. Arnold had just left for the Middle-East. Eve had volunteered for service in the Wrens. My two first cousins, my mother's nephews, who were both doctors, had joined the Royal Army Medical Corps; one of them had been sent to East

Africa and the other was in transit for India. Norman was still at the Judge Advocate General's Office in London, but there was no certainty that he too would not be posted overseas. And my own future movements were in the lap of the gods.

Christopher, the short-sighted Lloyds' underwriter, was the only one of my erstwhile OCTU room-mates I was ever to meet again. He had transferred to the Royal Artillery and he acted as forward observation officer with my company during our final attack to break out of the Normandy bridge-head. I never heard what became of the others, except George, the serene and quiet bank clerk, who won a posthumous VC in Burma. According to the citation he was leading an assault on a Japanese position when an officer hacked off his arm with a sword. Ignoring his wound, George continued the charge until he was killed by enemy fire.

CHAPTER 11

My recollections of the next few years are enmeshed in a tangled skein, consisting partly of discarded and partly of treasured memories.

I have never wanted to think, to speak, or to write about my own experiences in battle, and as soon as the war was over I made a deliberate effort to expunge them from my mind, except for the final episode which remained so stark and so vivid that it could never be effaced. For the sake of totality, however, it is necessary now for some of those dormant mental images to be reawakened.

My time in action comes back to me as a series of scenes and impressions rather than as a chronological sequence of events. I remember the moments of passivity as much as the moments of action. Crouching in a slit-trench when the shelling was at its heaviest; the shuddering of the earth at each explosion and the evil urgency of the screeching metal fragments streaking overhead. The incongruous sense of affinity with the insects which burrowed under the soil to escape from the predators stalking on the surface above. I remember the periods of silence as much as the periods of tumult; the tense and brittle stillness that could overhang the front line between the bursts of fury. I can recall the desolation of the tall trees with their foliage torn and disordered, and the branches which hung down from strips of bark like newly dismembered limbs. There were no bird-songs as all the birds had abandoned their nests when the bombardment had started. I can see again the captured objective directly after a successful attack; the enemy prisoners being marched away with their hands clasped together on the tops of their heads; the abandoned weapons, cartridges, clothing, and equipment strewn about at random; the dead, transformed in an instant from living beings into insensate corpses, lying where they had fallen, with pallid bloodless faces, staring eyes and fixed expressions of shock, horror, agony, or bewilderment.

Few soldiers, however battle-hardened, could look on death with equanimity, and you noticed them deliberately averting their eyes when they were passing the bodies of the men who had been killed in action. We used to bury the dead, both the enemy's and our own, as quickly as possible in shallow graves marked by rough crosses made from two lengths of wood or by rifles standing upright in the ground. It was necessary to notify the divisional chaplain of the map reference of one of these makeshift graves so that in due course the bodies could be reinterred in an authorised war cemetery. The men disliked being detailed for a burial party, which not only had to dig the hole but also to stow the corpse into it, wrapped in a blanket, while the Padre stood their side with bowed head reciting a short valedictory prayer.

On one occasion in Normandy my company sergeant-major reported to me that the men were even more reluctant than usual to take part in a burial. After a protracted spell of bitter fighting we had just made a small advance into an area which had previously been between the two front lines, and we had found a dead German corporal in the corner of a field where I wanted to set up my company headquarters. His body had obviously been lying there for some days as it was reeking with the putrid, sickly stench of decaying flesh, and was covered with maggots. I asked the Padre for permission to burn off the maggots with lighted petrol and he reluctantly consented. Directly the flames had gone out the sergeant-major and I shovelled the remains on to a blanket which we rolled up and deposited into the newly-dug grave. Afterwards, I had to go through the dead Corporal's wallet in order to identify him. It was stuffed with photographs of people and places near to his thoughts. One showed a happy, smiling group consisting of the Corporal himself in uniform, proudly displaying the insignia of his rank, flanked by a couple whom I assumed to be his parents, and his wife or girl-friend. When I looked at it I wondered if he had been deluded into believing that there was anything even remotely glorious about war.

We used to talk a great deal at OCTU about the prospect of going into action. We would often admit to each other our anxieties as to how we would react when we came under fire, and how well we would be able to contend with the prolonged strains of battle. I had another secret dread. I realised that if I survived long enough the time would come when I personally would have to kill or try to kill one of the enemy. In fact, it happened compulsively, without forethought, during my first engagement, when we were rushing a German position. I was carrying, as I always carried, a sub-machine gun, and I had a commando-knife in my belt for close combat. I saw the young officer in the half-light about six yards away from me coolly lifting his automatic revolver and pointing it in my direction. He was slender, fair-haired and boyish - not at all like the brutal images Captain Lacey had conjured up for us in our mad-minute bayonet charges against his straw-filled sacks.

I fired a burst at him from the hip. I saw the blood seeping through the front of his tunic and I noticed the look of pain and surprise on his face as his weapon tumbled from his hand. Then, almost in slow motion, he half-turned and collapsed full-length on the ground. He was dead before I reached him. We left the place immediately but for a while I had an urge to return there and to pray for his family above his body. Afterwards I kept telling myself that it might not have been my shots which had killed him as my men were firing all around me as they charged. But I knew the truth. I had seen my ranging fire kicking up the earth directly in front of him before I had raised my aim.

I was warned by a pacifist during the war that I would be haunted for the rest of my life by the things I was doing and the things I was ordering others to do. He was wrong. I have never had any feelings of guilt about the part I played in what was virtually a crusade against one of the greatest evils that has darkened the world this century.

Only one of my war experiences afflicted me with nightmares in after-years, but this emanated from claustrophobia rather than from self-reproach. We had been advancing in single file on either side of a narrow, overgrown lane soon after a landing, when we came under heavy mortar fire. I shouted to men near me to lie flat and just as I was getting down myself I felt a piece of shrapnel grazing my left leg on the outer side of the upper thigh. After a few minutes the firing ceased and I ordered the men to continue to advance. A company stretcher-bearer was standing near me at the time. He glanced down at my leg and exclaimed, "You've been hit, Sir." I told him it was merely a nick and was not even painful. "It's bleeding quite badly," he said; "You'd better let me have a look at it." I noticed for the first time the jagged tear in my battledress trousers, surrounded by a steadily extending dark red patch. By that time the sergeant-major had joined us. "You'll have to have a field dressing on that right away," he commented. "If you drop your trousers I'll put it on for you." I replied testily that had no intention of standing there in full view of my men with my trousers down to my ankles, but eventually he persuaded me to let him bandage the wound in the undergrowth at the side of the lane. When he had finished he said, "It's worse than you think, Sir. I'm afraid you must go back and have it seen to at the Regimental Aid Post. I think the shrapnel's still in your leg." As the blood was beginning to seep through the bandage already, and there was a numbness developing in my thigh, I reluctantly agreed. I knew roughly where the MO had set up his RAP, and I started to walk back towards it. After I had hobbled a few hundred yards I suddenly felt very sick, my wound began to throb, and the muscles of my left leg were seizing up. There was a low grassy bank along the verge and I decided to sit on it for a while until I felt better. A few minutes later a truck pulled beside me, driven by a sergeant who offered to take me to the RAP and helped me into the front passenger seat. The MO confirmed that a lump of shrapnel had penetrated my thigh. "It's impossible to see where it's come to rest without an X-ray," he said, "but wherever it is you'll have to have it removed. It will mean quite a tricky operation and we'll have to send you back to England to have it done."

I was then designated a "stretcher case" as I had difficulty in walking, and in the early afternoon I was taken by ambulance with three other wounded men to a tented casualty-clearing point close to a sandy beach. It had few medical facilities as we were only supposed to remain there for a brief period before being embarked in a hospital ship. The arrangements were being hampered because the whole area was coming under heavy shellfire and was intermittently attacked by low-flying aircraft. As a consequence, the evacuation of the wounded was principally carried out under cover of darkness. I was put into a bare tent with about 20 men lying close together on stretchers. Some of them were suffering from severe injuries and the long wait until nightfall was a considerable ordeal for them. One young private soldier was delirious and every now and then he would cry out, "Oh my leg! Help me, please!" Each time this happened a captain alongside him would reach out and clasp his hand sympathetically. Orderlies came in occasionally with urinal bottles or cool drinks, and during the evening they brought round a lukewarm, unpalatable meal for those who were well enough to eat it. When it was almost dark we were informed by a staff officer that our embarkation would take place two hours earlier than had been intended and would commence immediately. "A Jerry plane has been dropping flares near here, just off the coast," he said. "We think they've spotted our hospital ship so they'll guess there's something happening in this locality. We've got to get you on board as quickly as possible. This is going to be a rush job."

We were carried down to the beach in the half-light and

loaded into Ducks, the wheeled amphibious barges which looked equally ungainly whether they were trundling awkwardly on land or nosing labouriously through water. My stretcher was deposited with a long line of others lying laterally in the bottom of a Duck. We were packed in so close together that we could scarcely turn over without disturbing the men on either side of us. It was extremely uncomfortable but we could at least look up and watch the emergence of the stars. Then, to my dismay, the orderlies began to suspend another row of stretchers from racks just above us, and presently there was an impenetrable partition of canvas less than a foot from our faces, wholly obscuring our vision and seriously impeding our supply of fresh air. I had always been subject to claustrophobia and this confinement caused me considerable distress. There was an interminable delay before we started on our journey, and even when we reached the hospital ship there was another long wait before it was our turn to pull alongside the off-loading bay. I shall never forget my feeling of relief when the top layer of stretchers were removed and taken on board. This experience must have created a deep impression on my sub-conscious mind because for several years after the war I was having recurrent unpleasant dreams which were plainly connected with it. In one, I was back at St Anselms. I had been attacked by a crowd of bullying elder boys who had tied my hands together and had pushed me under the floor-boards of the sports pavilion. In another, I was in a building which had been bombed in an air-raid. I was lying on the floor under a pile of rubble which was pressing down on my body and smothering my face.

My career as an officer had started off very badly. The CO of the territorial battalion to which I had been posted was given a staff job soon after my arrival and the second-in-command, Major Wilson, assumed temporary command in his place. Wilson was an unintelligent pre-war regular officer, rank conscious, lazy, and incompetent. He had just as low an opinion of my abilities as I had about his, and he was continually asking my company commander for reports about me in the hope of hearing something to my detriment. Our adjutant was equally unimpressive. He had been a sergeant-major in the regiment in peace-time, but he looked more like a ledger clerk than a professional soldier. Whenever I saw him he was frowning and harassed, and he seemed quite incapable of coping with his responsibilities.

On two occasions I was selected to play for the divisional rugby 15 against other service sides. Even though Major Wilson had very grudgingly allowed me leave of absence for the matches, the adjutant created endless difficulties about my borrowing one of the battalion motor-cycles to get to Maidstone where they were taking place. In view of the uncooperative attitude adopted by both of them, when I was invited to represent the South-Eastern Command against a combined universities team at the ground of a London rugby club, my first inclination was to excuse myself from accepting. However, an artillery major in the division, a former English international, who had also been selected, offered me a lift in his car, so I wrote a formal letter to the adjutant asking if the acting CO would grant me permission to play. I received a brief reply informing me that Major Wilson would like to discuss the matter with me in private and wanted to see me in his office the following morning.

Wilson received me coldly and kept me standing in front of his table for several minutes while he fiddled with some papers. Then he said, "The adjutant has shown me your letter and this seems a good opportunity for me to tell you that I'm not satisfied at all about the way you're settling down in the battalion."

"I don't understand, Sir," I replied. "Do you mean that you think I'm inefficient?"

For a moment he looked flustered. "Oh no, it's nothing like that," he said. "Your company commander has a very high opinion of you. No, I'm referring to your general attitude. You seem to think that playing rugby football is more important than fighting the war - both the adjutant and I have noticed it. Your letter is the latest example. We're here in the front line with the Germans about to invade at any moment, and you want to go off miles away to play rugger. Supposing the invasion takes place in your absence? Your platoon would be left without an officer to lead them into battle. Probably that never occurred to you."

I pointed out that a similar situation would arise if I was on leave, or away on a course. This made him angry. He had called me before him, he said, to express his displeasure with my conduct and not to listen to my specious arguments. "I knew what to expect from you," he went on, "when I overheard you telling someone on your first evening in the Mess that you had hoped to be posted to the 1st Battalion. I suppose you wanted to spend the rest of the war in Malta? You imagined your military life was going to consist of tennis tournaments, cocktail parties, and moonlight swims."

I assured him that I had merely wanted to join a regular battalion, and that I had never imagined that the 1st Dorsets would remain in Malta for the duration of the war. He cut me short and informed me that he had decided to grant my application, but that this was the last time I would be given leave to play in a rugger match. Further, he added, he thought it would be better for both our sakes if I was to leave the battalion as soon as possible, and he would try to arrange a suitable posting for me.

During the following week I was transferred to a regimental training unit. I was extremely sorry to leave the battalion because I liked the other officers and I had become attached to the members of my platoon. A few months later I was invited to return by the new CO who had just taken over. He told me in his letter that Major Wilson had been sent to the Depot, and that my old company commander was very keen to have me back. But by then it was too late as I was about to embark upon a far more interesting venture than manning the coastline.

I never met Major Wilson again. Contrary to his suggestion, the 1st Dorsets, the battalion in which I was eventually to serve, only remained in Malta until the siege of the island had ended. They then trained for Combined Operations and, as part of the elite 231 Brigade, they took part in the initial assault landings in Sicily, Italy, and Normandy.

A group of us who were at OCTU together had arranged that, for the purpose of maintaining contact with each other, whenever we happened to be in London we would sign a book in a small, one-room drinking club near Piccadilly Circus, indicating how we could be contacted. The scheme expanded rapidly as we all introduced new participants, until eventually our book contained several hundred names. The only person I ever added was a cavalry captain with whom I had become friendly while we were both attending a street-fighting course. I gathered that he had some sort of staff job, but he never talked about the nature of his work. We continued to meet occasionally after we had returned to our units at the end of the course. One evening when we were dining together he suddenly asked me how I was enjoying being in the training unit. I told him I found it immensely dull and I was longing to do something more active. "I might be able to help," he said. "I can't promise anything but it's worth a try. You told me once that when you were young you could speak French pretty fluently. How well can you speak it now?" I told him I was extremely rusty and my accent was appalling. "You're probably being excessively modest," he commented, and he added vaguely, "Besides, if your French isn't good enough for what I have in mind, there are other things." He said he would discuss the matter with his commanding officer, and without elaborating any further he deliberately changed the subject.

During the next year I became proficient in the use of high explosives for the purpose of sabotage, in particular for blowing up railway steam engines. About 10 of us, all from different regiments and unknown to one another before, found ourselves living together at an officers' transit hotel in central London. We trained each day in a heavily-blitzed area of the Docklands, amidst the skeletons of rootless houses, the toppling chimney-stacks, the clouds of brick dust, and the acres of rubble, where we could let off our charges in safety. We were taught how to blast down locked doors with sticks of gelignite, how to scale the outer walls of buildings with linked toggle-ropes, and the best ways in which to enter or escape surreptitiously through upper-floor windows. Sometimes we were taken on expeditions along temporarily unused sewers, to show us their usefulness both for hiding places and for purposes of secret movement. Our instructor used to warn us, half-flippantly and half-seriously, that anyone who fell behind and lost his way would probably end up in a sewer which was working normally. We also learnt the best ways of wrecking steam engines, either with high explosives or by shovelling gravel through an opening at the front of the boiler. To make us more conversant with the mechanisms we were seeking to destroy, we took turns at driving an elderly engine on an inactive section of the line between Battersea Park and Victoria stations, under the surveillance of a professional train-driver.

This was the period in the history of the British people which Winston Churchill was to describe as "their finest hour," when there seemed no hope whatever of victory and very little prospect of survival, yet no one spoke of, nor even considered, the possibility of capitulation to the Nazis. It was a time of shortages and privation; food was rationed; fuel restricted; and most basic commodities were in short supply. The air raid shelter had become a habitual mode of existence and the wailing sirens an accustomed background to the ordinary sounds of the streets.

Each time I was returning to the transit hotel in the late evening and passing through tube stations in central London, I was amazed at the resilience of the people. They went down night after night, the men and the women, the old and the young, the children and the infants, to sleep in double-decker bunks along the entire length of the platforms, beside the passengers hurrying to their destinations. In the early hours of the morning they would emerge into the daylight not knowing whether or not their homes would still be standing. And yet, the daily round of activity, the friendly smile, and the jovial greeting were seldom lacking.

One evening towards the end of our course I was invited to supper by Rodney, the man who was teaching us to drive steam engines. He lived in a small, terraced house in Battersea Park, not far from the station, with his wife and their eight-year-old daughter, Rosemary, a bright, attractive, well-mannered child. We had a very pleasant meal which we had barely finished when the sirens blared forth. Rodney's wife hurried down to the shelter in their tiny garden with Rosemary, and I told Rodney it would be best if I went back to the hotel, as the air-raid might continue for the rest of the night. While we were talking bombs started to fall uncomfortably close and Rodney persuaded me not to go out for the moment, but to join them in the shelter. Immediately I entered the candle-lit bunker Rosemary exclaimed, "Oh, I'm so glad you're here, Tony. I won't feel frightened any more now with a soldier to guard me." Her words touched me with their simple faith, although they made me feel singularly inadequate. The all-clear did not sound until about four o'clock the following morning. Before I departed Rodney and his wife insisted that I should drink a cup of strong tea, laced with brandy, to speed me on my way.

Afterwards, Rodney and I kept in touch with each other for over a year. The last time he wrote to me he was shattered by grief. One night the blitz had been particularly heavy in south London and his house in Battersea had received a direct hit. He himself had had a miraculous escape, but when the rescue-workers had dragged his wife and Rosemary from the wreckage they were already dead.

By then I was becoming used to hearing of casualties - killed, wounded or missing - among my friends and acquaintances. Sometimes it was a boy with whom I had been at school; sometimes a former colleague at the Press Association; sometimes a member of the London Irish rugger club; and sometimes a person I had known casually before or after the outbreak of war. It had started with Denis, who had been mobilised on the eve of our trip to France during the last summer of peace. Jill had told me over the phone that his bomber had failed to return from a night raid on the Ruhr. We both thought there was every reason to hope he was still alive, but later it was reported that the Germans had found the remains of his body in his burnt-out aircraft.

About the time I received his sad news from Rodney I also heard that the man who had shared a room with me at the officers' transit hotel, a small, tough, cheerful Midlander had been killed whilst serving with the Partisans in

Yugoslavia. On the final night of the course we had gone out drinking together in the West End and had returned to the hotel in the early hours of the morning. Before he started to undress he had sat on the side of his bed, deep in thought. Suddenly he had inquired if I was a Christian. I told him I was, but that I found it difficult to accept the Christian dogma in its entirety. He had nodded. "That goes for me too," he said; "I'm never certain what I do believe and what I don't believe. I'd like to think that there's some sort of life after death. Otherwise the whole thing seems so pointless." He was silent for a while and then he went on. "Christians are supposed to practise humanity, aren't they? And yet, here's the pair of us being trained to be merciless killers, and we're enjoying every moment of it. It's a rum business."

I was in bed by then. "Yes," I agreed. "It's a very rum business."

It's odd how these snippets of semi-drunken conversation can linger in the memory, years afterwards.

CHAPTER 12

Towards the end of 1943 I was posted as a captain instructor to the recently established Anglo-American Battle School at Castlewellan in Northern Ireland.

Castlewellan in County Down was a compact little town, with a broad main street, at the foot of the beautiful, purple-tinted Mourne Mountains. The surrounding valleys are dominated by Slieve Donard, mist-capped and majestic, the highest peak in Ulster. The Battle School had been installed in the castle, from which the town derived its name, and there was a hutted camp in the grounds for the provision of additional accommodation.

Battle Schools, which were attended by junior officers and NCOs, had transformed the war-training methods of the British infantry. They sought to instil a spirit of resoluteness and aggression; they tried to develop initiative and independence; and they taught a practical form of elementary tactics based upon the known habits of the enemy. During the two or three week courses almost everything was done at the double. There were physical endurance exercises, gruelling assault courses with a constant accompaniment of high explosive detonations; section and platoon schemes with live ammunition being fired overhead; and lectures on such military skills as fieldcraft, patrolling, ambushes and night raids.

The senior officers in some United States infantry divisions preparing in Northern Ireland for the massive invasion of the European mainland were so impressed by this new approach to training that they proposed the formation of a joint Anglo-American Battle School with the American Army providing 50 per cent of the instructors and

50 per cent of the trainees. This suggestion was welcomed by the British and the Castlewellan project came into being.

The commandant of the school, a British lieutenant-colonel, was a Conservative Member of Parliament who had been a territorial army officer before the war. He was a quiet, kindly and courteous man, well-liked and immensely respected by everyone who served under him. He expected his staff to be hard-working and efficient, but he encouraged them to enjoy themselves when the day's work was finished. It was largely due to his attitude and his personality that the school achieved such a high reputation for the profitability of its courses and for the congenial atmosphere in which they took place.

There was never any rivalry or friction between the British and the American instructors. We shared equally in giving lectures, organising demonstrations, and conducting exercises, always working together closely and amicably. The fact that the Americans were receiving a far higher rate of pay than we were did not cause resentment, although it sometimes resulted in slight embarrassment when we went out with some of them in the evening, as they could be far more free with their money than we could be with ours.

Occasionally a party of us would spend a weekend in Dublin, travelling down by train from Belfast. Because the Irish Free State was neutral we had to obtain special passes and to wear civilian clothing. After the drabness and austerity to which we had grown accustomed Dublin seemed like a fairy tale city; the streets were a blaze of light; food and drink were plentiful; and the shops were well-stocked with articles of every sort at reasonable prices.

At the end of our weekends we would return laden with purchases for the Officers' Mess; and with silk stockings, perfumes, and boxes of chocolates for our wives and girlfriends.

I paid one brief visit to the Irish Free State, rather foolishly, without a pass and without permission. We had just finished a 36 hour endurance exercise and were preparing to bivouac for the night among the barren sand-dunes on Magilligan Point, where the waters of Lough Foyle merge with the surge and swell of the Atlantic Ocean. On the far side of the lough was the coastline of County Donegal and the twinkling lights of the Free State. Three of the American instructors had told me that they had been down to the shore and had arranged with the skipper of a small fishing boat to take them across to Moville, a town on the Donegal side, where they were going to have dinner. He had promised that he would be waiting at 11 o'clock to bring them back again to Magilligan. They invited me to join them and offered to lend me some civilian trousers and a sweater to wear. I hesitated at first. There was no possibility of obtaining the requisite pass and, in any case, although we had no further duties that day we were probably expected to remain in or near to the bivouac area. On the other hand, nobody would be likely to miss us, and we were not leaving Magilligan until six o'clock the following morning, so I agreed to go with them.

The fishing boat appeared on time and came in close to the shore so that we could wade out and clamber on board. The lough was choppy and the wind was rising while we were making the four mile crossing to Moville. When we reached our destination we landed at a proper quay and wandered round the town, visiting various pubs, before we went to a hotel for dinner. By the time we had paid our bill and left to retrace our steps to the quay all four of us had drunk a great deal and we were unconcerned that a gale was now blowing over the lough, which had become extremely rough. We met the skipper at the prearranged place and he immediately told us that the conditions had deteriorated so much he could not possibly take out his boat until they improved. We asked him how long we would have to wait and he shrugged his shoulders. The squall might die down before the dawn, he said, or it might last for another 24 hours. No matter how much we cajoled and entreated he remained adamant; there was no way, he insisted, he could risk his boat in such weather. A group of fisherman standing around listening to the conversation agreed with him that it would be folly to attempt the crossing at that moment. In reply to our questions, they doubted whether any of the local taxi-drivers would be willing, at that time of night, to undertake the long journey around the perimeter of the lough to Magilligan Point. In any event, as none of us had a passport or any other documents it was extremely unlikely that we would be allowed to re-enter Northern Ireland at one of the border crossing-points.

The only alternative seemed to be that we should ring up the military authorities from Moville and confess to our predicament. Inevitably, that would result in our being court-martialled for a very serious breach of discipline. While we were still discussing the matter two youths approached us and said that they would be willing to take us back in their motorboat if we made it worth their while. We offered them all the money we had left, the Americans contributing far more than I did, and they were satisfied with the amount. Their boat was even smaller than the one in which we had made our first journey. They told us to sit together in the stern, to hang on tight, and to bale continuously, otherwise we would become waterlogged. Crossing the lough in the gale should have been a petrifying experience but alcohol had given us a spurious intrepidity. I was impassively aware of the mountainous seas, the waves crashing over the gunnels, and of our puny craft being tossed around pitilessly by the elements. It would have been too dangerous to ground the boat at Magilligan, so we had to jump out waist-deep in the surf and wade ashore. When we paraded next morning our socks and our underwear were still ringing wet, but all four of us considered this discomfort was a very minor price to pay for the avoidance of a trial by court martial.

I had now been in the army for four years and I was longing to get back to civilian life and to embark upon my legal career. We were all aware that it would only be a matter of time before the Allies won the war, but we realised that some of the hardest battles lay ahead of us - the breaching of Hitler's vaunted Western Wall and the progressive liberation of all the occupied countries of Europe. Already preparations for the invasion were well-advanced, the whole of Britain was gearing itself for this one, last, supreme effort.

I felt more and more that I was in a backwater at

Castlewellan; I feared that I was becoming a non-combatant. I compared myself with the other members of my family. Arnold was the skipper of an Air-Sea Rescue launch in the Mediterranean and had just been mentioned in dispatches for gallant conduct in the face of the enemy. My first cousin was serving in the RAMC in Burma. Another cousin had recently been taken prisoner in Italy. Eve, who had been commissioned in the Wrens, had volunteered for foreign service and was expecting to be sent overseas at any minute. And I knew that many of my friends and former comrades-in-arms would be in the van of the invasion force.

I had gone to see the Commandant and I had told him that although I had been supremely happy at Castlewellan, I thought the time had come for me to return to my battalion. "I quite understand," he said; "in fact, I've been expecting you to make this request." He had warned me that these "desired" postings were often difficult to arrange, but he promised to ask my commanding officer to make a formal application to Northern Ireland District headquarters for my immediate return, on the grounds that I was urgently needed in the battalion. The Battle School, he assured me, would place no obstacles in the way of my transfer.

I rejoined my battalion a few weeks later, retaining my rank as captain, and I was immediately appointed to be second-in-command of my old company.

It was then that Emma entered into my life. I had heard of her beforehand from other officers in the battalion. Her name had appeared constantly in their letters - the gorgeous Wren who was billeted in the town to which they had recently been moved. It was generally agreed among them that if and when I returned I would find her as irresistible as they did themselves, and that I would be bound to fall madly in love with her. She was just my type, they told me; blond, bubbly, beautiful, slender, sweet and vivacious, but they cautioned me that I would be up against stern competition. Their eulogies about Emma only had the effect of making me mildly inquisitive to meet her, as I knew that no one can possibly envisage those indefinable characteristics which attract one person to another.

Our first meeting had been unpropitious from my point of view. We were both members of a fairly large party at an all-ranks dance, and I had hardly spoken to her the whole evening. On one occasion I deliberately sat down next to her at the table which our party had taken over. I began the conversation.

"I've heard a lot about you," I said.

"I've heard a lot about you too," she replied. "And I've been warned about you." She had seemed to be completely disinterested in me and was watching the dancers. I started to ask her questions about herself in an effort to draw her out, but she gave me such non-committal replies it led me to believe that she was finding me rather boring. Then we were joined by some of the others, whereupon she brightened and turned her attention to them.

During the following days I was not merely afflicted with injured pride; it was something that went far deeper. Emma had kept edging to the forefront of my thoughts, no matter how much I tried to exclude her from them. I was aware that I had become totally obsessed with her, and I could not help myself. Scarcely a moment passed without my recalling the nuances of her expression, the intonations of her voice, the symmetry of her figure, the grace of her movements, and the softness of her body when we had brushed together accidentally as we were entering the crowded dance-hall. I longed to meet her again and, at the same time, I dreaded that the sole outcome might be a further manifestation of her complete indifference towards me.

By chance, I found myself sitting next to Emma at a battalion concert for which her group of Wrens had been given tickets. She was altogether different from the last time we had met, chatting animatedly with me before the start and during the intervals. I saw her afterwards in the Officers' Mess and she had not seemed displeased when I went over and joined her. We spoke together for the rest of the evening, oblivious of the others in the room, and eventually she agreed to my seeing her home. While we were walking back to the house where she was billeted I asked her why she had been so unfriendly on the night of the dance. She admitted that she had made up her mind to dislike me from the things she had heard about me from the others, even before I rejoined the battalion. She had formed an impression that I was one of those men with a secret contempt for women, who pick them up at random and then discard them when they had served their purpose. "After we'd met that night," she went on, "I was furious with myself for liking you." I commented that she had a very strange way of showing her feelings. At that she had laughed and slipped her arm through mine. "I know I was simply awful to you," she said; "and I stayed awake half the night worrying about it. I was afraid you'd never want to speak to me again."

After that I used to see Emma nearly every day, depending on how frequently we could arrange to be off-duty on the same evenings. Sometimes we met for a drink; sometimes we had dinner together or went to a cinema; sometimes we could only see each for a few fleeting moments. I cannot recall our conversations in detail, nor all the subjects we discussed, and even if I were able to do so, it would be wearisome for others to read about them, so much was personal to ourselves. We were simply two young people falling ever more deeply in love with every hour that passed; we were in the exciting process of discovering each other's characters, attitudes, backgrounds, experiences, hopes, and dreams. Very soon, without realising what was happening, we both noticed that whenever we thought about the years ahead of us, we were assuming instinctively that we would be together; indeed neither of us could visualise a future in which we would be permanently apart. We talked about announcing our engagement right away, but we agreed that under the circumstances it would be better to wait until the war was over. In the meanwhile, we would consider ourselves as being physically, morally, and spiritually bound to one another.

Emma used to tease me because she said that I was showing signs already of developing into a sedate and pompous barrister. In spite of my protestations she undertook to "humanise" me. After we had seen a film she would insist that we ate our supper standing in a side-street at a fish-and-chip stall. She made me take her to local hops at which I was often the only officer present; and when a visiting circus set up nearby, complete with side-shows, she persuaded me into riding with her for half-an-hour in one of the bumper cars. She told me delightedly that all this would make me an easier person to live with after we were married.

One evening after I had seen her home I went into the Officers' Mess for a nightcap. The commanding officer was the only other person there. He bought me a drink and when the Mess waiter had gone he told me that he was glad I had come in alone because he had been looking for an opportunity to have a serious chat with me. "It's not concerned with military matters," he said, "I'm speaking now in my capacity of being in *loco parentis* to all the officers in my battalion, so if you want to tell me to mind my own bloody business you're at liberty to do so. It's about you and Emma." He paused expectantly, and when I made no comment he went on. "It's obvious to everybody that you're becoming extremely fond of each other. She's a lovely girl with a lovely disposition and I'd hate to see her getting hurt. She's very young - she's only 18 isn't she?"

I told him that she was just 19.

"That's still very young," he observed. "I realise that you're only 23 yourself, but let's face it, you've been around a bit. I merely wanted to ask you to be very, very careful not to hurt her."

I told him, truthfully, that I would never deliberately cause Emma to suffer any harm whatsoever - I loved her far too much. I added that we had every intention of getting married as soon as possible after the war.

"That's the best bit of news I've heard for a long time," he said. "I'd like to drink a toast to your future happiness together."

He had then rung for the waiter and had ordered two glasses of champagne.

Most people were aware that the invasion was drawing closer and closer, and would be bound to take place in the spring or summer of 1944. In early May Emma's group, which was working on preparations for the Allied landings, was moved down to a more centralised position in the Portsmouth area. Emma and I were heartbroken as we knew that our chances of seeing each other would from then on be few and far between, and might only occur when one of us was able to get an overnight pass. However, we resolved that we would communicate daily, either by telephone or by letter. As it turned out, hardly a day was to pass without our speaking on the telephone in the morning and writing to each other in the evening.

It was impossible for either of us to obtain any leave during this period because our duties kept both of us fully occupied. After we had been separated for two or three weeks I had received a message from the adjutant that he wished to speak to me urgently about a private and personal matter. I went to his office and he told me, in strict confidence, that leave for all three services was going to be stopped completely in the very near future. "The next few days may well be the last opportunity you'll have of seeing your beloved Emma before things start happening," he said, "and the CO is willing to grant you 48 hours leave starting at noon tomorrow. Please don't go too far away and let us know where we can find you if it becomes necessary." The next day happened to be a Saturday and Emma had been able to acquire a weekend pass at very short notice. I had suggested that I should go to Portsmouth and meet her there, but she had preferred to get right away from the places where we were stationed, so I had booked us in for Saturday and Sunday nights at a small hotel in the Cotswolds.

Her train arrived about half-an-hour after mine and I waited for her at the station. When we were in the taxi on the way to the hotel she asked me if we were putting up as "Captain and Mrs Smith". I told her that they would be sure to require our identity documents. She sighed. "What a pity," she said, "I suppose all the permanent residents will examine the register and we'll be branded a scarlet couple. But I don't care. I'm going to adore every minute of it." Although I had given our separate names when I had made the reservation on the previous day, we were welcomed without any disapproving frowns. After she had given us our room number the girl at the reception desk had said, "We have a dinner-dance here every Saturday evening. I hope you come to it. We like to get as many younger people as possible." The other guests at the hotel were mostly middle-aged or elderly couples, seemingly evacuees from their homes in towns and vulnerable localities. They smiled at us benignly, and a little shyly, when we met them in the corridors and when we were passing their tables in the dining room, as though they were indicating their indulgence of our moral turpitude, because of the abnormal conditions and because we were obviously much in love.

During dinner Emma told me that she too had heard the rumour about leave being stopped in the near future, so we were both aware that in all likelihood we would not see each other again before the invasion. We remained at our table until 11 o'clock when the dance finished. We were oblivious to the apathetic setting; the drab lighting; the regular residents together with a handful of junior officers and their partners shambling aimlessly round the floor; and the languorous music from the string quintet. We had made them play our chosen tune, "A Nightingale Sang in Berkeley Square," to which we had danced together so frequently in the past, and they repeated it at the end of the evening for our especial benefit.

Emma was full of plans for the future on that occasion; where we would live; how many children we would have; what countries we would visit on our holidays. "I'm not prepared to wait until you can afford to marry me," she said. "As soon as you're demobilised after the war, I'm going to come and live with you. I'll get a job and I'll keep you during you penniless days as a law student."

"I would never agree to that," I told her.

"Why not?" she asked. "You seem to have no scruples about taking me away for the weekend and seducing me. Why should you object to my coming to live with you as your mistress?"

When I made no reply she remarked sternly, "Captain Babington, not only are you a defiler of innocent maidens, but you're a bloody hypocrite as well."

At breakfast on the Monday morning Emma had said,

"I'll try very hard not to break down when we're parting. If I do, it will make it very much more difficult for you."

Throughout the weekend we had woven our fantasies, enthralled by our visions of the halcyon times ahead of us. During the final hours, however, we had come face-to-face with the stark reality of the present. I had thought that it might be preferable for us to say our goodbyes at the hotel in the privacy of our room; but Emma would not hear of it. Her train was leaving a short while after mine and she preferred to see me off at the station. In that way, she insisted, we could be together until the last possible moment.

There was only one person in the compartment when I had opened the door, a staff major wearing the flashes of the 21st Army Group. He had looked up from his newspaper and smiled pleasantly without speaking as I climbed in. Having deposited my suitcase on the luggage-rack I rejoined Emma on the platform for our farewell embrace. We had stood close together, tightly enfolded in each other's arms, until the guard had called to me that they were on the point of leaving. I had stayed in the open window, and as the train began to pull out of the station Emma, her eyes filled with tears, had turned away from me quickly so that I would not be distressed by her emotions.

The major glanced at me sympathetically. "These partings are hell," he said, "but let's hope it won't be for long. Your friend looks like a honey - a real dream-girl. I found it difficult to keep my eyes off her."

"Yes," I agreed, "she is a dream girl."

Already, the past few days were beginning to assume

the quality of a dream - a dream which had been terminated on the instant of waking.

I had sat with an open book on my knee, but I had not read a single word. An hour later we stopped at a busy junction and the major had told me that this was his destination. When he was leaving the train he shook me by the hand and said, "I hope you'll come through this all right, and that you'll soon get back to dream-girl. Your lot have a tough job on their hands - I know because I've been working on the plans."

During the remainder of my journey the compartment gradually filled up, all the other occupants being civilians. Everyone seemed to know that the invasion of occupied Europe was about to begin, and when I took down my suitcase, before getting out, they spontaneously wished me good luck in what lay ahead. One woman assured me that they would be praying for us continually.

CHAPTER 13

Whenever I recall the battle of Normandy my mind settles on Hottot - not on the place itself, but on the fighting all around it, which developed for our brigade into a minor Passchendaele.

Hottot, a relatively insignificant little village on the main road between Caen and Caumont, had become strategically important owing to the location of the opposing armies, and on June 19, 231 Brigade had been ordered to capture and hold it. Thirteen days had then elapsed since the Normandy landings, and it was obvious that the operation was not proceeding according to plan, since we had only penetrated inland to a depth of about 10 miles. The Germans, in skilfully prepared positions, well supported by artillery and tanks, were resisting all our onslaughts with grim determination. We had learnt to our cost that the Bocage countryside was ideally suited to the infantry defender as it abounded in small fields, surrounded by ditches, high banks, and thick hedgerows, which formed natural obstacles against advancing troops. To add to our problems a fierce gale was raging in the English Channel and had severely damaged our immediate life-lines, the two artificial harbours just off the coast. As a result, no reinforcements, materials, or supplies were coming ashore and our gunners were running out of shells.

The attack on Hottot had been timed to commence at 1300 hours in the hope that we would occupy the village before nightfall. My battalion was going to advance in the usual infantry formation, with two rifle companies leading and the other two following close behind them. The CO had told me on the previous evening that he wanted me to remain at battalion headquarters for the whole of the afternoon. We had very few captains left, he said, and I must be available to take command of one of the forward companies at short notice if it became necessary.

Early in the morning it had started to rain, a heavy downpour which was to continue for the next 24 hours, churning the hardened soil into a muddy morass. Battalion headquarters, consisting of a few vehicles and wireless sets, had been set up in a field at the side of a sunken lane. I had reported there to the adjutant with Private Rivers, my batman, at midday. By that time the water was dripping from our steel helmets, and our clothing was sodden under the groundsheets we had slung over our shoulders. The adjutant said, "I don't know what you're going to do with yourself, Tony, while you're waiting in the wings. I'm afraid we can't offer you any shelter from the elements." As he was very busy with administrative matters I wandered off for a chat with Laurie Lassman, the M.O., whose regimental aid post was a short distance away in the same field. Laurie would have preferred to be using a barn or an outhouse, but he had been unable to find a suitable building in the immediate vicinity, so he had had to content himself with a few blankets stretched out on the ground under the cover of a rectangular strip of tarpaulin suspended on four head-high posts. He was extremely worried about the impending attack, as in his opinion both the officers and men in the brigade were nearing the point of exhaustion after being almost continually in action for the best part of two weeks within the narrow confines of the bridgehead.

I had stayed with Laurie until the artillery barrage

opened on the enemy positions, 15 minutes before our leading companies were to move forward. I then went back to battalion headquarters and stood with Rivers, sheltering under some trees. Flashes were lighting up the sky behind us as shells screamed overhead. The Germans immediately put down an answering barrage. The ground shuddered as shells and mortar bombs exploded in the fields all round us. As the attack went in we heard sporadic bursts of rifle fire, interspersed with the even staccato thumping of the Bren guns and the frenzied jabbering of the fast-firing German spandaus. Presently, the casualties started to come in; the stumbling stretcher-bearers with their rain and blood-soaked cargoes; the walking-wounded, some limping painfully, others clutching an injured arm or shoulder. Very soon there was a steadily mounting queue alongside the Regimental Aid Post.

There was little activity at battalion headquarters. Both the CO and Major "Speedy" Bredin, the second-in-command, spent most of their time with the forward troops, only returning occasionally for fleeting visits. Hardly any information was coming back to the adjutant as most of the wireless sets with the attacking companies had been knocked out by enemy fire. At one point the intelligence officer emerged momentarily from his armour-plated truck to inform me that our attack was being held up at every point, and the other two battalions in the brigade were also encountering severe opposition.

About an hour later the CO drove up in his jeep, but did not get out. The adjutant and I hurried over to him. He told us that D company was being counter-attacked by infantry and tanks. It had been reported that five or six tanks - he thought they were Tigers - had broken through and were heading in our direction. "Tony," he said, "I want you to round up all the men you can find and form a defensive position round B.H.Q." With that he sped off again in the direction of the fighting. I asked the adjutant how many anti-tank rifles were available. "You must be joking," he replied. "We haven't even got a Bren gun here." The RSM who had overheard our conversation, mentioned to me that he had six "sticky bombs" in his truck which he kept to hand for emergencies such as this. These bombs were infantry weapons for close-range use against tanks. They were encased with a gummy covering; when primed it was necessary to affix them manually to the side or the top of an enemy tank, and they detonated after seven seconds.

For most infantrymen enemy tanks took on the fearsome aspect of animate and invulnerable monsters, because their armour was impervious to ordinary small-arms fire. I had decided that the only thing we could do was to prepare an ambush. I told the RSM to block the track with an empty three-ton lorry. While he was doing this I collected a dozen of the battalion headquarters' staff-clerks, drivers, and signallers - and positioned them close to the obstruction under the cover of the bank at the side of the track. I took one sticky bomb myself and issued the others to the RSM and four of the men. My plan was simple. We would wait until the column of tanks had been forced to halt, when the six of us would leap out, plant our bombs and dive for cover. In that way, I explained to my little party, with a confidence I was far from feeling, we would cripple six

Tiger tanks at one fell swoop.

After we had spent the best part of an hour crouching behind the bank, listening intently for the rumble of approaching tracked vehicles in the lane, I received a message from the adjutant - informing me that the tanks had turned about and were now heading back towards their own lines. He added the sad news that Lieut-Colonel Norie, our immensely popular CO, had been severely wounded while visiting one of the forward companies, and that Major Speedy Bredin had taken over command of the battalion.

Late in the afternoon the attack on Hottot had been discontinued and the brigade had been ordered to dig in in their new positions. Our battalion had had an unfortunate day. Apart from the CO, who died of his wounds before being evacuated to England, we had suffered about 100 casualties, including some of our most dependable junior officers and NCOs. I had returned to my own company which, although nominally in reserve, had been attacked from the flank and involved in a spell of heavy fighting. My company commander, Major Bill Meredith, was pleased to have me back again. He asked me to take out a reconnaissance patrol while it was still light with the object of discovering whether the Germans were occupying a dense copse a few hundred yards from our company front, in what had now become no-mans-land. A corporal and two privates volunteered to come with me. We had moved out with extreme caution as we had to cross an area of open ground. Having reached the copse without coming under fire, we searched it thoroughly, but we did not come across any Germans except three dead soldiers, none of whom looked more than 18 years old.

As company second-in-command I was responsible for seeing that the men were fed, and after they had finished digging their slit-trenches I had arranged for a hot meal to be sent up in containers from the cookhouse at our rear headquarters. It was dark by the time the food arrived, and though the rain was less heavy, a cool breeze had arisen which increased the discomfort of our drenched clothing. We had received orders that we must maintain a state of readiness all night because a German counter-attack was imminent; however, we were warned that we were only to call for artillery support if our situation became critical, as the shortage of shells was now acute.

The German gunners had the range of our positions and continued their shelling all night. Bill and I shared a slit-trench, one of us always being on duty while the other tried to snatch a few hours sleep, huddled under a groundsheet. There was plenty of work to be done; paying regular visits to the platoon areas to ensure the sentries were alert; checking reports from patrols and outposts; and dealing with messages received over the wireless from battalion headquarters. We stood-to at dawn, the conventional time for a mass attack, but, apart from the shells and the mortar bombs, the Germans showed no signs of activity. The rain had stopped, the breeze had died away, and the sun, rising above the trees in a cloudless sky, foretokened the warmth of the day ahead.

There was a fairly large farmhouse within the company locality, which we had assumed to be unoccupied, and after the men had been given their breakfast, Bill had gone to examine it in case the upstairs windows could be used for observation purposes. When he returned he told me he had been surprised to find that about a dozen civilians, whom he took to be farmhands, were camping-out in the basement. They had numerous bottles of calvados with them and most of them appeared to be drunk. He had been even more surprised to find that a mysterious girl was living on the ground floor. She professed to speak no English and had indicated that she could not understand Bill's French. He asked me to carry out a full search of the house and to instruct the occupants that they must all leave immediately.

I took Rivers with me and we entered the house through the unlocked front door. An attractive, dark-haired girl was standing in the hall watering a plant from an earthenware jug. Her white silk blouse, well-cut grey skirt, and elegant brown leather shoes looked strangely incongruous in such a setting. She greeted me coldly and explained, in French, that the farm belonged to her uncle who had gone to Caen on business the day before the Allied landings, and had been out of touch with her ever since. She herself worked as a secretary in Paris and had come to the farm for a week's holiday. I sent Rivers down to the basement to count the number of people there, and I told the girl I would have to search the house. She did not conceal her annoyance, but said she would show me around. I remarked that I was surprised by her inability to speak any English and I saw a flicker of a smile on her face - the only time she smiled while I was with her. "Your major is an arrogant man," she commented. "He did not treat me as courteously as you are doing. And his French is deplorable." She took me into all the rooms except one on the ground floor. When we reached it she turned to me and said, "I am using this one, Monsieur le Capitaine; I'm sure you don't want to examine a lady's bedroom?" I reminded her that I had been instructed to search the whole of the house, and with an irritable gesture she thrust open the door. "There!" she had exclaimed. "I hope you are satisfied!" It was a sparsely furnished room containing a bed, a table, and a cupboard. There was a clothes-line hanging by the window with some lingerie and blouses pegged on to it. She saw me looking at a framed photograph of an SS officer and she remarked, "I met him in Paris. As far as I know, he is still there." After my inspection was completed I told her that as the occupants of the house were now in the front line, and in great danger, they would have to leave the farmhouse without delay. I said I would send round a guide at eight o'clock the next morning to escort them back through the British lines. She responded angrily, accusing me of ordering them to their certain deaths because all the roads to the rear were under constant shellfire. While Rivers and I were walking away, she shouted after me from the front door that she would refuse to leave of her own accord, if I wanted her to go I would have to come in and drag her out.

I never found out if the farmhouse had been evacuated without trouble. That evening I was just preparing to take out a patrol when Bill Meredith had dashed up. "You'll be taking over "A" company, but Speedy would like to talk to you first. Tony Jones has just been killed - I don't know whether it was shrapnel or a sniper." It did not take long for Rivers to gather up his things and mine, as we were carrying all our belongings in our haversacks. When we were ready, I shook hands with Bill and we wished each other good luck. We were both sorry that our close association was ending as we had liked working together. "I'll miss having you around," he said, "but you've certainly earned your promotion, and I know you'll be a bloody good company commander." I replied, quite truthfully, that I would try to remember all the lessons I had learnt from him. That was to be the last time I ever spoke to him; he was killed a few days later.

Like Bill Meredith, Major Tony Jones was a regular, Sandhurst-trained officer who had been commissioned in the regiment during the mid-1930s. He had served with the 8th Army all through the desert campaign and had joined the lst Dorsets just prior to the landings in Sicily. Of all the company commanders in the battalion he had had the most combat experience, and I fully realised what an extremely difficult task lay ahead of me in trying to take his place.

I arrived at battalion headquarters to find that Speedy Bredin was about to leave for a meeting with the brigadier, but he delayed his departure to show me "A" company's position on my map. They had been one of the forward companies in the abortive attack on Hottot the previous day, and had suffered heavy casualties. They were now dug-in on a salient protruding into no-mans-land, where they were never allowed much respite from shelling, sniping, and raiding by enemy patrols. There were only two officers left, both lieutenants; and third platoon was commanded by a sergeant. "It will be a pretty demanding assignment for a brand-new company commander," Speedy had continued, in his usual imperturbable manner. "The main thing at the moment is to keep up the men's morale." As he turned to go he had said, "I'll get your promotion through as quickly as I can. It will probably be posted with my own - they've decided to give me command of the battalion." He had brushed aside my congratulations and had hurried off to his jeep.

"A" company had sent a runner to guide me to their headquarters. We had started out in the gathering dusk and it had become completely dark by the time we reached our destination. The runner had warned me that the sergeant-major was suffering from a bout of malaria, which he had contracted, as so many people in the battalion had done, during the campaign in Sicily. I found him lying in a slit-trench under a groundsheet, sweating profusely and slightly delirious. The first thing I wanted to do was to visit my three platoons, but nobody seemed certain of their exact location as Tony Jones had always done his rounds with his batman, who was also dead. Eventually, one of the signallers said he might be able to find them, but he was not sure as the night was extremely dark. I asked him to have a try and I had followed him along a ditch which ran in the direction of the German lines. We crossed a couple of fields and climbed a steep bank on to a track. I was beginning to feel increasingly doubtful if the platoons could be so far away when a spandau suddenly opened up in our direction at very close range. We threw ourselves flat on the ground as the air around us was filled with a cascade of brightly illuminated tracer bullets. After a few minutes the firing stopped and I could hear orders being shouted in German.

I whispered to the signaller that we were going back as quickly as we could. I had carefully noted the route we had taken and we managed to return to my new company headquarters without further mishap.

I had reconciled myself to the fact that there was no way I could locate my platoons until daylight, so I sat in a slit-trench with the intention of staying awake for the rest of the night. I dozed off towards morning and I was woken by a hand shaking my shoulder. I looked up and saw the sergeant-major leaning over the side of the trench. "It's time for dawn stand-to, Sir," he said. "Rivers is brewing-up some tea and when we've drunk it I'll show you around." Although pale and haggard he insisted he was fit enough for duty.

"A" company headquarters was at the side of a small field in which there were about 20 dead cows, all lying on their sides with their legs stretched out stiffly and their bellies grotesquely swollen with internal gases. The atmosphere reeked of the sickly-sweet stench of death. When we returned from visiting the platoons, the sergeant-major remarked dryly: "This isn't exactly the sort of place I'd choose for a holiday-camp. I hope they'll move us pretty soon." In fact, the company was to remain in that position for a further 17 days until the whole of 231 Brigade was relieved and sent back into reserve - the first time it had been out of the front line since the landing on D-Day.

In this type of warfare it had been inevitable that the nerves of some men in the front line should have given way. During the First World War they had been described as "suffering from shell-shock," during the Second, as "going bomb-happy."' An official committee, sitting in 1920, reported that the term "shell-shock" was a gross misnomer. The cases, they said, had been divisible into three categories; genuine concussion caused by an explosion, emotional shock, and nervous exhaustion. An eminent military historian had told the committee of his belief that the bravest man could not endure being under fire for more than a certain number of consecutive days, even if the fire was not very heavy.

When you were crouching in a slit-trench in an area under intensive bombardment you were constantly fearful of receiving a direct hit. The ordeal became more frightening still if the enemy were employing similar tactics to the Germans in Normandy and using a high proportion of air-burst shells, which exploded overhead, sending a mass of shrapnel hurtling down from above. I noticed that if a soldier was on the point of breaking down, the symptoms were usually discernible. He lost all interest in his personal appearance; he no longer washed or shaved himself properly, and he ceased to clean his boots. Later he developed a shake in his hands and a wild, hunted look in his eyes. I told my platoon commanders to be particularly vigilant for these early indications that one of their men was going bomb-happy, so that I could send him back to base straight away and minimise the demoralizing effect upon his comrades.

There were other ways of cracking too, and sometimes it could happen very suddenly without the slightest forewarning. It was like that with Private Lewis, one of the company stretcher-bearers. I thought that Lewis was a man with nerves of iron because even when the shelling was at its fiercest he would not hesitate to leave cover if he was needed to bring in a casualty. One day when the cry of "stretcher-bearers" went up he did not emerge from his slit-trench. I hurried over to see if anything was wrong and I found him lying face downward at the bottom of the trench, sobbing like a child. He had expended his reserves of fortitude until he had nothing left. Fortunately, we managed to place him in a permanent job at rear battalion headquarters.

In protracted trench-warfare conditions there was little that a company commander could do to prevent the onset of nervous exhaustion amongst his men, except to visit them frequently and to encourage them in any way he could. As a matter of elementary psychology, I arranged with my platoon commanders that the bodies of the dead should be removed as quickly as possible by stretcher-bearers, and taken to company headquarters, where they were laid out under blankets to await a field burial by the Padre. Every time a man was killed I had to write a letter to his next-of-kin, usually his parents or his wife. I always said that his end had been swift and painless, even when I knew that in reality he had died in the utmost agony.

After spending less than 24 hours in reserve, 231 Brigade was moved forward again to a different sector of the line. For the next five weeks we had taken part in a series of limited offensives designed to consolidate the Allied front before the eventual break-out from the Normandy bridgehead. During this time the Germans, ever-watchful, had remained unseen unless we probed into their positions, but the smallest activity on our part had drawn down a barrage of fire. The response had been so instantaneous it had almost seemed as though the tall, dark, motionless trees around us were somehow communicating our movements to the enemy gunners.

The break-out battles had began at the end of July, and 231 Brigade had carried out its last attack in the Normandy campaign on August 11 when it had formed the spearhead of a salient driven into enemy territory a few miles north of Conde-sur-Noireau. "A" company had been one of the forward companies in the battalion, with orders to seize and secure the high ground on the far side of a narrow valley. We had captured our objective without much difficulty and we prepared ourselves for a counter-attack. It never came. The following morning at first light I had sent three reconnaissance patrols into no-man's-land. They all returned with the same information; the Germans appeared to have abandoned the whole of the locality.

The lowly-ranking infantryman is seldom aware of the grand strategy of his Generals. He only sees the battle on a parochial level. In fact, the Germans had commenced a headlong retreat and were being squeezed by a pincer movement into an ever-narrowing gap, which thereafter became known as the "Falaise Pocket." Here, they were pounded by artillery fire from both flanks and savaged by incessant bombing from the air. Before they managed to extricate themselves, eight of their divisions had been annihilated.

It was difficult for us to believe that the desperate days of close-combat fighting were over; the costly slogging attacks to gain a mile or two of bitterly contested ground; the perpetual bombardment; the confinement to the slit-trench; the privation, and the lack of sleep. From then on the pattern of the warfare was changed. For the Germans it became the anguish of the hunted: for the Allies, the elation of the pursuers. In a redeployment of the British forces 231 Brigade had been attached as motorised infantry to the 11th Armoured Division, and had spent the next few weeks riding in troop-carrying lorries behind the tanks, stopping for meals by the wayside, and spending the nights in selected harbour areas. We had travelled at first through the Falaise Pocket where the roads were littered with the havoc of defeat. The wrecked and burnt-out vehicles; the discarded guns and equipment; the unburied bodies of the dead; the mutilated corpses of horses; and the mass of German prisoners, weary and dejected, marching back in captivity.

As we sped through the French countryside we were welcomed as liberators. People, gathered at the side of the road, waved, clapped and cheered. I was riding in a jeep with Private Wilson my driver, who had been a professional boxer in civilian life, and if we stopped, even momentarily, several girls usually dashed forward to embrace us and to thank us for coming to free them. Once, a very young couple made me stand beside the jeep so that they could photograph me with their baby in my arms. We soon grew accustomed to oft-repeated shouts of *Les Boches caput!* and *Bon voyage á Berlin*!

We used to have a very early breakfast and we would set off soon after dawn, leaving a fatigue party to clear up the harbour area. Our operational role was to follow closely behind the tanks, in constant readiness to assist them if they encountered any opposition. We also had the job of clearing the woods on either side of the roads. Most of the German soldiers we found in them were either stragglers or deserters, who were only too pleased to surrender at the first opportunity. We were working closely with the French Forces of the Interior, the FFI, who gave us useful information about any Germans hiding out in the localities through which we passed. As a rule we would continue our advance until the light was beginning to fail when we would halt in a new harbour area. The field kitchens were then set up to prepare an evening meal, and afterwards we slept in the fields under a single blanket. The most eagerly awaited event during these temporary stops was the distribution of the mail from home. Emma never missed a day in writing to me. Her letters were so ardent and so tender, they brought her very close to me. When I had finished reading them I was invariably overcome by a desperate yearning to be back with her again.

We stopped one evening at a harbour area on the outskirts of Arras, where we were told we would be remaining for the next 36 hours while the tanks were rested and maintained. Next morning, having spent a couple of hours on company administration and signing the passes for the men who wanted to get out, I had strolled into the town to see how the people were spending their first day after being liberated. A mood of joyful excitement pervaded the atmosphere. Shops and offices were closed and exuberant crowds were milling about in the streets. The cafes, bars, and estaminents were overflowing with revellers; many exhibited notices stating that they were offering free drinks to members of the FFI, but not, apparently, to the British troops who had helped to deliver them.

In the middle of a large square, crammed with onlookers, girls who had fraternised with German servicemen were having the hair shaved off their heads. Each in turn was dragged on to a platform and held roughly on a wooden chair while a man and two women went to work on her with scissors and razors. When they had completed their work she was hauled down again to be paraded around the city centre, with taunts and insults ringing in her ears. One of these processions of shame passed very close to me. I remember still the sight of the girl's ripped, blood-smeared blouse, and her face distorted by suffering, tears, and torment.

On our second day in Arras, 231 Brigade was placed under the command of the guards armoured division, which was going to lead a dash across the Belgian border culminating, it was hoped, in the liberation of Brussels, close on a 100 miles away. Our function was to be exactly similar to the one we had been carrying out with the 11th Armoured Division. We had started out at midday on September 2 and having overcome a strong pocket of enemy resistance in the early evening, we had travelled some 10 miles into Belgium before stopping for the night. We were on our way again as the dawn was breaking. We had made good progress until we reached Lessines, when our foremost tanks came under heavy fire from the direction of the town. The whole column had been halted and the 1st

Dorsets were ordered to disperse the Germans so that the advance might continue.

The local unit of the Belgian Maquis had told us that the bulk of the German forces had pulled out of Lessines leaving a rearguard detachment two or three hundred strong, which was holding a position on the southern outskirts of the town. Speedy Bredin had decided to send "A" company forward, supported by a troop of tanks from the Grenadier guards, and a platoon of medium machine guns from the Cheshire regiment. The skirmish at Lessines was the strangest battle in which I have ever taken part. The inhabitants were overjoyed to see us. As we moved along the street in single file with bayonets fixed, they collected in open windows, doorways, and entrances to shops, clapping and cheering; some of them offered glasses of wine or spirits to the passing troops. The Maquis, whose official task was to act as guides, were determined to join in the fighting against the "hated Boches" and a number of them, of both sexes, had attached themselves to each of our three platoons. A bronzed, sturdily-built girl with a sub-machine gun on her shoulder and a dagger in her belt, became my self-appointed bodyguard and followed closely behind me wherever I went.

I was rather anxious about carrying out an attack with a mixed Anglo-Belgian force in a densely-crowded urban area. Speedy's orders had been that after the enemy had been softened-up by the concentrated fire from the tanks and the machine-gunners, we were to go in and flush them out of the buildings with bullets and bayonets. House clearance was difficult and dangerous at the best of times;

and it was an operation of which "A" company had had no previous experience. Added to that, a high proportion of the men were recent reinforcements who had never been in action before. Fortunately for us the Germans did not resist for very long. As soon as the first few houses had been cleared they surrendered en *masse*, pouring into the street with their hands above their heads. The Maquis had marched off all the prisoners and had locked them up temporarily in the local gaol; they also took charge of the captured weapons and ammunition. When I was saying "goodbye" to the bronzed girl I noticed that she had acquired a mauser revolver which she had strapped on to her belt alongside her dagger.

The casualties sustained by the company had been extremely light - three wounded and one killed. Some civilians had removed the body of the dead man to the town mortuary. In later years he was to become a symbol for the people of Lessines of the day of their liberation, and a street was named after him in the neighbourhood where he had fallen.

We entered Brussels at five o'clock that afternoon. Speedy had previously told his company commanders that we would probably receive an ecstatic welcome, but he warned us that we were carrying out a military operation and we were not taking part in a victory parade. He wanted the highest standards of discipline to be maintained. The Germans had pulled out only hours before our arrival, he said; they were not many miles away, and they might counter-attack at any moment.

The liberation of Brussels was an exceedingly emotive

and a quite unforgettable experience for those who took part in it. The vast crowds, the uproarious applause, the flags waving on every side, and the men and women of all ages with tears of joy streaming down their faces. The Belgian police did their best to keep the way clear for us, but again and again the people filled the road ahead forcing us to stop. Every time this happened we were plied in abundance with flowers, fruit, and kisses. In the Boulevard Anspach, near the city centre, an attractive auburn-haired girl sprang into my jeep and settled herself precariously on the back of my seat with one of her legs over each of my shoulders and her arm enfolding my neck. A minute or two later another girl jumped in and sat on my lap. My driver, Wilson, had turned to me grinning, and shouted over the hubbub, "If you're too uncomfortable, Sir, we could easily change places." Our passengers were still on board when we drove through the Grand Place where several thousand voices were singing, "It's a Long Way to Tipperary." It was a matter of considerable pride that the song seemed somehow to associate us with the gallant soldiers of our fathers' generation.

On the second morning after our arrival in Brussels, 231 Brigade had been moved north to Antwerp to support the 11th Armoured Division who had battled their way into the town, but were now in urgent need of infantry support. We spent the next two weeks fighting in and around Antwerp, and establishing a bridgehead over the Albert Canal. It was apparent that the Germans had finished their retreat and were once again resisting with the same dogged tenacity which they had displayed in Normandy.

In the middle of September, 231 Brigade were with-drawn from the Antwerp sector of the front to take part in Operation Market Garden, a daring incursion deep into Holland to seize a bridgehead over the Lower Rhine at Arnhem. The thrust was to be carried out by Lieutenant-General Horrocks, the commander of 30 Corps, who had been my Brigadier in 1940. The airborne army was to play an important part, one American division landing at Eindhoven, another at Nijmegen, and the 1st British Airborne coming down furthest away at Arnhem. The guards armoured division was to lead the 30 corps advance, once again supported by our Brigade.

The airborne army had flown overhead while we were awaiting the order to cross the Dutch border. It was an amazing sight. The sky had suddenly become black with planes and gliders, flying majestically in formation at a low height through a continuous barrage of exploding ack-ack shells. No sooner had they passed than our advance had commenced. We had made much slower progress than had been anticipated, because we were endeavouring to open up and sustain a narrow corridor through a region where the Germans had concentrated their forces and were putting up a determined opposition. We were confronted by a number of SS divisions, fresh troops who had been held back intentionally for the final defence of the Fatherland.

30 Corps had succeeded in joining up with the American airborne forces, first at Eindhoven, then at Nijmegen where the bridge over the River Waal had been captured undamaged. We had tried to press ahead through the intervening 20 miles which separated us from Arnhem, but

the going was grim and our long slender salient was becoming increasingly vulnerable. Again and again the Germans had cut the road behind us, forcing us to turn about and clear them from our rear. Meanwhile the plight of the embattled 1st Airborne Division had become critical. On September 25, General Montgomery ordered the survivors to escape across the Rhine and to endeavour to reach the approaching British column. Few of them had been able to do so.

Five weeks later we were still in the locality which became known in the British Army as "the Island," the flat expanse, traversed by innumerable dykes, which lay between the Lower Rhine and the Waal. The fighting had been fierce and incessant with neither side gaining any appreciable advantage, and with both suffering heavy casualties in the bare and waterlogged terrain.

In the early hours of the morning on October 31, the sergeant-major awoke me while I was resting at "A" company headquarters. He told me that one of the platoon commanders was sending back alarming messages on the field telephone to the effect that he was being heavily attacked and doubted whether he could hold on to his position much longer. I took the sergeant-major and Rivers with me and went forward to investigate the situation. We were walking in single file along a hedgerow at the side of a small field and I remember thinking that the shells were landing closer and closer to us. Suddenly there was a frenzied screech - a searing of the air all round - followed by a fearful, crushing nothingness. I opened my eyes and tried to reorientate my swimming senses. There was a loud, continuous buzzing in my head. I fought hard to come to but I seemed to be wedged in the first fleeting phase of returning consciousness. Then Sergeant-Major Nicholls was kneeling beside me, bending over me. I head him shouting, "Rivers, get some stretcher-bearers as quick as you can. I'll stay here with him."

At first I thought I had merely been stunned by the blast from an exploding shell which had landed close to me, but I soon realised it was something far more serious, something the like of which I had never experienced before. I was not aware of any pain, nor even of any definite areas of physical discomfort: it was far worse than that, and far more frightening. I seemed to be drifting in a plane beyond the manifest limits of suffering.

The sergeant-major put his greatcoat over me. Someone tried to hold a water-bottle to my lips but I could not move and I had no idea how to drink. My brain seemed now to have lost all contact with my body. It was as though I was floating above myself looking down. I suddenly realised I might be dying; that my soul might be lingering over my mortal being for the final few moments before it started out on its journey. I began to pray, entreating God not to let me die, and that whatever was the matter with me, I would get better again.

I was lifted on to the back of a jeep which had been adapted for carrying wounded men, with a single stretcher slung across the hood supports. I knew I was holding on to life by a flimsy thread, and I felt convinced that I must force myself to remain conscious; that if I allowed myself to lapse into oblivion it would be the end. We drove away slowly along a bumpy track. The corporal in charge of the company stretcher-bearers was standing in the jeep beside me with an arm across my chest to hold me steady. I could hear shells falling in the fields on either side and tracer bullets from German machine-guns were streaking overhead.

The Regimental Aid Post was in a barn about a mile behind the front line. I was carried through the open door and laid on a trestle table. Our new MO, who had recently replaced Laurie Lassman, bent over me and appeared to be fiddling with the side of my head. He and his sergeant were discussing me in the third person, oblivious of the fact that I was taking in their conversation. The sergeant was against sending me back to the casualty clearing station. I looked as though I would not survive much longer, he said, and they only had one undamaged ambulance available for use. But the MO insisted that as I was still alive I must be given a chance. So I was taken out again and put into the back of an ambulance, where I was left alone.

After a short delay the ambulance began to move. I had never realised before the intense loneliness of being critically ill; the unremitting solitude in which your only proximate companions are the dark, stealthy images in the back of your mind. I tried desperately hard to keep awake, but my resolve was growing weaker and presently I gave way to the wave of blackness which welled up inside me. From then on I drifted between alternate phases of awareness and insensibility in a wearisome cycle of timelessness. Once when I came to, my stretcher was resting on a concrete floor in a long, narrow room with rows of other men on stretchers on either side of me. But usually when I opened my eyes I was travelling alone in the back of an ambulance, windowless, and dimly illuminated by a light in the roof. We always seemed to be travelling slowly; bumping, jolting, braking, and restarting.

I have a vague recollection of being wheeled along a corridor on a trolley by army orderlies, and a nurse in uniform walking beside me with her fingers on my pulse. I must have given some sign of recognition because she glanced down at me and said, "You're in hospital in Brussels. We're going to take care of you here."

They took me to a single room, laid me on the bed and undressed me. It was as though they were undressing some other person. I could still think clearly but I had receded even further from my body. Then everyone left the room except the nurse. She stood at the foot of the bed, looked at me intently and said, "I wonder if you can understand what's happening? If you can hear me, I want you to relax and not to worry. You're going to sleep now."

I think she must have given me an injection because I remember no more.

My next recollection is that the door was opened noisily, the light was switched on and the same nurse entered followed by two or three orderlies. She came up to the bed and said, "You're going to be flown back to England. You'll get better there." I think I passed out while they were lifting me on to the trolley.

I came to again in an ambulance which I presumed was taking me to an airport. There must be hope for me, I thought; otherwise they would not be sending me back to England - although I had heard that a number of severely-wounded men often died on board the ambulance-plane before the journey was completed. I knew that I must will myself to stay alive until we had touched down at the end of the flight. If I could survive that long I would stand a chance of recovering.

My memories of the air-journey are spasmodic and blurred. I know that the plane had a double row of bunks, one above the other, on either side of it, with a gangway down the centre. And there was a nurse, a pretty, dark-haired girl in American uniform, who was nearly always standing beside me in my moments of consciousness. From time to time she would speak to me comfortingly in a soft southern drawl. As I was in an upper bunk her head and shoulders were level with me. Often, I saw her face mistily, as though through a veil. Just after we had taken off she imagined, mistakenly, that I wanted a cigarette. She lit one herself and stuck it through my lips, but I did not try to hold it there and it rolled away across my chest. On another occasion, she was sponging my face after I had been sick and I noticed out of the corner of my eye that my pillow was saturated with fresh blood.

I still had no idea what was happening to me. During the flight I felt something stiff and cold on the right side of my chest. I puzzled about it for a while before it dawned on me that it was my own right arm, heavy, insensate, and totally paralysed. Although I continued to pray incessantly for recovery, I realised that the last vestiges of my strength were ebbing away. At one point I thought the end had come. Everything went dim and there was the sound of rushing water in my ears. I seemed to be drifting further and further from reality and from contact with my physical self. I heard the nurse's voice: "Steady old chap! Steady!" I saw her leaning over me with an arm round my shoulders. She appeared to recede gradually. Then she was no more.

The next thing I knew was that my stretcher was lying on the floor in the gangway and the motion of the plane had ceased. The nurse was kneeling beside me. When I opened my eyes she told me that we had arrived in England and that I would soon be safely in bed at a hospital. She had tucked a blanket round my neck and sat back on her heels. "I hope you'll be all right," she said. "You look a good sort. I like you." She had then leant forward and placed a hand on my cheek. It had still been there when I slipped back into oblivion.

Subsequently there were more · brief moments of awareness. Seen in retrospect they resemble fleeting pictures on a cinematography screen ... I was lying on a bed in a large room which looked like a hospital ward. There were rows of beds crammed in close together, each with its own bedside table, and a score of harsh lights shone down from the ceiling ... Middle-aged women in tweed costumes were bustling around holding trays. One of them came up and put a plate on the table beside me. "There you are," she said. "A nice plate of stew. You'll feel better when you've eaten something." I only wanted to be left alone. This place was noisy and overcrowded. I longed to be taken out of it. Some minutes later the same woman returned and reproved me for not having eaten anything. "Why don't you start?" she asked. "You're letting it get cold." She called out to an officer who was walking past. "Doctor! He isn't eating his stew." The officer walked up, looked at me, and said to her. "He's beyond it. We'll get him away quickly" ... An orderly in a white overall doing something to my head, working swiftly and with precision. He seemed to be chopping off my hair, as the clippings kept on falling across my face ... A man in a green smock, with a surgical mouth-mask, bending over me with a syringe in his hand. "Just a little prick," he said, "and you'll fall asleep immediately." I felt a sharp stab of pain in my left arm and a wave of sleep crept up my body until it had enveloped my brain.

PART II

THE AFTERMATH

CHAPTER 14

I was told by the Ward Sister on several occasions that my next-of-kin had not yet been located because my documents were still missing. I hoped they would be difficult to trace so that my mother, Emma, and my family would be spared from the anguish of knowing what had happened to me for as long as possible. And yet, I longed to see again the people who were closest to me.

One morning soon after my operation the Chief Physiotherapist came to see me. She said that my doctor thought I was now strong enough to start having treatment for my paralysed arm and leg. "We can't be sure how much movement you'll get back," she went on, "but a lot will depend on your own willpower."

From then on a young physiotherapist used to spend half-an-hour with me every day. Despite the fact that she knew almost nothing about me she managed somehow to keep up a bright one-sided conversation throughout these sessions. It was from her I first learnt that I was at Oxford in one of the women's colleges, St Hugh's, which had been taken over for the duration of the war as a hospital for head and spinal injuries.

A few days after I had started having physiotherapy I was visited by a small, frail lady in Red Cross uniform. She pulled up a chair beside my bed, sat down and said, shyly and half apologetically, "My name is Violet Brookes. I'm the speech therapist at the hospital and I'm going to teach you to speak again." She explained that she had been a singing teacher before the war, but she was now devoting herself entirely to her speech therapy work. Then she began to talk about the wonder of the human voice; how it could be used to convey passions and emotions, not only by a choice of words but also by the artistry of articulation As she warmed to her subject she seemed to lose her shyness. I watched her, fascinated. She was so diminutive, and yet her presence filled the room; she was as delicate as a china ornament, yet she exuded strength; her voice was quiet and bell-like, yet she was magnetic and forceful in every word she uttered.

"At present," she went on," you'll be totally mute, so I'll just come in every day and talk to you. When you begin to make vocal sounds later on, my lessons will really start. Until then, in your thoughts you must never visualise a future in which you are unable to speak, because between us both I'm quite certain we'll be able to get your voice back for you."

I was finding that one of the worst ordeals resulting from loss of speech was the interminable loneliness; the feeling of isolation, of being completely shut-off from a normal relationship with any other person. There was the sense of frustration too, for if I wanted anything other than my more obvious requirements it was often very difficult to communicate my need to the nurses by gesturing with one hand.

As I became more alert, I knew I would have to find some way of combating the long, restless hours of mental inactivity. Reading was a possible solution. I tried to indicate to a nurse who was tidying my room that I would like to see a newspaper, by putting my outstretched hand in front of my face, and running my eyes back and forth along it. She was puzzled at first; then she understood. "You'd like something to read? A paper, perhaps?" I nodded vigorously and she went off to find one for me.

She returned presently with a tabloid, which she held up so that I could see the headlines. I endeavoured to read them, but they meant nothing to me, as all the letters looked like characters written in an unfamiliar language. I shook my head and closed my eyes.

"Never mind," she said, "We'll try again when you're a little better."

It was apparent that I could neither read nor converse, and that the only mental diversion which remained for me was to delve into the swirling turbulence of my own thoughts. But this was a painful pastime as I found it difficult to recall the past without an overwhelming sense of sadness because so much was finished irretrievably. On that morning in Holland a part of me had died and a part had been reborn - but I was now a different person, destined to a vastly different existence.

My only reassurance during those cheerless days had come from my Christian faith, which had made it impossible for me to believe that I had been destroyed physically merely to be discarded on to a human rubbish heap. I felt that there must be some purpose in what had befallen me, some design which must make the whole thing meaningful. For my own part, the only course I could adopt was to pray incessantly for recovery, and to do everything in my power to assist the healing process, for I believed that God helps those who help themselves.

It was essential for me to find a way of communicating. The obvious solution was that I should learn to write with my left hand. When I was reasonably proficient I might try to write a novel. This would provide me with an interest and a motivation until I could progress to other forms of activity.

It was the Ward Sister, during her daily round, who had informed me that my papers had been discovered, and my relatives were being notified where I was. My mother had been staying at a small residential hotel in Bayswater when she received the War Office telegram. She had immediately phoned St Hugh's hospital, but she had only been told that I was very seriously ill and it would be advisable for her to visit me without delay.

She and Noreen had come down to Oxford by train the same day. They had taken a taxi from the station, and as they were turning into the entrance to the college they had been horrified to see on a large notice-board that it was a hospital for head-injuries. They were directed to the officers' surgical ward where the Sister saw them in her office. She asked them to wait there for a few minutes as the doctor wanted to have a word with them before they were shown to my room. It was the same doctor who had been with me when I was coming round from my operation. He warned them that I was paralysed down one side and unable to speak. I had suffered severe brain damage, he said, and my speech function had been entirely destroyed. There was still a remote possibility that I might learn to speak again with another part of my brain, but the surgeon who had operated on me considered it to be unlikely. Regarding my right arm and leg, it was too early to tell whether I would recover any movement in them, though the leg was probably less seriously affected than the arm.

I had known that my mother and Noreen were coming because they had sent me a message beforehand. I was longing to see them, but dreading their visit at the same time as I knew how devastated they would be at finding me in such a condition. They both behaved with considerable courage, concealing their true emotions and keeping up a cheerful conversation in which I was involved without being expected to participate. They told me all the news about the family, and my mother said that she had already been in touch with Emma, who would be applying for compassionate leave to come and spend a few days in Oxford. Mother herself intended to move into a local hotel so that she would be able to visit me more easily.

The doctor had asked them not to stay with me for longer than half-an-hour as he did not want me to become too tired. At the end of the allotted time they kissed me and hurried from the room without looking back. They told me later that they had scarcely closed the door behind them before both of them had broken down completely in the corridor outside.

After a few weeks my right leg had recovered a slight sensitivity and a small amount of very feeble movement. However, I had still been unable to utter a sound, and my right arm continued to lie heavily at my side without any life and without any feeling. Emma used to ring the hospital every morning and every evening to leave me messages and to find out the latest bulletins on my condition. She had been promised a few days compassionate leave, although we were not officially engaged, and one of the nurses had booked a room for her at a nearby guest-house.

Shortly before Emma's arrival in Oxford, the Ward Sister told me that I was going to be moved into a double room because it was felt that the company would be good for me. "You'll be sharing with a Norwegian paratroop captain," she said. "You'll like Anton enormously; everybody does."

As soon as the nurses had settled me in my new room Anton came over and sat on my bed. "I will look after you," he said, speaking in a delightful Norwegian accent. "I get to know your signals - anything you want. Later, I'll teach you how to talk. Try now. Say 'one, two, three'," he repeated slowly.

I tried to imitate him, but I could not produce any sounds.

"Don't worry," he said, "it will come. We try a little every day."

It was easy to see why Anton was so popular, as he was tall, blonde, very handsome and immensely charming. His head wound had been slight, scarcely penetrating his skull, and he was then undergoing his final medical tests to ascertain if he was fit enough to return to his unit.

Miss Brookes used to read my letters to me when she paid me her daily visits. Before she opened an envelope she would describe it to me. "This one is handwritten," she would say. "It has a London postmark and it looks to me as though it's from a girl who might be in her early twenties." She was seldom inaccurate regarding either the sex or the age-group of my personal correspondents. "Now," she would ask; "do you want me to open it?" Invariably, I would nod affirmatively. She dealt with typewritten mail in a more cursory manner. Sometimes she would study the contents of an envelope and comment irritably, "It's another one of those tiresome circulars. I suppose you'd like me to tear it up."

I had been in my new room for a few days when I received a message from Emma telling me that she would be travelling by train from Portsmouth to Oxford the following afternoon, and that if she arrived sufficiently early she would come to see me in the evening. I did not know how much she had been told by my mother or by the hospital about the effects of my wound, and I was very worried that she might not realise I was unable to speak. Anton seemed to sense my anxiety. He decided to cancel the arrangement he had made to dine out in the town with one of his numerous girlfriends, and he informed me reassuringly that he would be present when Emma came into the room. "I will explain to her everything about you," he said, "and then I will leave you alone together."

Anton had remained in the room for the whole of the next evening and for most of the subsequent two days awaiting Emma's visit, but she had neither appeared, nor had she sent any further messages. Then had come her letter from Portsmouth. It had been read out to me by Miss Brookes in a quiet and gentle voice whilst I was lying on my back with my eyes closed, listening to Emma's disembodied words and phrases scurrying above me and vanishing with the rapidity of shooting stars in a night sky. I had known exactly what she was going to say even before I heard it, because all this had happened once before in a distant dream. Consequently I felt a sense of detachment, as though I was viewing the scene as a bystander, a complete stranger who was uninvolved in the emotional turmoil which engulfed the participants.

In her letter Emma told me how she had gone to St Hugh's hospital soon after her arrival at Oxford, and how she had learnt about the full extent of my injuries for the first time from the Night Sister. How she had been too shocked to visit me that evening, but had returned to the guest-house where she had stayed awake all night in troubled thought. She said she had loved me as deeply as it would ever be possible for her to love any man, and all her thoughts had been centered around the life we would live together when the war was over. Now, suddenly, her visions of the future had been shattered into fragments. No matter how much we wished it otherwise, it could never be the same again; in our personal relations with each other we could never be the same people as we were before this had happened to me. If we tried to carry on now from where we had left off, we would only be blighting our memories of the blissfully happy times we had had with each other in the past. And so, she had decided to return to Portsmouth without coming to the hospital again, because she could not bear to see me in my present state. For the rest of her life she would remain in love with me, as I had been before our parting. She never wanted to fall in love with anyone else; nor would it be possible for her to do so. She ended with the terms of endearment with which she always finished her letters to me.

"The pages are very smudgy," said Miss Brookes. "She must have been crying a lot while she was writing."

CHAPTER 15

Both Miss Brookes and my unofficial speech therapist, Anton, were equally patient and persuasive, yet in spite of all their endeavours I still remained wholly mute.

Anton was with me when at last it happened. He had just said, "Repeat after me, one, two, three." Frustration and hopelessness spurred me on to make a supreme despairing effort. The sound I emitted was a choking, distorted, parody of speech.

He sprang up excitedly from his chair. "Do that again!" he commanded, and I complied with a similar articulation as before.

"You talked!" he shouted. "You talked."

Then he rushed out of the room yelling at the top of his voice, "Tony's talking! I've taught him! Tony's talking!"

The Ward Sister hurried in followed by a group of nurses and they all stood round my bed while Anton made me produce my new sound for their benefit. He wanted me to go on doing it, but the Sister intervened. "That's enough for the moment," she stated firmly. "You don't want to wear him out."

She told the nurses to go back to work and after they had gone she said to me, "I'm really pleased, Tony. You seem to have made a beginning at any rate. Don't expect anything spectacular; it will be years before you can speak in any way normally. Meanwhile, just keep on doing what Miss Brookes tells you - and for goodness sake don't start speaking with a Norwegian accent!"

Miss Brookes received the news calmly but with obvious delight. "Now we can begin your speech exercises," she said. "The first thing you must learn is how to form words."

From then on her daily visits became longer. For part of each session she would run through a sequence of vocal sounds and I would try to imitate them. After that she would read instalments of an Agatha Christie novel to improve my powers of concentration.

I was soon able to gabble as incomprehensibly as a one-year-old baby, but I had to rely on hand-signals whenever I needed anything, and I sometimes wondered if I would ever be able to speak intelligibly again. In other respects I was making a small amount of progress. Although there was as yet no sign of life in my right arm, my right leg was beginning to respond to treatment and my headaches were becoming less frequent.

Colonel Calvert came to see me soon after I had made my first utterance. He told me that I was now starting to speak with a "spare part" of the brain on the opposite side of my head to the gunshot wound. I had been exceptionally fortunate, he said, because it was very rare for the speech function to be bilaterally represented sufficiently for this phenomenon to occur. But he went on to warn me not to expect too much from my substitute voice. The fact that I would be able to talk at all was miraculous enough.

One morning Anton walked into the room with Sister and they both came up to my bed.

"Tony," said Anton, "I have had my final Medical Board. I get discharged tomorrow."

"I'm afraid it's true," the Sister added. "We hung on to him as long as we possibly could. Now, Tony, the problem is what we're going to do with you. I think, personally, that when Anton goes you'd be far better off in the big ward.

There's plenty of company there and you'd get lots of chances to practise talking."

The officers' section of the hospital was all on the ground floor. It consisted of a main ward and a number of single or double rooms for patients who were very ill. Next day, I was moved into the main ward, a large, bright room with a dozen or so beds around the walls, and windows which faced out on to a garden. I was put into one of the corner beds beside a window.

This was to be my first experience of ward life and I disliked it intensely. The monotony of the daily routine, the lack of privacy, the parochial humour, the forced jocularity masking the mood of bleak depression, and the constant stridency of the communal radio-set. On the other hand, of course, there were the kindness and efficiency of the staff , especially the VAD nurses whose unfailing cheerfulness partly counterbalanced, for the patients, the grimness of reality.

I was sedated at night to alleviate the pain in the left side of my head. Invariably I would wake up during the early hours of the morning, when the ward was in complete darkness and the only sound was the heavy breathing of the occupants, interspaced occasionally by someone crying out in his sleep. There was the bomber-pilot, shot down over the Channel, who repeatedly perpetually his final frenzied message to his crew on the intercom, telling them to bale out because the plane was on fire. And there was the very young infantry officer, wounded in his first action, who used to plead desperately in his sleep that he should not be returned to the fighting. The early morning was the time of my deepest despondency, when the comprehension of disablement seemed most frightening. It was particularly harrowing if I had just woken up from a dream in which I had been physically normal again.

When I had been in the big ward for a week or two the doctor said I could start to get up for a short while every day and to sit in a chair. On the first occasion I did this I felt very weak and unbalanced. After about five minutes I could sustain the effort no longer so I rang my bell and signified I wanted to be put back to bed. On the days which followed I gained confidence and I even began to look forward to my brief outings.

With every small improvement came a renewal of hope. I learnt to pronounce a few words - albeit haltingly and only by a great effort. Then a small amount of sensation began to return to my right arm and shoulder, and I found I could raise my right wrist a few inches above the blankets.

The doctor who was looking after me tested my latest movements.

"I'm afraid your arm will always be almost useless to you," he said, "but your leg is doing fine and might be quite strong eventually. As for your speech -" he hesitated - "you'll be able to take a limited part in conversation at the end of your treatment, but nothing more than that."

I remained in the corner-bed for the whole of that winter and for the early days of the subsequent spring. My memories of those months now are of the sameness of the daily round, of my slow but gradual progress, and of the people who were at one time or another my fellow-patients in the ward.

There was the Welshman in the bed next to mine when I was first moved in, who had been hit in the head by a sniper's bullet in Normandy and had lain in a coma for six weeks before he recovered consciousness. Although none of his limbs had been paralysed by his wound, he had obviously been affected mentally. He was allowed to wander about in his dressing-gown, but he seldom spoke to anyone and his favourite pastime was standing just inside the door of the ward endlessly switching the lights on and off until he was stopped by a nurse. He could also be malevolent. It was possible to raise or lower the top and bottom sections of my bed by turning a handle at the foot of the frame. Sometimes, when none of the staff were around, he would raise both sections as high as possible so that I was lying in chronic discomfort, shaped almost like a letter V. Whenever this happened one of the others would ring for a nurse who would reprimand him and readjust my bed. Once when it was snowing heavily he threw open the window beside me and watched delightedly as the flurries of snowflakes were blown on to my face and my blankets.

One of the saddest cases in the ward was an infantry captain from Birmingham whose spinal wound had caused him to be totally paralysed below the waist. Not only was he in constant pain, but he suffered considerable discomfort because of his inability to move the lower half of his body, and the nurses had to shift his position in his bed at frequent intervals. He was certain that he would recover the use of his legs fairly soon and he was always talking about rejoining his battalion in time for the massive offensive which the Allies were expected to launch in the coming spring. He kept pressing the doctors to tell him how long it would be before he could walk again. Eventually he was told that he would be a paraplegic for the remainder of his life. For the next few days he scarcely uttered a word, even to his wife. Then he was moved to a hospital at Birmingham, closer to his family and his friends.

Another sad case was the 19-year-old second lieutenant from a Scottish regiment, who was put into the bed next to mine when my Welsh neighbour left for a convalescent home. Although he was in the preliminary stages of coming to terms with his blindness he was invariably cheerful, and I wondered if he really believed the doctors when they told him that nothing could be done to restore his sight. His fiancée spent a lot of time with him and as she was a VAD herself she helped the nurses to look after him. It was necessary for someone to feed him at every meal. I once saw him trying to eat unaided and encountering immense difficulty in passing spoonfuls of food from a plate to his mouth.

There were others with whom I was destined to spend many months both in the ward and at Middleton Park, the St Hugh's convalescent home. A few of them became close fiends of mine and have remained so ever since. In the corner bed opposite my own was Desmond O'Meara, a handsome and charming young officer in an Irish Cavalry regiment who was very popular with the nursing staff. He had broken his back soon after he landed in Normandy, when a jeep in which he was travelling had run into a shell-hole and overturned. At first, both his legs were paralysed, but by the time I moved into the ward he was in the process of learning to walk again. Desmond's mother and mine were staying near one another in Oxford and they used to visit the hospital together every afternoon. Then there were the two inseparables, Richard Wheeler, a head-wound from the Battle of Alamein, and Michael Neville who had suffered multiple severe injuries when he had trodden on an anti-personnel mine in Italy. And there was Hugh Verney, a Subaltern in the Guards, whose bed was just inside the door. He had been shot in the head by a sniper in Normandy as he was leaning out of the turret of his tank, and he was partially paralysed down one side of his body. Hugh was usually one of the cheerful patients in the ward, although at times, like the rest of us, he was beset by a mood of intense depression.

Soon, I was able to enunciate a complete sentence, but only very slowly, with a pause after every word and with frequent mispronunciations. I found that as a necessary preliminary I had to formulate in my mind exactly what I intended to say, and that even when I had done so my phrases sometimes came out in a jumbled form with no coherent meaning. Miss Brookes continued to emanate calmness and confidence. "I'm extremely pleased with your progress," she kept telling me. "The day will surely come when you'll be speaking normally." Her lessons had grown longer now and she still finished them with a reading from an Agatha Christie novel. The ambulant members of the ward were following the stories with avidity and each time Miss Brookes took the book from her briefcase they all edged surreptitiously towards my corner of the room.

My arm continued to show little or no improvement and

I was shocked to see how quickly an unused limb assumes a wasted appearance. However, during the course of the winter my leg gradually strengthened. As soon as I was able to stand on it without falling over I was given a rubber-tipped stick and told that, provided I was very careful and not too ambitious, I could get up for short periods to hobble about the ward. In time I was allowed to put on my clothes with the help of one of the nurses. The muscles of my right leg and foot were still very weak so I had to wear a special shoe, fitted with a contraption called a "toe-spring" which kept my foot supported at right angles to my leg, instead of sagging down and tripping me up.

Most of the men in the ward appreciated that they would be permanently disabled, and spent hours discussing what they were going to do on their return to civilian life, bearing in mind that the scale of disability pensions was parsimonious in the extreme. There was a widely held view that few of us would ever again be fit enough for any normal occupation. Two of them said their parents had offered to pay them annuities for the rest of their lives so that they would never need to look for work. Others spoke of the large companies which after the previous war had found compassionate openings for severely wounded ex-servicemen, doubtless from mixed motives of gratitude and sympathy. They predicted that there would be similar employment opportunities after the present war. This sort of conversation made me shudder. With all my being I rebelled against the notion of becoming, or ever being regarded, as a permanent crock.

I had formed a resolution that no matter how lasting

were the after-effects of my wound, whether mental or physical, I would press ahead with the career which I had chosen for myself. I knew that if I were to take any other course I would spend my future years in bitterness and regret. The limits of my ambition were to qualify as a barrister, to be accepted as an ordinary individual by my legal colleagues, and to be able to fulfil a modest practice at the Bar. In a way, I saw what I was experiencing as a personal battle against fate and I decided to tap the only possible source of strength which lay open to me. I made up my mind to pray to God regularly and consistently for His assistance in carrying out my design. I still had my doubts about efficacy of prayer, but it was worth trying - anything was worth trying.

My progress was interrupted when I developed pleurisy in my right lung and I was confined to my bed for a painful week.

The long, cold winter had persisted stubbornly that year until the middle of March. And then, in an instant, the skies were no longer overcast and it was spring. In the early hours of the morning I could look out of the window beside my bed at the profusion of snowdrops and crocuses in the flower-beds, and the masses of green shoots on the trees. A new sense of hopefulness seemed to inspire the patients in the ward. "These next few months will make all the difference to the D-D casualties," Miss Brookes remarked. It was one of her idiosyncrasies that she looked upon everyone who had been wounded in France, Belgium or Holland during the previous year as being "a D-Day casualty."

I had been warned that as soon as the area of my wound

had healed sufficiently I would have to undergo another head operation. A protective metal plate would be grafted into the cavity on the left side of my skull, to limit the risk of my receiving another injury to the same part of my brain.

In the meanwhile, I was sent away on leave for a month, as it was thought that I needed a complete change from the hospital environment. Eve was stationed at a naval establishment on the outskirts of Bognor Regis and she booked rooms for my mother and me at a small, unpretentious hotel in the town, a few streets distant from the sea front. I was fairly mobile by then, being able to walk a few hundred yards with a stick, provided that my right foot was held up by a toe-spring. Whenever I was standing upright I was slightly unbalanced as my right arm tended to drag down, and I still had a certain amount of difficulty in controlling my right leg. As far as my speech was concerned, I could talk extremely slowly with a stammer, frequently muddling the words I intended to use. It was as though my brain had partially lost the ability to communicate with my voice and my limbs. I knew what I wanted to say and what movements I wished to carry out, but however clearly my mental messages were transmitted they were sometimes misinterpreted; and sometimes they were not received at all.

I was taken from Oxford to Bognor by a member of the Women's Voluntary Service in her private car. After more than six months in hospital it was thrilling to see the outside world again, to drive through towns and villages along highways and country lanes. I was fascinated by the sight of people, normal, healthy people going about their daily lives.

We stopped at a hotel for lunch. It was the first time I had been in a public place since my wound. I felt terribly embarrassed as I realised how conspicuous I must have looked with my stick, my arm hanging lifeless at my side, and my head loosely bandaged to conceal the scars which were not yet hidden by growing hair. I wished everybody would not stare so much, although I realised that their interest in me was compassionate rather than inquisitive.

My four weeks' leave passed quickly and quietly. The staff at the hotel could not have been more kind and helpful, always preparing my food so that I could eat it with one hand and assisting me in numerous other ways. My mother and I went out for a walk every morning, usually along the seafront, and Eve used to join us for lunch and dinner whenever she was free to do so.

I spent an hour each day in the privacy of my bedroom, working at the speech exercises Miss Brookes had prepared for me before I left Oxford. I also practised writing with my left hand. I was worried to discover that I had lost the ability to spell; and even more disquieting, that I was frequently unable to visualise the lettering or the structure of even the simplest words. As regards reading, I had brought several books to Bognor with me and I found that I could read fairly well but very slowly; my real difficulty was that when I came to the end of a line and flicked back my eyes to commence reading the next, I habitually went to the wrong part of the paragraph. I learnt later that as a result of my head-wound I had become an "acquired dyslectic", as well as being left permanently with a condition known as "dysgraphia" - the inability to write coherently.

By the end of the month I had discarded my toe-spring, though I was still walking with a limp and I needed a stick whenever I went out of doors. My hair had grown sufficiently for me to give up wearing a bandage round my head. With these developments I felt less noticeable and I was losing my embarrassment when going to public places. I travelled back to Oxford by train in the care of a lady from the WVS. At the station there she handed me to one of the St Hugh's VADs who accompanied me in a taxi to the hospital.

As I no longer required any regular attention I was put into a double room on the floor above the officers' surgical ward. I had been hoping that I could have my plating operation without further delay, but to my disappointment I was told that it would be several weeks more before I was ready for it. For the time being arrangements would be made for me to stay at Middleton Park.

Nearly all the officers on my new floor had finished their active treatment and were either awaiting their discharge, their final Medical Boards, or their transfers to Middleton Park. We passed our days aimlessly. We were served with our meals in a bare room downstairs, but there was no lounge or other place in which we could gather, so we spent our afternoons and evenings in the town. After lunch we usually went to a cinema, partly for the entertainment and partly because all the cinemas admitted patients from St Hugh's free of charge. After dinner, rather than going straight to our bedrooms, we would spend an hour or two in a pub or in the bar of a hotel. Even though we had been warned that those of us who had sustained penetrating head-wounds should not drink any alcohol for at least two years, I used to vary my perpetual glasses of tomato juice with the occasional half pint of beer.

Sometimes a few of us would be invited to a meal by people living in Oxford. We were always immensely grateful to them for entertaining us in their homes and for making us aware that we were still remembered. A lot of us were passing through a phase in which we were over-sensitive about what we imagined to be the unfeeling attitude of many of the general public towards us. There were occasions, of course, when strangers went out of their way to treat us with commiserative understanding. Desmond O'Meara once boarded a very full bus on returning to the hospital and he was immediately offered a seat by an elderly gentleman. At first Desmond declined to take it, but the man had insisted. "It's a privilege to do this for you," he said. "I can see that you've been doing something for me."

I do not think we realised the excessive war-weariness of the bulk of the civil population. They had endured five-and-a-half years of rationing, shortages, restrictions and drab living; with relatives and friends at constant risk in the armed forces. Five-and-a-half years in which the screw had been twisted ever tighter as the war had continued on its seemingly interminable course.

One morning at breakfast, soon after my return to St Hugh's, the man sitting opposite me inquired how often I was having fits. I looked at him blankly.

"Don't tell me you don't know about it," he said. "We all have them. Once you've had a brain injury you go on getting them for the rest of your life. I have one every two or three weeks."

When I next saw the doctor who was looking after me at the time I asked him if it was true that I would suffer from fits. He told me that nearly all the people with penetrating head injuries had them. "I'm rather surprised you've got away with it so long," he said, "in view of the position of your wound."

I wanted to know if there was any chance that I would avoid them altogether, but he refused to speculate.

"There are no certainties in medical science," he replied. "If you haven't had a fit during the first two years after you were wounded, you can be relatively confident. If five years pass without you having one you'll be absolutely safe. That's why you'll have to go on taking luminal for five years, even if nothing happens, to keep your brain damped down."

While I was waiting for my transfer I was taking daily lessons from Miss Brookes in her office. I had progressed to reading passages out loud from a book. Each time I stumbled or made a mistake she would tell me quietly to go back and read the words again. Once, when I had made more errors than usual, I asked if she thought my speech would ever be good enough for me to practise as a barrister.

"I'll let you know before you're discharged from hospital," she promised. "Of course it will only be my own opinion and I'm not a doctor."

"I wonder if I'm just kidding myself about the future," I said. "Quite apart from my speech defect, I'm told I'll probably have periodic fits."

She looked at me for a moment and then said firmly, "You must never give way to thinking like that. Courage and faith can overcome many disadvantages, and the achievements for which you've had to struggle hardest are always the most worthwhile."

The day before I went to Middleton Park I had a letter from Speedy Bredin, who was still commanding my old battalion. He said he was writing to send me his warmest congratulations because the French Provisional Government had just published an honours list and I had been awarded the Croix de Guerre with gold star. He sent me a copy of the citation, which referred to an event so utterly remote from the present that it seemed to have happened in a half-forgotten dream. By the same post I received a letter of congratulations from the adjutant, enclosing a Croix de Guerre medal ribbon, which he suggested I should ask one of the nurses to sew on my uniform.

I felt pleased and gratified to be associated in this way with the brave French men and women who had fought for the liberation of their country. However, I put the ribbon away and never wore it. Medals, for me, were now a thing of the past.

I knew that Emma would contact me again very soon. When she was over the initial shock of discovering the full extent of my injuries she would send me a message, write a letter or come to see me. I was constantly preparing for the discussion we would have about the future. I was going to tell her that she must not commit herself in any way until I had succeeded in passing my exams and I had been called to the Bar. If I could achieve that much it might be possible for us to resurrect some of our plans, some of the dreams we had shared together before the Normandy invasion.

Every morning when a nurse brought round the mail I searched eagerly through the envelopes she handed me for the sight of Emma's familiar writing. Each time the Sister approached me I longed for her to tell me that Emma had telephoned for news of my progress. On numerous occasions in the streets of Oxford I thought I saw her in the distance on a crowded pavement; a fleeting glimpse of her fair hair and her Wren uniform. I used to hurry to the place only to find it had been an hallucination.

But I still felt certain that the link which bound us together was indestructible.

CHAPTER 16

Middleton Park, the country residence of the Earl of Jersey, had become the convalescent home for St Hugh's hospital at an early stage of the war. It functioned as a separate military establishment under its own medical superintendent, and was fully staffed with a matron, nurses, physiotherapists and occupational therapists. The patients at any one time consisted of about 20 officers, all accommodated in the Earl's house, and upwards of a 100 Other Ranks living in a temporary hutted camp on the estate. All the patients remained under the care of the doctors at St Hugh's, who visited the home at regular intervals to keep a check on their progress.

The atmosphere in the Officers' Mess at Middleton Park was eccentric in the extreme. The two resident physicians, the medical superintendent and his assistant, were both long-retired lieutenant-colonels from the Indian Medical Service, neither of whom had had any previous experience of neurology. They lived in a world of make-believe in which they chose to confuse the convalescent home with an officers' recuperation centre at some hill-station in the Punjab, and it was quite apparent that they would have been much happier if we had all been recovering from bouts of malaria or falls on the polo field rather than from severe wounds sustained in action. Someone had once heard them lamenting together that we had all been so badly knocked about it was quite impossible for them to organise any of the normal social activities which formed such a necessary adjunct to the life of a Mess.

The idiosyncratic atmosphere in the house was augmented by the presence and conduct of the Earl's butler, who had continued his employment after the army had taken over. His position was an incongruous one as he had no place in the official establishment, but his firm and unobtrusive authority in domestic matters was never challenged. Dressed in a tail-coat, he used to supervise the serving of our meals at the large mahogany table in the dining-room. It sometimes seemed that he had not accepted the fact that Middleton Park had become a military convalescent home and he always referred to the officer-patients as "the guests", as though we were staying there for one of his master's prewar shooting parties.

The medical superintendent had made an arbitrary rule - he called it a "rehabilitative principle" - that patients with disabilities affecting the use of their arms or their hands should not be given any assistance at meal-times either by their neighbours at table or by members of the staff. As several like myself were wholly or partially paralysed in one arm it created a real problem for us. The main difficulty we faced was in cutting meat, and it was not unknown for a lamb chop to go gliding across the snowy-white tablecloth leaving a trail of vegetables and gravy behind it. When this happened the butler would dart forward with napkin raised to minimise the damage, while the medical superintendent, breaking off his conversation, would survey the scene in silent disapproval of such boorish behaviour in an Officers' Mess.

I was determined to get myself as fit as possible before my second head operation, and gradually increased the amount of exercise I was taking until I was walking about three miles every afternoon. Life at Middleton Park was boring and monotonous; the only entertainments arranged for the patients were a visit from a mobile cinema unit once a week and an occasional ENSA concert. Apart from that, we ate, we talked, we walked, and we slept. The conversation on the whole was fairly gloomy; the general view seemed to be that once the war was over the severely disabled ex-servicemen would be brushed aside and consigned to oblivion.

I knew that as soon as I had been given my final discharge from St Hugh's I would be invalided out of the army and returned to civilian life. At the beginning of May, after I had been at Middleton Park for three weeks, I could still get no information as to how long I would have to wait for my plating operation so I decided in the meanwhile to make some preliminary inquiries about taking my examinations for the Bar. At Norman's suggestion I wrote to Mr Cleveland- Stevens, the Director of Legal Studies at the Inns of Court, explaining my position and asking him for his advice. He replied at once suggesting that and I should come and see him as soon as I was well enough to do so.

Having made sure that my operation would not take place for at least a week, I asked the medical superintendent if I could have a 48 hour pass to attend to some important business in London. At first he was reluctant to grant my request because he believed that the strain might be too much for me in my present condition, but he eventually gave way with the warning that if I should collapse while was away I would only have myself to blame. I then made an appointment with Mr Cleveland-Stevens and booked myself a room for two nights at an inexpensive hotel in Kensington.

The war against Nazi Germany finished on the day I travelled by train to London. I took a taxi to my hotel, dined in solitude there, and went to bed very early; but I was kept awake half the night by the fireworks, the shouting and the singing in the streets nearby. I felt that I had no part in the celebrations, nor in the general mood of euphoria. These people were rejoicing, I thought, because their present tribulations were at an end: they were anticipating the joyous times which lay ahead of them. For some of us, however, the future would be a barren ordeal which would probably last us for the rest of our lives. During the early, sleepless hours in that narrow, over-heated hotel bedroom, I found it only too easy to be churlish and self-pitying.

The next day had been officially designated as "Victory in Europe Day," and the triumphal jubilation had continued. I spent the morning sitting in a corner of the deserted hotel lounge; everyone else seemed to have taken to the streets. I was feeling terribly alone. It was the first time there had been no attentive nurses or heedful relatives and friends to assist me in doing the innumerable things which I could not do for myself, and I had a feeling of utter helplessness.

In the afternoon I went by taxi to Lincoln's Inn for my appointment with Mr Cleveland-Stevens, a man of immense charm, who told me that his own son had been severely wounded in the fighting around Arnhem. He asked me a number of questions about the results of my head wound, and he wanted to know whether I really thought I would be able to manage the Bar exams. I replied frankly that I had been informed that my brain would not be able to cope with the strain, and that even if I succeeded in getting called to the Bar, my voice would never improve sufficiently for public speaking. He remarked that there had been several barristers in the past who had managed to practise successfully in spite of speech impediments.

"Supposing you try the exams," he suggested, "and if you can surmount that obstacle, you can see how much your voice had improved before you decide whether to go into practice or to apply for some legal appointment."

After I left Mr Cleveland-Stevens's office I went out into Chancery Lane intending to get a taxi back to the hotel, but taxis were very scarce and those which went past were invariably occupied. The alternative was to catch a bus, so I walked down to Fleet Street and made my way along the Strand. The streets were thronged with merrymakers all engrossed in their own jollifications. Outside Charing Cross Station I saw the stop I required. There were about 50 people waiting in front of me when I took my place at the end of the queue, and the few buses which pulled up were usually filled to overflowing.

I had been standing there for 10 minutes when I began to feel hot and dizzy. Fearing that I was going to faint, I left the queue and staggered down a side-street where I sat down in the doorway of a closed shop. A couple of drunken Canadian army lieutenants walked past. They saw me sitting on the low step and stopped, roaring with laughter. One of them came up to me and said: "Been having one too many, Sir? You should know when to stop at your age."

He rejoined his companion and they stood looking at me for a few moments before reeling away, still overcome with amusement.

After a while I felt a bit better and I went back to the queue which seemed to be about the same size as before. I was wondering how long I would be able to last out when another bus pulled in and I heard the conductress shouting out: "Two on top and one inside. I'm sorry, that's all I can take."

A murmur of annoyance went up from the crowd. Then I became aware of the voice of the conductress again: "Come on, Sir. There's room for you - you, Sir, the wounded officer at the back."

People in front of me were turning round and suddenly I realised they were looking at me. Nobody seemed to object as I went forward beside the queue and climbed on the platform of the bus. There were no seats on the lower deck but a girl sitting just inside the entrance stood up and offered her place, which I thankfully accepted because I was feeling utterly exhausted. When I tried to buy a ticket the conductress shook her head. "Not on your life," she exclaimed. "We haven't forgotten you yet, you know."

Soon after my return to Middleton Park I had been moved back to St Hugh's for my operation. I was put into a double-room in the officers' surgical ward with Ronnie Hutton, a Royal Engineers captain, who had received a shrapnel wound in the head at Nijmegen while he was serving with the Guards Armoured Division in the dash for Arnhem. We were told that we were both to have our plates put in by the same surgeon on the same day. Ronnie was not paralysed, and despite the severity of his wound he was hoping that he would be allowed to stay on in the army as a regular officer.

On the afternoon prior to the day of our operations, we were separately fitted for our plates. The craftsman noted the position and size of the gap in my skull; then he cut out a piece of tantalum from a large strip and hammered it into shape on his anvil while I sat on a chair watching him.

In the evening, contrary to the rules, Ronnie and I went out to dinner at a hotel. We arrived back at the hospital at around midnight and were immediately summoned to see the angry Sister-in-charge. She told us she would have to make a full report on our conduct with a view to disciplinary action being taken against us. We were both too drunk to care and we stood beaming at her with vacant benevolence. Eventually she realised that her words were having no effect on us and she burst out laughing.

"I shouldn't laugh," she said, making an effort to sound stern again. "You've been very naughty. For heaven's sake clear off to bed and we'll forget all about it. And by the way, best of luck to both of you for tomorrow."

A few days after our operations Ronnie and I were sent out to Middleton Park. Once again we were wearing bandages on our heads, though principally for cosmetic reasons as our heads had been shaved and our scalps were furrowed with unsightly scars. The routine at the convalescent home continued as before, with the same inactivity and the same boredom. The conversation was even gloomier than on my first visit, and more patients were having periodic fits. It was a great relief when a group of us, which included Ronnie, were taken back to St Hugh's for our Medical Boards.

Ronnie was graded as "fit for home duty," with every expectation he would be kept on by the army, and he was sent on immediate leave. My own Board was postponed for 24 hours so that I could undergo a long session of tests with a psychiatrist. Finally, when all the reports were available, I was shown into a room where an RAMC colonel and two majors were seated at a table with bundles of files in front of them.

The colonel motioned me to sit down, and when I had done so he told me that as a result of my wound they had no alternative other than to discharge me from the army on medical grounds.

"You'll never use your right arm again," he went on. "In addition, you'll always be a bit lame in your right leg, and you'll never be able to speak properly. You've certainly bought it in a big way. Have you any idea what you'll do in the way of work? We suggest farming."

"I'm going to be a barrister," I replied.

They all stared at me in surprise. Then the colonel said: "But that's quite impossible. What about your voice? And besides, you've been unfortunate enough to suffer a severe brain wound; you'd never pass the exams."

"I'm going to try," I persisted.

He shrugged his shoulders. "Well, if you won't take our advice, you won't. All I can say is this, don't be too disappointed when you find you can't study. We still think that farming would be the answer for you."

The colonel announced formally that the Medical Board

had decided I was permanently unfit for any form of military service in the future, and that I would be sent on indefinite leave the following day, pending my discharge. The Board were going to recommend that I should be granted a 100 per cent war disability pension.

Although I had been well aware that the result of my Board was inevitable, that did not lessen the impact of the decision. After nearly six years as a soldier I was now to become a civilian again. Presently I would fold up my uniform and put it away for the last time. The simple camaraderie of service life, the trusted fellowship of the Officers' Mess, would soon recede into the past. No longer would my well-being be regulated for me. I would be out in the world, fending for myself.

I went to Miss Brookes's room to tell her my news.

She asked me what the Board had advised me to do after my discharge.

"Farming," I replied; and I added quickly, "but I'm not going to take their advice. I still intend to read for the Bar."

Her face lit up. "Good!" she said. "I didn't want to influence you in any way. It won't be easy for you - ever. You'll have a hard struggle to study, and even when you qualify, as you most certainly will, you'll have to keep on fighting against your speech impediment for the rest of your life. But I'm sure that when you look back on it at the end, you'll have no regrets. Always remember to have faith in God and that will give you faith in yourself."

Desmond O'Meara, like Ronnie Hutton, had wanted to

remain in the army. His broken back had healed, but he had been left with a residual weakness in one leg and he would walk with a permanent limp. In spite of his disability the Medical Board at St Hugh's had graded him as "Fit for home service." Subsequently he had been posted as an Instructor to the Royal Military College at Sandhurst.

Desmond's father was in the colonial legal service, and for the last three years he had held an appointment as acting chief justice of the Sudan. Now that hostilities in Europe had ceased he was hoping to be repatriated very soon, as he had passed the official age of retirement. In the meantime, his wife was living at Polperro, the beautiful Cornish fishing village, to which she had become greatly attached. She had arranged for my mother to rent the cottage next door to her own for the remainder of the summer so that I would have somewhere to go when I was released from hospital.

The O'Mearas had had two children, both sons. Barry, Desmond's elder brother, was serving with the Special Air Service in Italy. During my final week at St Hugh's, Mrs O'Meara was notified that, after a recent engagement, Barry had been reported as "missing, believed killed."

After I left Oxford I spent a couple of nights at a hotel in London before travelling down to Cornwall. I was anxious to get my future sorted out as far as possible before I began my final period of convalescence, and I had arranged an appointment at an office in Whitehall with a representative of the Further Education and Training Scheme. The details of this project had just been announced by the Government. Any demobilised ex-serviceman who could establish that his call-up, or his voluntary enlistment, had interfered with his training for a career would be entitled to receive a grant which would enable him to complete his studies. As it seemed that I fulfilled all the necessary requirements, I had applied for a grant, both to take a law degree at a university and to sit the examinations for the Bar.

I was interviewed by a pleasant, middle-aged woman whose evident friendliness was tempered by the guarded manner and studied reticence of the professional civil servant.

My credentials, she said, made me admirably suited for the Further Education and Training Scheme. Obviously I had joined the forces at a vital stage in my preparations for a legal career, and in the ordinary course of events they would have had no hesitation in making me a grant to take a law degree at a university, and to cover my studies for the Bar. She paused and then continued, choosing her words with obvious care.

"I'm sure you will appreciate that as we're dealing with public funds we can't allow ourselves to be influenced by sentiment. We have to be satisfied before we make a grant that the recipient will stand a reasonable chance of completing the course successfully. In your own case we felt obliged to examine a detailed medical report on the after-effects of your very severe head wound."

I could guess what the report from St Hugh's would have said about my chances of passing any exams, and I was not altogether surprised when she told me that, although my application had been considered with great sympathy, they had felt that in my present condition it would be most unwise for me to be subjected to the competitive stresses of university life. However, she went on, since I seemed so determined to continue reading for the Bar in spite of my various disabilities, they had decided to make me a provisional grant which would enable me to take a correspondence course for the Bar exams with a legal crammer. The four subjects in the intermediate examination could be taken separately. I would be expected to sit for two of the subjects within a reasonable time, and provided I passed in both, my grant would be extended until I had taken my final. She added they had contacted Mr Cleveland-Stevens, the Director of Legal Studies, and he fully approved of their proposals.

Just before I had left St Hugh's the adjutant of my old battalion had written to me about the presentation of my decoration. He had said that General de Gaulle, who had become the head of the French Provisional Government, was about to hold an investiture in Paris and the French authorities would like me to attend it if I was fit enough to do so. I would have considered it a very great honour to have received my medal from the hands of General de Gaulle, but I felt unable at that moment to face the journey to Paris and the subsequent ceremony. In any event, I was anxious to put my military life behind me and was reluctant to re-awaken any past emotions in any way connected with it. So I declined the invitation. After two more unsuccessful attempts to get me to an investiture, the French gave up trying and sent me the medal through the post.

The three months I spent at Polperro were a period of

transition for me between the sheltered passivity of a hospital environment and the impersonal, bustling detachment of the world outside. Our cottage was close to the open coast, alongside the beautiful little fishing-boat harbour. We generally had members of the family or friends staying with us as we had ample accommodation. Every morning we used to walk along the cliffs to our favourite secluded cove, carrying luncheon baskets, papers and books, and we would spend the rest of the day on the beach. It was a relaxed existence and the weather was perfect. To my delight I found I was able to swim with one arm. After a little practice I became sufficiently confident to plunge off the rocks into deep water without sharing the trepidation of the people who were watching me.

I was concerned about the slowness of my reading, though I was finding far less difficulty focusing my eyes on the correct point on the page when I was starting to read a new line. My left-handed writing was becoming slightly more legible if I formed the letters carefully and unhurriedly, and also provided that I could wedge down the piece of paper on which I wrote to prevent it from sliding. On the other hand, my dyslexia and my dysgraphia were not improving at all; my spelling was appalling; I missed out whole phrases; and I was frequently afflicted with temporary amnesia when trying to visualise the construction of a word.

Even though I was following Miss Brookes's advice and reading aloud for an hour every day while I was alone in my bedroom, I did not notice my diction getting any clearer or any more fluent. It was customary for my friends to tell me that I was speaking far better each time they met me, but I suspected they were only being kindly and encouraging. I knew that I was not losing my stammer or my hesitancy; and there were still certain words and syllables I was utterly unable to pronounce.

Desmond spent a week at Polperro before taking up his job at Sandhurst, and his father arrived home while he was still there. Judge O'Meara was a man of considerable simplicity and immense charm. Although he had spent the whole of his working life in the Sudan he had never lost his soft, musical Dublin brogue. I saw a great deal of him after Desmond had left and we had many interesting discussions in which he always expressed a broad-minded, liberal viewpoint. He often spoke about his elder son Barry who was still posted as "missing believed killed." The Judge had collected all the information available from letters and reports, and had written a balanced summary hoping to convince himself that Barry might still be alive. However, from little things he said to me, I think he knew he was only fostering false hopes.

In the middle of the summer Judge O'Meara went into hospital suffering from what was believed to be acute appendicitis. It was discovered that in fact he had advanced, inoperable cancer, and he was returned home with the prognosis that at most he had barely a year to live. Mrs O'Meara, who had been a VAD during the First World War, insisted he must remain in the cottage until she was no longer able to look after him properly, and he agreed. Sometimes in the afternoon I used to sit with him on his favourite bench at the edge of the cliff s. He looked pale and drawn, and his youthful appearance had left him, but he faced death with resignation and courage, his principal concern being for his wife and his son whom he would leave behind him.

During the few months we spent at the cottage at Polperro, a General Election took place, the two atomic bombs were dropped and Japan formally surrendered to the Allies.

In company with so many other members of the armed forces I voted for the Labour Party at the General Election in July. Most of us were politically naive; all our thoughts and ideas had been concentrated on defeating the enemy rather than on the governance of our country when the war was over. However, we were vaguely aware that the Labour programme was more closely attuned to the Brave New World in which we all desired to live. We had no wish to return to the past, with its social injustice and its poverty; not to a Britain fragmented by class divisions and inequality. We were a little over-credulous, I suppose, of some of the plausible contentions and the suave assurances voiced by campaigning politicians.

All through the war both sides had been introducing weaponry which was more powerful and more destructive than anything seen before. I imagined at first that the atom bombs dropped by the Americans on Hiroshima and Nagasaki in August were merely a progressive development of conventional explosive devices. The general public at the time were still extremely ignorant about the devastating power and effects of nuclear fission. With the formal surrender of the Japanese on September 2, the Second World

War came to an end.

There were a number of younger people in Polperro that summer who sought continually to involve me in all their activities. In the gloomy discussions at St Hugh's and at Middleton Park I had heard it suggested that none of us would be accepted again as normal human beings; we would always be regarded as freakish and apart. I did not find that at all. I soon discovered that the more you can forget your own disabilities, the more they will be forgotten by those around you.

Before I left Oxford I had given my address in Polperro to the Sister in charge of the officer's surgical ward and she had undertaken, if Emma had phoned the hospital, to tell her where to find me. Every morning, every afternoon, and every evening I was expecting a message from her - but none ever came.

CHAPTER 17

After we left Polperro my mother had taken the lease of a ground-floor flat in South Kensington. It was part of what had once been a four-storey dwelling-house, built in the middle of the 19th century. Each of the floors and the basement were now self-contained flats, sharing a common hall and staircase. It was in a pleasant situation as there was a private garden-square at the back for the use of the surrounding houses, which was thoughtfully laid out with trees, tall bushes, lawns, flower-beds, and intersecting gravel paths. We had direct access to it through a french window.

In the days when the house had been a single residence our flat had comprised the principal living apartments. The rooms were spacious with high ceilings which made them very difficult to keep warm in cold weather, as there was no central heating. However, the Kenley Court furniture looked more in place in this commodious setting than it had done in the less stately ambience of our three previous homes.

South Kensington had the reputation of being an expensive locality in which to live, but our rent, like most of those in the borough, was controlled by the Rent Restriction Acts and was far lower than we would otherwise have had to pay on the open market. My own income was just sufficient for a modest way of life. I had been discharged from the army with a 100 per cent disability pension and this was augmented when I started studying with a small weekly maintenance grant under the Further Education and Training Scheme.

Arnold visited the flat on several occasions. Then, within three weeks of his return from the Middle East, the RAF sent him to Norway. Eve spent her embarkation leave with us before commencing her two-year posting to Malta. I missed her dreadfully when she had gone as I was increasingly troubled by loneliness. Nearly all my friends were still serving overseas and, in any case, I had a feeling that our paths had now diverged to such an extent it would be virtually impossible for us to recreate the old affinities.

Before she went away Eve had spoken to me frankly about my relationship with Emma. The time had come, she said, for me to accept the fact that Emma had broken off from me irrevocably, and I should cease to delude myself that she would ever return to me. I was bound to fall in love again, Eve went on, and when that happened it would give rise to all sorts of problems if I still retained an emotional commitment to Emma. I replied that I could not help myself; however fond I became of someone else in the future, my devotion would be infinitesimal compared with my love for Emma.

The first years of victory were years of hardship. Food, clothing and fuel were still rationed, shortages were widespread, taxation continued at exorbitant wartime levels, unemployment began to rise, and a host of bomb-sites and ruined buildings remained, as silent and forlorn as unburied corpses.

I used to work all day in my study-bedroom. The tutors guided my reading and sent me their own printed commentaries to be studied in conjunction with the authorised text-books. Every so often they would give a written test-paper which I would complete and return to them for correction. I was finding that neither my intellect nor my memory appeared to have been affected by my wound, but my tutors were deeply concerned about my untidy writing, my atrocious spelling, and the frequency with which I omitted words in my answers.

The principal hindrance to my studying was my medication. The luminal tablets I was taking to dampen down my brain were lessening my powers of concentration, making me permanently lethargic, and causing me to drop off to sleep continually during the daytime, even when I was working at my desk. I felt certain that I would not be subject to fits despite what I had been told by the doctors at St Hugh's, so I decided, very foolishly, to give up luminal completely. I did not disclose what I was doing to anyone, but I was ready to resume my prescribed dosage immediately if I had any forewarning of a possible epileptic attack.

A few of us who had been together in the officers' surgical ward used to meet from time to time to see a play in the West End and to dine at a restaurant afterwards. Michael Neville and Richard Wheeler were regular attenders. Michael had returned to his old college at Cambridge with the intention of studying law, but it had proved too much for him and he was now teaching at a preparatory school in the country. Richard, who had married one of the VADs at St Hugh's, was also a schoolmaster and taught at a prep school in St Leonards-on-Sea which was owned by his elder brother. Fortunately for Richard and Michael they had sympathetic and understanding employers as they both suffered from fairly frequent fits. Hugh Verney, who had joined us a few times, not only had periodic fits but he was afflicted by excruciating headaches whenever he had been reading for more than about five minutes. Desmond O'Meara came to only one of these reunions. He had been unable, with his disability, to cope with the life at Sandhurst and had been accepted for a temporary post with the Diplomatic Service in Belgrade.

During my first winter in London my erstwhile companions were gradually returning to England to be demobilised, and I was delighted to find that our former friendships seemed unaffected by what had happened to me. As my social life increased, my loneliness vanished. This was the era of the cocktail party. The jostling guests in overcrowded rooms; the haze of cigarette smoke; the half-heard conversations above the hubbub; the partial introductions, and perfunctory encounters. The average cocktail party was conviviality at its lowest ebb.

The Kensington flat was within easy walking distance of the Albert Hall and I used to go there regularly. Apart from the immense spiritual satisfaction I derived from listening to the music, it enabled me to escape wholly from myself. Directly the conductor had raised his baton all earthly things seemed to slip away and I was transported into the realms of the composer's fantasy. It was an immensely pleasing sensation to sit there, completely relaxed with my mind clear and receptive, and then to soar away, alone but never lonely, free but always guided. At the end of the journey I used to return to reality with a sense of tranquillity and peace. I think it is one of the fundamental truths of life that the faculty of perceiving beauty is often enhanced by suffering and by sorrow.

By slow degrees I was learning how to overcome the restriction of having only one usable arm in what was essentially a two-handed world. It often required a good deal of experimentation before I could devise my own techniques for carrying out many of the routine procedures of every day living, such as bathing, shaving, dressing, tying a tie, doing up shoe-laces, cutting food on a plate, or spreading butter on a slice of bread. When I needed a second hand I sometimes had to have recourse to my teeth, sometimes to my feet. My teeth were particularly useful for opening a letter or fastening a knot: my feet for gripping a solid object, for instance when I was removing the lid from a jar or the cork from a bottle.

Nevertheless, the problems of being one-armed were manifold. When I was carrying a parcel, a bag, a briefcase, or an umbrella, I was encumbered as much as a two-armed person holding something in each hand. This seldom caused any great difficulty until it came to clambering on or off a bus, or travelling on a crowded underground train. Another constantly occurring inconvenience was trying to sort out coins with one hand when making payment in a shop. As I was going around in the course of my daily life I had continually to plan ahead with regard to my immediate future movements. What was the safest route for me to take across the jolting carriage to avoid stumbling? How would I open the door through which I wanted to pass? What would be the best way to extract my wallet from an inside jacket pocket when it became necessary to do so? How would I ascend or descend the stairs ahead of me with the rails on the wrong side - or worse still with no side-rails at all?

The circulation in my right arm is very poor and when the weather is at all cold I need to wear a glove on my right hand. It is a slow and arduous process to fit each of my inactive fingers into the correct space. I have found that a woollen glove is slightly easier to manipulate than a leather one. If possible, when I am trying to adjust the glove, I like to go somewhere where I can sit down with nobody watching me.

I have never suffered from the slightest self-consciousness about my disablement, but I have noticed that it can cause some embarrassment to the people with whom I have come into contact. It is quite customary for someone, on being introduced to me, to hold out his or her right hand, and then to be overcome with confusion when I have clasped it with my own left hand. Usually when I make new acquaintances who know nothing about me I take the first opportunity of mentioning casually to them that as the result of a war-wound I have been left with a permanently paralysed right arm. I do this in the hope that it will nullify the unease which they might otherwise have felt if they had noticed my disability for themselves and had wondered how sensitive I am about it.

It cannot be over-emphasised that the vast majority of the physically handicapped have a burning desire to be treated as normal human beings, and this applies whether or not they are self-conscious with regard to their disablement. Naturally they appreciate being given assistance, provided it is done unobtrusively with the minimum of fuss. I am always immensely grateful if someone helps me on with my coat, opens a door for me when I am carrying anything, or places a table to my left when I am seated with a cup or glass in my hand.

As the date of my first examinations drew near, my tutors became increasingly concerned about my handwriting, my spelling, and my tendency to leave out complete words or portions of words in my answers to their test papers. They told me that these defects might well prejudice my chances of passing. I had additional worries of my own. I knew the exams would be a race against the clock and that if I tried to write at all hurriedly my writing would be completely illegible. Also, that once I was parted from my dictionary my spelling became even worse.

I decided to send a letter to the Council of Legal Education stating that I was still in the process of learning how to write with my left-hand and inquiring if it would be possible for me to be granted a little extra time to complete the papers. I received a prompt and courteous reply from the Secretary telling me that my request could not be granted, but offering me the services of an amanuensis who would take down my answers at my dictation in a private room adjoining the examination hall. Although I felt doubtful about my ability to dictate my answers in a concise and orderly form, I realised that if I used an amanuensis for the exams I would not have to worry about the speed of my writing, nor about my spelling and the other abnormalities brought about by my dyslexia or my dysgraphia. So I wrote to the Secretary, gratefully accepting his offer.

I took my first exams at Lincoln's Inn Hall on a beautiful

spring day. When I arrived in the morning I was shown into a small room where Mr Polden, my amanuensis, was already seated at a table with his pens and a blotter in front of him. We had a preliminary discussion in which he was kind, helpful, and reassuring. He told me he had been acting in this capacity for over 20 years and had assisted many disabled students in the period after the First World War, most of them one-armed or blind. When the time of commencement drew near he took a sealed envelope from his briefcase. Then he placed his watch on the table and waited until the hand was on the hour.

"Right," he said, "we'll begin now."

He broke the seal, extracted the examination paper from the envelope, and handed it to me. For the next three hours I dictated to him and he took down my answers swiftly in faultless copper-plate handwriting, giving me each page to check directly it was completed. Only once did he take a brief rest, when he produced two mugs and a thermos flask of coffee from his briefcase. We drank in silence for about five minutes and as soon as we had both finished we carried on again. There was another three-hour paper in the afternoon. Mr Polden seemed to be tireless; at the end of the day he was writing just as rapidly and just as neatly as he had been doing at the beginning.

That evening Norman took me to dinner at the Oxford and Cambridge Club. He went through my answers to the various questions with me, and eventually expressed the opinion that I had probably passed both papers. Fortunately for me his forecast turned out to be correct.

I decided to go to the south-west of Ireland for a month's

holiday before tackling the remaining two subjects in the intermediate examination. I had been attending a London hospital once a week to have physiotherapy for my right arm and the Ministry of Pensions arranged for me to continue the treatment at a hospital in Cork. I was willing enough to go on with weekly sessions for as long as it was considered advisable, although I was now reconciled to the fact that my arm would never recover.

A few weeks after my return to London I had a foreboding that I was about to undergo one of the unpleasant complications from my head-injury that I had been warned to expect. It started with severe headaches and transient spells of giddiness. Then one afternoon I was out shopping when suddenly I felt an unbalanced, reeling sensation and lights began to flash in front of my eyes. I would have fainted in the street but I managed to stop a passing taxi and I asked the driver to get me home as quickly as possible. In the evening I was feeling better, though still far from well, so I went to bed early in the hope that a good night's sleep would restore me to normal.

The next morning I woke up very early with a fierce headache. After breakfast I went out for a walk, but soon after leaving home I almost fainted, so I had to return hurriedly and lie down. My doctor did not know what was the matter with me; however he felt certain that it was some sort of complication from my wound, and he advised me to consult one of the neurosurgical specialists who had looked after me at St Hugh's. I phoned George Northcroft, the neurosurgeon who had been in charge of the officers' surgical ward and who, I had been told was always more than willing to help any of his old patients with their problems. George called round and saw me at the flat on the following day. He asked me for a full account of what had happened and then gave me a very thorough examination. Eventually, he confirmed that my present illness resulted from my brain injury. "It might have happened in any event," he said, "but very probably it had been precipitated by the strain of studying. There's no cure for this except complete rest."

He advised me not to continue with my course for another year or two, and to consider very seriously whether I should abandon my determination to be called to the Bar. "Now that this has happened once," he said, "it's likely to happen again if you go on pushing yourself. Why can't you be content with the miracle that you're still alive at all, without hanging on to your previous ambitions to carve out a successful career for yourself?"

It was a difficult decision for me to make. I could give up my studies at this stage without any sense of failure in the knowledge that my brain injury had forced me to do so. On the other hand, the disorder might only last for a few weeks, after which I would be able to carry on with tutors, trusting that it was never going to recur. Certainly I could not delay very long without informing the administrators of the Further Education and Training Scheme what had happened, and if I did that, the continuance of my grant would obviously be in jeopardy. I thought it best to wait for a month and then make up my mind.

After a fortnight my headaches began to ease off and my feeling of unsteadiness became less pronounced, so I decided to carry on with my studies. I had not told my tutors the reason why I had stopped working for three weeks and they probably assumed that I had been on holiday.

I took my next two exams in the same room as before at Lincoln's Inn Hall, one three-hour paper in the morning and another in the afternoon. Mr Polden was as imperturbable and proficient as ever. I found it much easier to dictate my answers to him on this occasion, partly because we were no longer strangers and partly because we were growing accustomed to working with each other. At the end of the day I was troubled by doubts and forebodings about the way in which I had dealt with some of the questions, but when the results were published a few weeks later I learnt with relief that I had passed in both subjects.

My doctor had told me not to start studying for my Bar finals until I was certain that I had recovered completely from the after-effects of my recent set-back, so I went off to stay for a while at a guest-house in an isolated locality on the west coast of County Cork. While I was there I spent most of my time in the open - walking, swimming and taking out a small boat with a few friends. I was soon feeling a lot better. My headaches became less frequent and less intense; the intervals between my spells of giddiness lengthened; and fewer of my nights were marred by prolonged insomnia.

Most of the residents at the guest-house had only come there for short holidays and I never saw very much of them, except at meal-times. The only two people with whom I became very friendly were Tom Barry and his wife.

"General" Barry, as he was always called, had led an IRA Flying Column during the Irish troubles of 1919-1921, and had become one of the best known of the anti-British guerrilla commanders. Tom and I often visited one of the local pubs together in the evening and as two old soldiers we used to swop yarns about our experiences in action. He was particularly interested in the exploits of the Special Forces and the activities of the underground movements in Occupied Europe. He told me that he had always respected the soldiers of the British Army and he had regretted having had to fight against them. One evening a young potman, clearing away empty glasses from a table beside us, had remarked to him, "You must have enjoyed yourself, general, ambushing British troops during the Troubles." Tom had replied sternly, "One never enjoys killing and maiming brave enemies. It's all part of the bloody business of warfare."

Just before Eve returned to England from Malta in the autumn of 1947 she became engaged to Lieutenant Peter La Niece, a Naval officer who was then serving as gunnery officer in the Cruiser HMS Ajax. They were married in London in March the following year. After their honeymoon in Ireland Peter was posted to the shore establishment at Gosport, on the staff of the 5th Submarine Flotilla, and they moved into a rented flat in Portsmouth.

The English winter of 1947-1948 was one of the coldest on record. Owing to a national fuel shortage, factories had been faced a shut-down, and domestic users had to endure power-cuts at set times every day. I was working flat out for the Bar finals, and I recall my periodic sense of frustration when the lights and electric fires were suddenly cut off. There was nothing for it but to put on an overcoat and to resume reading, hoping that the failing temperatures would not impair my concentration.

Although more than two years had elapsed since the end of the war, Britain had seen little of the harvest of victory. Food rationing continued interminably; clothing could only be bought in exchange for coupons; scarcities, non-fulfilment and shoddy performance were still blamed entirely on wartime restrictions. It was as though an epidemic of inertia had infected the whole country.

Norman had been demobilised early on account of his age, and had immediately returned to the Bar. He had joined the chambers of the Honourable Victor Russell, an elderly and much-respected barrister, and he had soon developed a large and varied practice. Norman told me that if I managed to get through the final examination he would take me as his pupil for a year, as a year's pupillage was a necessary prelude to practising at the Bar. After my pupillage was completed it would be necessary for me to find a set of chambers in which I could become a tenant. It was always a problem, Norman said, to find a set where there was plenty of work, but he had every hope that when the time came I would be offered a tenancy in Victor Russell's chambers.

One morning a month before the commencement of my exams Michael Neville rang me to say that he was going to the theatre that evening with Richard Wheeler and they were going out to dinner afterwards. "Why don't you tear yourself away from your text books for a few hours and join us?" he asked. Although I still had a vast amount of revision to get through, I thought I needed a break so I consented.

We went to a new Noel Coward revue, which I was enjoying immensely when I suddenly began to feel I was developing a temperature. During the second half of the show I became progressively worse and worse, and I wondered whether I would be able to remain until the final curtain. Eventually I could stick it out no longer. I made a hurried apology to the other two, left the theatre and took a taxi home.

The next day my doctor called round to examine me. He told me I was suffering from pneumonia and I would have to stay in bed for at least a fortnight, during which time I must not try to study at all.

"Will I be able to sit for my finals?" I asked him.

"I would prefer not to speculate about that for the time being," he replied. "It will depend a great deal on how quickly you get over this illness - and, of course, on the absence of complications."

The pneumonia took its course and I was well on the way to recovery when I contracted pleurisy in my right lung.

"That settles it," said the doctor. "You won't even be fit enough to travel to the examination hall by the date of your exams."

I wrote to the Council of Legal Education withdrawing my name from the list of candidates and explaining the circumstances. I enclosed a certificate from my doctor stating the nature of my illness and expressing his opinion that it would be necessary for me to remain indoors for the next few weeks. The Secretary replied sympathetically saying that, provided I felt up to it, the Council would allow me to take the examination at home, with Mr Polden acting in the dual capacity of invigilator and amanuensis. With some misgiving my doctor consented to this arrangement taking place.

The exam lasted for three consecutive days, with a three-hour paper every morning and another every afternoon. Mr Polden sat at the desk in my bedroom and I dictated my answers to him from an armchair at his side. I found the strain considerable, especially during the afternoon sessions, and directly they were finished I used to go straight to bed. When I went over the questions in the six papers later on I realised that most of them seemed almost to have been designed to cover the parts of the various subjects which I knew best. None the less, I felt fairly gloomy about the results as I had been too tired to think clearly after the first couple of hours each day.

I remained in London until the announcement of the results. Norman had found out first, as he had sent one of his pupils to inspect the lists as soon as they were exhibited at the office of the Council of Legal Education. He rang me immediately he knew. He was short and to the point. "Congratulations, Tony," he said, "you've passed."

We arranged that I would take a long holiday as my illness had left me in a low condition, and that I would only start my year's pupillage when I was feeling really fit again. The Middle Temple had granted permission for me to be called to the Bar *in absentia*, which would mean that I would not have to return to London to take part in the ceremony.

A distant cousin of mine living in County Donegal on the rugged shores of Lough Swilly had turned his family home into a private hotel, which he was running very successfully. When I booked a room there for a month he insisted on my paying a far lower rate than his ordinary charges, although it was approaching the height of the summer season.

I was determined to recuperate as quickly as possible, and I spent my time in Donegal swimming, going for long walks, and climbing small mountains, a formula for recovery which had always worked with me before. As the days passed I tried to persuade myself that I was beginning to feel better, but I knew it was not true. My cough persisted, I continued to lose weight and my lack of energy became more apparent.

Directly after my return to London my doctor arranged for me to have a chest X-ray. He told me the result over the telephone.

"I'm afraid you've got a tuberculosis lesion in your right lung," he said. "I'm fixing an appointment for you to see Dr Ernest Lloyd in Harley Street; he's one of the leading physicians in the treatment of tuberculosis. I have absolutely no doubt that you'll be cured. This is nothing to what you've been through already."

I was stunned by the news. In those days TB was still regarded by the general public as one of the principal incurable killer diseases. It was widely believed that people suffering from it were constrained to drag out the last months of their lives in a gloomy sanatorium, surrounded by other patients who were under a similar sentence of imminent death.

On my first meeting with Dr Lloyd, at his consulting rooms in Harley Street, he struck me as being slightly distant and a little pompous. I was to discover later that he was the epitome of kindliness and he possessed a never-failing sense of humour.

He had studied my X-ray plates and jotted down notes for several minutes before he spoke to me. Then he looked up and said, "You already know the cause of your illness. In all probability this is another result of your head-wound."

"Have I got it badly?" I asked.

"I cannot tell until I know how well you'll respond to treatment," he replied. "But we must fight this thing together, you and I. I will do all that medical science enables me to do - the rest will be up to you."

He then told me I would have to go into Brompton Hospital in Fulham as soon as he could get a bed for me, and later on he would like me to go to Midhurst Sanatorium in Sussex.

I inquired how long my treatment would last.

Dr Lloyd stood up, came over to me and put his hand on my shoulder.

"We mustn't think of time," he said. "And you mustn't worry about your career or your plans for the future. It will require all your concentration and all your will-power to overcome this disease."

As he showed me to the door he added, "Rest is our chief weapon. Complete and absolute rest."

CHAPTER 18

I was in bed at home for two weeks before being admitted to the Brompton Hospital.

I had been informed in a letter from the Ministry of Pensions that their medical advisers had accepted that my tuberculosis was the result of my head wound, but that as I was already assessed as being 100 per cent disabled it would not be possible to increase my pension any more. However, the Ministry would assume full liability for the cost of my treatment for the disease, and if it was necessary for me to enter hospital I would be entitled, since I was an officer-pensioner, to go in as a private patient.

The Brompton dated back to an era when hospitals had been constructed with a mindless emphasis on practicality and without any comprehension of the psychological reactions of the patients. It must have been one of the most dreary and depressing-looking buildings in London. Inside, it was drab and bare, and seemed to reek of discomfort, desolation, and death. The long, dark corridors smelt unpleasantly of polish and antiseptic; and they echoed interminably to a metallic clanging in the background as lids were hammered off the tops of oxygen cylinders.

I was put into a two-patient room, already occupied by Bert, a youth of 18 who was awaiting major surgery. He told me that his tuberculosis had been discovered more than two years before while he was still at school, and he had been confined to bed ever since. This was his second stay at the Brompton. During the previous year he had been returned home because the doctors had decided that there was nothing more that could be done for him. Then he had taken a turn for the better and his disease had become sufficiently stabilised for him to undergo an operation on his infected lung.

Bert was the only child of adoring parents who had been devastated by his illness. His father worked as a self-employed plumber in north London, and although his means were fairly modest he had determined that his son should be treated in the private wing of the hospital, regardless of the expense.

In spite of the difference in our ages Bert and I found we had a lot in common. He had become an avid reader; I had the impression that when he immersed himself completely in the imagined happenings of a novel it enabled him to break free for a while from the perpetual bondage of the sick-room. He had also developed a taste for music and used to listen for hours to concerts broadcast on the radio.

On my first day in the room, I was visited by Dr John Batten, Dr Lloyd's house physician. He explained to me that my tuberculosis was still at an active stage and that it had caused a cavity to develop in my right lung. I was going to be placed on a régime of "absolute rest," which would mean that I must not leave my bed at all, even for the purpose of visiting the toilet. I would have to remain as still as possible, avoiding all unnecessary movement, and I would be washed by the nurses. "When we have the cavity under control," he said, "or better still, when it is scarred over, Dr Lloyd will decide what to do with you next."

I was told by Bert, from his experience of the treatment of tuberculosis, that when the disease was quiescent they would be almost certain to give me an artificial pneumothorax, a method of keeping the lung partially deflated by pushing air through the pleura at regular intervals. If that did not work, he added, they would probably want me to have the same operation as he was about to undergo himself.

I realised that this unexpected spell of enforced idleness must not be entirely wasted, so I spent a few hours every day reading Plato's *Dialogues* and Lecky's *History of England in the Eighteenth Century*. For my lighter literature I chose the novels of Somerset Maughan and Dostoevsky.

In the private wing we were allowed to have visitors every afternoon as well as for a short while in the evening. Hardly a day passed without a visit from a member of my family or some of my friends. My mother, Noreen and Arnold came to see me regularly, and Eve, whose social life in Portsmouth kept her fully occupied, usually managed to get to the hospital once or twice each week.

Dr Batten liked to do his rounds in the morning. He was always relaxed, cheerful and optimistic. He had firm belief that a complete and rapid cure for tuberculosis would be found in the very near future, and that in the meantime the present methods of treatment could generally prove effective in controlling the disease. His visits were entirely informal; he used to sit on the side of my bed discussing the news, books and plays, making me feel that I would soon be out again living a normal life. Dr Lloyd went on his rounds at the Brompton every Saturday afternoon. His visits were the height of formality. He would be ushered into the room by the Sister, followed by the Staff Nurse and a flock of younger physicians. Invariably he would have a kindly word for me and would assure me that I was making good progress.

I generally managed to keep myself in good spirits as I felt certain that, all in good time, I would recover and be able to practise as a barrister. Occasionally, however, I was weighed down by a mood of a dark depression. Supposing my disease could not be arrested? Would I have the courage to endure the long, weary battle against a death which approached gradually with a fearful, unrelenting inevitability? Or, if they partially cured me, it might mean that I would have to see out the rest of my days as a semi-invalid, pushed around in a wheelchair with constant nursing and medication. I wanted to be the same as other people; I longed to merge into crowds unnoticed, to live as they lived, feel as they felt, and to be accepted as one of them.

Bert's operation was to take place in three stages, a fortnight apart. It would entail the removal of most of his ribs on one side of his chest and the permanent closing down of one of his lungs. He had the first stage when I had been in the room for about two months. One afternoon a nurse painted the upper half of his body with jodine and wrapped him in an operation gown. Before she left she gave him a premedication injection and told him to lie still until they were ready for him in the theatre. He was hot and uncomfortable and terrified out of his wits; but the nursing staff were fully occupied with other duties and no one was available to try to reassure him. It seemed an age before the theatre orderlies came in, lifted him on to a trolley and trundled him away.

Bert returned a few hours later, still unconscious from

the anaesthetic. His mother and father came in to sit with him that evening. It must have been a very distressing experience for them as he was just in the process of coming round, and for most of the time he lay with his eyes closed, groaning. Before they went home they begged me to keep an eye on him, and I promised them that I would ring for a nurse whenever I thought he needed attention.

For three or four days Bert was in constant pain, but he endured it with great courage, and his mood was buoyant when he was told that the first stage of his operation had been entirely successful.

Before he went to the theatre for his second stage, I had my "AP" as an artificial pneumothorax was always called. It was carried out by Dr Lloyd on a Saturday morning in front of a group of junior doctors and nurses, who stood around my bed watching him attentively. First of all he gave me a local anaesthetic which made my chest feel stiff and heavy. For the next half an hour he was busy with needles and tubes, working in absolute silence. Then he straightened up.

"Good," he said, "it seems to be all right at the moment. You'll have to lie almost motionless for 24 hours until it settles down."

He patted me on the shoulder and left the room, followed by the others.

After a few moments Bert inquired how I was feeling. I told him that I felt fine apart from the soreness in my chest. We could not see each other as I was still surrounded by screens.

"Would you like to hear some music?" he asked.

"Yes," I said, "provided it's cheerful."

He turned up his radio and the room was suddenly animated by the joyful strains of the mazurka from the opening act of *Coppelia.* I closed my eyes and listened. There had been an occasion long before when I had watched *Coppelia* with Emma at my side. I saw again the flawless grace and precision of the corps de ballet; I recalled the ecstasy of the audience. At that moment my thoughts had taken wings and I had drifted timelessly far from my hospital bed, the tubes and the needles.

After a week it had become clear that my AP was far from perfect, and it was undecided whether or not it should be abandoned. Despite its imperfections, Dr Lloyd was in favour of retaining it for a while: on the other hand, a senior surgeon, who had examined my latest X-rays, thought it should be discontinued immediately and that I should undergo a similar operation to the one which Bert was having. Finally, another consultant physician was asked for his opinion and he agreed with Dr Lloyd that for the time being my AP should be retained.

During the period in which the future of my treatment remained in doubt, Dr Batten had kept my lung deflated by pressing more air into the pleural cavity around it every few days. He would enter the room, followed by a nurse wheeling a medical trolley. I had to lie on my side and Batten would press a hollow needle connected to a rubber tube into the right side of my chest. He would then pass air through the tube until he was satisfied that my right lung was scarcely functioning.

When I had been in the Brompton Hospital for three

months I asked Dr Batten how long it would be before I could resume a normal life. He replied that it was too soon to answer my question with any degree of accuracy. I would have to go to Midhurst sanatorium first, and the waiting list there was so long that I would probably have to wait until the early spring before they had a vacancy for me. It would then be for the consultants at the sanatorium to decide when I was fit enough to be discharged. Later, I repeated this conversation to Norman and he assured me that I could commence my pupillage with him whenever I was ready to do so.

Bert was taken to the theatre a second and a third time. He withstood the operations well and suffered no complications. Gradually his tuberculosis had ceased to be active.

Christmas passed by; the second Christmas I had spent in hospital within five years. There was the same forced hilarity, the same simulated joyfulness and then once more we returned to the dreary round of blanket baths, bedpans, inactivity and boredom.

Since my first day in the Brompton I had kept a diary in which I recorded my thoughts and my reactions. I had some idea that it might help me to stand aside and to see myself impersonally, for I recalled that Oscar Wilde had written in his moving account of his own experiences, "To become the spectator of one's life is to escape the suffering of life."

Just before midnight on the last day of the year, I wrote in my diary:

"I have never lost confidence and I will not do so now.

I still hope to be cured by next summer and to resume work in the autumn."

Early in January, Dr Lloyd told me that he was pleased with my progress and that henceforth I could have two pillows in my bed instead of the one to which I had been previously restricted. In February he gave me permission to get up once every morning to walk along the corridor to the nearest lavatory. My chart, which until then had been marked "Absolute Rest" was now altered to "Once a day - toilet."

Bert was ahead of me; he was allowed to sit in an armchair for half-an-hour every afternoon. His mother and father had been there the first time he had left his bed. They had stood watching him spell-bound, with tears of sheer happiness clouding their eyes.

The sanatorium at Midhurst did not have a vacancy for me until the beginning of March, after I had been in the Brompton Hospital for very nearly six months. I travelled down to Sussex in the back of an ambulance. Noreen came with me as I had been told I must arrange for some relative or friend to accompany me on the journey. I sat up in the stretcher bed looking out of the window at my side. I was fascinated to see again the busy London streets, the people, the cars, the buses and the shops. Later, when we had left the urban areas behind us, I was surprised by the greenness of the fields, the bushes and the trees, because I had last seen the countryside the previous September, and the images of the early autumn were still implanted in my memory.

In outward appearance Midhurst Sanatorium resembled

a hotel or large country club. Everything about it was hospitable and friendly.

I was put into a medium-sized single room on the first floor. Almost the whole of the outer wall was taken up by windows and a glazed door, which led on to an unpartitioned balcony, extending along the side of the building. When I looked out I could see two tall magnolia trees, smothered in blossom, surrounded by a well-kept lawn; and beyond them a profusion of flowers stretching away to a thick pine forest. The gentle slopes of the South Downs in the background looked deceptively close and well-defined in the lukewarm sunshine. Here, I thought, was a place where I was bound to recover.

Several of my fellow-patients came in to see me on the day of my arrival; from them and from the nursing staff I learnt about the internal administration of the sanatorium.

Midhurst was entirely self-contained with its own shop, post office, and hairdressing salon inside the main building. The sanatorium was not arranged in wards as such, but the equivalent unit was the "floor" consisting of about 20 patients in the charge of a Sister with her own staff of nurses and orderlies. The male and female patients had separate floors; otherwise there was no segregation of the sexes.

The patients were passing through different stages in their recovery from tuberculosis, varying from those who were still completely bedridden to those who were on the verge of their discharge and were going out for a couple of short walks every day. It was expected that patients who were up and about would carry out certain duties to assist those who were still immobile, such as posting their letters, distributing their newspapers, and buying what they needed from the sanatorium shop. The person responsible for the allocation and fulfilment of these tasks was the "Floor Representative." All the floor representatives were ex-officio members of the patients' General Purposes Committee, which also had its chairman and other officers, including an entertainments secretary who was in charge of the internal broadcasting system, connected to earphones in all the bedrooms. The committee met regularly to consider the interests of the patients and to liaise with the sanatorium staff.

The participation of the patients in so many of the arrangements concerned with their own welfare was a unique feature of the Midhurst administration. It served to create a sense of fellowship between them and the medical authorities.

As a general rule, Midhurst only accepted patients who were thought to have a good chance of recovery, and the medical routine was designed to provide a very gradual return to a fairly normal lifestyle. On my arrival I was graded "ILO" which meant that I was allowed to walk along the corridor to the lavatory once every day. For the rest of the time I could sit up in bed, except during the "rest hour" between midday and one o'clock in the afternoon, and between half-past five and half-past six in the early evening. Rest-hours, the beginning and the end of which were indicated by electric gongs sounding throughout the sanatorium, were compulsory for all the patients. While they were in progress we had to lie down on our beds; although we were allowed to read and to listen to the radio, talking and writing or any form of activity were strictly forbidden.

All the ambulant patients on my floor came to visit me during my first few days in the sanatorium. Several were senior serving officers, including a general, a Naval captain, and a brigadier, but for the most part they were men about my own age who had contracted tuberculosis whilst in the forces during the recent war; a number of them had been prisoners in Germany and the Far East. The youngest patient on the floor was an 18-year-old public schoolboy.

An event which we either looked forward to in hope, or dreaded in apprehension, was the weekly round of Dr Geoffrey Todd, the Medical Superintendent of Midhurst. It was then that we learnt of our prospects for the immediate future - in particular, whether we were going to be upgraded, left on our present gradings, or considered for the possibility of surgery.

I always had plenty of people, both family and friends, who came to see me at Midhurst. The sanatorium encouraged patients to maintain as close a contact as possible with the world outside, and very few restrictions were imposed on external visitors in regard to the times or to the duration of their visits. Eve used to drive over from Portsmouth frequently and my mother, Arnold or Noreen would come down from London on a Sunday afternoon.

In spite of the imperfections of my AP, which were mechanical rather than medical, Dr Todd thought that it should be continued for a few years and that I should need weekly refills of air while it lasted. My tuberculosis was now quiescent and I was allowed, slowly and gradually, to progress through the escalating sanatorium grades, each of which enabled patients to spend more time out of bed and increased their permitted mobility.

As a rule I was upgraded every fortnight. I passed through the initial stages of advancement. For two weeks I was allowed to walk to the lavatory whenever necessary and then for another two weeks I was at liberty to wander around on my own floor in my dressing-gown, visiting other patients and sitting in their rooms. Next, the milestone of getting up for dinner, and the thrill of putting on clothes for the first time after over seven months in pyjamas. Then successively being allowed up for tea and dinner; for lunch, tea and dinner; and finally for all meals including breakfast. The most advanced grade was known as "Exercise." This consisted of going out by yourself or with other patients for carefully measured walks in the vicinity of the sanatorium, first every morning and later both in the morning and in the afternoon.

At first it was all excitement. Walking about fully dressed; the companionship at the tables in the dining-room; and the casual affability of the lounges. However, the initial exhilaration soon gave way to a sense of anti-climax. This was a closed, secluded society. The inmates, for the most part, had a wraith-like intangibility. They seemed to have detached themselves from their previous existence and to be half-afraid of ever returning to it. Both in conversation and in outlook they were entirely parochial. Their lives were governed by the sound of the electric gongs which directed them where they must go and what they must do, and apart from that, the majority were content to pass their days in apathy and idleness.

The whole regime was devised to spare the patients from the traumas, the responsibilities and the worries of normal living; its side-effect was to weaken their self-reliance and their resolution. There was a patient on my floor, a town planning officer, who had been at Midhurst for a long time and had become thoroughly institutionalised. Despite the fact that he had a wife and family, and his job was being kept open for him, he dreaded being discharged from the sanatorium. A week before he was due to leave he appeared to have had a violent haemorrhage during the night, saturating his sheets and pillowcases with blood. The Floor Sister was suspicious. She sent his bed-linen for analysis and it was discovered that the stains had been caused by red ink.

It was inevitable that there would be flirtations and romances among the patients, who had so much time on their hands and so little to occupy their minds. Dr Todd appreciated the situation and was tolerant about it. However, he cautioned us frequently that both parties in an act of sexual intercourse expended the same amount of energy as they would have done in taking a five-mile walk, and that any of us who indulged ourselves that way might cause a serious setback in our treatment. I doubt very much if there were many patients foolhardy enough to disregard his warning.

Geoffrey Todd was an Australian who had come to Britain as an army doctor in the First World War. He remained here to specialise in chest diseases and had become one of our leading consultants in tuberculosis. He had never lost his obvious Sydney accent; a lot of people thought that he had deliberately maintained it. Somehow it fitted with his laconic manner, and his succinct, positive approach to every decision he was required to make. I found myself working with him fairly closely as I was elected to be chairman of the General Purposes Committee, and I learnt to admire and to respect him. He was always anxious to keep abreast of the views of the patients on every aspect of the sanatorium routine, and he told me once that his position as Medical Superintendent required him to be as much a psychologist as a physician.

It was Dr Todd who suggested to me that I should write a mock trial to be acted by the patients and broadcast over the internal system. There were several professional actors and actresses passing through the final medical grades at the time and they all supported this proposal enthusiastically. With their assistance I wrote a semi-humorous script about the trial of a nurse for the attempted murder of a doctor at a sanatorium. We rehearsed every evening for a week and then gave the actual broadcast before an audience composed of staff and patients. The performance was well-received, the ability of the cast compensating for the shortcomings of the plot and the dialogue.

I had been going out for a one-mile walk twice a day for several weeks before Dr Todd told me that I was well enough to be discharged, but he warned me that I would have to live very quietly for the next year, going to bed early and lying down for an hour every day in the afternoon. Arrangements would be made, he said, for me to attend a clinic once a week to get my AP refilled with air.

"I know you're not going to take my advice," he went on, "but I'm going to give it to you none the less. Even if your tuberculosis remains dormant you won't be fully cured for four or five years. I think you'd be very foolish to try to practise at the Bar. You'd have much more chance of staying fit in some non-exacting sedentary occupation."

"I still intend to be a practising barrister," I told him.

He shrugged his shoulders. "Very well," he commented. "It's for you to choose between giving yourself the chance of making a complete recovery, or embarking on a course which might well land you up in Midhurst again."

It was then the last week in July and I had been told to continue my convalescence for the remainder of the summer. This fitted in with my plans as the best time for me to commence my pupillage would be at the start of the legal term the following October.

Noreen and Norman were living in a flat in the Temple. They had recently rented a house in an Essex village so that they could leave London at the weekends and during the vacations. They were going to be there for the whole of August and they had suggested that I should stay with them for a few weeks directly after my discharge from Midhurst.

During the afternoon on my last day at the sanatorium I received a telephone call from Eve.

"Norman had a stroke this morning," she said. "He's now in a London nursing-home, and he's still unconscious."

"Probably he's been overworking," I suggested. "He may be in need of a good rest."

"It's far worse than that," she replied. "The doctors say he won't come round again - it's a matter of hours."

Norman died that night.

I was reluctant to impose myself as a guest on Noreen at such a time, but she insisted that I should come to stay with her. She intended to be at their country house for the month of August, as her 11-year-old daughter, Miranda would be home from boarding-school for the summer holiday. Noreen assured me that they would both appreciate my company during so sad a period in their lives.

CHAPTER 19

Soon after Norman's death his close friend, Conolly Gage, offered to take me as a pupil in his stead. I was immensely grateful because, although I did not know him at all well, I had always found him charming, likeable and amusing.

Conolly, who was then in his mid-forties, had been a member of Norman's small set of chambers which had closed down in 1939. Throughout the war he had served in the Judge Advocate General's Department and directly he was demobilised he had joined Norman in Victor Russell's chambers, where he had soon built up a busy common law practice. He also took a keen interest in politics and was a staunch Ulster Unionist. Since 1945 he had represented one of the Northern Ireland constituencies in the House of Commons.

In those days the Bar was generally regarded as a predominantly male occupation for the well-to-do. The difficulties, both of starting and continuing in the career were widely recognised. It was extremely hard for the new entrant to find himself a tenancy in good chambers, and if he was successful in doing so he could only expect to earn a very meagre income for the next three to four years; even established barristers were often haunted by the lurking spectre of brieflessness. In spite of these discouragements there was never any lack of candidates for the profession.

During the immediate post-war years the Inns of Court were overcrowded with wishful and aspiring pupils, as the customary annual intake of newly called barristers had been swollen by a six-year backlog of ex-servicemen. The numbers were further increased by the fact that more girls than ever before were reading for the Bar.

*The author's father
and his elder brother
Sydney at their home
in the south of Ireland*

*The author's father
on his graduation
from Trinity College, Dublin*

The author's mother
at the time of her marriage

The author's elder brother
Arnold as a cadet
on board H.M.S. Conway,
the merchant navy training ship

*The author's first term
at prep school in 1928*

*The author when he was
first commissioned
in the autumn of 1940*

*A group of wounded officers (the author is second from the right)
at St Hugh's College, Oxford,
which was used as a military hospital in the war*

*The marriage of the author's sister Eve
to Lieutenant Peter La Niece R.N. in 1948*

The author as a Circuit Judge in 1972

The author with Mr Justice Warner, leader of the British delegation
(second from left) and two foreign delegates at a meeting
of the International Society of Judges in Oslo

At a meeting of the International Society of Judges in Senegal

*The author with a newly-called barrister and his family
after a call-to-the-Bar ceremony in the Middle Temple*

A happy occasion when Princess Diana, a Royal Bencher of the Inn, was dining in the Middle Temple in November 1990

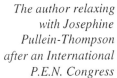

The author relaxing with Josephine Pullein-Thompson after an International P.E.N. Congress

A family gathering with Peter La Niece and some of his family

MESSAGE FROM PRESIDENT ROBINSON

I am very pleased to convey warmest congratulations to Judge Anthony Babington on his election as an Honorary Bencher of King's Inns. It is an honour well deserved and I join with the members of King's Inns in celebrating the occasion and in extending a welcome to him and to their other guests from the Middle Temple. I remember my own great pleasure when I was made an honorary member of King's Inns and of the Middle Temple.

At a time when the links between our two islands are growing ever stronger and when we have so much in common, including the similarities in our legal systems, the close ties that have long existed within our respective legal professions are increasingly important. The election of Judge Babington as an Honorary Bencher further strengthens those links and is very welcome.

MARY ROBINSON
PRESIDENT

A message of congratulation from Mary Robinson,
then President of Ireland, when the author was elected an
Honorary Bencher of King's Inns, Dublin, in July 1995

There were seven barristers in Victor Russell's chambers, three of whom had two pupils each. The six pupils occupied a small room in which each of us had his own table. Apart from accompanying our Masters whenever they went into court, we were supposed to assist them with their paper-work. A pupil would select a set of case-papers, still awaiting his Master's attention, and would write out his own draft for the pleading, divorce petition, opinion or whatever else was required by the Instructing Solicitor. In due course the Master would discuss the draft with him and, if necessary, would point out any errors it contained.

Apart from the barristers and the pupils there were four secretaries in chambers, who had a room to themselves. There was also a clerk's room for Fred, the senior clerk, and his two assistants.

Fred had to arrange the barristers' work, negotiate their fees and manage their accounts. For this he was richly rewarded as he received 10 per cent of all their professional earnings. In a way, he was the most important person in chambers, and this was certainly his own view of his position. The other clerks were paid fixed salaries. The younger of the two, who was still a boy, was never entrusted with any real responsibility; he made the tea every afternoon, carried books in and out of court for the barristers, and ran messages. Fred, as he sometimes reminded the pupils, had himself started his own working life in the Temple in such a manner as that.

All my fellow-pupils had served in the army during the war, with the exception of a South African who had been too young for military service. There was a good deal of friendly rivalry between us as we were aware that the chambers had room for another member, and although none of us had been promised a tenancy at the end of his pupillage, Fred had hinted darkly that someone would be kept on to fill the vacancy.

We represented the new style of entrants to the barristers' profession, as only one of the six of us was a man with private means. All the rest had their own plans for financing themselves during the lean years which would lie ahead of them if they should be fortunate enough to find places in chambers and to get started in practice. The most common method they chose was lecturing on legal subjects at night-schools. Some people preferred to work at home, correcting papers submitted by students reading law on correspondence courses, but I was told this was tedious work, and very poorly paid. Others took part-time jobs entirely unconnected with the law. A pupil in one of our neighbouring sets of chambers was regularly employed in the evening by the Savoy Hotel restaurant assisting with the washing-up.

Directly I commenced my pupillage I started to write short, chatty articles for motoring journals about various aspects of the law which affected the car driver. These were nearly always accepted for publication. I wrote occasionally for country magazines as well, on such rustic matters as the legal liability of the owner when his dog worries cattle or sheep. With the money I earned from writing and my disability pension, I was enabled to meet my living expenses and to avoid running into debt.

Apart from a tendency to tire quickly I was feeling

reasonably fit. For the initial month of my pupillage I only came to the Temple in the morning and I spent the afternoon resting at home. After that, I gradually increased my working hours until they were the same as those of the other pupils in the chambers. Noreen had kept on her Temple flat and she gave me a key so that I could go in every day after lunch to lie down for an hour.

On Wednesday afternoons I had to go to the Brompton Hospital at three o'clock for my weekly refill of air to keep my right lung sufficiently deflated. The general refill-clinics at the hospital were very crowded, and I had been told that in order to avoid a long wait, I could join a special small clinic which had been started for doctors and nurses with APs. As there were usually only four or five of us there we seldom encountered any delay. Even so, I often thought how difficult it might be to keep my appointments every week after I had started in practice.

Meanwhile I was enjoying my pupillage immensely. Apart from the valuable tuition I was acquiring from watching Conolly at his work, I was being initiated into the calling I had always longed to follow. I was experiencing from the inside the congenial fellowship of a barristers' set of chambers; I was witnessing the immutable conventions and the inviolable code of conduct which govern the whole of a barrister's professional life.

When Conolly Gage was appearing in court his other pupil, John Newey, and I sat in the row behind him with his Instructing Solicitor. We were meant to take a longhand note of the evidence given by the witnesses, so that he would know exactly what they had said. My dyslexia greatly impaired my capability as a note-taker - my sudden confusion as to the shape of words and the absurdities of my spelling. In the course of time I developed my own phonetic form of shorthand, completely unintelligible to any one except myself, which I could transcribe with a fair degree of accuracy. After a case was finished Conolly would discuss it with his pupils telling us the ways in which he had tried to handle the various witnesses.

As well as his civil work Conolly had an extensive divorce practice. Several times a week during term-time he would hurry across the Strand to the Royal Courts of Justice with a bundle of undefended petitions in his robe-bag. At that time the English divorce law had reached the heights of fatuity. Most of the undefended petitions had been connived in advance and the court proceedings for the granting of a decree nisi was usually a pompous charade. The entire hearing would last for about 15 minutes, with the petitioner giving evidence on oath concerning the disintegration of the marriage. In theory, all the faults were on the side of the absent respondents. Petitioners who had committed adultery themselves were under a solemn obligation to make a full confession in writing, and to "humbly crave" that discretion should be exercised in their favour. There was a tense moment when the Judge was reading the discretion statement and deciding whether the facts set out in it would justify him in overlooking the venial act, or if the grant of the decree must be refused. It was usually stated in these statements, which were invariably settled by counsel, that at the moments when they fell from grace the petitioners were feeling "lonely and depressed." It must have been taken for granted by the divorce Judges that a natural prerequisite for adulterous lovemaking was the state of loneliness coupled with the depression of one of the participating parties.

Most days I lunched in Middle Temple Hall, where a group of about 20 of us always sat at the same long table. It was a random convergence of men from different chambers who had no previous links with one another. The only factor we had in common was that we were all in the process of starting at the Bar. A simple relationship was soon established between those of us who habituated what we were presumptuous enough to regard as being "our table." Several of my lunch-time companions became my close friends and have remained so ever since. Others remained casual acquaintances. Later, they went their various ways in pursuance of their careers; one ended up as a Law Lord and two spasmodic lunchers at the table became Cabinet Ministers.

We all felt a considerable pride in our membership of the Inn. We never regarded it as a soulless institution or a purposeless anachronism. It meant something very real to us. Each time we entered Middle Temple Hall we were conscious of its age-old traditions and the permanence of its values. The atmosphere was impregnated with history - in part, the living history of England: in part, the history of lawyers and the law. We felt a curious sense of proximity to the ghosts surrounding us, so that the past and the present merged together in a timeless continuity.

Middle Temple Hall, which had been built during the reign of Queen Elizabeth I, looked particularly impressive on the evenings when dining was taking place. The long tables under the magnificent double hammerbeam roof; the elaborately-carved oak screen, flanking the minstrel's gallery; the walls adorned with panels bearing the coats of arms of the past Readers, who at one time were responsible for the teaching of the Inn's students; and at the far end, the massive portraits of former monarchs dominating the High Table at which the elders of the Inn, the Benchers, were sitting.

I only dined in Hall on special evenings. There was an occasion when the Queen, our Royal Bencher, was present, and another when Winston Churchill and Clement Attlee both attended as guests. This was the first time that most of us had seen Churchill in the flesh. After dinner we crowded around him begging him to say a few words. He removed his cigar from his mouth, smiled benignly and proclaimed above the clamour, "Jolly good luck to all of you!"

One summer afternoon towards the end of my pupillage I met Conolly Gage in Kings' Bench Walk when I was returning from lunch.

"I've been waiting for an opportunity to get you on your own," he said. "It's about time we had a little chat about your future. Let's take a turn in the garden before we go back to chambers."

We strolled through the iron gateway to the spacious lawn of the Inner Temple garden where other barristers were ambling around in the warm sunshine.

Conolly was silent and thought for a while. Then he said, "I find it difficult to tell you this, Tony. You're one of the people to whom we all owe a huge debt - a debt we can never adequately repay, but I think it's time for you to face the facts and to accept your limitations. The Bar is a harsh taskmaster; even for the 100 per cent fit it's hard enough. For someone with your disabilities it would be quite impossible. For instance, your voice - your hesitancy of speech. It would be an awful handicap in court. Then there are your physical disabilities, your arm and your leg; to say nothing of your TB and your collapsed lung. I think you'd be far better off, and far happier, in some quiet office job. I'm sure the Government Legal Service would fit you in somewhere, in view of your war record."

I told him that the last thing I wanted was the chance of being "fitted" into a sheltered position, mainly for reasons of compassion. My only desire was to carry on in my chosen career as a barrister; to work beside my colleagues in chambers, sharing with them all the vicissitudes of their professional lives. Above all, I wished to be treated by them as an ordinary, normal human being.

"Very well," he said. "I've offered you my advice, but it's quite obvious you don't intend to take it. I'll give you all the help I can in finding yourself a tenancy somewhere."

After a moment he went on, "There's one thing more you should realise. No head of chambers will take on a new tenant without the agreement of his clerk, and the clerk will almost certainly ask Fred what he thinks of you. I'm afraid Fred's going to tell him all about your health problems, with the inevitable result. A senior clerk relies on the tenants in his chambers for his income, and I'm afraid, to put it bluntly, most clerks would consider you a bad bet."

It soon became apparent that none of the six pupils were

going to be offered places in our present chambers, so we all had to commence the dispiriting task of trying to find vacancies elsewhere. That was a time before the introduction of a Government-financed legal aid scheme, and the costs of civil litigation were borne entirely by the litigants. This meant that far fewer people were willing to go to law. In consequence, unless a barrister at the outset of his career had personal contacts with solicitors who were willing to send him work, it was extremely difficult for him to get started in practice.

In a busy set of chambers there were various ways in which the senior clerk could find work for a new tenant. The most common method was by arranging for him to have a "returned" brief. Time and again the barrister who had been briefed originally would find at the last minute that he was unable to do the case, either because he was tied up in a trial which was taking longer than had been anticipated, or because two of his cases had been listed on the same morning in different courts. The clerk would explain the predicament to the Instructing Solicitor and would inquire whether the brief could be returned to another member of chambers. In all likelihood the solicitor would agree and the transfer would take place.

On other occasions a solicitor would want to brief a particular barrister who was not going to be available on the day of the hearing. The clerk would usually suggest that the brief should be entrusted to someone else in his chambers, and he would often add, whether or not it was true, that "Mr So-and-so" had recently been doing a lot of cases of a similar sort to this.

Tenancies in active sets of chambers were very difficult to obtain. There were plenty of other chambers, however, with very little work, which were only to pleased to have a new tenant who would pay rent and would contribute to the general expenses, even though he was destined to come in each day to an empty desk.

I sent innumerable letters to heads of chambers asking if they would consider me as a new tenant, but the answer was always the same; either they were full already or else they were keeping their future vacancies for their own pupils. Eventually, I remembered that when Mr Justice Pritchard had signed my call papers he had told me that I must not hesitate to come and see him if I needed his help, so I wrote to him about my difficulty in finding a tenancy. The day he received my letter he sent me a message that he would see me next morning before he went into court, in his room in the Royal Courts of Justice.

Mr Justice Pritchard, universally known as "Freddy" Pritchard, was one of the most popular Judges on the High Court Bench, mainly because of his incessant kindliness and his impish sense of humour. He was short and slight in stature but he bristled with energy. A lot of people expected that one day he would become Lord Chief Justice.

When I was seated in an armchair in his room, he said, "I'm very sorry you're having trouble finding chambers. Norman told me shortly before he died that Victor Russell intended to offer you a tenancy when you'd finished your pupillage - but it doesn't seem to have worked out that way."

"Perhaps the clerk didn't like the idea," I suggested,

remembering Conolly's words.

The Judge nodded. "Yes, that's a definite possibility. Most clerks have their own ideas."

I asked him to tell me very frankly if he thought I was foolish in wanting to practise at the Bar.

"Why ever not?" he exclaimed.

I mentioned that my speech would never be normal.

"There's nothing at all the matter with it," he said emphatically. "If you think this is the life for you, you should stick it out, no matter what happens, and in spite of what anyone says to you."

A week later Freddy Pritchard rang me at home to tell me that he had spoken about me to Gerald Howard, a well-known King's Counsel and a Member of Parliament. "Gerald wants to meet you as soon as possible," he said, "and if he likes you he'll take you into his chambers."

The following morning I phoned Gerald Howard and he arranged to see me that afternoon. When I called at his chambers he was still in court, but he had left a message asking me to come back again at six o'clock, and meanwhile to have a talk with Arthur, his clerk.

Arthur took me into Gerald Howard's room and we both sat down. I told him right away that I had been severely wounded in the war, and I said that if he preferred to have people in chambers who were perfectly fit, I would understand.

"I know all about what happened to you, Sir," he replied. "If Mr Howard wants you to join us I certainly wouldn't raise any objections; in fact we would all welcome you here. "We're a happy set of chambers and I'm sure you would like the other tenants."

Arthur then told me what rent I would have to pay and how much I would have to contribute towards chambers' expenses. He explained that they were not a busy set, but they had a steady supply of work coming in. Gerald Howard spent a great deal of his time on his parliamentary activities. The senior junior, Garth Moore, was a Cambridge don who did most of his legal work from his rooms at the university. Next after him on the list of members came Edward Robey, a son of the great comedian George Robey, who had spent a number of years in the Director of Public Prosecutions' office and who now had a large criminal practice.

"The other members here," Arthur went on, "are younger men, like yourself, who took part in the war. Two of them actually passed their exams in prison camps."

Later that evening I met Gerald Howard. He was middle-aged, tall and portly with a dignified Edwardian appearance. In manner he was charming, if somewhat remote. After talking to me for about 20 minutes he offered me a tenancy in his chambers. He apologised for having no spare accommodation, but he told me that I could move my desk into a corner of his large room, which he very rarely used as Arthur generally sent round his papers to the House of Commons.

My new chambers were on the first floor of an unmodernised building in which there was no lift and no central heating. Nevertheless, they were extremely comfortable. Gerald Howard's room was well furnished with his capacious oak working table in the centre, a few leather armchairs, and shelves full of legal volumes on all the walls. My own desk was put in a corner by a window overlooking the broad expanse of King's Bench Walk. Every morning when I came in there was a closely packed coal fire blazing cheerfully in the hearth.

The atmosphere in chambers was relaxed and friendly; the clerks were most obliging, and other tenants seemed to accept me as a colleague right away. It was customary for all of us to gather in one of the rooms every afternoon for a cup of tea and a chat. On these occasions I learnt quite a lot about the peculiarities of the Judges who sat permanently at the Old Bailey and at London Sessions. I was told that a plea in mitigation on behalf of a convicted defendant must be adapted according to the temperament of the Judge on the Bench. Some of them paid particular regard to war service; some to youthfulness; some to encroaching age; and some to domestic circumstances. One of them, known to be romantically inclined, was especially lenient to defendants with pregnant girl-friends; if the lady in question could be produced in court it was particularly advantageous.

I was reconciled to a long period of inactivity before I could hope to get any work, so I passed the time writing articles for magazines. During my second week as a tenant Arthur gave me two returned briefs, the first a plea in mitigation in a London Magistrates' Court, and the second a simple, undefended divorce petition. In my third week, he managed to get me a two-day Poor Prisoners' Defence at Kingston Quarter Sessions, returned to him by another set of chambers which had no one available to do it. Although my client was convicted by the jury, the Instructing Solicitor told me he was pleased with the way I had handled the case, and he promised to send me more work in the future.

I had been aware of the stabbing pains on the right side of my chest for several days before I was forced to admit to myself that they were a physical reality. Also, I knew that I was running a slight temperature. But I continued to hope that these symptoms were not indicative of any serious trouble, and that they would vanish as suddenly as they had started.

At length I could deceive myself no longer; the pains were becoming more persistent and my temperature seemed to be creeping higher. Reluctantly I rang up the Outpatients Department at the Brompton Hospital, and I was told to come round for an examination without delay.

I was seen by the duty physician who peered at my chest through an X-ray screen.

"Yes," he said, "just as I thought. You've got some fluid on your right lung - an attack of pleurisy. It shouldn't be serious. Go to bed and rest for two days; then come back and we'll look at you again."

After two days I was feeling worse and I was having a certain amount of difficulty in breathing. When I returned to the Brompton I was seen by the same doctor. In the X-ray room he spent a long time examining my chest through the screen. "I'm afraid there's a lot more fluid since you were last here," he said. "We'll have to detain you as an emergency patient. You live very near, so your night things, and whatever else you need, can be sent round."

My heart sank at the prospect of another confinement in the Brompton Hospital. The long hours of enforced idleness, the absence of privacy, the servility of helplessness and the condemnation to an indefinite sentence of detention.

In desperation I said, "Must I go into hospital? Couldn't I rest at home?"

He shook his head. "That would be quite impossible. I cannot let you out of here in your condition. You're very ill and in need of constant observation."

He went away to arrange for my admission and returned a few minutes later accompanied by a porter, wheeling a chair. In spite of my protests he made me sit in it.

"I'll come and see you during the evening," he said. "You'll be starting on antibiotics immediately and we'll give you something to help you sleep tonight."

Under the post-war Labour Government officer-pensioners had lost the privilege of being treated in hospitals as private patients, so I was taken to a public ward containing 10 beds only one of which was vacant. I heard later that the previous occupant had died that morning.

Each of the beds had a wooden chair on one side of it, and a small locker on the other.

I was wheeled to the empty bed and a nurse put screens around it.

"You'd better sit in your chair until your pyjamas arrive," she said. "And you'll have to arrange for your day-clothes to be taken away. There's nowhere to keep them here, and you probably won't be needing them again for quite a while."

CHAPTER 20

My second spell at the Brompton was unpleasant in every respect. This was partly due to my mental state, for I was plumbing the lowest depths of dejection, bordering on despair. I had recently been presented with an ideal opportunity to start on my career at the Bar, and now it was being snatched away from me: I had imagined that I had come to terms with the after-effects of my war wound, and now I was back again in hospital, indefinitely excluded from leading a normal life. It was also partly due to my physical condition. I was running a high temperature; I was never free from the pain in my chest; and the antibiotics I had been prescribed - PSA to be taken orally and streptomycin given as a deep injection - caused me to suffer from perpetual nausea.

My fellow-patients in the ward were an agreeable lot. They were all suffering from pulmonary tuberculosis or, like me, from a complication resulting from the disease. We came from a diversity of occupations. The man in the bed opposite mine had been a constable in the Palestine Police, and my immediate neighbour, who came from the south of Ireland, had been working as a barman in a West End night club. The youngest patient there was a student at the London School of Economics.

I found myself detesting ward life more than I had ever done before. It was not only because of the lack of seclusion, but also because of the continual noise. The shouted conversations, the ribaldry and banter which lasted all day long; and added to this was the incessant jarring sound of distant pop music, as most of the patients used to hang their headphones, switched on, over the tops of their bedsteads.

The meals they gave us were served from a trolley; the food was unappetising and indifferently prepared.

Certain of the regulations imposed on the public patients at the Brompton were totally anachronistic and bore an unpleasing resemblance to the administrations of a workhouse. The admission of visitors to the hospital was an example. Visiting periods were restricted to an hour on Tuesday afternoons, an hour on Friday evenings, and two hours on Sunday afternoons. Relatives and friends had to queue up outside the porter's lodge until the exact moment when they would be permitted to enter the wards. When visiting-time was ended nurses would go round ringing hand-bells, and anyone who remained at a bedside for more than a few minutes after this would be requested to leave. Frequently when a patient had visitors he was taken away to the X-ray department and he might not be returned to the ward until the visiting period was almost finished. It struck me that this was an utterly insensitive procedure. Indeed, I thought at the time, and I have not altered my opinion, that patients undergoing a long and wearisome illness in hospital should be allowed to see members of their families or their friends every day of the week.

Dr Lloyd, my consultant, came to see me on my first Saturday in the ward.

"I can't tell you how sorry I am that this should have happened to you after everything else you've been through," he said. He told me that my AP would have to be abandoned. His main concern at that moment was to get rid of the fluid from my chest. When this had been accomplished he would decide what to do with me next. In the meanwhile, he wanted me to remain sitting up in bed, all day and all night, to counteract my breathlessness.

From then on I was given an aspiration every few days by Dr Lloyd's new house physician. This was a painful process in which he drove a hollow needle into my chest and endeavoured to suck out all the fluid with a syringe. However, each time he did this another pleural effusion took place and I was back where I started.

I wrote to Gerald Howard telling him it looked as though I would be away for quite a while. He replied expressing his sympathy and saying that he had instructed Arthur that I was not to pay any rent or chambers expenses until I was well enough to return to work.

October passed and November without my showing any signs of improvement. My aspirations were discontinued since they were failing to achieve their purpose, but I still had to go on taking PAS and receiving streptomycin injections. Apart from that, Dr Lloyd told me I would just have to wait as patiently as possible for my fever to subside.

And so I spent my third Christmas in hospital within the space of seven years. Once again the tokenism - the synthetic jollity, the paper decorations, the holly and the mistletoe. Once again the underlying reality - the nostalgia and the constant yearning to be back at home.

After supper on Christmas Eve the choir from a local church went round the hospital singing carols. On Christmas Day the ordinary medication was continued but no temperature or pulse readings were taken. A special lunch was served in a lobby, the ambulant patients seated at a long table, and the others eating in their beds, which had been wheeled out of the ward for the occasion.

One morning early in January the Ward Sister said to me, "I've been intending to move you into a side-room, but I haven't had a place for you until now. You'll be moved today. It's much quieter there and I know you'll prefer it."

When my fellow-patients heard that I was leaving them, the LSE student, who was allowed to walk about in his dressing-gown, offered to find out where I would be going. He returned to the ward from his investigations and sat on the end of my bed.

"I'm afraid it's bad news," he said. "They're going to put you in a double room and the windows are just above the kitchen, so you'll get the cooking smells coming up all day long. Worse still, you'll be sharing with a man who's dying very slowly. He's elderly and very bad-tempered."

I was moved into my new room before lunch that day. At first appearance it was bare and bleak. There was a minimum of furniture, a brown linoleum floor, two beds side by side and a window facing out into a courtyard flanked by another wing of the hospital. Mr Trotter, my room-mate, eyed me when I was wheeled in, and then turned over and went to sleep. I was aware of his lean, gaunt face surmounted by a mass of grey hair, and the outline of his shrivelled body under the blankets.

The smell of cooking pervaded the room, as the student in my old ward had warned me that it would. A rancid, greasy stench seeped through the open window.

During the afternoon Mr Trotter spoke to me in a weak, tired voice.

"I hope you won't have many visitors," he said. "I like

quiet - absolute quiet. Don't try to talk to me - I hate chatter. I want to sleep most of the time."

I told him that although I usually had quite a lot of people visiting me, I would do my best to cause him as little disturbance as possible.

The following day several of the nurses came in to see me and to inquire if I liked being in my new room. This was the cause of Mr Trotter's first complaint about my behaviour - the first of a long succession.

"I thought you understood that I wanted absolute quiet," he said angrily. "You must stop these nurses from coming here to gossip with you. Either that, or I'll have to ask Sister to move you elsewhere."

I felt very sorry for him as he seemed to have given up the will to remain alive. In the past he had been a fairly successful architect, and I gathered from what he told me in one of our rare conversations that he had earned quite a lot of money. He was then a widower. His two children came in to see him from time to time, his daughter, who was working as a secretary, more often than his son, an accountant. Neither of them showed any affection for him, and they never brought him flowers or any other presents.

At the end of March, after I had been in hospital for more than six months, my temperature began to subside, but the fluid showed no signs of dispersing.

"That's a start," said Dr Lloyd approvingly. "It's taken a long time, but now it's happening."

He studied my latest X-rays thoughtfully.

"It's difficult for me to decide what to do with you next," he went on. "Normally there'd be the possibility of an operation - a major one. However, we must face the fact that you've been through so much already and there's bound to be a limit to what your constitution can stand. Alternatively, I could start getting you up with your chest as it is, and let you go back to a very restricted way of life."

"You mean, the life of a semi-invalid?" I inquired.

"I wouldn't put it like that," he replied. "There would still be plenty of things you'd be able to do."

He looked at the X-rays again, and then put them down on my bed.

"I think I'd better talk to Mr Price Thomas about you," he said.

At that time Clement Price Thomas was one of the leading thoracic surgeons in Britain. He came round to see me during the following week accompanied by his Registrar, the Ward Sister, and four young junior doctors. He walked up to the side of my bed while the others hung back in respectful silence. I took to him immediately. He was a small, neat man with a kindly manner and without a trace of self-importance or pomposity. We chatted first about a cousin of mine who had once been his surgical registrar. Then, after a pause he said, "I've just been looking at your case-history and your X-rays. You've had a very severe attack of pleuritis which has left your right lung in a bit of a mess, and it isn't going to improve with medical treatment. If you left the hospital with your chest in that condition, you'd live with a sword of Damocles hanging over your head, and you'd probably be back here again inside of 18 months."

I asked him what he thought should be done. I was

annoyed with myself because I sounded so hoarse. I felt in many ways like a condemned prisoner in the dock awaiting the Judge's sentence.

"I want you to allow me to operate on you," he said. "I want you to grant me carte blanche to open up your chest and to do whatever I think is necessary. Once we have put our hands to the plough there can be no turning back. I'll try to remove only one of the two lobes of your right lung, but I might have to take out the whole lung. You can rest assured that I'll leave as much of it as I possibly can. Do you want to think about it before giving me your decision?"

"No," I replied, again in a hoarse croak. "I'll agree to have the operation."

He patted me on the shoulder. "Well done, old chap. Well done," he said quietly. "I'll tell Dr Lloyd what we've agreed."

With that he left the room, followed by the others.

Mr Trotter had been lying on his back with his eyes closed, not sleeping but listening to what was taking place. As soon as they had gone he remarked, "Before your surgery they'll probably move you back to the main ward where they can keep you under observation."

I detected a note of hopefulness in his voice.

I told him I was going to ask Dr Lloyd if I could have my operation at Midhurst, as Clement Price Thomas usually operated there on one day every week. If that could be arranged I might be going down to the sanatorium quite soon.

"I'm afraid you haven't been too happy with me as your room-mate," I added.

His gaze was fixed on the ceiling.

After a moment he said, "You're quite right, I haven't. It isn't anything you've done - it's just something about you. I've heartily disliked you from the moment they brought you into this room."

Then he turned on to his side and went to sleep.

Dr Lloyd agreed immediately with my suggestion. He told me that as I was now on Mr Price Thomas's waiting list I would get a bed at Midhurst within the next two or three weeks. When I asked him about my chances of returning to the Bar he seemed reluctant to commit himself. All I could get out of him was that if I only lost half a lung, and there were no complications, I might be fit enough to practise again, but he still thought I would be wiser to go into some more restful occupation.

While I was waiting for my transfer to the sanatorium I was visited by a girl who lived in the village where Noreen and Norman had their country house. After we had been chatting for a while she told me that an aunt of hers would like very much to come and see me.

"My aunt might be able to help you," she said. "She does healing work and apparently she has some special gift for it. I gather that she just waves her arms about and the sick seem to recover."

People had tried to interest me before in faith healers and wonder remedies to get my paralysed arm functioning again, but I had always declined as I took the view that it was better to persevere with conventional medicine.

My visitor indignantly denied that she was attempting to put me on to a quack commercial cure. Her aunt, Emily

Winteringham, was working as an unpaid volunteer, she said, and her organisation was supported by almost all of the principal Christian denominations.

Eventually we arranged that her aunt would visit me before I left the Brompton and would explain to me how she might be able to help in my recovery.

Mrs Winteringham appeared a few days later during an evening visiting period. She was a lady with a pleasing personality and I liked her from the start. Her manner was bright and humorous, understanding and kind, warm and sincere. In spite of all her manifest normality, she sometimes wore the detached expression of the visionary. We talked for a while about general subjects. Then she asked me how much her niece had explained to me about her work. I replied that I merely knew that she could wave her arms in the air and the sick were miraculously cured.

At that, she burst out laughing.

"Oh no!" she exclaimed. "I can assure you I don't practise any form of black magic - and I play no personal part in curing the sick. I simply intercede on their behalf.

She told me she worked for the Church's Council of Healing, which had been started by the Archbishop of Canterbury at the close of the Second World War. They believed that healing was a threefold process involving the body, the mind, and the spirit. They offered no substitute for the doctor or the surgeon; they only sought to approach curative treatment from an additional angle. If I was willing, she said, she would give my name to one of their prayer groups who would pray for the successful outcome of my operation.

I asked her what I would have to do myself.

"Nothing very much," she replied. "Of course it would help if you could bring yourself to believe in the efficacy of our prayers for you. And perhaps before you go to sleep at night you could tell God that you trust in Him and that you know he will ordain that the best will happen to you."

I told her that I already believed in the power of prayer and I would like her to do what she had suggested.

She stood up. "Good," she said. "Now I must go and visit some more people. I'll look you up at the sanatorium, and you must keep in touch with me. From now on we'll be praying for your recovery."

The Ward Sister told me it would not be possible for me to be taken down to Midhurst by ambulance, as the National Health authorities had made a regulation that ambulances must not be used for journeys of more than a limited distance unless the patients were totally incapable of walking on their own. The most she could do for me, she said, was to send me to Waterloo station by ambulance, and to arrange for another ambulance to be waiting for me at Haslemere, the nearest railway station to the sanatorium.

A friend of mine who had heard of these tentative arrangements said that he would be only too pleased to take me down to Midhurst in his car. I accepted the offer very gratefully as I was feeling somewhat apprehensive at the prospect of embarking on a train journey after I had spent all these months in bed, many of them with a very high temperature.

I asked the Ward Sister if it would be possible for me to go home for a day and a night immediately before I was driven to the sanatorium. She could see no objections to this, provided I continued taking my medication, and she promised to put my proposal to the doctor. I think she understood what was passing through my mind. She knew I had been warned that although there was no reason for believing my operation would not be successful I should, nevertheless, be aware of the risks which would be involved in carrying it out. I did not think I was going to die just yet, but I wanted for a brief moment to recapture the happiness and contentment of my home life in case I should never return there again.

On the morning I left the Brompton Hospital I put on my clothes for the first time since the day of my admission. Noreen picked me up in a taxi soon after breakfast. I felt once again the excitement of seeing the people, the traffic, the shops, and all the wonderful normality of the outside world. I was sorry to have to undress immediately I arrived home, but my regret was tempered by the pleasure of being back in my own bedroom.

My mother would have liked to get the whole family together in the flat. However, that was impossible because several members were not in England. During the previous year Arnold had been offered a very good job with a large food-exporting firm in Auckland and he and Helen had decided to emigrate to New Zealand with their two young children. Peter, now a lieutenant-commander, was at sea serving as the flotilla gunnery officer of the Fourth Destroyer Flotilla, but Eve managed to come up to London for the day bringing her baby son with her.

I had agreed with the other members of my family that

we would not tell my mother anything about my operation until a short while before it happened, so as to shorten the time she would spend in worrying about the outcome.

My brief interlude at home passed all too quickly. In the afternoon a few of my closest friends came in to see me, so I put on my dressing-gown and had tea with them in the sitting-room. When they had gone I went to bed again. My mother, Noreen and Eve had dinner with me in my bedroom, balancing their plates on their knees.

After I put out my light for the night I deliberately tried to keep myself awake because every minute at home was so precious to me, and I begrudged the hours of insensibility which would separate me from the morning. Ever since that conversation with Mrs Winteringham my fears about my operation had been dulled, and I had become much more relaxed and more confident. Finally fatigue overcame me and I drifted off into a tranquil sleep.

My friend collected me with his car just before noon the following day. It was warm and sunny, and he drove at a leisurely speed, stopping for a picnic lunch directly we had reached the open countryside. Then we resumed our journey and arrived at the sanatorium about an hour later. A pretty, auburn-haired nurse showed me to my room, on a different floor from the one I had been on last time, and she insisted that my friend should stay for a cup of tea. When he had gone she told me to undress and get into bed as the floor-doctor would be coming to see me very soon.

Everything in my room was spotlessly clean and freshly painted; the french windows leading on to the balcony were wide open. I went over and looked out. I saw once again the magnolia trees in full blossom, the wisteria-covered alcoves, and in the distance the gentle slopes of the South Downs. I thought of my room at the Brompton, the yard outside, the stale smells from the kitchen, and Mr Trotter permanently crotchety and glowering. As I started to undress I could sense all around me the same atmosphere of serenity and peacefulness that I remembered from my first stay at Midhurst.

Later in the afternoon I was visited by Dr Grant, the floor-doctor, an Australian in the mid-thirties with a natural and amiable manner. He told me I was to remain in this room until Mr Price Thomas was ready to operate on me, when I would be moved over to the surgical block. He did not know how long I would have to wait: probably it would not be more than a month or two. Meanwhile, I would have to stay in bed, but I could get up to use the toilet whenever necessary, and I could take a bath a couple of times a week.

During the evening I had a succession of visits from the other patients on the floor. Most of them were coming to the end of their treatment and were up and about all day. They seemed a cheerful and congenial group of people. I liked particularly our floor-representative, a retired air vice-marshal, who had a quiet charm and dignity; and also, my next neighbour, a playwright with an irrepressible sense of humour.

After I had been back at Midhurst for about a week it had become customary for most of the other patients on my floor to bring their evening milk drinks into my room and to stay there chatting until the night nurse came round and told them it was time for bed. I realised that they had adopted this routine to keep up my spirits, and to stop me from ruminating too much on what lay ahead.

The days passed fairly quickly in spite of my physical inactivity. I read a lot and I had borrowed a record-player and a number of records, mostly Beethoven, Mozart, Haydn and Chopin. Several other patients on the floor were fond of music and we used to have regular concerts in my room.

One morning Clement Price Thomas and Dr Todd came in to see me. Both of them stood at the side of my bed for a moment looking at my temperature, respiration and pulse charts. Then Price Thomas laid a hand on my arm.

"Well, old chap," he said, "the time has come. If you're still willing to go ahead with it, I'd like to operate on you next week. But before you give your final consent, there's one more thing you should know. In view of the paralysis in your right side, if I have to remove the whole of your right lung it may - and it probably will - result in a certain amount of bodily disfigurement. I hope that's not going to alter your decision."

"No," I told him. "I've made up my mind and I'm not going to change it."

"I think you're quite right," Dr Todd commented. "Sometimes we have to risk these consequences when we're dealing with a condition which can only be cured by pretty drastic surgery."

As they were leaving the room Clement Price Thomas turned to me and remarked.

"Bad luck isn't rationed in life, Babington. If it was you'd have nothing to worry about for many years to come."

On the same day Mrs Winteringham turned up on an

unexpected visit in the afternoon while I was having tea.

"I got into my car after lunch," she explained. "I didn't know where I intended to go - I just drove on as the spirit moved me. Then I saw a signpost pointing to Midhurst, so I knew my destination at once."

I told her my operation had been fixed to take place the following week, and she seemed delighted.

"I'm certain that everything's going to work out for the best," she said, "and it will be such a tremendous relief when you get it all behind you."

She did not stay long as she and her husband, a London solicitor, were going out to a dinner in the City that night. Before she left she asked me to let her know the date and the time of my operation so that the group which was looking after me could pray for its successful outcome while it was still taking place.

A few days later I was transferred to the surgical block.

On the last evening before I left the floor all the ambulant patients brought their milk-drinks into my room and toasted the success of my forthcoming operation with Ovaltine and Horlicks. The air vice-marshal apologised most graciously for the obligatory absence of champagne.

CHAPTER 21

My room in the surgical block was small and comfortable. The windows looked out on to a tree-bordered path, known as the Pine Walk, which skirted the sanatorium building and wound away into a thick forest.

I moved there on a Sunday morning, the day before my operation. I had anticipated that the fear and the dread, suppressed for so long, would surface suddenly in my mind during those final 24 hours, but to my surprise I continued to feel calm and relaxed.

The sanatorium Chaplain came in to see me before taking Morning Service. He was a middle-aged, ex-naval padre, who was extremely popular with the patients of every religious denomination. During my first stay at Midhurst I had discovered that he had been a keen oarsman in his younger days, and we had often discussed the various down-Thames regattas at which we had both rowed.

He sat down in the armchair at the foot of my bed.

"Well," he said. "How do you feel about the op?"

"Not as bad as I expected - so far!" I replied.

"Good," he said. "In a very short while it will all be over. You'll be very much in my thoughts tomorrow. I'm sure it's going to be successful. Everything turns out all right in the end for those who love God."

He promised to look in on me again when I had fully recovered from the effects of the anaesthetic.

Noreen and Eve came together in the afternoon. They had told our mother the day before that I was about to have an operation, but they did not go into the details or explain how serious it would be. Nevertheless, she had been very distressed about it and they had had the utmost difficulty in dissuading her from accompanying them to the sanatorium.

I was delighted to see them, but the last moments before they had to leave were harrowing for all three of us. They both had tears in their eyes when they kissed me good-bye.

In the evening I listened to a broadcast concert from the Albert Hall on my radio. The principal work was Beethoven's Seventh, which had always been one of my favourite symphonies. The last movement was drawing to a close when the night nurse, a slim, attractive blonde called Nicky, entered with a tray of medicines and pills.

She told me that she too was very fond of music, and she was having piano lessons every week on her days off. We chatted for a while about our best-loved composers until, after a glancing at her watch, she said reproachfully: "You mustn't detain me here any longer. I have other patients to attend to when I've settled you down for the night. The doctor wants you to take two tablets to make you sleep. I'll be waking you at half-past five in the morning with a cup of tea and some dry toast - I'm afraid it will be the last meal you'll get for some time."

After I had taken my pills she opened the windows and drew the curtains. Then she came over to my bed.

"Are you worried about tomorrow?" she inquired.

"A bit," I replied. "I don't want to die yet. There are so many things I still want to do."

She asked what sort of things I was thinking about and I told her I wanted to visit the Shakespeare Memorial Theatre at Stratford and the opera at Glyndebourne. I added, "It's only when you're facing the possibility of death that you realise how wonderful it is to be alive."

"Try not to worry about it," she said. "If you do, it will keep you awake, and we don't want you to be tired out in the morning."

But that did not happen. Even as she switched off the light and closed the door behind her the tablets were already beginning to take effect.

I did not wake up again until Nicky brought in my breakfast tray and placed it on my bedside table.

"There's no need to hurry," she told me. "When you've finished this you can get up and shave."

I was amazed how tranquil I felt about what was going to happen to me. I was certain it had something to do with Mrs Winteringham and my unknown friends of the Churches' Council of Healing who were praying for me that day.

Nicky came in to collect my tray while I was standing by the basin shaving.

"Good-bye and good luck," she said. "You'll be all right. I was looking at your case-papers last night; this is nothing compared with what you've been through in the past. I'll see you again this evening."

As soon as the day staff came on duty the procedural preparations for my operation commenced. I was given an operation smock to wear and thick woollen stockings, which came up well above my knees. A nurse shaved the hair from my chest, and then gave me the premedication injection.

"This will make you a bit drowsy," she remarked as she inserted the needle. "It wouldn't be a bad idea if you could get a short sleep. They won't be collecting you for half an hour."

She drew the curtains and went out.

Next the loneliness, the heat, the discomfort and the thirst. At last the period of waiting came to an end. The door opened and the theatre orderlies in their white overalls, bustled in with a trolley. And finally the anaesthetist, standing beside me and speaking in a low, kind voice. "I'm the chap who's going to put you to sleep."

In that moment I realised that I was able to look on death without fear; the dark phantom had suddenly lost its terror. I found myself repeating in my mind, 'let the best happen to me.'

I closed my eyes and heard the anaesthetist say: "Hold out your good arm, please. Just a little prick and you'll feel nothing more."

When I came to it was as though I had been in a heavy sleep for several weeks. I felt enfeebled and exhausted.

I opened my eyes fully. Dr Grant and the Day Sister seemed to be giving me a blood transfusion in my foot, and a nurse was standing beside me with her thumb on my pulse. There was something pressed tightly over my mouth and I tried to pull it away, but the nurse grabbed my hand.

"No! Don't do that," she exclaimed. "You still need oxygen."

I was desperate to know the extent of the operation. I lifted the mouthpiece temporarily.

"Doctor, I want you," I croaked. I was so hoarse I could scarcely speak.

He told me to wait for a moment as he was busy. After

he had completed the blood transfusion, he turned to me and asked what was worrying me.

I said weakly. "Was Price Thomas in good form?"

A broad grin spread over his face.

"If he'd been at Lords," he replied, "he'd have scored a certain century."

I lifted the mouthpiece again. "What did he do?" I asked. Dr Grant moved closer to me before answering.

"He removed half of your right lung - the infected half. But it took a long time. You were in the theatre for more than five hours. Relax now and don't talk. You'll need all your strength to recover from what you've been through."

The Sister bent over me with a syringe. "This will ease the pain a bit and send you to sleep," she said, as she gave me an injection in the arm.

The next time I opened my eyes the overhead light was on and it was dark outside the window. Nicky, a watch in her hand, was timing my pulse. When she noticed that I was awake, she whispered.

"I'm glad it went off so well. You'll be able to go to Glyndebourne next summer after all."

Mrs Winteringham rang Noreen in the evening to find out the latest news about my condition. She said that she and another person, who was also praying for me, had both had a sudden intuitive feeling around three o'clock in the afternoon that everything was all right.

Noreen informed her that I had had a lengthy and successful operation which, according to the sanatorium, had finished at 10 minutes to three.

For the next few weeks I was rarely left alone for long during the daytime. Nurses came in constantly to take my temperature, read my pulse, to wash me, to change my dressings or to give me pain-killing injections; a physiotherapist saw me every morning to put me through a course of breathing exercises; and Dr Grant visited me two or three times a day to probe my chest with his stethoscope and test my blood-pressure.

During the night everything was quiet. I found it difficult to sleep for long as I had to sit bolt upright in bed against a wall of pillows. I would wake up feeling cold and stiff with a crick in my neck. If I rang my bell Nicky would bring me a cup of tea and sometimes, when she was not busy, she would stay and talk for a while. Then she would settle my bed-clothes, put out the light, and leave me to try to get to sleep again - or to wait as patiently as possible for the morning.

As my strength commenced to return my thoughts focused increasingly on the future. After I had fully recovered from my operation there seemed to be no reason why I should not return to chambers and try once more to practise as a barrister. I had no illusions regarding the additional disadvantages I would have to face. I would have been away for 18 months and it would be necessary for me to start again from scratch. Even more harmful for my prospects would be the perpetual question mark concerning my health; the fact that many people would not take my aspirations at the Bar at all seriously. I had received several letters from my colleagues in the Temple, doubting the wisdom of my professed intention to return. They pointed out the shortage of work for beginners in a highly competitive profession. The struggle to gain a foothold, they said, was keen, hard and unsparing. Many of my contemporaries had given up already, and had drifted away to safe, salaried jobs in the civil service or in commerce.

While I was still in the surgical block I received a visit one evening from Freddy Pritchard. I was impressed once again by his kindness as he had driven down from London after sitting in the High Court all day, and he looked extremely tired. He wanted to know when I would be returning to chambers and I told him that Dr Todd did not want me to work again until early in the New Year. Freddie said that the date would fit in admirably with what he was going to propose. He was due to go out on the North-Eastern Circuit in mid-January and he would like me, if I felt up to it, to accompany him as his Marshal. I eagerly accepted his invitation as I knew that this would be an excellent reintroduction to my life at the Bar. A Marshal acted as the Judge's ADC and social secretary. He lived at the Judge's Lodgings, accompanied him everywhere he went, and sat beside him on the Bench. Marshalling with Freddie Pritchard would be a most congenial and a most instructive experience.

I remained in the surgical block for three weeks before it became necessary to move me out in order to make room for another patient. Dr Grant had done his best to get me back to my old floor, but as there were no rooms available I had to go to the special floor reserved for officers in the services, or those who had held commissions in the past. It was run on much stricter lines than the rest of the sanatorium by an ex-army nursing Sister who did her best to incorporate an element of military discipline into the customary tolerant Midhurst routine. The patients on the officers' floor had a reputation for being unsociable and morose. This was generally attributed to the fact that they were looked after by a squad of male army nursing orderlies, and not by a bevy of solicitous nurses.

I was not looking forward to being in the charge of "the Dragon," the name by which the autocratic Sister was known throughout the sanatorium. However, once I had moved on to the officers' floor I found it easy enough to get on with her because I complied meticulously with all her regulations, no matter how irksome or unnecessary I considered them to be. As soon as I was sufficiently mobile she invited me to become the floor representative. She told me that I was the only one of her patients who fully appreciated the need for the strict rules which she imposed on us.

Conolly Gage wrote me a letter urging me to think again about returning to the Bar, now that I had been away for such a long time. By chance, he said he had heard that there was a vacancy in the Parliamentary Draftsmen's Office. He had written to the First Parliamentary Draftsman, whom he knew, telling him that I would be admirably suited to fill the position. He had also asked Freddie Pritchard to add his own recommendation. Conolly went on to say that the parliamentary draftsmen were all barristers and their function was to formalise government legislation before it was put before Parliament, so that they had to work very closely with government departments.

This placed me in a quandary. I did not fancy the idea of becoming a civil servant, neither could I feel any enthusiasm at the prospect of spending the rest of my working life drafting Acts of Parliament. On the other hand, I had to accept that my chances of establishing a practice at the Bar were extremely remote, and as I was now 30, if I was going to adopt another career I would have to do so pretty soon. Therefore, with some reluctance, I followed Conolly's suggestion and wrote to the First Parliamentary Draftsman applying for a job in his office.

He sent me a somewhat chilling reply saying that he would be pleased to grant me an interview, but he wanted me to realise that positions in his office were much sought after and I would be up against very strong competition. He told me to notify his secretary as soon as I was discharged from Midhurst and she would arrange an appointment for him to see me.

For some time before this I had been troubled by intermittent pains to the right side of my stomach, becoming slightly worse each time they occurred, but only lasting for a few days before disappearing completely. One of these attacks came on when I had just been promoted to the grade of "lunch, tea and dinner." I reported to Dr Grant, who told me he thought I might be suffering from acute appendicitis, and ordered me back to bed for two days while various tests were carried out. He came to my room to tell me the result. It was not appendicitis after all, he said. It appeared to be some sort of digestive ailment about which nothing could be done. Probably it would not get any worse, but if the pain became severe I could take analgesics for it. Although the future outlook seemed so unpropitious I was thankful that I would not have to undergo another operation.

I reached the final sanatorium grade "Exercise," without any other setbacks. One morning when I was looking at the newspapers after returning from my measured walk, I was shocked to read that Freddie Pritchard had been taken ill the previous day and had been rushed into hospital. I immediately telephoned Noreen to find out if she had any more information about him. She told me that he had suffered a severe stroke and was now in the London Clinic. According to the latest reports it was doubtful whether or not he would live.

The following week I received a letter from another High Court Judge, Sir Geoffrey Streatfeild, whom I had met on one previous occasion when he had been sharing a room with Freddie in the Judges' corridor at the Royal Courts of Justice. He was writing to me, he said, because he knew that Freddie Pritchard had intended to take me on Circuit with him as his Marshal early in the New Year. Sadly, this would now be impossible. Even if Freddie recovered from his stroke it was most unlikely he would ever be able to sit on the Bench again as he was completely paralysed down one side. After the Christmas vacation, Sir Geoffrey continued, he himself would be going out on the Northern Circuit and he would be delighted if I would come as his Marshal. He added that we both had something very important in common, as two years before one of his lungs had been removed by Clement Price Thomas. He could appreciate just how I would be feeling when I went back to work for the first time, and if I ever wanted a day or two off he would fully understand.

While I was still at the sanatorium Dr Todd was awarded a knighthood in the Birthday Honours List. Immediately after I had left, Mr Price Thomas carried out an operation on King George VI at Buckingham Palace and became Sir Clement Price Thomas.

By that time I had reconciled myself to the certainty that Emma had vanished from my life forever. But I frequently had dreams in which she had returned to me and everything was once more as it had been in the past. I would see her walking towards me, quickening her pace in the final moment before we came together. In the instant of waking I would still feel the tightness of her arms around my neck, the softness of her body pressed to mine, and the gentle fondling of her lips. And then would come the awful shock of awareness; the realisation that it had only been a taunting fantasy; and the sense of abandonment, of utter desolation.

I was shopping one morning at Harrods soon after my discharge from Midhurst, and I met a man who had joined my battalion as a second lieutenant a few months before the invasion of Normandy. We went to a restaurant for a coffee and sat at the table for almost an hour discussing old times. He had kept in far closer contact with the regiment than I had done, and he was able to give me the latest news about most of the officers whom we both had known.

Just before we parted he remarked, "By the way, I suppose you heard that your old girl friend Emma got married last year?"

I replied, trying to make my voice sound casual, that

Emma and I had been out of contact with each other since the war.

"I've forgotten who told me," he said. "Apparently her husband is farming somewhere in Rhodesia."

I hoped he would stop talking about her. I wanted him to get up and leave because I felt a sudden overwhelming need to be alone.

After a moment he went on. "She really was a smasher, that girl. I always envied you - quite a lot of us did. We all thought you and she would get married after the war, but obviously it didn't work out like that."

I looked away from him so that he could not see my expression.

"No," I agreed, "it didn't work out like that."

CHAPTER 22

My interview with the First Parliamentary Draftsman was a waste of time for both of us. He had decided before he had seen me that I was entirely unsuited for a job in his office, and I had already made up my mind that I did not want to work there.

I had the feeling that we were merely going through the motions.

After a brief, formal introduction he had sat down behind his desk and had invited me to sit in a chair in front of it. His manner was cold, distant and humourless. What concerned him most, he said, was whether I would be able to cope with the sort of work a parliamentary draftsman had to do.

"All the people I take on have the highest academic qualifications," he went on. "I notice that you have never even taken a university degree. You had a gallant war record, but I must not allow that to cloud my judgment. I'm only interested in your competence to perform the sort of difficult and highly intricate responsibilities I would have to entrust to you."

We left it at that, and for the rest of the time we had talked about general matters. When he showed me out he wished me good luck in my career at the Bar, as though to finalise the prospect of his offering me a job in his department.

As soon as the interview was out of the way I paid a visit to my chambers in the Temple to settle the date of my return to work. I was most distressed to find that my name no longer appeared on the list of tenants either at the entrance or outside the door on the first floor.

I found Arthur by himself in the clerks' room, and he was obviously surprised to see me. When I raised the matter of the removal of my name from the boards he seemed a bit embarrassed about it.

"Frankly, Sir," he said, "none of us thought you'd be coming back here again. I got the impression from Mr Howard that you'd decided to give up the Bar."

Gerald Howard was at the House of Commons, so it was impossible to contact him there and then, but Arthur promised to let him know as soon as possible that I was once more fit and I would like to return to chambers.

A couple of days later I received a charming and apologetic note from Gerald. "I don't know what gave me the impression you were not coming back to us," he wrote. "You've been away for such a long time and I heard you were having a very drastic operation, so I suppose that I stupidly drew the wrong conclusion."

He congratulated me on my recovery and told me I would be welcome to share his room again directly I had finished my spell of Marshalling.

I made a point of finding out as much as possible about Mr Justice Streatfeild before the Assizes commenced. I discovered that, like me, he had never been to a university. During the First World War he had joined the army at the age of 17, pretending he was a year older, and had subsequently transferred to the Royal Flying Corps to train as a pilot. He had been awarded the Military Cross for gallantry in air battles over the Western Front. By the end of the 1930s he was one of the leading silks on the North-Eastern Circuit, and shortly after the Second World

War he had been appointed to the High Court Bench. I was told that he was very happily married and had three attractive daughters, all of whom were single.

During the Christmas vacation the Streatfeilds invited me to dinner at their Kensington house. All three of their daughters were there as well, and I had a chance of seeing what a close-knit, devoted family they were. Lady Streatfeild was natural and homely. She told me that she would be coming on Circuit with her husband, and that while we were staying in the Judges' Lodgings she would do any small sewing repairs to my clothes which became necessary.

One morning in mid-January I travelled by train from London to Liverpool with the Streatfeilds and two other High Court Judges, one of whom was accompanied by his wife. We had a reserved first-class compartment and the three Judges' clerks were in a separate first-class compartment nearby. Although Geoffrey Streatfeild did his best to put me at my ease I felt rather like a junior army officer would feel if he was thrust suddenly into a group of generals.

I had not met either of the other Judges before. Gordon Wilmer, the elder of the two, struck me on first acquaintanceship as being both haughty and aloof, an opinion I was to modify later. His wife, a vivacious lady, was moderately friendly. Colin Pearson, a recent appointment to the High Court Bench, was going out that day on his initial Circuit, and in consequence he seemed slightly shy and subdued. He was reputed to have a brilliant legal mind, and in fact he was destined to finish his judicial career as a Law Lord.

Directly the train pulled out of the station Gordon Wilmer lit his pipe. I wondered, as the atmosphere in the compartment became thickened with tobacco smoke, whether he was aware that one of his fellow-passengers had lost a whole lung and another had lost half a lung.

Just before one o'clock Geoffrey Streatfeild suggested that we might all go along to the dining-car for lunch. Gordon Wilmer agreed to this, but proposed that as the dining car would be filling up, "the Marshall" should hurry on ahead and book two tables. Lady Streatfeild said she would go in advance with me.

The two senior Judges with their wives sat at one table, and Colin Pearson and I sat at another. While we were sipping sherry before we started lunch he said to me, "I know just how you must feel today. We're new boys together in a way."

We were met at Liverpool station by the Under-Sheriff and three chauffeur-driven limousines, which took our party to the Judges' Lodgings, a large house on the outskirts of the city. The domestic arrangements there were presided over by a permanent housekeeper and each of the Judges had his own butler to look after him. When I went up to my room after tea I was pleasantly surprised to find that Geoffrey Streatfeild's butler had unpacked my suitcase for me and had laid out my evening clothes on the bed. He came round later to see if I required any assistance in tying my bow-tie, and he looked faintly disapproving when I told him that I always wore a tie with a made-up bow.

In the train I had sat next to Lady Streatfeild and she

had prepared me for the formalistic procedures I would encounter at a Judge's Lodgings. It was not like staying in a private house, or even in a hotel, she said, because a Judge on Assizes was the direct representative of the Monarch. As such, he even had a perfect right to precede his wife when they were both passing through a door, but no Judges went that far. Nevertheless, she went on, I would notice that whenever we went in to meals in the Lodgings the senior Judge present would invite the ladies to lead the way.

I went down to the drawing-room early that evening, as part of my social duty as a Marshal was to pour out aperitifs for the others.

My last function of the day was to say grace before we all sat down at the dinner-table.

My time at Judges' Lodgings was interesting, pleasurable, and relaxed. After breakfast, which was our only informal meal, Geoffrey Streatfeild and I used to go for a brisk half-hour walk. He had to take sleeping tablets every night and I think he liked to clear his head in the fresh air before starting the day's work. Although I never heard him complain, I suspected that he still suffered a good deal of pain resulting from his operation.

We would all assemble in the drawing-room at 10 o'clock, the Judges in robes, the Sheriff and the Under-Sheriff in court dress, and the Sheriff's Chaplain in clerical vestments. As a Marshal, I had to wear a morning-coat and to carry a black top hat. The three Judge's clerks would be waiting for us in the hall when we were going out, and the cars would pick us up at the front door to drive us in convoy to the courts, preceded by a police car.

Geoffrey Streatfeild was the Judge in commission at the Liverpool Assizes, so he presided over the principal criminal court. The Sheriff, the Under-Sheriff and the Chaplain sat on the Bench to his right; I was beside him to his left, and next to me was Mr Fanthorpe, his clerk.

"Fanny" Fanthorpe, a small, elfish man, with snowy-white hair and a placid temperament, had been Geoffrey Streatfeild's clerk for many years at the Bar. When Geoffrey was appointed a High Court Judge Fanny had insisted on accompanying him, although he could have earned a far larger income by remaining as senior clerk of a very prosperous set of chambers. He was treated as an old retainer by the entire Streatfeild family and he adored them all. Fanny and I became firm friends from the moment we first met.

During the interval which is known in the idiom of lawyers as the "short adjournment" we would be driven back to the Lodgings for lunch. We returned there again when the courts rose late in the afternoon, and tea would be served to us in the drawing-room by the staff. Before we started to change for dinner I used to go with Geoffrey Streatfeild to his study, where he would work for an hour or two on the trial taking place before him. From my point of view this was an immensely instructive period of tuition, as he used to discuss with me not only the legal issues involved, but also the manner in which counsel on both sides were conducting their cases.

Sometimes the Judges entertained guests to dinner at the Lodgings, and I would be responsible for sending the invitations. Quite often they would be asked out to dine by private individuals, societies or organisations, and I was always included in the invitation. The local branch of the Law Society, and the Liverpool Bar, both gave formal assize dinners at which there were numerous speeches, some good and some bad.

The Marshal's only official duty in court was to adjust the black cap on the Judge's head before he passed a death sentence. Fanny, who was responsible for administering the oath to witnesses, suggested that I should swear in some of them to increase my confidence in my voice. It was the first occasion on which I had uttered in public since my head wound; I found it an awesome experience, even to stand up and to repeat aloud the few words that were required of me. After I had done it a few times my nervousness lessened, though it never vanished completely. ·

Geoffrey Streatfeild had only one murder case in his list at Liverpool, the first murder trial I had ever sat through from start to finish. The defendant was a girl in her mid-twenties, charged with killing her illegitimate baby. I have described her appearance in an earlier book, and my recollection of her remains unaltered:

"She would have been attractive, even beautiful, but her eyes were dulled with the shock of her predicament, and her pale face was ravaged with torment and hopelessness. For two-and-a-half days she sat in the dock facing us ... I can picture her still. The dark hair, resting on her shoulders; the thin, drained face; the slight motionless body in a plain black dress, leaning slightly forward in the hard, upright chair, and flanked on either side by two equally immobile women prison officers."

It was a tragic story. Her husband, a vicious ruffian with a record of crimes of violence, had been away from home for several years serving a sentence for a particularly brutal assault. During his absence she had cohabited with a worthless young waster, the father of her child, who had given evidence for the prosecution. Under cross-examination he had admitted without shame that she had been keeping him and that he had never even tried to get work.

Then suddenly and unexpectedly she had been told that her husband's release from prison was imminent. The young man said in evidence that when he had heard the news he had slipped off secretly, taking his possessions with him, and leaving the girl a note telling her that she would never see him again. The day he left her, in a moment of desperation, she had killed her baby by beating its head against a wall, and had planned to dispose of the corpse before her husband arrived home. She had made a full confession in writing to the police, which she had later repudiated. At her trial she gave evidence to the effect that she did not know who had caused the baby's death.

The defending counsel had hinted to the jury that even if they thought that his client had committed the terrible act they should only find her guilty of manslaughter, and not of murder. However, Geoffrey Streatfeild had directed them in his summing up that on the facts before them a verdict of manslaughter would not be a possibility.

The jury retired to consider their verdict early in the afternoon, and while they were deliberating, the High Sheriff, the Chaplain and I went to the Judge's room with him. Geoffrey Streatfeild was opposed to capital punishment and hated passing a death sentence, which at that time was the mandatory penalty for murder. The Chaplain shared his views, and he told me he did not at all relish the prospect of pronouncing from the Bench, as was his duty after the sentence, the sombre invocation "and may God have mercy on your soul."

Fanny, who was a stickler for the correct performance of court procedures, was worried because he thought that I would not be able, with one hand, to open out the black cap, which was kept folded flat. By rights, he told me, I should be standing behind the Judge's chair when I did this. However, he proposed that he should keep the cap out-of-sight at his feet as the jury were returning to court. He would lean down and open it out while the foreman was delivering the verdict. He would then pass it surreptitiously to me so that I could take up my position behind Geoffrey Streatfeild's chair with the black cap already unfolded.

The jury were still out after three hours. I concluded that one or two of them were holding out against convicting the girl because they felt sorry for her and did not want her to be hanged. Fanny believed it was more likely that they were trying to make up their minds whether to recommend her to mercy. Even if they did so, he thought it was very unlikely that the Home Secretary would recommend a reprieve as it had been a brutal and premeditated killing.

At about seven o'clock in the evening the jury had

indicated that they were agreed on their verdict and the court reassembled. While the jurors were filing into their places I was aware of Fanny bending forward and fiddling busily with the black cap on the floor between us. The girl was standing in the dock, her face even paler than usual. The female prison officers on each side of her had moved in close so that they could support her if she collapsed.

The foreman read from a scrap of paper in his hand. "We find the defendant not guilty of murder but guilty of manslaughter. We recommend her to mercy."

I head the audible sigh from the public gallery and the girl slumped down in a dead faint.

Geoffrey Streatfeild immediately adjourned the court. When she had recovered sufficiently he returned and sentenced her to three years' imprisonment.

We were joined at Liverpool by another High Court Judge, Mr Justice Finnimore, a tall, gangling man with a reticent manner. Although never unsociable or lacking in courtesy, he was a bachelor of the sort who always seem slightly ill at ease in the company of women. He brought his own Marshal to the Lodgings with him, so after their arrival I only had to say grace before dinner on alternate evenings.

After the Liverpool Assizes had closed, the four Judges, together with entourages, were driven to Manchester for the commencement of the Assizes there. We moved into the Manchester Judges' Lodgings where the pattern of life for me was much the same as it had been in Liverpool, except that Geoffrey Streatfeild was taking civil instead of criminal cases. I was finding that with the frequency of the social occasions I had to attend with the Judges, I was getting less self-conscious about my speech defect, and I was gradually overcoming my reluctance to take part in casual conversation out of fear of saying words which I could not pronounce properly.

Geoffrey Streatfeild had finished his last case at Manchester two days before the other Judges had completed their lists, so we returned to London ahead of them. During the train journey I left the Streatfeilds for a while to keep Fanny company, as he had a reserved compartment to himself. He loved to talk about the times when he had been running the busiest set of chambers on the North-Eastern Circuit, and I never tired of listening to his reminiscences. At one point he broke off and remarked, "It's a great pity you weren't a member of my old chambers. I'd have got you started in next to no time."

I told him truthfully that I would have had few worries about my future at the Bar if he had been my clerk.

"You'll do all right nonetheless," he assured me. "And I don't doubt that you'll end your career by being made a Judge."

I replied laughingly that my ambitions did not extend to such dizzy heights. The only thing I wanted to achieve was to build up a reasonable practice as a junior barrister, and if I was able to do that I would be altogether content.

"Well," he said, "you know best what you want out of life, but whatever happens to you, I hope you will write a book about your recovery. It would be such a wonderful encouragement for other people with disabilities."

My first day back in chambers was very like the day I had started there as a tenant 18 months before. Arthur was in the clerks' room reading a newspaper when I came in. After congratulating me on my recovery, he said, "I'm afraid I've got nothing for you at the moment. There's been a general slump in the Temple for the last few weeks; even our regular solicitors have been sending us very little work."

He told me that only two members of chambers were in court that morning. Most of the others were not coming in until the afternoon.

I left him and went into Gerald Howard's room to sit at my empty desk. It had been exactly the same on the first day - the same silent telephones, the same sterile inactivity, the same frustration.

I made up my mind that I would start writing articles for motoring journals again. I would also take up the suggestion which Fanny had made to me on the train, and I would try to write a book about my recovery. It was to be a simple, straightforward account, written anonymously, and I would stress the divine help I believed that I had received throughout my illnesses. If it was ever published, I hoped that only my family and my closest friends should be aware that I was the author.

From then on I used to arrive at chambers every morning almost as early as the clerks, in case a barrister should be required at very short notice for a returned brief or an urgent application.

In those days, any unrepresented defendant at Assizes or Quarter Sessions could ask to have a "Dock Brief," provided he was able to provide the sum of two pounds, four shillings and sixpence as payment for his counsel. He would be led to the centre of the court and told to point to the barrister whom he wished to defend him. Dock briefs, or "dockers" as we called them, were normally allocated at the beginning to the first day of a session. As the counsel selected by the defendant could not refuse to accept the case, barristers with established practices used to take good care to be out of the courtroom while the defendants were making their choice.

There was a collection of out-of-work barristers in the Temple who habitually attended the first morning of each session of the various courts in the central London area, hoping to be picked out for a docker, or better still financially, of being granted a legal aid defence by the clerk of the court. These people knew that they were parading their brieflessness before their colleagues, but they sank their pride since it was for most of them their only foreseeable chance of appearing as advocates in a courtroom.

I joined the Dock Brief brigade, encouraged by Arthur to do so.

"After all, Sir," he said, "it's one of the ways of getting started if you have no tame solicitors to send you work - much more helpful than sitting in chambers writing articles for magazines."

Every month I marked in my diary the opening day of a new session at the Old Bailey in the City, the County of London Sessions in Newington Causeway, and Middlesex Sessions in Parliament Square.

There were usually between 20 and 30 of us, though

sometimes there were as many as 40, so if you were not in court on the early side you were liable to find that all the counsels' seats were already occupied. People held different theories as to where you should be sitting to have the best chance of being picked out for a docker. The front row was the most favoured position, some preferring to be towards the left and others towards the right of the courtroom.

The defendant would stand at first with his back to the rows of counsel, while the procedure was explained to him. Then he would be told to turn round and to make his choice. If he pointed to you, you would rise majestically and bow, to indicate your acceptance of the brief. We always tried to avoid being next to one of our more devious colleagues who was adept in springing quickly to his feet and bowing when the defendant was actually pointing to a barrister sitting beside him.

If you were selected, you hurried off to interview your client, either in the cells or in some quiet corner of the court building. Almost every docker was a guilty plea, so it was a matter of seeking desperately for something to say in mitigation of sentence. Often you barely had time to complete your notes before the case was called on in court.

If you had not been chosen for a dock brief it was still advisable for you to hang around for a while in the hope of being given a Poor Prisoners' Defence by the clerk of the court. Generally, these were cases in which unrepresented defendants had entered pleas of "not guilty" in spite of the apparently overwhelming evidence against them. It was clearly understood that the primary duty of the counsel in such circumstances was to persuade the defendants to admit their guilt, rather than running spurious defences and being branded as liars by the verdicts of juries.

One of the workless barristers, a habitué of London Sessions, had achieved a considerable reputation for his ability to induce the most recalcitrant defendants to change their pleas from "not guilty" to "guilty." This made him extremely popular with the court clerks who entrusted him with numerous Poor Prisoners' Defence briefs. Eventually he was disbarred for professional misconduct when it came to light that he had never belonged to a set of chambers, nor had he ever had a clerk.

On my third or fourth visit to London Sessions I had received a legal aid brief from the court to represent a Polish bookkeeper, charged with theft by embezzlement. Both the manager and the assistant manager of the firm which employed him alleged that when they had asked him to explain his defalcations he had broken down and had confessed to his dishonesty.

As the clerk was writing my name on the brief, he said, "No doubt you'll point out to him that he hasn't a chance of getting off. If he persists with his plea of 'not guilty,' he'll only be wasting court time and public money - and he'll get himself a stiffer sentence in the outcome."

When I interviewed my client he emphatically maintained that he was innocent. According to him, he had been framed by the manager and his assistant to account for the thefts which they had been carrying out themselves, as they had regularly defrauded their employers. This was well known to the staff, he said, and several of them were willing to give evidence on his behalf.

In view of his instructions I applied for his legal aid certificate to be extended as I would require the assistance of a solicitor to prepare the defence witnesses' statements. The clerk of the court frowned and commented dryly, "I hope our Polish friend isn't stringing you along."

Apparently the jury did not think he was doing so, because after a three-day trial they acquitted him of all the charges on the indictment.

CHAPTER 23

Slowly and gradually work began coming in. When the regular chambers' solicitors became used to me they did not mind if I took over their returned briefs, and occasionally they gave me cases of my own. I had joined the South-Eastern Circuit and several solicitors in Kent and Sussex began sending me legal aid defences, undefended divorces, and small county court actions.

Within a short while both the army and the RAF had added my name to the lists of barristers they could call upon to act as defence counsel at courts martial overseas. Britain had not yet abolished compulsory national service and had a large number of soldiers and airmen stationed abroad. They still remained subject to the British civil law, and any junior officer or other rank who was being court-martialled for a serious criminal offence could apply to be legally assisted at his trial. If the application was granted, which it usually was, arrangements would be made for a practising barrister to be brought out from London to conduct his defence for him.

I used to go over to Germany every few months and I greatly enjoyed my trips. The Services ran special trains from Liverpool Street station to Harwich every evening, and they had their own ferry for the overnight crossing to the Hook of Holland. At the Hook several trains would be waiting to take soldiers and airmen to various parts of West Germany. Barristers going out for courts martial would be met at their destinations and driven to the units to which they were going to be temporarily attached. Although we retained our civilian status we were granted the honorary rank of brigadier by the army, and of group captain by the

RAF, for the purposes of travel and accommodation.

The most irksome court martial at which I ever appeared was the occasion I defended a second lieutenant on charges of manslaughter, driving under the influence of alcohol, and the commission of a number of military offences. On a bitterly cold night in the depths of winter he and another lieutenant had taken their company commander's jeep without his permission and had gone out for the evening to a town near to the barracks where they were stationed. After a few hours of hard drinking they had set forth on their return journey in the early hours of the following morning, and had offered a lift home to a private soldier in their regiment who was, so I gathered, as intoxicated as they were themselves. My client was at the wheel, and according to prosecution witnesses he was travelling at great speed on an ice-covered road. He lost control of the jeep on a bend and crashed into a clump of trees on the verge. The two officers were lucky to escape with cuts and bruises, but the private soldier was killed instantaneously.

The two officers were jointly charged. Since their defences were identical it would have been time-saving and practical for both of them to be represented by the same counsel; however, one of them chose to be defended by a major in his battalion, who prided himself on his ability as an advocate. Unfortunately, my client's name appeared second on the charge sheet so that the major had the right to cross-examine the prosecution witnesses before I could do so myself. At the outset of the trial the Judge-Advocate, a professional barrister, suggested tactfully that it might be advantageous for both the accused if I was permitted to cross-examine first, but the major would not hear of it. A short while later he protested because the prosecuting officer in opening the case had called me his "learned friend" and had merely referred to himself by his rank and his name. If we were going to adopt these forensic niceties, he said, the prosecutor should have alluded to him as "my gallant friend," in the terminology of the House of Commons.

For two days I had undergone the agony of watching the major cross-examining and squandering most of the best defence points by his ill-considered questions. At the close of the prosecution case I submitted that the charge of manslaughter had not been substantiated by the evidence. I began by saying that I had hoped to make my submission on behalf of both the accused, but "my gallant friend" did not wish to be associated with it; nevertheless, if my contentions succeeded they must inevitably apply to his client as well. The Judge-Advocate upheld my legal arguments and the court dismissed the charge of manslaughter against both the accused. After that, my client changed his plea to "guilty" on all the other charges, as I had advised him that he had no defence to any of them. The other accused officer followed the same course, much against the wishes of the major. In the outcome, the two of them were suitably punished for their irresponsible behaviour without either of them being dismissed from the Service.

I only once went to Germany in company with another barrister on a joint-defence, and this turned out to be the most eventful of my many trips, though not on account of anything that happened during the trial. My co-accused was defended by my friend Kenneth Harrington who later became a metropolitan stipendiary magistrate. We were appearing for two RAF sergeants alleged to have taken part in a series of homosexual orgies with a group of young airmen. Kenneth's client had made a long written statement to the investigating officer, and I was particularly anxious to know what he had said as it had not been sent to me with my brief. As Kenneth and I were both rather busy at the time we agreed to go through the statement together on the train from Liverpool Street to Harwich, but we were sharing a compartment with two senior officers' wives, so we could not discuss the case at all. On the boat they had put us into separate two-berth cabins, and both our fellow-passengers were already in them when we came on board.

The following morning at the Hook we found that we had been allocated a reserved compartment to ourselves on the train. As it was not due to leave the station for another 40 minutes Kenneth proposed that he should read out his client's long statement which, he said, amounted to a detailed confession, while everything was quiet and peaceful. After he had finished the first three or four pages a red-faced brigadier stormed in from the corridor.

"I don't know who the hell you are," he shouted angrily, "but your disgusting conversation can be heard very clearly through the open windows in the next compartment - where there are three lady passengers. I intend to report the matter to the authorities. Meanwhile, I order you to keep your revolting discussion to yourselves or I'll have to hand you over to the military police!"

We had the utmost difficulty in convincing the brigadier that we were barristers coming over to take part in a joint defence. We eventually did so by producing our wigs and gowns from our suitcases.

The court martial took place at the aerodrome a few miles on the German side of the Dutch border. We finished the case late in the afternoon, and the RAF Legal Service made arrangements for us to return to England on the ferry the following night. This left us with a clear day, and we decided to visit the Arnhem military cemetery at Oosterbeek where a number of men from both our old battalions were buried. We were planning how we would get there in the bar of the Officers' Mess before dinner when a Dutch colonel came up and told us he had been listening to our conversation.

"I am driving to Amsterdam early tomorrow morning," he said. "I shall be passing through Arnhem and I would be delighted to take you there."

We gratefully accepted his offer, and he asked us to be outside the Mess, ready to start, at seven o'clock.

Next morning when we came out of the Mess after a hurried breakfast the colonel was waiting for us in his car. He suggested that Kenneth should sit in the back and that I should take the front passenger seat where there was more leg-room. He had already switched on the engine when he bent down and brought out a large parcel which he placed on my lap.

"I am doing you a favour taking you to Arnhem," he said. "Now I ask you to do me a little favour in return. I bought this movie-camera yesterday. If I declare it at the

Dutch customs I will have to pay heavy duty on it, but you two are only passing through Holland on your way home. If you pretend it is yours no one will have to pay anything."

By the time I had taken in what was happening we were speeding towards the Dutch frontier. I told the colonel I could not possibly agree to what he proposed and I asked him to stop so that we could talk it over, but he brushed aside my protests and said he was going to cross the border on a little-used road where the customs officers were not at all thorough.

I was still sitting with the movie-camera on my lap when we pulled up at the frontier-post. Our passports were checked and we were asked to stay there for a few minutes because the customs officers were still at breakfast.

We sat in the car in silence. The wait seemed interminable. I had made up my mind to deny that the camera was mine, and I was wondering how the colonel would react at my refusal to accept responsibility for it.

After about quarter of an hour a police inspector came up and apologised for the delay. He did not know why the customs officers were being so long, he said, but if we assured him that we had nothing to declare he would allow us to proceed on our way.

The colonel was jubilant. As we drove away he thanked me fervently for my co-operation and said he had known from the start he could rely on me. As a mark of his gratitude he insisted on taking us all the way to Oosterbeek, although it was off his direct route.

We had arranged to join the Services boat train when it stopped at Arnhem that afternoon. We would get to the

Hook about six o'clock and the ferry did not sail until midnight, so we intended to leave our suitcases in our cabins and to dine at a restaurant in the town.

We separated in the war cemetery and each of us went off in search of the graves of the members of our battalions. There were very few people about at the time and there was a stillness all around - not a brooding, oppressive silence so much as a sense of spiritual tranquillity, an ethereal quiescence.

I soon found the 1st Dorsets graves. I walked slowly along the orderly rows of simple, white headstones, reading the names on each one. Afterwards I paused for a while thinking of the men who lay buried there. I saw them as I had seen them last, before the ending of their short lives. That is how they would always be remembered, for death had bestowed on them the mystical timelessness of eternal youth.

I had expected to be saddened by my visit to the cemetery, but I had not anticipated that it would be such an immensely moving experience to stand beside the graves of the men I had known. Kenneth told me that he had been affected in the same way.

We left Oosterbeek in time to have an early lunch in the town-centre of Arnhem. It was a warm autumn day so we chose a restaurant with pavement-tables where we sat and watched the crowds hurrying past in the busy street. Actuality for them, I thought, was their present-day existence: the cemetery, a few miles distant, has become a relic of their history.

When we went to the station in the early afternoon we

were dismayed to find out that the Services train was not stopping at Arnhem that day. However, the obliging station master, on hearing of our predicament, offered to stop it for us, and the necessary message was conveyed to the engine-driver. For some reason which was never explained to us, the train halted a few hundred yards before it reached the station, and Kenneth and I, accompanied by a railway official, had to walk along the line to get to it.

Even then the predicaments of that incident-prone trip were not yet ended. In the evening when we were about to leave the ferry for a leisurely dinner in the town, we were stopped at the head of the gangplank by a military police sergeant who told us that the officer in charge of troops on the ship had made an order that once a man had come on board he was forbidden to return to the shore again. We tried to persuade the sergeant that the rule did not apply to us because we were civilians and not service personnel, but he remained adamant. He could not allow us to disembark, he said, unless we obtained special permission to do so.

We found the OC troops, an RASC captain, sitting at a table heaped with papers in the cabin which he used as an office. I noticed that he wore no campaign ribbons on his uniform although he looked old enough to have served during the war.

He glanced up peevishly as we entered and asked us what we wanted. I left Kenneth to do the talking as he could speak with all the authority of an ex-major in the Coldstream Guards. Kenneth asked him to pass a message to the sergeant to the effect that we were civilians and he had no authority to stop us from going ashore. The captain interrupted him.

"As far as I'm concerned," he snapped, "while you're on this ship you're both under my command. I've made an order and you'll bloody well obey it. I'm forbidding you to leave the ship."

When Kenneth told him we had every intention of dining on shore, he warned us that on our return we would be placed under close arrest and would spend the night in the hold he used as a guardroom.

We then went back on deck, and I followed Kenneth as he strode purposefully down the gangplank. The military police made no attempt to impede us.

We returned to the ferry about an hour before she was due to sail. As I climbed up the gangplank - I was ahead of Kenneth this time - I saw the sergeant and several of his men standing in a group apparently waiting for us. As soon as I stepped on to the deck the sergeant sprung to attention and saluted.

"Sir," he said, "the OC troops presents his compliments and he hopes that both of you will do him the honour of joining him in his office for a drink."

The captain was scarcely recognisable from our previous encounter. He was now all smiles, deference, and affability. Having invited us to sit down and to make ourselves comfortable he produced three glasses and a bottle of duty-free cognac. While he was pouring out drinks he apologised profusely for his previous behaviour and begged us not to report him to the War Office. He seemed immensely relieved when we assured him that as far as we were concerned the matter was best forgotten.

We were still drinking cognac in his office when the ship sailed out of the harbour.

I was still getting the periodic bouts of pain at the side of my stomach which had been investigated at Midhurst sanatorium. They were becoming more and more severe, but as I had been told that I was suffering from a complaint for which there was no effective treatment there was nothing I could do except to dose myself with painkillers until the attacks had worn off.

One morning I had to go to Lewes prison for a conference with a man whom I was defending at Sussex Assizes the following week. During the train journey from London the pains started, and this time they were far worse than they had ever been. I managed to get through the interview with my client, and to return home, before collapsing on my bed.

Throughout the afternoon and evening, and for most of the night, I dosed myself liberally with analgesics. Just before dawn I woke up in excruciating agony, and I could stand it no longer so I phoned my doctor. He came round to see me immediately and carried out a cursory examination.

"You have a ruptured appendix," he said, "and peritonitis. You'll have to be operated on at once."

With that he went to the telephone and rang for an ambulance.

I recovered from my operation quickly and I was back at work a month later. It was a great relief to know that the true cause of my recurrent abdominal pains had been discovered and eradicated.

I had started work on my book. I was calling it *We Who Are Left*, and I was dedicating it to the war-disabled of all nations and all those who have helped them. As it was to be a simple, straightforward account of my own experience after receiving my head wound I had decided to write it in the first person. I would not be inhibited from revealing my thoughts and my emotions because, if the book was ever published, very few people would know I had been the author; it would be described as "written anonymously" and I was not referring to people by their correct names.

I did not intend to mention Emma. I felt that the memory of how much we had meant to each other was too personal, too precious, and too hallowed to be shared with others. Nor was I going to allude to my problems of dyslexia and dysgraphia, as I feared that if my true condition was ever discovered it might well prejudice my future at the Bar.

It took me just over a year to finish the book. I was suffering from insomnia at the time, but however badly I had slept I used to wake up very early, so I could generally fit in about an hour's writing before I went to work. I wrote again at home in the evenings, and in chambers during my spells of brieflessness.

My progress was slow as I frequently had to check my spelling in a dictionary. Sometimes there was an added complication if I had completely forgotten the formation of the word I was trying to look up, or the sequence of the letters in the alphabet.

I wrote the whole book in longhand and then sent it to a professional typist, who assured me that she could read my writing without much difficulty. I had no idea to which publishers I was going to submit it, but I had prepared myself for numerous setbacks and discouragements when I had started to hawk round the manuscript. However, while it was still being typed, a cousin of mine by marriage, at that time a leading surgeon in Dublin, gave me an introduction to Mr Johnston Abraham, the chairman and managing director of William Heinemann's medical section, who had published two of his own books.

I went to see Mr Johnston Abraham, at his suggestion, taking my manuscript with me. He put it on a corner of his desk, promising to look at it as soon as possible. Then he questioned me about my progress at the Bar. Just before I left his office he said, "You're lucky enough to have a first-class profession, and you seem already to have surmounted the first few hurdles. But authorship is a different matter. Masses of people try to write, and hardly any of them ever succeed in getting anything published. It's one of the sad facts of life that every would-be author has to face."

From then on I waited anxiously for Mr Johnston Abraham's opinion. At first I dreaded coming home in the evening and finding that my manuscript had been returned with a terse note to the effect that it was wholly unsuitable for publication. When I heard nothing for six weeks I took heart; it seemed to indicate, at least, that he had not condemned the book out-of-hand after reading only one or two chapters.

After three months I could bear the suspense no longer, so one afternoon I phoned Mr Johnston Abraham's secretary and asked her what was happening. It was obvious that neither my name nor the title of my book meant anything to her, but she promised to make some inquiries and to let me know the result. An hour later she rang back to tell me that she had located my manuscript, piled up with some others in Mr Abraham's room. She could only conclude that he had just put it aside intending to read it and had forgotten to do so. In view of the long delay, she said, she would bring it to his attention directly he came in the following morning.

I did not hear from Mr Johnston Abraham again, but within a short while I had a telephone call from Owen Evans, one of the directors of Heinemann Medical Books. He said he had just finished reading my manuscript.

"I was very impressed with it," he went on. "However, it isn't suitable for our sort of list, so I've passed it to my brother, who is a director of Heinemann's general publishing company. I don't want to raise your hopes too much as he mightn't share my views of its merits."

I did not have to wait long before I received a letter from Dwye Evans making me an offer for the publication of my book. He told me, when I called in to see him, that he was unhappy with the title *We Who Are Left*, which sounded more suitable for the autobiography of a Labour party politician. Also, he was reluctant to publish it anonymously, and he would much prefer to name me as the author.

After a great deal of thought I altered the title to *No Memorial* - words taken from the well-known verse in

Ecclesiasticus, Chapter 44:

"There be of them, that have left a name behind them,
That their praises might be reported.
And some there be, which have no memorial;
Who are perished, as though they had never been born."

Eventually I agreed, still with some misgiving, that *No Memorial* should be published under my own name.

I was slowly picking up more work on the South-Eastern Circuit, particularly in Maidstone and Canterbury.

The Circuit covered a wide area, with the counties of Norfolk, Suffolk and Cambridgeshire on its northern edge, and extending down to include Essex, Kent, Surrey and Sussex. The majority of the members tended to practise in a single county, or perhaps in two neighbouring counties. We were all subject to the jurisdiction of the Wine Committee, presided over by the leader of the Circuit, who was addressed on formal occasions as "Mr Senior." The rest of the committee were mostly distinguished Queen's Counsel. The honorary secretary, called the Junior, was usually a comparatively unknown barrister just making a little headway on the Circuit. He was chosen by the Wine Committee and held office for a year.

After I had been in practice for a few years I was very surprised when I received an invitation to become the Circuit Junior. Arthur was delighted, although a lot of extra work would fall on him, as he said that as well as being a personal honour for me, it would result in a certain amount of kudos for the chambers as a whole.

During my year in office I tried to pay regular visits to the towns on the Circuit where Assizes were taking place. It was by no means an arduous task as they were mostly within easy reach of London, and by custom the Junior was given a court legal aid brief by the Clerk of Assize if one was available. At each of the towns there was a designated Bar hotel where barristers could obtain lunch or dinner in the comfort of a private room.

I had to keep in close contact with the leader of the Circuit, Tristram Beresford, an elderly, eccentric Queen's Counsel, who throughout his life at the Bar had been known by the nickname "Chimp." Small in stature and pugnacious in temperament, he was always a distinctive figure as he strutted round the Temple in his black top hat and his grey spats.

On one occasion his pugnacity almost landed me in a position of extreme embarrassment. The Clerk of Assize had mentioned to me that there had been complaints by the Judges about the competence of several of the counsel who had appeared before them on Attorney-General's nominations. There was a system at that time by which the Attorney-General kept lists of the barristers on every Circuit whom he could nominate to represent the Director of Public Prosecutions at Assizes or at Quarter Sessions. The process of allocating the briefs was usually administered by the Attorney-General's clerk.

I reported what I had been told at the next meeting of the Wine Committee, and the general opinion was that the leader of the Circuit should raise the matter tactfully with Sir Reginald Manningham-Buller, the Attorney-General. However, Chimp insisted on sending Sir Reginald what he referred to as one of his "strong letters," in which he suggested that something underhand might be taking place in the selection of counsel from nominations.

When Sir Reginald asked him to come and discuss this serious allegation, Chimp's ardour began to cool. Having failed to persuade any of the senior members of the Wine Committee to go with him when he saw the Attorney-General, he told me it was my duty as Circuit Junior to accompany him and to lend him my support.

On the day fixed for the meeting Chimp phoned me to say he was too busy to leave his chambers, and that I would have to see the Attorney-General on my own. I flatly refused.

The next day Chimp wrote an apologetic letter to Sir Reginald withdrawing his imputation, and the whole affair passed into oblivion.

The South-Eastern Circuit used to hold their annual dinner in Middle Temple Hall every July. There was generally a large attendance. All the Judges who had sat at any of our Circuit towns during the past year were invited, as well as the High Sheriffs of all our Circuit counties. The Junior always had to make one of the after-dinner speeches; this was considered to be a traditional ordeal of his office. I had never spoken before a large gathering before and was dreading it.

On the evening of the dinner Chimp came up to me just as the guests were assembling.

"Junior," he said, "this is a massive hall with a very high ceiling, and we don't have a microphone, so for goodness sake remember to speak up. I'm making the first speech, and you mustn't be deceived by the fact that I seem to be talking in quite a low voice; I've been trained as an actor, and can assure you that my words will be audible in every corner of the hall."

Chimp had proposed the toast of "The Guests". After his first few sentences people at distant tables began to shout, "Can't hear, Mr Senior. Speak up!".

This increased my own apprehensions. However, when I was replying to the toast of "The Circuit", even if my audience couldn't hear me properly they were kind enough to listen without interrupting.

CHAPTER 24

On the day *No Memorial* was published I had a case at Dartford Magistrates' Court in the morning. After it was finished I went back to London, lunched in Hall, and spent the afternoon working in chambers. I felt a vague, illogical sense of disappointment. For the previous few hours my first book had been on sale to the public, yet as far as I was concerned the process seemed impersonal and remote; the normality of my own actions and the customary behaviour of those around me had trivialised the whole occasion. Early in the evening I said good-night to Arthur and left for home. I made the journey, as always, standing unsteadily in an overcrowded, jolting underground train from the Temple to Gloucester Road. The day ebbed to a close without the occurrence of anything in any way notable or unique.

For the next two or three weeks I scanned the literary pages of countless journals, but *No Memorial* was never mentioned. I had made up my mind that the book was going to be completely ignored when a very favourable review appeared in *The Daily Telegraph*. From then on it was reviewed extensively in national and provincial news-papers, and in magazines. It was serialised by the *Liverpool Echo* as the story of a miraculous recovery. I never inquired how many copies of the book were printed. At any rate, they had all been sold within the first few months, and Heinemann's had informed me of their decision that the demand was not sufficient to justify a reprint at that particular moment.

I received many letters from people who had read the book. Some of them wrote to congratulate me on my recovery; others, who were suffering from ill-health or from various forms of disability, told me that they had derived considerable help and encouragement from reading of my experiences. I also heard from Eileen Molony, a BBC Talks Department producer, who was about to prepare a series of broadcasts on the D-Day landings and thought I might be a possible speaker. She took me out to lunch at a restaurant in Soho to discuss her programme, but during the meal told me that my hesitancy of speech would make it difficult for me to take part. Before we parted she brought up another project which did not involve the BBC. She was planning to write a novel about a murder trial at the Old Bailey, and she invited me to become her co-author. The book was to be divided into four sections, each of which would be written in the first person by a different character who had been directly involved. Her proposal was that she should deal with the case as it had appeared to the defendant and to a member of the jury: I would describe it from the point of view of the defence counsel and the Judge. It seemed an interesting idea, but it never came to anything.

I had spent the whole of the previous year writing a novel, which I had shown to Heinemann's. They had not liked it at all, and so I had made up my mind to abandon my aspirations to authorship for a few years and to concentrate my time and energy on building up a practice at the Bar.

By then the Ministry of Pensions had ceased to summon me for regular medical examinations and I had been graded as 100 per cent disabled on a permanent basis. I still had to go to the Brompton Hospital every six months for a chest X-ray and an out-patients appointment with Dr Lloyd, but

I was trying desperately hard to put my ill-health behind me and to live a perfectly normal life.

Noreen had sent her daughter Miranda to her old school, Cheltenham Ladies College, and she had managed to get a most interesting job as social secretary to Mrs Lakshmi Pandit, the Indian High Commissioner to London. Mrs Pandit, a sister of Pandit Nehru the Prime Minister of India, was regarded at that time as one of the world's leading women in public life. She had already held several important diplomatic posts including appointments as Indian ambassador in Washington and in Moscow. I saw a lot of Mrs Pandit during her years in London for she treated Noreen as a member of her own family and being Noreen's brother I was frequently invited to the High Commissioner's Residency in Kensington Palace Gardens. She was a wonderful hostess with a natural warmth and a genuine liking for people.

Mrs Pandit enjoyed nothing more than an opportunity to forgo her public duties for a while and to relax in the company of her circle of private friends. These comprised a blending of the famous and the unknown. On the one hand, there were celebrities in the arts, in literature, and in national affairs: on the other, ordinary men and women whom she had met through her numerous activities. Margot Fonteyn and Yehudi Menuhin were two of her especial favourites. But it did not matter how undistinguished a person happened to be in the easy sociability of these gatherings at the Residency for we were meeting together in the commonality of Mrs Pandit's friendship.

In those days a high proportion of the students at the Inns of Court were black and they used to return to practise in their own countries as soon as they had been called to the Bar. One morning I was listening to the radio while I was dressing and heard a young Nigerian barrister describing his student days in England. He had come to London, he said, proud to belong to an Inn of Court and keen to meet some of the more senior fellow-members, but during the two years he had spent there he had never spoken to a Bencher, nor even to a practising barrister. When dining in Hall he had felt like an interloper and he had invariably hurried away directly the meal was over.

A few days after hearing the broadcast I was lunching in Hall and sitting next to Hubert Munroe, one of the regular group at our table. I told him about the Nigerian barrister and asked him if he thought we could do anything to make our overseas students feel more welcome. Hubert, who was in revenue chambers, was one of the most successful of my contemporaries and already had a substantial junior practice. I had broached the subject with him because I knew him to be a passionate idealist and an ardent campaigner for reform. He said that he himself had been very worried by the indifferent attitude adopted by the Inns to all their students, whether or not they came from overseas. He would have liked the Middle Temple to introduce a system whereby every student who joined the Inn would be allocated to a "sponsor." The sponsors would be practising barristers who would have the duty of befriending their students, dining with them in Hall from time to time and introducing them to the customs and traditions of the Inn. However, he was extremely doubtful if the majority of our Benchers - "the aloof untouchables" - as he called them, would consider that his scheme was either necessary or desirable.

I had suggested to Hubert that we should discuss his idea with Freddie Pritchard, as he was one of our most senior Benchers and I was sure he would view it with favour. Freddie had had to retire from the High Court Bench because his stroke had left him with a paralysed arm and a very lame leg. He had recently been appointed Director of Legal Studies at the Council of Legal Education, so he had an especial interest in the welfare of Bar students. We had seen Freddie in his office and, as I had expected, he thought that Hubert's proposal was excellent. He said he would arrange for us to explain it to the Treasurer of the Middle Temple in the hope that he would decide to give it a trial.

The Treasurer, one of the most senior Benchers, held office for a year. During that time he was virtually in control of every activity which took place in the Inn, although he exercised his authority in the name of all the Benchers collectively. Our Treasurer then was Mr Justice Gorman, a High Court Judge. He listened carefully while we outlined the proposal, asking a number of questions for clarification. We told him that the scheme would be still more effective if there were special "sponsorship nights" when sponsors would have dinner in Hall with their students, and when, at the end of the evening, Benchers would circulate among the tables chatting with the diners.

Finally, the Treasurer gave us his decision. He did not want to discourage our initiative, he said, and therefore he would allow us to try out our project for two years, but the Inn could not adopt it as an official procedure until they were satisfied it would be successful. At the moment, he went on, he felt very doubtful if many barristers would be willing to act as sponsors, or if many students would want to dine with them in Hall. With regard to our suggestion that Benchers should circulate after dinner on Sponsorship Nights, he would leave it entirely to them whether or not they chose to do so. He advised us to form a small committee to administer the scheme and assured us that the staff of the Inn would give us their full co-operation.

The committee we set up consisted of Hubert as chairman, and three other members, of whom I was one. The Sponsorship Scheme was an immediate and lasting success, but we had to run it on an unofficial basis for five years before it was formally adopted by the Inn. Plenty of barristers took part and the students found it a very pleasurable form of initiation to the spirit and the fellowship of the Middle Temple. In time, the other three Inns of Court started their own schemes on similar lines.

There was a strong rumour in the Temple that Gerald Howard was going to be appointed a High Court Judge. If that should happen, Garth Moore would very probably decline to take over from him as head of chambers because he was becoming increasingly bound up with his work as a don at Cambridge. The next person in seniority was Edward Robey, but he had applied to the Lord Chancellor for a job as a metropolitan stipendiary magistrate and he would probably be leaving us quite soon. After Edward, there was nobody of sufficient standing who could fill the breach, and there was a real danger that our chambers might disintegrate. This was a very worrying thought and I was wondering if I ought to make a few inquiries with a view to finding myself a tenancy somewhere else.

I was doing a fair amount of work in Kent, mainly at Maidstone and Canterbury. A barrister appearing frequently in both towns was John Mathew, the son of the Director of Public Prosecutions, and we became very friendly. John, who was considered to be one of the most promising of the younger counsel on the Circuit, was a member of a leading set of criminal chambers, headed by Maxwell Turner, the Senior Treasury Prosecuting Counsel at the Old Bailey. After we had been against each other in a case in Maidstone, he had offered me a lift back to London in his car. On the way he told me in confidence that Max Turner intended to ask Gerald Howard to become head of their chambers. If Gerald agreed, Max would invite me to join them too. My delight at hearing this was tempered by the thought that if Gerald was really about to become a High Court Judge he would probably see no point in moving. However, John said that Max was quite sure he would not be appointed at the moment as the Government were going through a period of considerable unpopularity and they would be most reluctant to fight a by-election in a marginal seat like Gerald's.

A week later Gerald phoned me at home to tell me that he had agreed to take over Max's chambers at the beginning of the next quarter, and it had been decided that I should go there with him. He said he wanted to break the news to Arthur himself and he asked me not to mention it to anyone in chambers until he had done so.

From then on Gerald ceased to visit chambers at all and had had all his papers and briefs delivered to him at the House of Commons by our junior clerk. I felt certain that he was staying away deliberately to put off telling Arthur about our move. As the days passed, his arrangement with Max Turner became an open secret in the Temple and I was afraid that Arthur would get to hear about it from one of the other clerks. I rang Gerald on several occasions to tell him of my concern. He always replied, somewhat vaguely, that he would come in and speak to Arthur very soon. But nothing ever came of it.

About a week before the move was due to take place Arthur met me at the door of the clerks' room when I had just returned from court. He looked pale, tense and unsmiling and asked me if we could have a private talk in my room. Directly he had closed the door behind him he told me he had heard from another clerk that Gerald Howard was taking over Maxwell Turner's chambers and that I was going there with him. He wanted confirmation from me that this was merely a groundless rumour. I had to admit that it was quite true, but I added that I would prefer not to discuss the matter any further with him until he had spoken to Gerald Howard about it.

I could see that Arthur was deeply shocked by what I had told him, and he was struggling to hold back his tears. He had been Gerald's senior clerk for a number of years and regarded him with a kind of reverential devotion. He looked down at the floor for a few minutes and then muttered, partly to himself, "I don't believe Mr Howard would treat me like this - I just don't believe it. There must be some mistake."

Gerald was at the House of Commons that afternoon, working in his room, so I suggested to Arthur that he should go there in a cab straight away to see him. He took my advice. I do not know what happened at their subsequent meeting but I heard later that Gerald, who was a wealthy man, had undertaken to pay him a substantial sum of money as compensation for his future loss of earnings. However, I realised that Arthur could never be recompensed financially for the injury which he had suffered to his pride, or for the shattering of his trust in human reliability. I had liked him from the start and always regretted that Gerald had not told him about our move as soon as the details were arranged.

Several years after the war people in Britain were only permitted to exchange a very small amount of sterling into a foreign currency for the purpose of spending a holiday abroad. This imposed a severe restriction on overseas travel, but it did not rule it out completely. Soon after the publication of *No Memorial* three of us, Charles Potter, John Davies and I, all members of the Middle Temple and all very junior tenants in our respective chambers, went for a motoring trip to north-west Europe in a long vacation. During the war Charles had served in a tank regiment which had supported my brigade in the Normandy landing. John, a Welshman, had been unfit for service in the forces and it was the first time he had been out of the British mainland. We used Charles's car, a small, dilapidated convertible, and toured for a few weeks in France, Germany,

Holland, Austria and Switzerland.

It was quite impossible to plan a holiday in the United States of America on your personal currency allowance. However, it was still feasible if you had friends or relations who would put you up for your visit. Peter, now a Lieutenant-Commander, had been posted to the British Navy Staff in Washington DC as staff officer (Gunnery) for what was likely to be a two-or-three-year appointment. He and Eve, together with their three small children and a nanny, were living in a furnished house on the outskirts of Washington. The Navy had insisted that they had a resident nanny because it was essential that they should both be free to take part in the heavy round of social commitments which they would be expected to fulfil. When they had been in Washington for about a year Eve and Peter invited me to stay with them. I travelled out cabin class on the *Queen Mary*, living for five days in the height of luxury. I had booked a two-berth cabin, but the man who was supposed to be sharing it with me never turned up and I had it to myself.

Transatlantic crossings in a liner were a memorable experience, not least for the attention which was paid to the comfort and the entertainment of the passengers. The food was superb and all too plentiful, so I tried to get as much exercise as possible by swimming in the pool or walking briskly round the decks. Every evening there was a choice of dancing, cabaret or a cinema. There were periods of relaxation too. Sitting in a wicker chair enfolded in a blanket in some sheltered part of the deck, and gazing out at the varying moods and swiftly-changing patterns of the illimitable ocean. I have a vivid recollection of the end of the voyage; sailing slowly and majestically into New York harbour; the excitement and the immensity of the towering buildings on the skyline.

The Americans are by nature friendly and hospitable, and they had met so few private visitors from Britain during recent years that I was inundated with invitations the whole time I was in Washington. I was asked repeated questions about British politics and the British economy in the aftermath of the war. I did my best to provide adequate answers. I was surprised, and not a little flattered, to find that my opinions were being treated with a respect which they very rarely received from my friends in England.

I spent an interesting morning with Charles Rhyne, the chairman of the American Bar, watching a case being argued in the United States Supreme Court. Charles had suggested that I should come with him because he was taking his client, Liberace, the well-known entertainer, who was to be in Washington that day for a consultation regarding his forthcoming libel action in London against the *Daily Mirror*. I joined the others at the entrance to the court, Charles, his wife Sue and Liberace accompanied by his Hollywood lawyer. Liberace was idolised by the American public and he obviously expected and revelled in this universal adoration. When we were leaving the court building at the midday adjournment we had to fight our way down the broad steps through throngs of Liberace fans, a high proportion of whom were enraptured schoolgirls. Charles took us to lunch at one of the leading Washington hotels. Again the mobbing continued - on the pavement as we walked from our taxi; in the hotel vestibule, and even in the restaurant. Liberace's place at the table was surrounded by candelabras, and the kitchen staff came up in turn to shake him by the hand. Our lunch-time conversation consisted of a virtual monologue by Liberace about his tremendous successes on a recent European tour. His principal characteristic seemed to be his enormous conceit.

At the end of my holiday Peter had lent me some dollars to enable me to stay in New York for a couple of days before I flew home.

The American Bar Association were holding their annual convention in London that year, and before I left Washington, Charles Rhyne had asked me to tell the Attorney-General, Sir Hartley Shawcross, that they would be bitterly disappointed if they were not addressed by Winston Churchill on some occasion during their visit. Immediately after my return I wrote to the Attorney-General and conveyed Charles's message to him. In his reply Sir Hartley had said that unfortunately the desire of the American lawyers would be impossible to fulfil. Churchill's mind was now so clouded he could not be relied upon to make a coherent address. It would be far preferable for them to remember him as the great British wartime Prime Minister than to see him in his present condition.

I gave a cocktail party at the flat in celebration of my move to Maxwell Turner's chambers. A few days before it took place the wife of a colleague of mine at the Bar rang me to ask if they might bring along an old school-friend of hers who was staying with them. I told her it would be quite all right. Ruth, she said, was a doctor, practising abroad, and was very keen to meet me.

The three of them arrived at the party with a cluster of other guests so I did not have a chance to say much to them. Ruth was a woman in her early thirties, slim, dark-haired and attractive. Later, when the party was in full swing, I found her in a corner of the crowded room standing in front of a small bookcase on the top of which was a photograph of me in uniform, taken soon after I had been commissioned.

When I came up beside her she said, "I've often seen that photo before."

I was curious. "Where was that?"

"At Emma's. I thought you'd been told why I wanted to meet you so much. I was Emma's GP in Rhodesia - as well as being her closest friend. We used to see each other nearly every day after her marriage had broken up."

"I never knew how her marriage worked out," I said.

"It didn't last long. It was a disaster. She was dreadfully unhappy. After Tom left her she put up that photo of you on the table beside her bed. She talked about you a lot. She told me the whole story."

Suddenly I felt a gleam of hope. "Is she still in Rhodesia?" I asked.

Ruth looked surprised at my question.

"You never heard? She died of cancer three years ago. She was only a little over 30 at the time."

I said, "If we'd married soon after the war we'd have had more than 10 precious years together."

Ruth placed a hand gently on my arm. "You might have

had a lot more than that. We don't yet know the cause of cancer. Personally, I believe that it can be caused by excessive emotional distress - for instance, by continuous grief. Emma always blamed herself for not returning to you. She fell in love with you the first time you met, and she remained in love with you for the rest of her life."

CHAPTER 25

Maxwell Turner's chambers at 5 Paper Buildings in King's Bench Walk were on the first floor of an old block, with a stone staircase and an antiquated lift. Before Gerald Howard and I arrived, there were eight members. They all had busy practices except for one man, a retired Naval officer, who spent part of his time sitting as a deputy chairman of Quarter Sessions either in London or in Kent. The chambers were extremely short of space as they only had three rooms for all the barristers and a small room for the two clerks. This did not cause any inconvenience in the morning when the tenants were usually in court, but it sometimes presented difficulties in the late afternoon when more than one person wanted to hold a conference.

In the early stages of their careers most barristers like getting publicity in the press, partly to satisfy their own egos and partly in the hope that it will bring them more work in the future. *The News of the World* was a very popular newspaper with the Bar because in their reports of trials they usually mentioned the names of the counsel, and when they did so they always spelt them correctly. The first few cases of mine to be reported did nothing to boost my reputation as they were mostly of trials in which I had appeared for the defence and the prisoners had been sentenced to long terms of imprisonment.

Soon after I had joined my new chambers I was briefed for the defence in a case at the Old Bailey which received a lot of publicity at the time. My client, a man in the early thirties, was charged with conspiracy to corrupt public morals and also with living on the earnings of prostitution. He had published several editions of a brochure called *The*

Ladies' Directory, advertising the services of London prostitutes. Each girl had a page to herself showing her photograph, scantily clad, and giving her telephone number. She also listed her specialities in well-recognised erotic codes, such as "stern disciplinarian", "corporal punishment", "bondage", and so on. I was instructed by a very experienced criminal solicitor, Victor Lissack. We both took the view that in the conspiracy charge the prosecution would lay heavy emphasis on the perversion aspect of the advertisements, and we knew they would be exhibiting some of the paraphernalia such as whips, manacles, and strait-jackets, which had been seized by the police from the prostitutes' premises. All this would be bound to have a significant effect on the minds of the jury.

Our client denied that he had been aware of the exact meaning of the idioms used in the advertisements, or of the sexual deviances practised by his advertisers. Unfortunately, every copy of the directory had contained a notice inviting the prostitutes to discuss the wording of their entries with him. For this and several other reasons both Victor and I thought it would be better if he did not give evidence. After a good deal of persuasion he reluctantly agreed to accept our advice.

The prosecution were calling several of the prostitutes who had advertised in the directory, and our client assured me that they would do everything they could to help him. In particular, they would totally refute any suggestion that they had ever corrupted the young. He wanted me to put to each one that all the men who came to her were middle-aged and sexually sophisticated. I had followed his instructions when I cross-examined the first of the girls. She reacted indignantly and told the court, with evident pride, that most of the 'punters' were young men in their early twenties, and even youths in their late 'teens'. I did not repeat my question with any of the other prostitutes for fear of getting a similar reply.

At the close of the prosecution case I made a submission to the Judge that the evidence had not substantiated either of the charges, but he ruled against me. We called no witnesses for the defence. After a fairly lengthy retirement the jury found the defendant "guilty" and he was given a short prison sentence. Victor Lissack and I saw our client immediately after the trial and we advised him to appeal on a point of law. Although he accepted our advice he decided that his interests would best be served by having another solicitor and another counsel.

The point of law which I had taken with the Judge was rejected by the Court of Criminal Appeal and subsequently by the House of Lords. However, the *Ladies' Directory* case lives on as one of the principal authorities in law regarding conspiracies to corrupt public morals.

Although I had decided not to embark on another book for a while, I still had the urge to write in the limited time available to me. I completed two full-length plays both of which were accepted by a literary agent but were never performed on the stage. I then turned to radio drama. My efforts were all rejected by the BBC who used to return them to me with kindly and detailed criticisms. However, two of my plays were broadcast in Australia and two in Canada. I think that if the BBC had accepted any of my work I might have kept on writing for the radio, because I enjoyed writing dialogue. As it was, I gave it up and concentrated my attention on the law.

Thomas, my new clerk, told me that there was to be an appointment on the Circuit of a second Prosecuting Counsel to the Post Office, and he urged me to apply for the job. The Post Office solicitors had to send all their Assizes and Quarter Sessions cases on each of the Circuits to the counsel who had been appointed by the Attorney-General to prosecute for them. In spite of its size, the whole of the South-Eastern Circuit had always been covered by one barrister. The present incumbent of the position was Michael Havers, a future Attorney-General and Lord Chancellor. The amount of Post Office work, mainly thefts of mail and savings bank frauds, was increasing all the time, and Michael had found that it was allowing insufficient time for dealing with the remainder of his substantial practice. He had suggested that the Circuit should be split into two parts, the north and the south. He himself would keep the northern counties, and a separate counsel should be nominated for the counties of Kent, Sussex and Surrey. His proposal was officially agreed and applications were invited for the new appointment.

I felt that it was a waste of time for me to apply, but to satisfy Thomas I did so. A few weeks later I received a message that the Attorney-General, Sir Reginald Manningham-Buller, wanted to see me the following afternoon in his chambers at the Law Courts. I was uncertain whether this meant that I had been placed on a short-list or that I had, surprisingly, been selected for the job.

Sir Reginald had been detained at the House of Commons when I called round to see him and I had to wait for almost an hour before he returned to his chambers. He was a large, thick-set man with an easy, cheerful manner. He told me he had carefully considered all the applications he had received and he had decided that I was the best person for the appointment. He added that Mr Justice Streatfeild had recommended me and so had the leader of my Circuit. He offered me his congratulations, and I left him, scarcely believing that this had really happened.

Hubert Munroe, with whom I had helped to found the Sponsorship scheme in the Middle Temple, was continually exhorting me to join the Liberal Party because, he said, my political views were very closely in accordance with theirs.

Hubert was a staunch, almost a fanatical, Liberal. He had stood for Parliament unsuccessfully at the General Election immediately after the war and had continued to nurse the same constituency as a parliamentary candidate ever since. Eventually I succumbed to his argument that the party was so small numerically, and their opinions were so little heeded, that anyone who shared their philosophy should become a paid-up member and should help to spread their beliefs. I joined the local South Kensington Liberal Association, making it quite clear to the committee that I had neither the time not the energy to play an active part in joined constituency affairs. After I had been a member of the association for a little over a year Hubert telephoned in chambers to tell me excitedly that he had put my name forward to be the next Liberal candidate for South

Kensington, and he was certain I would be adopted. I protested that this was about the last thing I wanted. I asked him to withdraw my nomination without delay, but I undertook that when the next General Election was approaching I would assist in the canvassing and campaigning. I fulfilled my pledge when the time came, and every evening after work I trudged round with the others calling at unwelcoming houses in an effort to whip up support for Liberals in one of the safest Conservative seats in the country.

I had accepted an invitation from Dame Isobel Cripps to join the Council of Management of Students Residential Centres (SRC), a charitable trust set up after the war to open and manage multi-racial hostels for young people of both sexes. Dame Isobel, the widow of Sir Stafford Cripps the Labour statesman, was a remarkable lady who devoted herself tirelessly to humanitarian causes. I had met her at one of Mrs Pandit's receptions and we had discussed the difficulties which were encountered by overseas students at the Inns of Court in finding somewhere to live while they were in London. SRC had just opened their first hostel, a large house in Wimbledon which accommodated about 30 residents cheaply in comfortable conditions.

The chairman of the Council of Management was the Earl of Lucan, a great-grandson of the general who had ordered the charge of the light brigade at Balaclava. He had been a junior Minister in Clement Attlee's post-war Labour Government and was now retired from active politics. Lord Lucan was a quiet, withdrawn and dignified man. He had a certain amount of difficulty in controlling our meetings which were apt to become stormy and acrimonious. Dame Isobel Cripps was a visionary, and although practical and clear-sighted herself, she had gathered together in her various projects a group of people who were mostly dedicated philanthropists, but some of whom were either temperamentally unbalanced or were of dubious sincerity.

I had had no idea that the management of a single hostel would entail so many problems. During my first year on the Council we had a series of crises. The sudden departure and replacement of the warden, the protracted illness of the chef, friction among the staff, and a male student who almost died from an overdose of drugs. Whenever an emergency arose Lord Lucan was inclined to ask me if I would go down to Wimbledon to investigate what was happening.

In due course Gerald Howard was appointed to the High Court Bench and Maxwell Turner went to the Old Bailey as a permanent Judge. Dr Lloyd had started to inquire, on my routine visits to the Brompton Hospital, how long I would have to wait before I could get some sort of settled employment, because he was becoming increasingly concerned about the amount of travelling I was doing on the Circuit. I told him that I was determined to remain in practice until I had sufficient experience and sufficient reputability to justify me in applying to be considered for the lower judiciary. I had set my heart on becoming a metropolitan stipendiary magistrate, but vacancies for the job were few and far between, and I realised that I would be up against strong competition from other members of the Criminal Bar. When I thought that the time was ripe, or nearly ripe, I sent a formal letter of application to the Lord

Chancellor's office at the House of Lords.

It was the custom that a barrister who wished to be considered for an appointment to the lower judiciary should inform the Lord Chancellor, whereas preferment to High Court Bench took place without the need for any such application. Metropolitan stipendiary magistrates were appointed by the Monarch on the advice of the Lord Chancellor, and it was well-known that before a candidate was short-listed for a vacancy a careful investigation was carried out of his background and ability. I suspected that, even if I was thought suitable in every other respect, my medical history might prove a decisive impediment to my selection. I felt certain that I could do everything that was required of me in spite of my difficulties in reading and writing, and to a certain extent in speaking. As far as I could tell, my judgment was unimpaired and my memory for facts was normal. I still woke up in the early morning with a splitting headache once or twice every week, but it usually passed off by half-past nine or ten o'clock before I went into court. I had been afflicted with continual insomnia since my head-wound and had learnt to live with it. The worst feature of those long wearying hours of sleeplessness was the worry about how exhausted I would feel in the morning and whether I would be fit to cope with the next day's work. My anxieties were considerably diminished after my experience of literally staying awake all night before the start of a fateful RAF court martial in Germany. I had been defending a Wing Commander, a well-known pilot in the Battle of Britain, on charges of driving while under the influence of alcohol and assaulting a civilian. The trial had taken place at Cologne during a sweltering heatwave. I shall never forget my small and stuffy bedroom in an Officers' Mess, and the sultry, airless night. In the morning I had contemplated asking for the case to be adjourned, but I was afraid I would look absurd when I gave the reason for my request. As it was, I had carried on. It turned out to be one of those rare cases for an advocate when every question I asked elicited the reply for which I was hoping. In the late afternoon my client was acquitted of both charges.

In reply to my letter of application, I received from the Lord Chancellor's office a questionnaire requiring details of my education, academic qualifications, war service record, the state of my practice, my professional income, and my health. I was also required to provide the names of a few people who would be willing to act as referees on my behalf. In my answers to the questions I mentioned my head-wound and the fact that I was assessed as being 100 per cent disabled. I was then asked for a detailed medical report from a neurosurgeon or a neurologist who had up-to-date knowledge of my condition.

George Northcroft, who had looked after me throughout my time at St Hugh's, was then the senior neurosurgeon of the Brook Hospital at Woolwich. I went to see him there and he agreed to write the report. After giving me a thorough medical examination and asking me numerous questions he told me he would inform the Lord Chancellor that the after-effects of my head-wound would not in any way interfere with my work as a metropolitan magistrate.

A few weeks later I received a message that Sir Thomas Skyrme, the Secretary of Commissions in the Lord

Chancellor's Office, would like to see me at the House of Lords. At my interview with him I faced a lot more questions about my practice, and he wanted to know if my disabilities caused me to tire quickly or to become bad-tempered. Finally, he warned me that there were at that moment, a number of able and well-suited candidates waiting to become metropolitan magistrates. I took this to be an indication that my chances of being appointed were exceedingly remote.

My hopes were revived when I was invited to sit as a temporary deputy chairman at the County of London Quarter Sessions for four weeks. My clerk, Thomas, assured me that this meant I was being tried out for a job on the Bench. The trouble was, he said, that my instructing solicitors would think so too, and would be disinclined to send me briefs in the future as they would be looking out for new barristers to do their work. In the initial stages I felt very strange and very isolated sitting on the Bench in a crowded courtroom. Most of the counsel who appeared before me were my friends or acquaintances. However, none of them ever took advantage of our previous relationship, or of my inexperience and the impermanence of my authority. I found that summing-up at the end of a case was the most formidable task with which I had to contend. It was necessary to explain the law to the jury in language intelligible to a lay person, and to summarise the evidence as concisely as possible in a way that would accentuate the issues of fact they would have to decide in reaching their verdict.

After my four weeks at the County of London Sessions

had ended I returned to my practice. I did not know whether I had done well or badly, and I had no idea what sort of reports had been sent to the Lord Chancellor's Office about my performance of my judicial duties. If I had created an unfavourable impression I presumed that I would hear nothing more from them, and their prolonged silence would be the only indication of my failure. I tried to prepare myself for the worst, but knew I would be bitterly disappointed if it happened. I had found my brief spell as a deputy chairman immensely enjoyable. It was not that I was beguiled by the supremacy of the Judge in his own court, or by the deference with which he is treated there. It was rather that I had found the work so absorbing, so stimulating, and so full of human interest. I had come to realise that I did not possess the proper temperament for a good professional advocate, who must be capable of advancing a proposition with persuasive assurance even though it wholly differs from what he believes to be the truth. I would have infinitely preferred the function of an arbiter who hears the arguments of the disputants and endeavours to achieve a just result.

I knew that even if I was to get a judicial appointment it would not happen very soon. Fortunately I was kept very busy for the next few months so I did not have a lot of time to worry about it. I sat on several occasions for a day or more as Deputy Recorder of Gravesend. The Recorder, Petre Crowder, was parliamentary private secretary to the Attorney-General, and he sometimes found it difficult to fit in his sittings with all his other commitments. I was only too pleased to take his place whenever I was invited to do so because I wanted to gain as much experience as possible. Thomas told me it was a hopeful sign that I was authorised to act as a Deputy Recorder by the Lord Chancellor's office. They would not have permitted it, he said, unless they thought that I was reasonably competent. Usually the Mayor of Gravesend sat beside me on the Bench and during the short adjournment we would go into the Mayor's parlour for coffee and sandwiches.

I had been briefed to appear as a junior counsel for the defence in a murder case at the Old Bailey. I was to be led by Paul Wrightson, now the head of our chambers, who had just become a QC. Our client, with three other Scotsmen, had been involved in a drunken Saturday evening brawl against four men from Liverpool outside a public house. No weapons had been used but one of the Liverpudlians had been savagely kicked to death, and the four Scotsmen had been jointly charged with murdering him. As each of the defendants was separately represented by two counsel, and there were a number of witnesses called by both the prosecution and the defence, the trial lasted for more than a fortnight. When I returned to chambers at the end of the second day, Thomas told me that the Lord Chancellor's office had been inquiring how long it would be before the case was finished and I would be free. They had asked him to inform them directly the Judge had begun his summing-up. I told Paul about this and he felt sure I was about to be appointed a metropolitan magistrate.

During the closing stages of the trial Paul Wrightson's voice was becoming increasingly hoarse and he asked me to make the final speech to the jury in his place. "After all," he said, "it seems fitting that you should do it as it's very probable that this is the last brief you'll ever have." Sadly, it turned out to be the last brief he himself ever had before he was diagnosed as suffering from untreatable cancer of the throat.

In the outcome, only one of the Scotsmen was convicted of murder. He had denied taking part in the kicking but traces of the victim's blood group had been found on the toecaps of his boots. The other three, including my client, were found guilty of manslaughter.

The morning after the trial ended I received a letter informing me in the customary phraseology that the Lord Chancellor was 'minded' to recommend me to the Queen for appointment as a metropolitan stipendiary magistrate, and that I must not mention it to anyone apart from my clerk. Soon afterwards Sir Robert Blundell, the Chief Magistrate, asked me to lunch with him at his club. He told me that I would be starting at Bow Street on the following Monday. He had tried to arrange for me to be sworn in on the preceding Friday, but he had been unsuccessful. "The Treasury took the view," he said, "that if you were sworn in on Friday they would have to pay you for three whole days before you actually started work. So you will have to take the oath at the Royal Courts of Justice first thing on Monday morning and then get a taxi round to Bow Street, where we will have a full day's list waiting for you." He added with a wry smile, "Don't expect to be reimbursed for your cab fare. You'll have to get used to the cheese-paring ways of the Treasury from now on."

I had not anticipated that my appointment to the

humbler judiciary would have any news value whatsoever. To my surprise on the Monday morning several national newspapers ran stories about what they called my 'miraculous' recovery from severe war-wounds, and highlighted the fact that it had been thought that I would never be able to speak again. One of the tabloids published a feature article about my war service and my subsequent career at the Bar.

I was sworn in by Lord Widgery, the Lord Chief Justice, at half past 10, and in accordance with my instructions from Robert Blundell I caught a taxi outside the Royal Courts of Justice and was driven to Bow Street where a couple of photogprahers were waiting for me by the magistrates' entrance. I was met inside by Mr Minden, the chief clerk, who showed me to my room and had a hurried talk with me about my list. He told me that I was being thrown in at the deep end as I was going to sit in the court which dealt with all the arrests which had taken place since the previous Saturday afternoon. It was after 11 o'clock before I walked to take my place on the Bench. I was aware of the thronged courtroom, the upturned faces, and the inquisitive eyes. Directly I was seated a couple of barristers waiting for their cases to be called on welcomed me on behalf of the Bar, and then the maelstrom of frenzied activity commenced. Bow Street was the busiest Magistrates' Court in London - probably, the busiest in the whole of Britain. The tempo was frantic. Case followed case with scarcely a pause. First, the overnight arrests, the drunks, the prostitutes and the unlicensed street-traders. Next the more serious offenders, the muggers, pickpockets, burglars and car thieves. Police officers and advocates were springing up continually to make applications, and documents kept showering on my desk. Mr. Minden my clerk, seated on a lower level in front of me, firmly and imperturbably controlled the sequence of events, guiding me from time to time on matters of procedure. In the afternoon the pace subsided and I dealt with motoring offences, of which summonses for dangerous or careless driving took the most time. When I finished my list at five o'clock I felt that I had certainly done a full day's work.

I settled down quickly and happily to my new life. The other three stipendiary magistrates at Bow Street were always pleasant, helpful and ever ready to guide me through my initial difficulties. Our rooms were adjoining on the first floor of the building. Sir Robert Blundell had by far the largest as the Chief Magistrate's room was used for his conferences and for the monthly meeting of all the metropolitan magistrates. Next door to him was his deputy, Kenneth Barraclough, and lastly, a room shared by Geraint Rees and myself.

Robert Blundell, who had been in Max Turner's chambers before I joined them, was a wealthy bachelor of the old school. He lived at a comfortable flat in Mayfair and used to spend most of his spare time at one of his three West End clubs or during the summer months, at Lords. His slightly detached, apathetic, attitude towards his subordinate colleagues was often mistaken for lethargy. In truth, the scenario of perfection as far as he was concerned, was that his Bench of magistrates should perform their daily duties with discreet competence, avoiding both controversy or complaint. On my first day at Bow Street he said to me, "I want you to remember, Tony, that there will always be at least one reporter in your court, and any provocative remarks or contentious comments you make may be regarded as newsworthy. The less I see your name in the papers the better I'll think you are doing your work."

Within a few weeks of my appointment, in a moment of thoughtlessness, I forgot to heed Robert Blundell's warning. I had been trying a case in which the defendant was charged with carrying out a series of frauds on betting-shops. At one o'clock the prosecuting counsel, a man I knew very well, asked me to hear a very short expert witness before I adjourned. The witness was a bookmaker, he said, who would merely be testifying that if a person makes a hundred bets at least one of them is almost sure to be successful. "Probably you know that from your own experience, Sir," he added with a smile.

Although I only backed horses extremely rarely I replied jokingly that all my last 100 bets had been unsuccessful.

Going home in the tube that evening I was appalled to see a short paragraph about my remark in an evening paper under the heading of 'The punter on the Bench'. Another evening paper had written it up under the headline: 'Bow Street Magistrate admits gambling losses'. That was not the end of the matter, as shortly after I arrived at the flat I received a phone call from the racing correspondent of a national daily who wanted to know if I had used any particular method in making my unfortunate run of bets.

During the first summer at Bow Street there was a long spell of particularly warm weather, and there were a number of reports in the papers of young women appearing topless in the streets, mostly at seaside resorts but also in a few inland towns. No one seemed to be at all sure whether or not a female who fully exposed her breasts in a public place was committing any criminal offence, and it was apparent that if the custom spread the courts might have to rule on the matter.

Early one afternoon in July a 30-year-old married woman posed for a snapshot on Westminster Bridge with the upper half of her body completely naked. The bridge was fairly crowded at the time, and two men complained about her behaviour to a police constable. As a result, she was summonsed under an old London county council by-law, alleging that she had committed an act of indecency to the annoyance of passers-by. A week later two sisters in their early twenties, both cabaret singers, arrived by car for a film *premiére* in Piccadilly. They were wearing evening dresses and had wraps around their shoulders. As they walked through the crowd on the pavement outside the cinema they allowed their wraps to fall, revealing their topless dresses underneath. They were summonsed under the same by-law.

Robert Blundell called me into his room and told me I was going to try all three cases. "Whatever you decide," he said, "a whole lot of people are going to be furious with you. But you're the youngest metropolitan magistrate on the Bench at the moment, and you should be more 'with it' than the rest of us. Apart from that you'll have longer to live down your unpopularity."

The three cases were listed on the same afternoon. When

I returned to Bow Street after lunch there was a large group of photographers and television cameramen outside the main entrance waiting for the women and the witnesses to arrive. The reporters could not all fit into the press seats in my court and a lot of them had to stand round the dock with their notebooks in their hands. The Westminster Bridge case was called on first and then the two sisters were tried together. All three defendants pleaded "not guilty." According to the *Daily Express* account next morning, the magistrate repeatedly had to stop laughter in the packed public benches as witnesses spoke. Having heard the evidence I convicted the three of them. As these were in the nature of test cases I granted conditional discharges to each of the women, as well as ordering them to pay two guineas costs.

The letters started to come in right away, mostly anonymous, mostly abusive. One man wrote that he had seen my photo in a newspaper alongside a photo of the woman who had exposed herself on Westminster Bridge. "Your ugly face would cause me to suffer far more annoyance," he said, "than a glimpse of her shapely naked tits." A lady, who signed her name, told me she was writing to the Lord Chancellor to get me sacked. I was obviously in sympathy with these three dreadful females, she went on, otherwise I would have sentenced them to long terms of imprisonment. It was people like me, in her opinion, who had ruined a once-great nation like Britain.

Bernard Levin was then a columnist on the *Daily Mail*. He devoted a whole article to an attack on my narrow-mindedness. A few days later T.E. Utley sprang to my defence in *The Sunday Telegraph* and said that I had stated the case for society. I cannot recall the exact words I used when I gave my judgment, but according to *The Sunday Telegraph*, when seeking to define indecent behaviour I said:

"In every civilised community at any one time there are certain conventions of decency in public places which are generally accepted and generally approved."

That was my reasoning at the time, and even now I do not think it was faulty. At any rate, the defendants appealed against my decision and all their appeals were dismissed.

After the Bow Street indecency cases, women ceased to appear topless in the streets. Perhaps it was because of the convictions, or because a few days later the weather became much colder.

CHAPTER 26

During the initial months I was sitting at Bow Street I had walked down to the Middle Temple for lunch nearly every day. The regular users of our table in Hall insisted on giving a dinner to celebrate my becoming a metropolitan magistrate. It was held in a private room at a fashionable restaurant in the West End, and about 20 people attended. I realised with a pang of regret that my ties with the Inn would gradually loosen now that I had ceased to practise. There was a convention at all four Inns of court that if a barrister who was not already a Bencher was appointed to the lower judiciary, he would become permanently ineligible for call to the Bench. I knew that as the years went by most of my group of friends would become Benchers or would leave the Bar, and then the Middle Temple Hall would hold nothing for me but a host of pleasant memories.

The members of my chambers also gave me a dinner on my appointment. As we sat chatting and drinking after the meal was over, I begged them all to let me know if I ever developed any bad traits as a magistrate which were objectionable to the barristers appearing before me. They promised me that they would do so.

I had never joined a London club because I did not think I would have sufficient time to make use of it. Now, however, my lifestyle would be different. The only club I wanted to join was the Garrick, but I knew that the membership was fairly small and I had been told the credentials of the candidates were examined with meticulous care before they were elected. The first time I had gone there I had been invited to lunch by a man I did not know who had just read *No Memorial*. I had walked up the steps to the entrance behind a tall, stooping man with a hooked nose, who turned out to be T.S. Eliot. It was a great thrill for me as I had always been fascinated by his poetry and his plays. My host and I lunched at a side table in the coffee room, the walls of which were covered with old theatrical paintings, and I had immediately been conscious of an atmosphere of sociality and friendship. It was Edward Robey, then sitting as a magistrate at Marlborough Street, who suggested to me that I should become a member. He offered to propose me himself, and advised me to get a publisher to act as my seconder as he thought I would stand more chance of being elected if I was not sponsored by two fellow-lawyers.

When your name had been entered in the candidates' book at the Garrick, any member who knew you and would like to see you elected could sign your page. In those days there was a waiting period of about six months before a candidate was considered by the committee. Such is the popularity of the club that the waiting time since then has gradually crept up to six years. Immediately after my election Ted Robey introduced me to the chairman, the secretary, and the key members of the staff.

The Garrick is only a few minutes' walk from Bow Street and I started using it regularly for lunch, though I still went down to Middle Temple Hall once or twice a week. "We don't regard ourselves as being merely a club," said a member to me on one of my early lunch-time visits. "We prefer to look on ourselves as being a large family." I soon discovered what he meant. There were certain Garrick conventions with which everyone automatically conformed.

If a new member entered the Bar alone, someone would speak to him. When you went into the coffee room for a meal you sat at the first vacant place on either side of the long table, and you were obliged to chat with your neighbours. These and other customs of the club encouraged cordiality among the members.

Naturally, it increased the allurement of the club for me that so many well-known actors lunched there habitually. I often saw Kenneth Moore, Donald Woolfitt, Donald Sinden and Frank Lawton; sometimes I sat next to one of them at the table, and I invariably found them to be both interesting and charming. Others whom I saw on occasion included Laurence Olivier, John Gielgud and Alec Guinness.

My excitement at belonging to the club, and my devotion to it, have never lessened. Most of the members feel the same way as I do. Somebody sitting next to me at dinner on one occasion remarked, "If one could be sure that the after-life would have the same ambience as the Garrick; it would help to take the sting out of death."

The metropolitan magistrates at Bow Street had a special responsibility connected with the protection of young persons below the age of 21 who went overseas on engagements as professional entertainers. We would see them with their agents before they left the country, to make sure the terms of their contracts were in order, and that suitable arrangements had been made for their accommodation and welfare. We saw them again when they returned at the end of their travels to find out if they had been looked after properly. We carried out the interviews, sometimes with individuals, sometimes with groups, in our rooms before we went into court for the morning list. The Chief Clerk knew that I enjoyed this duty so he frequently asked me to do it. The procedure was informal and relaxed, and after a while a lot of faces became familiar. The Dagenham Girl Pipers and the Bluebell Girls were very popular with the Bow Street staff, and the actress Hayley Mills was a particular favourite. I generally found that the young entertainers had no complaints about their treatment when their engagements were in Western Europe and America had come to end. However, several girls who had gone out to the Middle East as dancers or singers had had unpleasant experiences or had run into trouble with the managements employing them.

As a metropolitan magistrate I had to sit for four days a week. There was seldom any preparatory work to be done in the evenings or at weekends as we usually started on a fresh list of cases every morning. It seemed to me that this was the ideal job for a part-time writer and I decided to begin another book. I chose for my subject the history of punishment in Britain.

Before Judges or magistrates sit in a criminal court for the first time they have to make a personal appraisal of their attitude towards their new responsibility for passing sentence on their fellows. My own approach to the matter was very simple. I believed that offenders could be divided into three categories: those who needed help, those who deserved mercy, and those who merited punishment. I had never considered it to be either inhuman or purposeless for some wrongdoers to be sent to prison, nor did I think it improper for the element of retribution to be taken into account, and I felt quite certain that deterrent sentences could be a potent factor in the discouragement of crime.

Now that I had the time, I wanted to look at as many prisons and other penal establishments as possible so that I would get a better understanding of the nature of the sentences I was passing. I mentioned this to Barry Swinney, one of the four probation officers at Bow Street, and he willingly agreed to make the necessary arrangements for me. From then on I paid regular visits to various prisons, borstals and detention centres, usually accompanied by a court probation officer. The Governors were always helpful in showing me round and discussing their problems with me. They often gave me the opportunity to speak to the staff and the inmates about the conditions and routine.

Punishment must of necessity be disagreeable; otherwise it lacks its fundamental purpose. However, the punitive aspect of imprisonment should be confined to the deprivation of liberty. Prisoners should not be subjected to an overcrowded and primitive environment, calculated discomfort, and long empty hours of boredom, as was the case in most of British prisons at that time. During the next few years I went on a study-tour, organised by the Magistrates' Association, to examine the Norwegian penal system. I was most impressed with the prisons we were shown. The inmates lived in austere, but not unpleasant conditions; they were employed all day for modest wages in the prison workshop; and in the evenings they were allowed facilities for exercise and recreation. I also visited Finland on a similar tour and I was equally impressed with the Finnish penal system.

Soon after I went to Bow Street Lord Lucan died and we were faced with finding another chairman for the Council of Management of Students' Residential Centres. There was a suggestion that we should invite the new Lord Lucan to take over from his father, but it was decided that he would almost certainly refuse as he was not interested in charitable projects. Several years afterwards he suddenly disappeared and he has not been seen since. Rather to my surprise, our honorary secretary informed me that he had canvassed all the other members of the council and it was the unanimous opinion that the vacant chairmanship should be offered to me. Without any hesitation I accepted.

Once my appointment had been officially confirmed we launched an appeal with a view to opening a second international hostel. It was very difficult to raise money for such a purpose, as this was a period when student organisations were staging disorderly demonstrations, sit-ins, and minor riots. In consequence, the general public were becoming increasingly exasperated with their behaviour. We did not employ a professional fund-raiser, but we wrote endless letters to private individuals and to charitable trusts. Eventually, with the funds we had managed to raise and a grant from the British Council, we bought another large house in Wimbledon, not far from our existing hostel. After it had been furnished and staff had been employed, it was opened for us by Sir Cyril Black, the MP for Wimbledon.

It was customary for newly-appointed metropolitan magistrates to sit at Bow Street for a while, under the watchful eye of the Chief Magistrate, before being sent on to another court. Robert Blundell and I used to get on particularly well with one another, and he kept me at Bow Street for more than two years, despite the fact that there were several more appointments during that time. At length, he told me he would have to send me temporarily to fill a vacancy at the recently opened court in Wells Street, very near Oxford Circus. I did not remain there very long before I moved to Marylebone Magistrates' Court in the Paddington area, where I remained on a permanent basis. It was now impossible for me to get down to the Middle Temple for lunch, and it was even difficult to get to the Garrick unless I finished my morning list on the early side and none of my colleagues needed my assistance. Normally I lunched with the other magistrates in a private room which was made available to us by the landlord of a public house nearby.

I had called my new book *The Problem of Punishment*. My literary agents placed it with Pergamon Press at Oxford, which was owned by Robert Maxwell, the publishing tycoon and Labour MP. It was to be brought out by a Pergamon subsidiary in London with offices not far from the Marylebone court. The editorial department did not like my title and changed it to *The Power To Silence*, a quotation from Johnson's *Sermons*, 'The power of punishment is to silence, not to confute.'

A few publishers and others at the Garrick told me I was foolish to get mixed up with a man like Robert Maxwell, who even then had a bad reputation. They warned me that I might have difficulty in getting royalty payments, and that I would be done down all along the line. After his mysterious death Maxwell came to be regarded as an arch-villain on account of disclosures about his dubious financial transactions, and his massive defalcations from the *Daily Mirror* staff pension fund. All I can say is that in my own dealings with him in connection with my book, I invariably found him to be scrupulously fair and honest. In addition, he was very helpful to the students' residential centres as he arranged for all our printing to be done by the Pergamon Press, free of charge. I met Robert Maxwell too rarely and too fleetingly to form any definite opinions about him. I remember him as a person who could exercise a quiet charm, and yet who had a chilling quality in his distant but decisive manner.

Before *The Power to Silence* was published I had had to obtain clearance from the Lord Chancellor's Department. They were very hesitant about granting it at first, especially as the book was about punishment, but they eventually assented on my undertaking that the subject-matter was entirely historical and that I had not commented on the present-day British penal system. When the review copies had been sent out, a few weeks before publication, Alix Palmer, a girl who wrote regular feature articles for the *Daily Express*, rang up to say that she would like to discuss the book with me. I was not sitting next day so she came to see me at my flat. It was only after she had left I recalled that under the 'Kilmuir Rules' an edict issued by Viscount Kilmuir when he was Lord Chancellor, members of the judiciary were strictly forbidden to grant interviews to the press. But the deed was then done and there was no going back on it. I had to reconcile myself to the expectation of being severely reprimanded. I hoped the consequences would be no worse.

Alix Palmer's article was published two days later under the heading: "Do We Really Know How to Punish Criminals?"

The problem, she wrote, was fully discussed in my book. She described me with journalistic licence, as a London stipendiary magistrate 'who had quickly acquired a reputation for fairness and understanding towards both the criminal and Society.' She quoted me, no doubt accurately, as saying that this was the age of the hooligan and the thug, and upholding imprisonment as a necessary punishment, but severely criticising the conditions in our prisons.

To my surprised relief I did not receive an imperious summons to present myself at the Lord Chancellor's Department. The book was published in due course and was reviewed a lot more widely than I had anticipated. The fact that it was recommended by the Book Society as one of the best books of the month was less of an honour than it might have been because Robert Maxwell had then taken over control of the Book Society.

The editor of a magazine supplement of one of the national Sunday newspapers wrote to tell me that he was planning to have a feature on the history of punishment in Britain in a future issue, and he would like me to contribute an introductory article on the subject. I rang up Sir Thomas Skyrme, the Secretary of Commissions, to make sure there would be no objection to my doing this. I said that I was prepared to give a similar undertaking to the one I had given before the publication of my book, and that any fee I received for the article I would make over in full to the Barristers' Benevolent Association. There was a pause for a moment. Then he said in a reproachful tone, "I'm very surprised indeed at your making such a request. You ought to know that the Kilmuir Rules forbid members of the judiciary to write for the press."

"Even historical articles?" I asked.

"Yes," he replied emphatically. "Even historical articles."

Robert Blundell had suffered for years with high blood pressure and gout. Ever since I had been a magistrate his health had been deteriorating visibly and I was not entirely surprised when I heard that he was very ill in the Charing Cross hospital. I visited him there one afternoon and found him in a small, bare single room, propped up in bed by a pile of pillows. He looked pale and tired but he seemed to be quite cheerful in spite of the fact that he was intermittently in considerable pain. He hated being in hospital and he was longing to be discharged so that he could go down to Brighton for his convalescence.

After we had chatted for a while about general topics, he said suddenly, "I've decided that when I start working again I'm going to get you back to Bow Street - unless you prefer to be out in the sticks."

I told him I would like nothing better than to return. He was becoming more and more sleepy but he asked me to stay a bit longer. Eventually, he fell asleep and I left his room as quietly as possible.

I never saw Robert Blundell again. He died in Brighton while he was convalescing. Frank Milton, whom I did not know at all well, was appointed Chief Magistrate in his place and, as was customary, received a knighthood a few months later.

As I became used to being on the Bench my various disabilities scarcely troubled me at all. A Magistrates' Court did not have a shorthand-writer so the rapidity with which the witnesses could give their evidence was governed by the speed with which the clerk could take down what they were saying. This gave me enough time, despite my dyslexia, to make adequate notes for my own purposes. My insomnia caused me no concern for I had found that if I had four or five hours' sleep during the night it was perfectly sufficient for the day ahead of me. My morning headaches still persisted with the same frequency. However, if I took analgesic tablets before I left home to go to court they had almost invariably passed off before I started my first case.

As regards my physical defects, the most gratifying compliment I could be paid was when people said to me, "You manage so well that when I'm with you I keep forgetting you can only use one arm."

About a year after my transfer to Marylebone I became aware that the front portion of the large scar on my head was becoming increasingly inflamed and swollen. For a time I coated the sore patch with ointment, but this did not bring about any improvement. I still hoped it would get better without treatment although I realised it was getting worse. The barber, who had been cutting my hair for years, peered at the scar and said, "I don't like the look of this at all; it seems to be infected and it's oozing."

I could disregard it no longer, so on my next day off I

went down to Woolwich to consult George Northcroft at the Brook Hospital.

George examined the inflamed area and said, "I'm afraid the forward edge of your tantalum plate has pierced your scalp and caused an ulcer. I'll have to operate on it as soon as possible."

I asked him about the nature of the operation and he told me that he would have to reopen part of my old scar, peel back the scalp, and cut off the front of my plate. "You should only be in hospital for a week or 10 days," he added, "and then you'll need another two or three weeks to recuperate before you return to work."

The Lord Chancellor's Department were extremely helpful and sympathetic when they heard what had happened, and immediately told me that I would be granted sick leave until the end of my convalescence. Frank Milton assured me that he would have no difficulty in finding another magistrate to relieve me until I was able to return.

Then came another spell of the old, dreary routine of blanket-baths, bandages, dressings, headaches, pain-killers, discomfort, and general incapacity. When I returned to work I felt fully recovered except for a continuous throbbing in my head. George had told me he could do nothing to alleviate this, but he was certain it would pass. Sure enough it began to lessen after a few weeks and then gradually disappeared.

It was soon after I was back at Marylebone that an organisation called the Vietnamese Solidarity Campaign started to hold massive demonstrations in London, which invariably developed into riots. We were inundated with cases arising out of these disorders, usually the defendants were charged with provocative behaviour or assaulting the police. I formed the impression, and so did the other magistrates, that although the bulk of the demonstrators were sincere and peaceably inclined, there was always a certain element which was intent on a confrontation with the police. I regretted to see that quite a lot of the offenders who appeared before me were students from red-brick universities who had come up to London in special coaches for the specific purpose of taking part in the rallies.

About this time Justice, the British section of the International Society of Jurists, had arranged to hold a one-day conference on the granting and refusal of bail. Frank Milton had agreed to attend and he told me he would like me to go with him.

The conference took place on a Saturday at the Lord Chief Justice's Court in the Strand. Just as I was preparing to leave my flat that morning Sir Thomas Skyrme telephoned me to inform me that he had also been invited to attend. "Naturally I don't intend to speak," he said, "and I assume that you won't do so either. Bail is a sensitive subject and a public statement about it by a member of the judiciary could easily be misquoted or misinterpreted."

I never discovered whether Frank Milton had received a similar admonition. If so he ignored it as he made a number of very intelligent observations in the course of the discussions. I know that he shared my irritation regarding the absurd rigidity of the Kilmuir Rules.

At the end of the day, it was decided to set up a Justice working party to investigate and report upon the bail system. Frank proposed that I should be a member, and this appeared to meet with general approval, although I had made scarcely any contribution towards the proceedings.

Less than a year after my operation at the Brook another ulcer had formed in my scalp, and George Northcroft had had to cut back my tantalum plate once again. Before I was discharged from hospital I asked him if the trouble was likely to recur.

"I can give you no assurance that it won't," he said. "Once a plate has started to go wrong, the outlook is unpredictable."

In view of his reply I had made up my mind that if this happened again in the near future I would have to resign from the Bench, as I could not continue taking sick leave so frequently.

For three or four months we had been seeing each other practically every day, and we had been continually in each other's thoughts.

We had dinner together the evening before she flew back to New York. It was then I asked her to marry me. She took my hand in hers and told me very sadly and very tenderly that it would not be possible.

"You're haunted by a ghost," she said. "Emma is always there. Even in our most intimate moments I never feel I have you to myself. I couldn't share my marriage-bed with a husband and the ghost of a woman he still loved."

After she had spoken, I think we both realised that this was the last occasion on which we would ever meet.

CHAPTER 27

Robert Blundell used to say that he intended to write a book on the history of Bow Street Magistrates' Court, but in fact he had never even started to collect the material for it. During the last year of his life he told me he knew that he would never get down to carrying out the necessary research and he hoped that I would decide to write the book myself.

It was an interesting story and well worth telling. It had commenced in 1740 when Thomas De Veil, a Justice of the Peace for Middlesex and for Westminster, had transferred his magistrate's office to a house in Bow Street, on the opposite side of the road to the present court building. At that time there were no professional police and no Magistrates' Courts in Britain. Justices of the Peace had been responsible for investigating crimes, and they performed their judicial duties in their own homes or offices. De Veil had converted the ground floor of his Bow Street house into a courtroom.

When De Veil died in 1746, Henry Fielding, the novelist and playwright, had taken over his house and his magisterial responsibilities and had been succeeded in turn by his blind half-brother Sir John Fielding. The Fielding brothers had initiated the Bow Street Runners, the first detective force in Britain. Sir John had also introduced the Bow Street Horse Patrol, consisting of parties of well-armed, mounted constables who rode round the streets of the metropolis during the hours of darkness to make them safer for the inhabitants. A Bow Street Foot Patrol had been started 10 years after Sir John's death. The old Bow Street office had finally closed in 1881 on the opening of the new court.

I called my book, *A House In Bow Street*, a title I took from Walford's 1813 *London Gazetteer* which stated about the old office:

"In Bow Street is a house celebrated all over the United Kingdom and, it may be said, the whole world ..."

I did most of my research in the Middlesex records office, the City of Westminster Public Library and among the numerous documents in the Bedford Estates collection. The book was published by Macdonald, after I had given the customary undertaking to the Lord Chancellor's Department that the subject-matter was entirely historical.

I had negotiated with the immediate landlords of my flat in South Kensington on behalf of a little syndicate consisting of my sister Noreen, two friends and myself, and we had purchased the lease of the whole house for a period of just over 40 years. We had then sub-let one of the flats to each of ourselves, so that we remained co-tenants of the house but we were the individual sub-tenants of our own flats. The fifth flat, in the basement, we sub-let to two girls, both freelance artists, and we used the rent they paid us to defray the general expenses connected with the servicing and upkeep of the premises.

I used to spend most of my leave periods travelling abroad, sometimes staying with relatives or friends, sometimes going on a trip by myself. When Eve and Peter were overseas they always invited me to come and stay with them for as long as I liked. I visited them twice in Malta where they had a pleasant house overlooking St Paul's Bay. The second time I was there Peter, then a commander, arranged for me to be allowed on board his ship while they were out on a six-day cruise to test some new equipment. On a later occasion I stayed with them in Singapore when Peter was captain of HMS *Triumph* which was then stationed there. After I had left them I travelled up Malaysia by train, stopping for a few days at Kuala Lumpur, Ipoh and Penang. On my way home I spent a week in Bangkok.

I had formed a close friendship with an American family, namesakes of mine, who lived at St Louis in the middle-west, and I used to visit them frequently. Charles Babington had written to me out of the blue to tell me that he and his wife Sarah were coming to England on vacation, and he was anxious to meet any Babingtons who might be his relatives. I had asked them to a dinner party at my flat. It was an unpredictable encounter for all of us since they knew as little about me as I knew about them, but it proved to be a tremendous success as we took to each other at once. Charles's great-grandfather, who had emigrated to the United States, had come from Dublin so we felt it was very likely that we were distant cousins. Charles and Sarah had two sons, who were both at university reading law when I first met their parents. I went over to St Louis for the wedding of Kip, the elder of the two. At the reception Charles had insisted that I should say a few words on behalf of all the unadventurous Babingtons who had remained in Ireland.

Arnold and Helen were very keen for me to stay with them in Auckland, as we had not seen each other for such a long time. Some neighbours of theirs had a daughter, Raewyn, who was coming to London for a year or two to attend a drama school and Arnold tentatively suggested that I might think of accompanying her when she returned to New Zealand at the end of the course. Raewyn's parents had asked me to keep an eye on her while she was over here, and I had promised to do so. It was a pleasant duty because she was a bright, lively, and very attractive girl. Not surprisingly, she soon formed a group of friends of her own age and became immersed in their social activities. However, we had an agreement that she would keep closely in touch with me and would come out to dinner with me once a month so that I could feel I was not neglecting my responsibilities.

After her course at the drama school was finished Raewyn did not go back home immediately. She was enjoying herself over here and she seemed to have no difficulty getting parts in plays, sometimes at West End theatres, sometimes in the provinces. Eventually, at one of our monthly dinners, she told me she had decided to return to New Zealand because a production company there had offered her the lead in a play they were going to take out on tour. She said that she had an additional reason for leaving London; she was about to become engaged to her boy-friend and she thought they should separate for a while to make absolutely sure of their feelings for each other.

We arranged to fly out to Auckland together. We both wanted to stop off for a few days at San Francisco and at Hawaii, which were on our route. Raewyn had a friend who was a travel agent so we left it to him to book our air tickets and to reserve our hotel accommodation for us.

Everything worked out well for the initial stages of our journey. We had left San Francisco on an evening flight to Hawaii and landed at Honolulu after midnight. We were told by the taxi-driver who took us from the airport to our hotel that we had arrived in the middle of a festival and the town was very crowded; it was lucky we had booked our rooms in advance, he remarked. The night manager at the hotel spent several minutes studying the register. Then he looked up and shook his head.

"We have no bookings in either of your names," he informed us, "and in any case, we're absolutely full."

I asked him if he could get us in somewhere else and he replied that it would be a waste of time for him to try because all of the hotels were full until the festival was over. He glanced at the register again.

"There's only one possibility," he said. "The couple who booked our special honeymoon room haven't shown up yet and it doesn't look as though they'll be coming tonight. I'm willing to cancel their booking and to give the room to you for the three nights you're in Honolulu."

When Raewyn inquired whether it contained a couch on which one of us would be able to sleep. He looked surprised. "No," he said, "there is no couch. But I can assure you that the bed is sufficiently wide for two and is very comfortable."

Raewyn reminded me firmly that she was on the point of announcing her engagement and she insisted that it would be unthinkable for us to share the honeymoon bed for three nights. She persuaded the reluctant night manager to telephone innumerable hotels in the district, and eventually he found one with two vacant single bedrooms.

My visit to Arnold and Helen was disappointing in only one respect; I would have liked to have seen something of New Zealand, but I was caught up in a non-stop round of parties given for me by their immensely hospitable friends. As a result, I remained in Auckland the whole time. After two weeks, I flew to Canberra to stay with some cousins on their sheep station. I then went for a few days to Sydney where the Pergamon Press representatives had fixed up for me to give two broadcast talks and to be interviewed twice on television. I found that my principal claim to fame was my judgment with regard to topless dresses.

On my way home I spent a few days in Hong Kong.

I had been commissioned by Macdonald, the publishers of my book on Bow Street, to write a history of Newgate Gaol and of prison conditions in Britain from the year 1188, when Newgate came into existence, until 1902, when it was finally demolished. I had finished the manuscript before my trip to New Zealand and I received the proofs soon after my return. James Callaghan, a popular and successful Home Secretary in the Labour Government which had just lost office, agreed to contribute a foreword to the book. I had never met him before he came to a publication party at my flat, and I was deeply impressed as were my other guests, by his modest and unassuming manner.

During the week in which the book was published I was invited by the BBC to be interviewed about it on their early morning current affairs programme *Today*. The organisation for getting me to the studio in time was most impressive.

First of all I received an alarm call on the telephone. Then, having allowed me sufficient time to bath, shave and dress, a car drew up at my door to take me to Broadcasting House, where I was shown into the *Today* waiting-room. It was reminiscent of visiting the dentist or a doctor's surgery, except that there were no magazines and in a corner there was a trolley containing tea, coffee, cereals and toast.

The Lord Chancellor's Department had given me permission to make the broadcast provided that I did not comment upon prison conditions in Britain after 1902. The two presenters came into the waiting-room for cups of coffee while the weather forecast and the seven o'clock news bulletin were being read. Robert Robinson, who was going to interview me, told me that he intended to ask me for my assessment of the state of the British prison system at the present moment. Apparently he had not heard about the restriction which had been placed on me and when I appraised him of it he remarked rather testily that he could not see why I had been asked to come on the programme at all.

He opened the interview by reading a typewritten introduction which stated that throughout the long history of Newgate Gaol the prisoners had existed in deplorable conditions and had been treated with diabolical brutality. Then he put down the script and observed that most people might wonder why such a sordid topic should have been chosen as the subject-matter for a book - but it had been and the author was sitting there beside him. It seemed a most discouraging commencement for our discussion. His subsequent questions almost suggested that my interest in

Newgate must emanate from a morbid fascination with the depravity of gaol. Anyhow, my publishers were very pleased with the broadcast, and told me not to worry about the content of the interview; the very fact that it had taken place on a popular programme like *Today*, they said, was bound to have a considerable impact on my sales.

The Justice Working Party on bail had completed their deliberations and issued their report. As the members held such widely differing views we did not produce any really constructive proposals, except for our recommendation that the courts should have a more effective method of finding out about the background and circumstances of defendants when deciding whether or not they were likely to abscond if bail was granted. I expected our report to be pigeon-holed and quickly forgotten by the government department to which it was submitted, and I was quite surprised to receive a letter for Sir Frank Milton telling me that the Home Office had decided to set up their own working party to inquire into the entire procedure for granting and refusing bail in the Magistrates' Courts. He had been asked to appoint two metropolitan magistrates as members, he said, and he was nominating me as one of them.

I had never sat on any sort of governmental committee before and found it a most interesting experience. We had an excellent chairman, one of the top civil servants at the Home Office. The membership of the Working Party was mostly made up either of people actively involved in the courts, such as magistrates, magistrates' clerks, and senior police officers, or of Home Office personnel who were concerned with some aspect of courts' administration. Soon after we started work the chairman and I had a serious difference of opinion. I had written to him proposing that our report should contain a recommendation that defendants on bail who failed to surrender at the appropriate time, without a good reason, should be committing a specific criminal offence. At that time defendants, whether or not they had any means, were admitted to bail on their own recognizance, with or without sureties. If they absconded and were rearrested the only way the courts could punish them was by ordering the forfeiture of the recognisances; when they were unable to produce the necessary sums of money they were sent to prison in default. This procedure had always struck me as being thoroughly unsatisfactory, and singularly unfair to impecunious bail-jumpers. The chairman thought that my criticism was unwarranted and he asked me not to raise the matter in our discussions. But I was determined to do so. When he refused to put my proposal on the agenda for any of our meetings I set it out in a memorandum which I circulated to all the members. I was delighted to find that a sizeable majority of the Working Party shared my views.

Peter had been posted to America the previous year on the staff of the United Kingdom Polaris project, and he and Eve had taken a house in Washington. Their sons, Jeremy and Christopher, were at a boarding school in England, and daughter Fenella was attending an American day-school. During that summer, while the children were all at home for their holidays, they were planning to drive up the west coast from California to the Canadian border, and they asked me to accompany them. I was delighted to accept their invitation as I was going to be in New York about that time in connection with the American publication of my book on Newgate Gaol.

Several people had suggested to the chairman of the Working Party that before we issued our report we ought to examine the experimental bail systems in New York and Washington, but he had to tell them that our budget did not include the expenses of overseas travel. I offered to look at both of these experimental systems at my own expense while I was in America. The chairman consented and authorised the Home Office to make all the necessary arrangements for my visits. Peter and Eve were going to drive to California with the children at the start of the trip, and we agreed that as soon as my work was completed I would fly to Los Angeles where I would join them at their hotel.

On our return journey I parted from the others at Salt Lake City and I travelled back to New York by Greyhound coach, spending a night at Kansas on the way.

In due course the Working Party published its report, which was generally well-received. Within the next few years most of our proposals were implemented by Parliament under the provisions of the Bail Act. In particular, defendants were no longer to be bailed in their own recognisances. If they failed to surrender to it "without reasonable cause" they would be committing a criminal offence. The courts were given much wider powers to impose conditions when granting bail, and every defendant was to be entitled to bail except in certain specified circumstances. The chairman had plainly forgiven me for my opposition to his views because he nominated me to act as our spokesman on a television programme when I would have to answer questions about the report. Surprisingly enough the Lord Chancellor's Department had no objection to my doing this.

I had been a metropolitan stipendiary magistrate for nearly eight years when it was announced that the structure of the superior criminal courts in Britain was going to undergo a radical alteration. Assizes and Quarter Sessions were to be abolished and the jurisdictions of both would be transferred to a new type of tribunal known as a Crown Court. There would be Crown Courts in every part of the country, sitting almost continuously throughout the year. There was also to be a new type of Judge called a "Circuit Judge", who would try every sort of case, criminal, civil and matrimonial.

At a quarterly meeting of the metropolitan magistrates just before the Crown Courts came into being, Sir Frank Milton told us that Lord Hailsham, the Lord Chancellor, would like two or three suitable members of our Bench to be appointed Circuit Judges. Those of us who wished to be considered, he said, should notify the Lord Chancellor's Department forthwith, but he emphasised that no one ought to apply who would not be proficient in dealing with a Circuit Judge's very wide jurisdiction. I felt that I had been away from civil and matrimonial work too long to justify me in submitting my name, so I thought no more about it.

Frank Milton was a member of the Garrick. I met him there a few weeks later when we were both having a drink in the bar before lunch. He mentioned that he had just been at the Lord Chancellor's Department for a discussion about the metropolitan magistrates who wanted to become Circuit Judges.

"I was rather surprised to see that your name wasn't on the list," he added. I told him the reason.

"The majority of your colleagues don't share your inhibitions," he said. "Within three days of our last quarterly meeting over 80 per cent of them had sent in their letters of application. But it's not too late even now, if you'd like to change your mind and apply."

He then offered to arrange for me to see a man called Hume Boggis-Rolfe who was dealing with appointments to the Circuit Bench. "He would understand how you feel about it," Frank assured me, "and he would be the best person to advise you whether or not your uncertainty is justified."

I saw Hume Boggis-Rolfe in his room at the House of Lords. He told me that if I applied to become a Circuit Judge, and if the Lord Chancellor decided that I was suitable, it would be possible for me to be relieved of my duties as a metropolitan magistrate a week before my official appointment, so that I could spend five days sitting alongside a County Court Judge as an observer. I agreed with him that this should be sufficient time to remind me of "the feel" of a civil court. I sent off my application the same day.

Very soon afterwards I received a letter in the morning post telling me that the Lord Chancellor "was minded" to recommend me to the Queen for appointment as a Circuit Judge. It was intended that I should be sworn in on the following Monday and that I would start sitting at Hertford Crown Court on the Tuesday. I was not to mention my forthcoming appointment to anyone, not even to the chief clerk at my court, until it had been officially announced.

Fortunately, my morning list finished early that day, so I took a taxi to the House of Lords where I saw Boggis-Rolfe again. He was most apologetic. "I should have told you," he said. "The Treasury objected to your sitting for a week as an observer at a county court. They considered that you shouldn't be paid for doing nothing. I'm afraid the whole thing has moved a lot quicker than I had anticipated." Before I left his room I had told Boggis-Rolfe that I had already run into difficulties because the clerk at Marylebone had wanted to adjourn several of my part-heard cases to dates later than the end of the week. He appreciated my problem and said that I could inform the chief clerk, in strict confidence, about my appointment, as it would be impossible for me to come back and sit as a magistrate once I had become a Circuit Judge.

Ede and Ravenscroft, the legal costumiers in Chancery Lane, offered to dress me for my swearing-in as I would have to wear a court coat, breeches, black hose, buckled shoes, lace cuffs, a silk gown and a full-bottomed wig. The items of attire which they could not make for me in time they would lend me for the occasion. I had been given a list of the apparel I would have to buy and warned that the Circuit Judges' outfit allowance which I would receive from the Treasury could not possibly cover the cost of everything I needed.

I hired a chauffeur-driven car for the morning on the

Monday and I took Noreen with me to see me sworn-in. We went first to Ede and Ravenscroft's shop where my clothing and trappings were laid out in readiness. I emerged from the changing-room, hot and uncomfortable, with the feeling that my medals would probably become unpinned and my stockings were about to fall down. At the House of Lords we were conducted to a waiting-room, and presently the Principal Secretary arrived to explain the procedure to me. By this time I was becoming increasingly ill-at-ease and only half-listened to his words of instruction ... when the short procession entered the Lord Chancellor's room I was to place my white gloves on the lectern in front of me ... I would pick up from it the first of the two parchment sheets on which the oaths were written ... I was not to start reading it aloud until the Lord Chancellor told me to do so ... after I had read the second oath I would replace the parchment and pick up my gloves ... it all seemed so rigid, formal and impersonal.

Since my brain injury I had always had considerable difficulty in reading aloud, especially when I was at all nervous. Lord Hailsham was sitting behind his desk eyeing me coldly and critically as I held up the first parchment, waiting to commence. For a few moments the silence was tense, and then he told me to take the oath. I started off slowly and haltingly. After a few lines I stumbled over a word, mispronouncing it. I was about to carry on when the Lord Chancellor interrupted. "Start again, and this time read it properly," he ordered irascibly.

I did not remain at Hertford Crown Court for long before I was relieved by another Judge who was going there permanently. I had been appointed to sit on the South-Eastern Circuit which meant that I could be sent anywhere in the Home Counties, but I had been informed unofficially that after a while I would only have to go to courts in the Inner London area. For the next few months I had to phone the Circuit office every Friday morning to find out my programme for the following week. It usually consisted of one-day sittings at various County Courts and Crown Courts, interspersed with frequent days in the family division at the Royal Courts of Justice in the Strand. Although this routine entailed a fair amount of travelling, both on ordinary trains and on the underground, I enjoyed the changes of location and the wide variety of cases I had to try.

Several of my friends and some members of my family had asked me whether I had been wise, in view of my health problems, to exchange the settled routine and the four-day week of a metropolitan magistrate for the itinerant existence and the greater responsibility of a Circuit Judge. However, I was still determined, even in middle age, that my disabilities should not impede me from leading a normal life and fulfilling a normal career.

One Saturday morning I woke up early with a throbbing pain in the top of my head. I looked in the mirror and my fears were confirmed; an ulcer had formed on the edge of my metal plate.

After breakfast I went to see my doctor, Steven Sebag-Montefiore. He examined the sore carefully and said, "Yes, it's another ulcer all right, and rather a bad one - it's turning septic. I'm afraid you'll have to go back to the Brook

Hospital."

Another operation, I thought. More time away from work. And the probability that my scalp would ulcerate yet again in the none-too-distant future. I could not go on taking these perpetual spells of sick-leave. I had already made up my mind that if I had any further trouble with my plate I would resign from the Bench on medical grounds. Now I would have to do so.

On the Sunday morning I had taken up my pen to write to the Lord Chancellor when something made me hesitate. I decided that before I took such a crucial step I would go to church and pray for guidance, so I walked along to Holy Trinity, Brompton, arriving there in time for Matins. My ulcer was aching and I felt extremely self-conscious because Steven had put a large dressing on my head. Nearly everyone I had met in the street had glanced up at it and then had shyly averted their eyes.

When I left the church I knew exactly what I had to do. Directly I arrived home I rang Steven and informed him that before I went to the Brook I would like to have a second opinion from a leading neurosurgeon. I wanted to know if there was anything at all that could be done with my plate to prevent the constantly recurring ulcers.

"I completely agree with you," Steven said. "I'll make an appointment for you to see Campbell Connelly. He's a consultant at Barts, and in my view he's the best neurosurgeon in England today."

I saw Campbell Connelly as an emergency patient during the following week. Having read Steven's report and examined my head, he told me that I would have to have the entire plate removed. Otherwise it would be a source of continual trouble.

I asked him if it would be possible for me to have a new plate in its place.

He shook his head, "That would be impracticable," he replied. "It would almost certainly become infected and it would cause more ulcers."

We arranged that he would operate on me at King Edward VII's hospital for officers in Beaumont Street as soon as a bed was available. When I pressed him about my condition in the future he said that he would prefer to discuss my prognosis after the operation - when he had seen what was happening under the plate.

CHAPTER 28

Campbell Connelly came to see me in my room at King
Edward VII's hospital the morning after my operation.

"It was all very satisfactory," he said. "The hole in your
skull had filled over with a coating of fairly hard gristle. It
won't afford you the protection you would have with your
plate but it should be sufficient to withstand any moderate
impact. I'd recommend you to leave it the way it is and
unless you're unlucky it will see you through."

I was thankful then that I had not mentioned the
possibility of resignation to the Lord Chancellor's
Department.

I remained in hospital for another 10 days, until I had
finished with antibiotics, drainage tubes and dressings.
Apart from an occasional headache I had felt very little pain
and I spent a good deal of the time sitting in a chair beside
my bed reading or writing. A month or two before, Henry
Bailey-King, a publisher I knew at the Garrick, had
commissioned me to write a history of the Rule of Law in
Britain. It was a subject which required a considerable
amount of research and I had brought numerous notes with
me in the hope that I would feel well enough to do a little
work on the book.

When I started work again I was sent to a small
temporary Crown Court at Woodford in Essex. It was
accommodated in a house, formerly a rectory, and contained
two courtrooms, one of which had been added as a
hastily-built extension. As the third Judge I sat in the church
hall next door, making my entrances and exits through the
backdrop curtains on the stage. From time to time we
borrowed a neighbouring Magistrates' Court building and

used it for a fourth Judge.

The senior Judge among the three of us, who was very conscious of his status, had practised law for years in a British colony and when it had achieved independence he had returned home to start afresh at the London Bar. In many ways he was a caricature of the Empire-building English gentleman; certainly, his views and the comments he expressed on contemporary affairs dated back to another age. The clerks at the court usually referred to him as "the chairman" although there was no such officially recognised position as we were just a group of co-equal Judges exercising our jurisdictions separately. His daily moment of manifest ascendancy came about when he presided at the head of the table during the luncheon adjournment and he was able to dominate the conversation. On several occasions he had been quoted by the national press; for instance, when he had forbidden women to enter his court in trousers, or when he had criticised solicitors for appearing in front of him wearing gaudy ties.

When I had been sitting at the court for a week the Chief Clerk came to see me in my room.

"This is rather awkward," he began, "but I thought I should speak to you about a couple of matters before things go any further. First of all, I hear that you have been granting bail to some defendants during the short adjournment. The chairman has issued a directive that they should always be kept in custody; otherwise they are apt to delay over lunch and not to be back on time for the afternoon session. Secondly, your clerk had told me that one day you rose at quarter-past four: the chairman wants every court to remain sitting until four-thirty.

I told him politely but forcefully that I would not tolerate any interference with the way in which I conducted my judicial business, except from the Lord Chancellor's Office, the Court of Appeal, or a Presiding Judge of the Circuit.

I had no more trouble in relation to "local rules," except on one occasion. I had been trying a fairly long case when the defence counsel came to see me in the morning just before I went into court. He complained that his instructing solicitor's clerk had been prevented from entering the courtroom by some member of the staff because she was wearing trousers. The clerk in question, who had been with the counsel every day of the trial, was a pretty, dark-haired girl of about 19 or 20. Up to this point she had always worn a rather brief mini-skirt, and when she stood tiptoe in front of the dock to speak to her client, which had happened very frequently, I had noticed that several men on the jury seemed to be paying far more attention to her than to the witness giving evidence.

I told the defence counsel that I had no objection whatsoever to his solicitor's clerk appearing in my court in trousers. He went away appeased, but returned a few minutes later and said that the girl was too upset to come into court. She felt she had been insulted and she was now in tears. I asked him to tell her from me that I was quite sure she looked just as attractive in trousers as she had done in a mini-skirt, and hoped she would forget all about it.

When I went into court, she looked up and gave me a quick, shy smile. After that we carried on as normal.

I did not enjoy being at Woodford Crown Court. Quite apart from the irksome atmosphere of the Judge's luncheon room, every morning I had a tedious and uncomfortable journey in an overcrowded underground train. It took over an hour, with one change en route. At the end of the day I would travel back to London in similar discomfort.

Nevertheless, the work at the court was interesting. Two cases in particular stand out in my memory. The first was a retrial, because on an earlier occasion the jury had been unable to agree on their verdict. Three men were jointly charged with carrying out a smash-and-grab raid at a jeweller's shop in the early hours of the morning. Although the street had been deserted at the time, a 15-year-old schoolboy had watched the crime being committed from his bedroom window close by. The following day he had picked out all the defendants at identification parades. The prosecution had placed great reliance on his evidence, but at the first trial he had said that he had not seen the culprits at all clearly and he was not sure if he had identified the right people.

I expected him to be equally indecisive when he gave his evidence before me. To my surprise, he stated clearly and unhesitantly that the men he had seen at the window of the jeweller's shop were the three defendants in the dock. Quite naturally, one of the defence counsel cross-examined him about his previous evidence. The boy explained that he had been afraid to tell the truth because he had been accosted by two men outside the court and they had told him that if he identified any of their mates he would get his face slashed.

The defence counsel did not conceal his disbelief. "I

suppose," he suggested sarcastically, "that these men who frightened you so much were large and ferocious-looking?"

The boy agreed that they were.

"And no doubt," counsel went on, "One of them had a massive scar across his face?"

"That's right," the boy replied. "It was on his left cheek." And then, before the counsel could ask another derisive question, he blurted out, "If you don't believe me you can see for yourself. They're both in court now!"

At that moment two large men rose hurriedly from their seats in the public gallery. They were making for the exit when I ordered the police to detain them. Unfortunately, there was insufficient evidence to charge them with any offence. However, the incident made a profound impression on the jury and they convicted all three defendants after a very brief retirement.

In the second case which I remember particularly well, I was trying four men on a charge of robbery. They all had appalling records and I had refused to grant any of them bail. On the third or fourth day it was reported to me that a prison officer had overheard a conversation between them in the van bringing them to court that morning. Apparently they had formed the impression that the jury was very much against them, and they had agreed on a manoeuvre which they thought would force me to stop the trial. One of them was going to sack his counsel and would then tell me he was incapable of conducting his own defence. It would be too late for another barrister to take over; the jury would have to be discharged and the case would start afresh.

Before I sat that day I informed the defending counsel

about the prison officer's report, and I asked them to tell their clients that if anyone carried out this ruse, the trial would still continue. In spite of this warning, during the afternoon one of the counsel had applied to withdraw from the case as he had been dismissed by his client. I agreed to his request, but I told the defendant concerned that unless he gave me a valid reason for his action I intended to terminate his legal aid and to let him carry on with his own defence. He protested that I was treating him most unfairly and said he was going to appeal against my ruling.

From then on the defendants tried ceaselessly to coerce me into stopping the trial. For instance, when the court was temporarily evacuated as the result of an IRA bomb threat, prison officers had placed coats over the men's lower arms to conceal the fact that they were wearing handcuffs, and they deliberately raised their arms above their heads in front of the jurors. As soon as the hearing was resumed the defence counsel submitted that their clients would now be unfairly prejudiced if the trial continued, because the jury knew they were in handcuffs, and therefore in custody, and would guess that they had bad records.

As one of the defendants had started to give evidence he broke off suddenly and leant forward in the witness box with his hands clasped to his face. I inquired if he was all right. He looked up and asked me vaguely, "Who are you and why are you dressed up like that?" He glanced round the courtroom and then turned back to me. "What am I doing here?" he said. "Who are all these people?"

I adjourned the case and ordered that he should undergo a mental and medical examination. Next morning

I received reports on his condition. I was not surprised to learn that the prison doctors could find nothing wrong with him and were convinced he was just shamming. I recalled him to the witness-box and told him to carry on with his evidence, but he insisted that he had lost his memory and was therefore unable to answer any questions about past events.

Even then the saga was not ended. The night before I started my summing-up the church hall was set on fire by an arsonist. Although it was extensively damaged, the end of the building where all the exhibits and other documents were kept remained unscathed. I was able to finish the case in the local Magistrates' Court. All four defendants were convicted, but none of them appealed against my repeated refusals to discharge the jury and restart the case.

To reach the Judges' luncheon room in the old rectory, I used to walk past the church through the graveyard. The church, which had only been built very recently, was said to be a good example of modern ecclesiastical architecture, and I had made up my mind to have a look at the inside when I had time to do so. The opportunity came when I had just sent out a jury in a case of some complexity. I was anticipating that they would stay out for quite a time, and there was no other work for me to do so I told my clerk where I was going, and without removing my wig or robes went into the church. It was empty except for a middle-aged woman kneeling down in the front pew, deep in prayer. She noticed me for the first time when I was walking back from the altar. I saw the look of terror in her face as she put up her hand to her mouth and suppressed a scream. It took some minutes for me to explain who I was and to assure her that the day of judgment had not yet come to pass.

I did not remain at Woodford for long before I was sent to sit at the Old Bailey for two months.

When the structure of the superior criminal courts was reorganised, the authorities in the City of London had insisted that the Old Bailey should be allowed to maintain many of its long-established traditions. As a consequence, it was unlike any of the other Crown Courts. The influence of the City was strong, with its dignity, its rituals and its hospitality. The Judges lunched every day as guests of the Sheriffs. You learnt your position at the vast rectangular table from a seating-plan delivered to you in your room every morning before you were ushered ceremonially into court. You had to go into lunch wearing your wig and robes, the High Court Judges in scarlet, and the Circuit Judges in black court-coats and black silk gowns. It was always a three-course meal, though generally the food was light, and it was served without any delays. Most of the Judges prevented the uniformed attendants from refilling their glasses with wine and they declined to drink port with their coffee.

I had not been told beforehand that Circuit Judges sitting at the Old Bailey were supposed to be dressed in black. On my first day there I wore my usual Crown Court attire, a long navy blue robe with a wide strip of mauve down the front, and a red sash over my left shoulder.

As soon as I had entered the room where we met for drinks before lunch Sir Karl Aarvold, the Recorder of London and the senior permanent Judge at the Old Bailey, came forward, looked me up and down and said with a perfectly straight face, "Ah! You must be the visiting Judge from Ruritania."

After I had completed my two months at the Old Bailey I sat for a while in the family division at the Royal Courts of Justice, and at Wandsworth County Court trying civil cases. I was then moved to a temporary Crown Court at a converted house in St James's Square. As it had no canteens or catering facilities, we had to adjourn every day at one o'clock for an hour-and-a-half to enable everyone to go out for a meal. We used to find that during the afternoon sessions the Judges were constantly receiving notes from the male jurors who wanted to visit the toilets. We assumed that these frequent interruptions were not entirely unconnected with the diuretic qualities of the beer in the pubs nearby.

The situation of the court suited me admirably. It was only four stops from South Kensington on the Underground; and it was within easy walking distance of the Garrick, so I went there for lunch every day. Apart from that, the London Library, from which I regularly borrowed books, was close at hand on the other side of St James's Square.

I had just completed my history of the Rule of Law in Britain when Henry Bailey-King's publishing house was taken over by a larger firm. They circulated a letter to all their newly acquired authors welcoming them and assuring them that their contracts would be fulfilled. However, a short time later they wrote to inform me that economic necessity had compelled them to decrease the size of their list and they had regretfully decided to discontinue the publication of all books connected with the law.

Henry was very concerned by this turn of events. He put me in touch with Barry Rose, a successful legal publisher in Sussex, who read my rejected manuscript and instantly accepted it. Barry was an extremely likeable man and exceptionally generous to his aspiring authors. Every time he wanted to discuss any aspect of the production or the promotion of my book he would invite me to dine with him at Simpsons restaurant in the Strand. During these dinners our conversations would range over a wide variety of subjects, and invariably they were cut short when Barry suddenly realised that he would just have time to catch the last train back to Chichester. While he hurriedly collected his hat and coat, I used to dash out and arrange for the doorman to call a taxi for him.

I stayed at St James's Square until the opening of the new Knightsbridge Crown Court in Hans Crescent, a stone's throw from Harrods. I had been promised that I would be one of the four permanent Judges there, but that I would also sit for a month every quarter at Wandsworth County Court, and for an occasional stint at the Old Bailey. In fact, this was to remain as my working pattern for the remainder of my time on the Bench.

Knightsbridge Crown Court was within half-an-hour's walk of my flat. It had originally been built as a hotel and had then become an international students' hostel. Finally, it was taken over by the Office of Works and hastily converted into a complex of 10 courtrooms, together with all the other appendages which were necessary for its new function.

Such was the backlog of cases awaiting trial in London

that Knightsbridge was opened even before the preparation of the building was complete. On the first day I sat there the carpets were still being laid, the furniture was being moved in, and the electricians were finishing off the wiring. The atmosphere of the new court was happy and enthusiastic from the start. We all felt that we were taking part in an incipient venture and everyone seemed determined to make it successful. We had no Judges who were unduly difficult, the staff were efficient and courteous and we were fortunate enough to be working in the midst of the glitter and vitality of the West End of London. There was an additional advantage for me as I had just been elected to membership of the Special Forces Club in Herbert Crescent just round the corner. From time to time I went there for lunch, or while I was awaiting the return of a jury late in the afternoon.

For several years past I had been having less and less to do with the Middle Temple, so it came as a complete surprise when I received a telephone call from Captain John Morison, one evening when I was at the Garrick. John, a retired Naval officer, was now the Under-Treasurer, the virtual chief of staff of the Inn. "I'm glad I've managed to locate you," he said. "I wanted to break the news to you as soon as possible and to offer you my congratulations. You've been elected a Bencher. I understand it's the first time on record that they've elected a member of the lower judiciary."

I suppose that every honour is magnified in the eyes of the recipient if it is totally unexpected. The Middle Temple had played a large part in my life and had meant a great deal to me. I thought back to the far-distant day when, at the age of 19 I had entered the Under-Treasurer's office, awestruck, but eager and proud to enrol as a student of the Inn. And the years immediately after the war when the Benchers had seemed so mighty and so far removed. Then the long period of weakening ties and the awareness that the inner citadel was closed to me forever.

John Morison contacted me again a few days later to tell me the date on which I would be called to the Bench. It was to be an exceptionally large Bench-call on that particular evening as there were four of us, the other three being senior practising Queen's Counsel.

Each Inn of Court had its own way of inducting its new Benchers; it was generally agreed that the method employed by the Middle Temple was more demanding for the initiates than those used by any of the other Inns. Our ceremony was enacted on an ordinary dining evening when the Hall was filled with students keeping their terms and barristers who had been working late in chambers. The four of us had been asked to arrive early and to sit together at a table close to the dais. The wait seemed interminable. Suddenly the discordant hum of mingling conversations was hushed, and everyone stood up as the Head Porter, with his mace in his hand, led in the Treasurer, followed by the other Benchers two abreast. They walked along the length of the Hall in majestic procession and formed up around the High Table, which was believed to have been presented to the Inn by Queen Elizabeth I.

Before grace was read, and while Hall was still silent, the Catering Manager approached the place where the four of us were standing. Loudly and clearly he called out our names, and then repeated the prescribed words which transformed us into Benchers. "With the compliments of the Treasurer and the Masters of the Bench, you are invited to take your places with them on the High Table."

While the assembly applauded politely we mounted the dais to shake hands with the Treasurer and the other Masters, knowing that the main ordeal of our inauguration was yet to come.

At the end of dinner, as the Benchers were preparing to file out, we four had to stand in front of a bust of Edmund Plowden, who had been Treasurer in 1564 when the building of the Hall commenced, and bow three times to all those present. We then retired to a Benchers' room called the "parliament chamber" for coffee, fruit and liqueurs.

After the toasts had been drunk the Treasurer welcomed each of the newcomers in turn and invited him, in accordance with the Inn's tradition, "to give an account of himself." No one had seemed able to tell us in advance what sort of exposition about our lives was expected from us, except that it must be brief, modest, amusing and informative; and that it should not resemble an after-dinner speech. We knew that our audience, which included Government Ministers, senior Judges and leading counsel, would be jocular but critical. It was an awesome prospect.

Being a Bencher was not only an honour, it was also supposed to involve a responsibility for taking part in the management of the Inn. Control was exercised through a number of coordinated committees which looked after every aspect of our corporate activities. To my immense pleasure I was put on the Students' Affairs Committee. Benchers were expected to have dinner in Hall as often as possible, and I made a point of dining at the High Table at least once a week. The atmosphere among my new colleagues was friendly, relaxed and informal. Apart from the Treasurer, who held office for one year, we ranked in the Inn as equals, and by custom all Benchers called each other by their first names. When precedence was necessary it was governed by the length of time we had been Masters of the Bench.

One of my friends at the Bar, writing to congratulate me on my election, remarked that I was now a member of the two best clubs in London - the Garrick and the Middle Temple Bench.

I was inclined to agree with him.

Eve and I had promised our mother that, if possible, she could spend the closing moments of her life at one of our homes, as she had a horror of dying in the unfriendly isolation of a hospital ward.

In fact, she maintained her health and independence until she had passed the age of 90, when she became ill with severe heart failure. At that time, Eve was living in a Naval house at Portsmouth where Peter, then a rear-admiral, was serving as Flag Officer Spithead. However, there was ample accommodation in my flat both for mother and for the nurses who were looking after her.

My mother's own family were immensely devoted to her. We all owed her a great deal for the love we had received from her and for the way in which she had bound us together in affection for each other. I never could forget the months she had stayed in Oxford, visiting me without fail every afternoon even when I was lying in bed speechless and immobile. I often tried to imagine what she must have endured in seeing me in that condition and knowing the gloomy prognosis that the doctors were holding out for my future.

When mother became critically ill Arnold flew back from New Zealand for a week to see her. Eve used to come up frequently from Portsmouth, and Noreen, who was still living in the flat above mine, visited her daily. We knew that her life was ebbing to its close and we could only wait in sadness for the end.

Eventually she developed pneumonia - the doctor, after his examination, called it "the old people's friend." That evening the nurse who had been on duty all day offered to stay on with the night nurse.

At two o'clock next morning one of the nurses knocked on my bedroom door and told me that my mother had just died, very peacefully. I rang Noreen and when she came down we went together to our mother's bedside to bid her our final farewells. Then we went to the sitting-room and had cups of tea in silence with the nurses.

I went back to bed, but I did not sleep again that night, I kept thinking of my mother and my mind was filled with memories of her. She had seemed so ageless, so eternal, it was difficult to realise that I had seen her for the very last time.

In the morning life would go on without her, though it would not be the same - when someone very close to you has died your world can never be quite the same again.

CHAPTER 29

My book on the history of the Rule of Law in Britain was published by Barry Rose in simultaneous hardback and clothback editions. It received a number of fairly favourable reviews in legal journals, and some American universities added it to the lists of "background reading" they were recommending for their law students.

This was not my first association with the American academic milieu. Several years earlier Dr Howard Gotlieb, who organised the special collections of manuscripts for the Mugar Memorial Library at Boston University, had written to ask me what became of my own manuscripts after my books were published. He was most reproachful when I told him that I always tore them up, and he requested that for the future I should send them all to him for inclusion in the Special Collections. I willingly agreed. It was a simple process for me as each time I had a manuscript ready for him I would notify his shippers and they would call at my flat to collect it.

Every few years Dr Gotlieb used to give a reception in London, usually at the Savoy or the Dorchester, for English writers who donated their manuscripts to Boston. These gatherings were memorable for their lavish hospitality and their extremely convivial atmosphere. Howard Gotlieb was a charming, solicitous host who was determined that all his guests should enjoy themselves. His authors included well-known novelists, biographers, historians, leading politicians and a host of other celebrities, which added to the interest of his parties.

My life was becoming increasingly busy both professionally and socially. I had met Josephine

Pullein-Thompson, the children's writer, who was working part-time as general secretary of the English Centre of International PEN, and at her suggestion I had become a member. The English Centre had no premises of their own, but the London Sketch Club in Chelsea lent them rooms for their offices and meetings. Josephine was a very active and efficient organiser. Almost every week she arranged a talk or a discussion on some literary topic, in addition to regular quarterly dinners and various other functions.

International PEN was an association of writers; the initials stood for Poets, Playwrights, Essayists, Editors and Novelists. It had national centres all over the world, which usually met together at an annual congress. The association was non-political and non-partisan, but it was ready to denounce any government which had imprisoned authors or journalists solely for the opinions they had expressed in articles and books.

The next PEN congress after I became a member was being held at Rio. Every national centre was entitled to send two official delegates, whose hotel bills would be paid by the hosts, as well as any other members who wished to participate at their own expense. The English Centre had already nominated as their delegates, Francis King the novelist, who was then their president, and Josephine Pullein-Thompson. The air fare to Brazil was expensive and we had been warned that the cost of living in Rio was high. Consequently, the English party at the congress was going to be very small. My travels abroad had never taken me to South America and it was a part of the world I wanted to visit so I added my name to the list of participants.

A few days before the congress commenced some hospitable Brazilians in London gave a buffet supper party in honour of the English writers who were going to it. During the course of the evening an attractive dark-haired girl sat down on a sofa beside me. She seemed to know who I was because she addressed me as "Judge." She came from Rio, she told me, but she was now living in Putney with her husband and their baby son. She said that her father had a large house close to the hotel where we would be staying and she was going to arrange for him to make contact with me.

"I feel certain that you would like each other very much," she went on. "Daddy is what you call here a 'business magnate' and he is very fond of entertaining, as you will see. As soon as you return from Brazil you must visit me in Putney, and you can tell me all about your trip."

The officials from the international headquarters of PEN, which was based in London, were flying on the same plane as the members of the English Centre. Also with us were David Fletcher, the President of the Scottish Centre, and his wife Susan. David, whom I had never met before, had started his professional life as a publisher and was then the editor of *Blackwood's Magazine*. Susan was a schoolteacher. At Rio airport a group of journalists, photographers, and television cameramen were waiting patiently for the incoming delegations. We must have looked an unimpressive lot with our crumpled clothing and tired faces after our lengthy overnight flight.

The next evening there was a big reception at the congress hotel, attended by the President of Brazil and members of the Brazilian Government. The notabilities had just arrived when Peter Elstob, the International Secretary of PEN, told me there was a strange rat-like little man looking for me. "Mr Ratty doesn't speak much English," Peter said, "but he's waving around a photo of you and a rather beautiful girl sitting extremely close together on a couch."

I found Mr Ratty at the other side of the room, holding in his hand a photograph which had been taken at the supper-party in London the previous week. We found it very difficult to communicate with each other because his English was atrocious and I could speak no Portuguese at all. However, he managed to get across that his daughter had asked him to look after me and he would be inviting me to his home within the next day or two. He also asked if, when I returned to England, I could take back a present for his grandson in Putney. I replied that I would be delighted to do so, provided it was very small and very light, as my suitcase was full up already.

He nodded, "Of course, he said, "very small, and very light."

The invitation to his house never materialised. In fact I did not see Mr Ratty again until our final evening in Rio. I was in my bedroom preparing for the congress farewell dinner when I received a message from the reception desk at the hotel that he had come round with another man to say "goodbye" to me. A few minutes later they were shown up to my room. Mr Ratty explained that he had brought along a friend of his who spoke good English, to make conversation easier. His companion, who looked like a gangster, was carrying a white plastic bag which he placed on my bed, telling me that it contained the present for the grandson in Putney. I asked him what it was, and he replied vaguely, "just food - baby food." I told him that if it was unopened I would need a shop-receipt to show to the customs officer at Heathrow, and he said immediately, "But you are a Judge - they won't examine your luggage." I assured him that in England members of the judiciary were subject to the same customs checks as everyone else. At that, they both smiled and shrugged their shoulders.

As soon as they had gone I examined the white, plastic bag, and I found that it contained four identical fairly large round tins. They were very heavy and their lids were firmly secured with layers of wide tape. I was meeting some of the others for pre-dinner drinks in one of their bedrooms so I took the tins with me to show them. We all agreed that they would not weigh so much if they contained drugs. The general impression was that they were full of coins, jewellery, or gold. At any rate, they seemed most unsuitable for the little grandson's suppers. A group of us were flying to Salvador early next morning, so before I went to bed that night I wrote Mr Ratty a note telling him that I could not take his present back to England as he had not supplied me with a receipt. Therefore I was leaving it with the hotel reception for him to collect.

Francis King could not come to Salvador with us because he was going to Chile on a lecture tour. Before we parted company in Rio he asked me if I would like to serve on the National Executive Committee of the English Centre of PEN. I hesitated at first for fear of undertaking too much; as I foresaw that during the next few years I was going to become increasingly involved with my responsibilities at the Middle Temple. Nevertheless, it would be a new and interesting experience to work with writers and to see the way in which they approached the various matters which came before them. So I told Francis that if I was invited to join the committee I would willingly consent.

I was thoroughly enjoying my duties at the Middle Temple. Soon after we returned from Brazil I was appointed chairman of the Student Affairs' Committee, one of the most rewarding offices in the Inn, which brought me into frequent contact with the very charming young people on the students' own committee, and also with Jean Austin, our excellent students' officer.

Twice a year Jean Austin had to organise weekend training courses at Cumberland Lodge in Windsor Great Park. These were always conducted in a relaxed, informal manner and the students enjoyed them immensely. Apart from helping to arrange the programmes, I was responsible for recruiting a "tutorial team," of Benchers and practising barristers from the Inn. I never had any difficulty as invariably more people wanted to come than were actually needed.

Cumberland Lodge, a royal house in a royal park, was built around the middle of the 17th century. In 1947 the King and Queen granted it by trust deed to the St Catherine's Foundation, an educational charity founded principally to serve the needs of students. Since then the house had been in constant use for conferences and residential courses. It was comfortable, beautifully situated and efficiently managed by a permanent staff.

Queen Elizabeth, the Queen Mother, often stayed at the Royal Lodge nearby. As patron of the St Catherine's Foundation and the Royal Bencher of the Middle Temple she took a special interest in our weekend visits, and when she was in residence she generally invited a large group from Cumberland Lodge to come round to the Royal Lodge for drinks before lunch on Sunday. On these occasions she greatly enjoyed meeting the students, especially those from overseas.

I had never relished the idea of meeting royalty. I imagined that the protocol and the artificiality would turn the whole occasion into a nightmare. I pictured the squad of equerries standing-by to cover up my gaffes or to rush me away if they were sufficiently outrageous. I was afraid I might neglect to use the address of "Your Majesty" or "Your Royal Highness" in the first few sentences I spoke, or fail to sprinkle my replies with an adequate number of "Sirs" and "Ma'ams" thereafter. I thought that I might commit an inadvertent solecism by introducing a new topic of conversation, failing to laugh uproariously enough at a royal witticism, or appearing to show a lack of deference in some other way.

The first time I attended Cumberland Lodge after I had been appointed chairman of Students' Affairs I was asked by the Treasurer to take our party to the Royal Lodge on the Sunday morning. I went on a little ahead of the others and I was shown into the spacious room where the rest of the guests had already forgathered. The Queen Mother came forward to meet me in the doorway. I had often been told that she had a wonderful knack of putting people at their ease and I found immediately that this was true. She was so warm, so kindly and so natural. She wanted to know if we were being well looked after at Cumberland Lodge and being given enough to eat. I told her truthfully that the students were thoroughly enjoying themselves.

"I'm so glad," she said. "I always think it's most important with young people to give them a lot of good grub!"

As the students entered the room I presented them to the Queen Mother one by one. When we were about halfway through, she turned to me suddenly and said, "I do think it's marvellous of you to know them all by name when you've only been together just over a day."

I admitted that I had a list hidden in my hand, and I had already told them beforehand the order in which they would come in.

"That was very thoughtful," she commented.

When all 20 students had been presented, the Queen Mother asked me, with a twinkle in her eye, what would have happened if they had come in in the wrong order. She seemed highly amused when I told her that I had given specific instructions that whatever names I used when presenting them were going to be their names for the next hour.

Apart from students' affairs my principal responsibilities in the Inn were as Master of the Revels and chairman of the Middle Temple Historical Society. The Revels had started in the Elizabethan era and had once lasted for several days immediately before Christmas. The event took place on a single evening in December, and consisted of a supper in

Hall followed by an entertainment put on by our own barristers and students. It was always a popular and well-attended function as the sketches and the musical items were usually of a very high standard. I took no part in the actual performance, my position being more like that of an administrative manager. The Historical Society had been formed very recently under the aegis of Dame Veronica Wedgewood, the historian, who was an honorary Bencher of the Middle Temple and who had agreed to become its first president. We used to arrange after-dinner talks in Hall given by well-known speakers, and quarterly supper parties for our own members.

One morning in court I felt suddenly that I was going to faint. There was a throbbing in my ears, lights danced before my eyes and my skin became cold and prickly. An important cross-examination was taking place, which was being followed attentively by the jury, and I did not want to interrupt the proceedings if I could possibly avoid doing so. After a few minutes the sensations passed leaving me feeling limp and slightly sick. I thought I had undergone some sort of temporary after-effect of my head-wound and I tried not to worry about it, but I could not help being concerned that this should have happened such a long time afterwards.

I did not go the Judges' dining room during the short adjournment because I neither wanted food nor company. Instead, I asked my usher to bring me a cup of coffee in my own room. Somehow I managed to get through the afternoon session and then went home by taxi. I intended to go straight to bed, and if I did not feel better in the morning to get in touch with Steven Sebag-Montefiore, my G. P. When I was opening my front door I began to feel similar sensations to those I had experienced in court that morning, only this time they were far worse. I remember starting to walk across the hall and then I blacked out. The next thing I knew I was lying face down on the floor. I staggered to the phone and rang Noreen, who fortunately was in her flat. I asked her to come down as soon as possible because I felt terrible and I had just fainted.

Noreen telephoned Steven right away to tell him what had happened and he arrived at my flat 20 minutes later. He inquired about my symptoms and after examining me briefly he told me that this was nothing to do with my head-wound. "You're having an abdominal haemorrhage," he said. "I'll have to arrange for an ambulance to take you to hospital without delay." I asked what was causing it. "I can't tell at this moment," he replied, "The main thing we've got to do is to stop the bleeding."

I was taken by ambulance to the Middlesex Hospital where it was found that I was suffering from a perforated duodenal ulcer. I was relieved when I was told this because I was afraid that it might be something far more serious. Steven admitted to me afterwards that he had been so concerned about my condition when he saw me at my flat that he had advised the hospital I might require an immediate emergency operation.

Noreen had managed to contact the chief clerk of Knightsbridge Crown Court that evening to explain to him what had occurred. He told her I must not worry about the case I had been trying as he would arrange for another Judge to go to my court and discharge the jury.

After two days of treatment at the Middlesex my bleeding had stopped completely and I was hopeful of being allowed to return home. The next morning I asked the Ward Sister how long she thought they would keep me there. She replied that a surgeon would be seeing me that day and it would all depend on what he decided. He came round with my house doctor early in the afternoon. "I've been looking at your case history and your X-rays," he said, "It's clear that we've now got your trouble under control, but I'm afraid it's almost certain that this will happen again - and probably very soon - unless you agree to having an operation."

I had heard all about the operation for duodenal ulcers. "That would mean having half my stomach removed wouldn't it?" I inquired.

He laughed, "Oh no! Nothing so drastic as that. But it would be a major operation nonetheless."

I asked him when it could be done because I had been selected as one of the English delegates for the International PEN Congress in Tokyo in three months' time.

"If you were to have it done immediately," he said, "you should be all right by then. I could fit you into my list tomorrow afternoon if you gave your consent to me now."

"All right," I told him. "I'd like you to go ahead and do it then."

Much as I disliked the idea of undergoing more surgery I was glad in a way that I would only have such a short time to think about it.

After the operation was over the surgeon came to see me again and told me it had been successful.

I thanked him for performing it so skilfully and I added, "I suppose I'm forbidden to drink from now on, and I'll have to go on a special diet?"

He shook his head. "No," he replied. "There are no restriction on alcohol, but try not to drink on an empty stomach. There are no dieting requirements either, but it would be better if you avoid spicey food. I don't think you're going to have any more trouble with duodenal ulcers in the future."

I was afraid that I might not be able to go to Tokyo after all, as I was troubled by persistent post-operation pains in my stomach. Although they did not lessen as the date of the congress approached I decided not to cancel my trip in spite of them. I had always wanted to visit Japan and this seemed too good an opportunity to miss. The pains ceased miraculously the day before my flight and never came back again.

The Japanese were superlative hosts, and outside our programme of working-sessions they arranged for us a constant round of visits, excursions, receptions and banquets. We were accommodated at one of the leading hotels in Tokyo where the facilities and the service were excellent. The hotels in Japan have a charming custom of lending their residents bedroom slippers, and kimonos to wear at night. When the chambermaids clean the bathrooms every morning they leave in them a new toothbrush, a small tube of toothpaste and a disposable razor. The only difficulty I encountered in Tokyo was finding my way around on the underground system as the names of the stations were written in Japanese characters.

After the congress had finished all the delegates were invited, as guests of the Japanese Centre of PEN, to spend three days in Kyoto, once the capital city and now the cultural centre of Japan. We went there on a high-speed "bullet" train, having been advised previously that the stop at Kyoto station would be exceedingly brief and that once the automatic doors on the train had been reclosed they would not be opened again for any passengers who failed to alight in time.

Before returning to England I joined a group of delegates who were flying from Tokyo to Beijing. There were seven of us, four English and three Germans; all males except Josephine Pullein-Thompson and a translator from London. We were met at Beijing airport by our designated guide, a tiny slip of a girl who told us that we would find her name unpronounceable and we were to call her "Miss Koo." From the start she ruled us with a rod of iron. A minibus was waiting to drive us to the city and once we were on board Miss Koo informed us that we had been allocated to the Beijing Hotel. She added that hotel accommodation was very short at that moment so we would all have to share double rooms, except for one member of our party. It was generally agreed that I should have a room to myself as I was getting severe attacks of cramp in my right leg which necessitated my getting out of bed three or four times every night and walking around for about five minutes. Miss Koo warned me that if there was a sudden influx of tourists at the hotel they might have to put someone in with me, but if possible it would be a "similar type" of person to myself.

"What is your occupation?" she asked me.

"I'm a Circuit Judge," I replied.

She nodded and wrote something in her notebook. "If they have to move someone into your room," she said, "they will try to select a Circuit Judge - but naturally, he might come from any part of the world."

During the week we stayed in Peking we visited all the recognized tourist attractions such as the Red Square, the Forbidden City and the Great Wall. Every evening on returning to the hotel I used to open my bedroom door expecting to be confronted by unfamiliar items of luggage and clothing. But it never happened. At the end of our stay Miss Koo told me that the hotel had had several large intakes of tourists since our arrival. "You are very lucky to have kept a room to yourself," she said. "It has only happened because there have never been any Circuit Judges to share it with you."

From Peking we flew to Canton, where we had another guide, a far less redoubtable lady than Miss Koo. After a few days there we travelled by train to Hong Kong where we parted from our German companions and returned to England.

For some months I had been looking for a cottage in Kent - a place where I could spend weekends and vacations for the time being, and at which I might live permanently when I retired. I had no roots in any English county, but I had chosen Kent, partly because Eve and Peter had just bought a house at Yalding and partly because my out-of-London work at the Bar had been mainly at Maidstone or Canterbury. Peter had left the Navy as a rear-admiral and was now working for an international money-broking company in the City. Eventually I managed to find the exact home I wanted in the beautiful village of Chilham, six-miles to the south-west of Canterbury. It has given me infinite enjoyment ever since.

Thydon Cottage had been built in the sixteenth century as three separate, but adjoined residences for the inhabitants of the village. Much later the three were converted into a single four-bedroom house, still retaining the beams, the inglenook fireplaces, and other characteristics of the Tudor period. The front door opened directly on to a hill leading up to the old, Elizabethan Square, bordered by the grounds of Chilham Castle. At the back of the cottage there was a patio, which could be a suntrap on a summer day, and a secluded well arranged garden. In the distance the gentle slopes of the North Downs rose from the far side of the Stour Valley. I turned one of the bedrooms, with this view from the window, into my study.

I could not move into Thydon Cottage for some months after the conveyance was completed, because the roof required extensive repairs and the rooms needed redecorating; also, I was having central heating installed. I used to go down to Chilham most Saturdays to see how the work was progressing. The people there were friendly and hospitable. One lady, who was particularly kind, took infinite care in introducing me to the habits and the outlook of the village. "We are all equal down here," she told me once. "So if you ever come 'the London Judge' you will make yourself most unpopular." I invited her to my house-warming party which was to take place on my first weekend at the cottage. She accepted and asked who else I was inviting. I told her the names of my other guests and she looked at me in horror.

"You can't possibly invite the butcher and the sub-postmaster with the élite of the village!" she exclaimed.

I reminded her that in Chilham everyone was equal.

"Quite so," she said severely. "But there are times when it is necessary to exercise a little discrimination."

Steven Sebag-Montefiore had been giving me some injections before I went to an overseas conference. "Now that you have your shirt off," he said, "it might be a good idea if listened to your heart - I haven't done so for some time." When he removed his stethoscope from my chest he told me I had a slight heart murmur. "It's probably nothing much," he added, "but we'll have to have it properly investigated."

The cardiologist saw me in his consulting room after I had undergone a series of examinations, X-rays and tests. He was a small man in his 60s with a rather aloof and solemn manner. He motioned me to sit down on the chair in front of his desk and addressed me in a quiet grave voice. "We've found out what's wrong with you," he said. "You have a defective aortic heart-valve. Naturally you'll want to know how we're going to treat it. I'm afraid that this is a condition for which no treatment exists. Until recently it was terminal; now, however, it is possible for the defective valve to be removed and an artificial one to be inserted in its place. It's a very serious and a very dangerous operation of course, but a few highly skilled cardiac surgeons are performing it successfully every week. It's going to be several years before you need to have it done. Meanwhile, you can still keep on with your job and lead a normal life. You'll have to come and see me at regular intervals and I will tell you when the crucial moment has arrived."

CHAPTER 30

I had never heard of the International Judges Association until Mr Justice Jean-Pierre Warner invited me to join the English delegation for their forthcoming meeting at Dakar in Senegal.

I discovered later that the IJA, or the Union Internationale Des Magistrats, had been formed in 1953 by a group of European nations as a non-political forum in which Judges from all over the world could meet together annually to discuss their common problems and to compare their systems of law. None of the original organisers had known who to approach in London regarding British participation. Eventually, a letter outlining the scheme had been sent to the Magistrates' Association, the national society of the Justices of the Peace, in the mistaken belief that it was the representative body of the British professional Judges. The letter was dealt with by a lay magistrate, a successful businessman who was not a qualified lawyer. Instead of referring the matter to the Lord Chancellor's Office or consulting with anyone else in authority, he had appointed himself as the official delegate of the British judiciary and had begun to attend the annual meetings in this capacity. He was a personable man with ready charm and he soon became a popular figure in the Association, where it was naturally assumed that he was a full-time Judge, empowered to speak for his colleagues.

IJA had grown rapidly and was still growing, both in numbers and repute. By 1980 it included countries in Europe, South America, Africa, the British Commonwealth, the Middle East and the Far East. It also achieved consultative status with the Council of Europe and with the

United Nations. In due course the significance of the Association had become known to the Lord Chancellor's Office. Although they were lukewarm about its usefulness as an organisation, they felt that since Britain was a member, her judiciary ought to be properly represented. Accordingly, a Lord Justice of Appeal was appointed convener of the British delegation and a Scottish High Court Judge was nominated to support him. By this time the magistrate had become so firmly entrenched that it was virtually impossible to remove him, and he was allowed to continue as the third member of the team.

After a few more years the Scottish Judge dropped out and had not been replaced. The office of convener had changed hands several times before it was taken over by Mr Justice Warner. Jean-Pierre Warner was ideally suited for the appointment. His mother was French and in consequence he was bilingual. Before his elevation to the High Court Bench he had served as Advocate-General to the Court of Justice of the European Communities in Luxembourg so he was well used to working and socialising with lawyers of other nations.

The IJA had three permanent Study-Commissions on each of which every member-country could be represented by two Judges. Jean-Pierre sat on the first Commission which dealt with judicial administration; Britain had no delegate on the second, which dealt with civil law and procedure, and the magistrate sat on the third which covered all aspects of the criminal law. After he had taken over as Convener, Jean-Pierre lost no time in pointing out to the Lord Chancellor's Office that as most of the larger

European nations sent their full entitlement of six delegates to the annual meetings of the Association, the British were displaying an obvious lack of enthusiasm for its objects by only sending two, and by not being represented at all on such an important Study-Commission as the second. As a result of his persistence I was appointed as an additional delegate to fill the vacancy.

The subject which had been chosen for the second Study-Commission at Dakar was "The Equality of Husband and Wife in Marriage." Before the meeting commenced the delegates who were to take part in the discussion had interchanged the answers to a questionnaire on the rights and remedies available to both spouses in the legal systems of their countries. Most of the papers I received from the other delegates were written in English or in French; however, a few were in German and were translated for me by a Middle Temple girl, just starting at the Bar, whom I had known as a student. She refused to accept any payment for her trouble, but allowed me to take her to dinner at the Garrick as a token of my gratitude.

The meeting that year took place towards the end of October. When the three of us left England it was raining and bitterly cold: when we arrived in Dakar the sky was clear and the temperature was in the upper 80s. Our hotel was situated on the coast, with a large swimming-pool by the water's edge. The Study-Commissions used to start work early and concluded their morning sessions around noon. We would then go down for a swim before having lunch in the pool-side restaurant. The afternoons were spent in a further working session or in sightseeing. The other delegates were a friendly crowd; most of them had been coming to the meetings for some time and regarded them, to a certain extent, as annual reunions. Before going to Dakar I had firmly believed that the British system of law was universally esteemed by the lawyers of most nations and was considered to be the finest in the world. I soon discovered that this was by no means the case. The delegates on my commission thought their own systems just as good as ours, and in some respects superior to it. Furthermore, they were critical of the apparent reluctance of the British judiciary to attend international legal seminars and of their seeming lack of interest in the laws of other countries. They viewed with slight amusement the lofty prefixes which British Judges added before their names.

From then on I became a permanent member of the second Study-Commission. Jean-Pierre achieved his desire of increasing the British representation on the IJA from three delegates to six, when a Lord Justice of Appeal from Northern Ireland, as well as a High Court Judge and a Sheriff from Scotland were added to our delegation. We still remained the only country in the Association which required its delegates to pay their own fares to the annual meetings.

Our delegation at the IJA were acutely embarrassed by the fact that we were continually accepting the hospitality of other member-countries without ever returning it. There was little or no prospect of offering ourselves as hosts in the foreseeable future because we had been informed that the Treasury would not be willing to bear the cost. Therefore, we were all astounded in the closing session of a meeting in

Oslo when our magistrate delegate rose to his feet and invited the Association to come to London for their meeting the following year. He told us afterwards that a group of his wealthy business friends were willing to pay for everything and no government subsidy would be necessary.

The delegates at Oslo, who had received the magistrate's announcement with excitement and acclaim, were destined for disappointment. Nothing more was heard about the impending London visit and, in fact, during the ensuing year the IJA held no annual meeting for the first time since it had been formed.

I was planning to write a book on the history of discipline in the British Army. I had been given an introduction to John Andrews, the Chief Librarian of the Ministry of Defence library in Whitehall, who took a kindly interest in my project and guided me in my research. One afternoon I was in his library studying an official publication about punishments in the army during the First World War when I came across a table showing that between 1914 and 1920 a total of 346 officers and men had been sentenced to death by courts martial and executed by firing squads. Apart from 37 of them, who were convicted of murder, all the rest had committed military offences, mostly desertion or cowardice. I asked John where I could find the details of these cases. He told me that the files were in the Public Records Office at Kew, but that no one was allowed to see them as they were closed to the public until 75 years after the trials had taken place.

I was determined to inspect the files if it was in any way possible for me to do so. I went to see the Judge Advocate General, Harold Dean, and put my request to him. I pointed out that several books had been published during the previous few years which gave wildly exaggerated figures for the number of men who had been executed, and horrific, invented accounts of their trials. The secrecy regarding what had really occurred was only serving to foster rumours and speculation. Even when the files were finally opened for public inspection under the 75-year rule they would only become available very gradually over quite a long period and it would be difficult to form an accurate assessment of their contents until they had all been seen. Harold Dean told me he could see the force of my argument. He said that he had read a couple of my books and considered me to be a careful, objective and non-sensational writer. He was willing, therefore, to submit my application to the Ministry of Defence, together with his personal recommendation that it should be granted.

Much to my surprise the Ministry of Defence decided to allow me privileged access to all the court martial files I wanted to see. They laid down three conditions. First, that I showed my manuscript both to them and to the Judge Advocate General before passing it to a publisher; secondly, that my book did not mention the names or the regiments of the executed men; and thirdly, that I did not make known the fact that I had seen any closed documents in carrying out my· research. I willingly gave my consent. I then encountered a new difficulty. The files could not be removed from the Public Records Office, which did not open at the weekend, and I could not possibly get down to Kew sufficiently early to examine them on a weekday afternoon. When I told Harold Dean of the problem he kindly offered to draw out the closed files in batches, and to keep them locked up in his office where I could look at them. Twice a week, from then on, I used to go to his offices at the top of Whitehall after I had finished in court in the late afternoon. I generally arrived there when all the members of his staff had left, but he had lent me a key and had put a room at my disposal in which I could work for as long as I liked.

It was an engrossing yet distressing experience to read through the files in the deserted stillness of the Judge Advocate General's offices. I knew that I was probably the first person to have looked at them since they were stowed away during the distant years of the First World War. As I studied each case I pictured the scene at some estaminet just behind the line, or in a dugout lit by candles. The three officers who constituted the court sitting side-by-side at a trestle-table; the accused soldier standing nervously in front of them; the prosecutor fulfilling his relentless task; and the young defending officer ineptly groping for a question to ask or a point to put forward in mitigation. It all came out from the notes scribbled down in pen or pencil by the Presidents of the courts while the witnesses were giving their evidence.

At first I read the files with a completely open mind, but I soon became convinced that few of the executed soldiers had received the most elemental form of justice. They had been tried by officers who had no judicial training and who, for the most part, were given no legal guidance. The cases for the defence were seldom adequately presented, and when matters were raised which might have established the innocence of the accused they were rarely investigated. After the trials had finished the papers were passed to a succession of senior commanders for their opinions as to whether or not the sentence should be carried out. They had usually approved the death penalties without making any inquiries regarding the backgrounds or the circumstances of the condemned men. The whole process was made even more oppressive by the fact that the decision of a court martial was virtually unappealable.

The Duke of Wellington had once said that all punishment was imposed for the sake of example, so using his words, I called my book *For the Sake of Example*. Directly it was completed I gave it to Harold Dean to read in accordance with my undertaking. He had no complaints whatsoever about my treatment of the trials, but he objected to several of my comments on the arrogant behaviour and the lack of intelligence of certain of the more senior officers in the pre-1914 British Army. However, he accepted my contention that these observations were not based upon any of the closed documents which I had been allowed to inspect, so he could not rightfully ask me to modify or to delete them. For their part, the Ministry of Defence approved my manuscript without requiring any alterations.

For the Sake of Example was published by Leo Cooper in conjunction with Secker and Warburg. Leo warned me that when the book came out it would probably create a great deal of interest and the media were bound to ask me how I had obtained my information. I took up this point with the Ministry of Defence and they agreed to absolve me from the requirement that I must not disclose my privileged access to the records. An official in the Lord Chancellor's Office told me there would be no objection to me being interviewed about the book, provided that I did not enter into any discussion regarding the restoration of capital punishment for murder.

Immediately after the publication of *For The Sake Of Example* I was interviewed about the book on a BBC television documentary and on a number of national and regional radio programmes. One of my broadcasts caused me an anxious moment. It was for *The World This Weekend,* the Sunday afternoon feature on Radio 4 which, I was told, had a very large listening public. Because I would be down at Chilham the Presenter had arranged that he would ask me the questions from London and I would answer them from an unmanned BBC studio in Canterbury. He assured me that although there would be no one there to assist me, I would have a set of clear and simple instructions telling me what to do. At the agreed time on the Sunday I arrived at the studio, which consisted of a single room full of equipment on the first floor of an office building. The microphone was standing on a table with a keyboard, a telephone, and a large card of printed directions beside it. I sat down and adjusted the necessary knobs and switches. After I had completed the preliminaries I was required to phone a Kent number and report that I was ready to begin. When I tried to do this I found, to my consternation, that I had rung a local radio station and was receiving a recorded message to say that they would be closed until Monday morning. I searched around frantically for some other number to call, aware that the vital minutes were slipping away. Fortunately, I found a letter from Broadcasting House lying in a drawer. I explained the situation to a girl on their switchboard and she immediately put me through to the Presenter who was waiting anxiously to hear from me.

Arnold and I used to write to each other once a week. I had only seen him on two occasions since he had gone to New Zealand during the year before I was called to the Bar, but we had remained very close because of our regular correspondence. In spite of the length of time he had been away I always had a lot to tell him because he liked to hear news of every member of the family and of all his erstwhile English friends. For his part, he used to describe his life in Auckland with Helen and their children. He had a wonderful gift of communication and when I was reading his letters it seemed as though he was actually present, speaking the words he had written.

It was a great shock, when Arnold was undergoing one of his rare illnesses, to hear from Helen that he had been diagnosed as suffering from lung-cancer, which was considered to be inoperable. My cousins in Canberra had invited me to stay with them again and had suggested that I might combine my visit with another trip to New Zealand. It was apparent there was no time to lose so I started to make my arrangements immediately. I intended to break my flight for a few days in Delhi on my outward journey, and to stop off for a while in Singapore on my way back. I had just booked my air tickets and arranged my hotel accommodation en route when I received a telegram from Helen telling me that Arnold was dead.

Noreen and Eve were as saddened as I was by the news. We each had our own separate memories of Arnold and we had still regarded him, in many ways, as being the head of our family.

One morning after I had returned from Australia I was telephoned by Lord Justice Eveleigh. He told me he had been asked to appoint a couple of delegates to represent the British judiciary at a four-day colloquium to be held at Louvain-la-Neuve in Belgium and organised by the Commission of European Communities. The subject to be discussed was "Legal equality between women and men in the European Community." He could not get away to attend it himself and neither could Jean-Pierre Warner, so he was inviting a Scottish High Court Judge and me to form the British judicial delegation. There would be quite a lot of work to do beforehand, he said, as the two of us would have to be conversant with the British position in regard to any of the points which might arise. We would have to study the various relevant Acts of Parliament, White Papers and Statutory Instruments, as well as the Community Directives and judgments of the European Court on the matter. My travel and subsistence expenses would be paid by the organisers and my time in Belgium would be treated for statistical purposes as being ordinary working-days in court.

I told him that I would be very pleased to take part, and thanked him for nominating me.

There was a formidable amount of reading to get through so I started on it at once. A short while before the colloquium began I received my tickets and my travel instructions from Brussels. By the same post I had a letter from the Lord Chancellor's Department informing me that as my attendance at Louvain could not be classed as being part of my judicial function, the period I spent there would have to be deducted from my annual allocation of leave. I was so annoyed that I immediately wrote to Lord Justice Eveleigh asking him to nominate another Judge in my place. He rang me to know why I had changed my mind, so I told him what had happened. I said I was disgusted by the fact that I was going out as one of the two British representatives at an important conference of the European Community, and yet my presence there was being regarded as a glorified vacation. He entirely agreed with my attitude and he promised to take up the matter himself.

A few days later an official from the Lord Chancellor's Department invited me to come and see him, bringing with me all the details about the colloquium so that he could reconsider his previous decision. I suspected that this was merely a face-saving exercise, so I was not altogether surprised at the end of our meeting when he told me that he was now satisfied that my trip to Louvain could be treated as a part of my official duties as a Judge.

Most of the other countries were represented at the colloquium by fairly large delegations, including Judges from their highest courts. I was having a drink with the

Convener one evening and I congratulated him on the success of his arrangements. He thanked me and added, "I'm only too pleased that you and your Scottish colleague have come. We never expected that Britain would send any Judges at all."

By chance I became involved with another particularly pleasing international responsibility.

It had started when about a dozen successful Dublin barristers decided to join an Inn of Court in London and to get called to the English Bar. Under the existing regulations they were entitled to do this without passing any additional examination. They chose to become members of the Middle Temple, partly because it had had connections with Ireland in the past, and partly because they had been told that it was the friendliest of the four Inns. Nevertheless, they were expecting to encounter a certain amount of hostility when they came over for Call Day, as the IRA had carried out a series of particularly brutal murders both in Northern Ireland and in England a short while previously. To their surprise they were received with the utmost cordiality. During his speech after the Call ceremony had ended, the Treasurer welcomed the Irish contingent to the Inn and invited them all to join the Benchers for drinks before dinner. Peter Sutherland, the Irish Attorney-General at the time, was already a member of the Middle Temple. He happened to be in London on government business and he came to Hall to see his fellow-countrymen being called. The Treasurer heard he was there and asked him to dine with the Benchers at the High Table.

After dinner that evening, while I was having a cup of coffee in one of the Bencher's rooms, a waiter came in to tell me that the Irish would like to see me in Hall. "They want you to have a drink with them, Master," he said, "and they want to speak to you about something important."

There was always a convivial atmosphere in Hall after a Call Day dinner, with the newly-called barristers, most of them wearing their wigs and gowns for the first time, celebrating their achievement with their families and friends. When I joined the Irish they were grouped around a table drinking champagne. After we had been chatting for a few minutes they told me they were so appreciative of the way they had been treated that they would like to show their gratitude by entertaining a party of about 20 Middle Templars in Dublin for a weekend. They asked me if I would discuss their proposal with the Treasurer.

Our Treasurer that year was Sir John Arnold, the president of the family division. I went to see him next day and I told him about my conversation with the Dublin barristers. He said that we must certainly accept such a kind invitation and he put me in charge of the arrangements for the visit. We agreed that he should lead our party himself, and that it should not consist entirely of Benchers, but must include a sizeable proportion of the younger members of the Inn. He added with a smile, "and make sure you choose people with strong heads."

The Middle Temple visit to Dublin was a huge success. The Irish could not have been more hospitable. Every member of our group was accommodated in a private home;

we were entertained to dinner in the Hall of the Kings Inns, and there was an incessant round of parties the whole time we were there. During those few days a lot of mutual misconceptions were put right and a number of lasting friendships were formed. My own host and hostess were Nicky and Ellenor Kearns who lived in a fairly large house on the outskirts of the city. They had three young sons who were delightful boys and full of character. I first met them on the Saturday morning at breakfast. Ellenor, in an effort to speed their washing and dressing, had told them they were about to meet a renowned soldier. When they entered the dining room they regarded me with a certain amount of awe. But it did not last for long. As soon as they had settled round the table one of them asked me in how many wars I had fought. After I told them I had only taken part in one I saw their faces fall and their disillusionment was obvious. I knew then that my brief moment of stardom was irrevocably ended.

The next year the Middle Temple invited a group of Judges and barristers from the Kings Inns to come to London for the weekend and we endeavoured to entertain them as well as they had entertained us on our visit. Again, the event was entirely successful. Soon afterwards I was staying in Dublin and I had dinner with Nicky Kearns and Peter Sutherland, who was still the Attorney-General. We had a long discussion about the very warm relationship which had arisen between our two Inns and how it might be preserved in the future. We all agreed that if these reciprocal weekends were to take place every year it would strengthen our existing links, and it might even make a modest contribution to the cause of Anglo-Irish friendship.

From then on the Kings Inns and the Middle Temple used to entertain each other in alternate years. I was invariably asked to supervise the Middle Temple arrangements for these events, whether we were going to Dublin or the Irish were coming over to London. I invited three young barristers, whom I knew to be enthusiastic about the project, to join me in an unofficial standing committee. We never had any formal meetings, but we dealt with all our business at "working-dinners," which were extremely pleasant occasions and generally took place either at the Special Forces Club or at Simpson's Restaurant in the Strand.

The members of the family had known for some time that Eve was ill, but none of us had thought that her illness would be fatal. When she was admitted to hospital our principal concern had been how long she would be detained before she came home again.

Noreen had phoned me in the morning just before I left for court. She had been in tears and had spoken with difficulty. "Eve died an hour ago," she said. "Peter has just told me. He asked me to break it to you."

It is impossible, on the instant, to comprehend the death of someone you love deeply. Finality and everlastingness are equally difficult to envisage. For several days Eve was constantly in my thoughts, as she had been in the fullness of her life. I suppose that she and I had been as fond of each other as a sister and a brother ever can be. While we were growing up we had always been together. We had shared our wakening realisation of the world around us; our pleasures and excitements; our doubts, our sorrows, and our fears. When in adulthood we had gone our separate ways we had seemed to maintain contact by some form or extrasensory awareness which could constrict the greatest distances which divided us.

While I stood in prayer beside her newly dug grave I felt as though a part of me had died with her.

CHAPTER 31

Circuit Judges could retire on full pension after serving for 15 years or more, provided they had reached the age of 65. They were entitled to continue, if they wished to do so, until they were 72.

On my 68th birthday I notified the Lord Chancellor's Department that I wanted to retire in six months' time. I had then been on the Bench for 24 years - eight years as a metropolitan stipendiary magistrate and sixteen as a Circuit Judge. I still enjoyed the work and I still felt fit enough to do it, but I had always realized that I was under a greater strain than the majority of my colleagues because of my dyslexia, my dysgraphia, and the defect in my speech. I had constant difficulty in keeping up with witnesses when I was making notes of their evidence in court, and my voice became excessively tired when I had to sum up in a long case or to deliver a lengthy judgment. Furthermore, I had been enabled, after my head wound, to accomplish all I had endeavoured to accomplish - I had lived a normal life in my chosen profession.

I looked forward to spending more time in Chilham. I wanted to avoid the discomfort and stress of travelling in the Friday evening rush-hour; the jostling crowds on the underground; the packed compartments; the habitual turmoil at Charing Cross station; and the frantic dash to catch my train. Then, having to leave my cottage every Sunday afternoon for the return journey just when I had started to relax.

I might have imagined it, but the birds seemed unusually fearless in my garden at Chilham. While I was sitting on the patio working or reading the sparrows and robins would caper on either side of me. The blackbirds and thrushes, with infinite dignity, would roam about the lawn, sometimes passing a few feet away from my chair. I had a nesting-box for tits and even though it was very close to the cottage it was generally occupied for a few weeks in the early spring. Every year the house martins, welcome guests, would settle on my roof and at dawn and dusk they would make their swift sorties among the invisible swarms of flying insects. There were other species too, occasional visitors, like chaffinches, wood pigeons, collared doves, and pied wagtails. The only unwanted birds were the starlings who, in spite of their colourful summer plumage, I continued to regard as acquisitive and graceless marauders.

My final six weeks as a full-time Circuit Judge were spent at the Old Bailey. On my last day there I finished early and caught a taxi to Knightsbridge Crown Court, arriving just before the commencement of my farewell party, to which I had invited everyone who worked in the building. There were the customary speeches and toasts; the conventional presentation of a parting present. When it was over I gathered up my belongings from the room which had been my chambers for more than a decade and left it to my successor. In the evening I entertained some of my closest friends to dinner in a private room at the Garrick. Charles Potter, who was by then a leading silk at the revenue Bar, insisted on saying some flattering words about my time on the Bench, and all my guests drank to my health and happiness in retirement. At midnight my permanent judicial appointment came to an end.

I did not intend to retire completely because I had been

asked to continue sitting as a Deputy Judge on a part-time basis. But I knew it would not be the same as before. In future I would go to any court where I was needed. I would have no roots and no ties; the listing-officers, the clerks, and the ushers would be virtual strangers to me. Every Judge likes to create the atmosphere in his own court. This is hard enough to do even when you have your usual staff around you who are used to your ways. It is much more difficult when you are only a transient wanderer.

I spent the first few weeks of my retirement reading crime novels.

Tim Heald, the president of the Crime-Writers Association at the time, had asked me to serve on a panel which was going to choose the two best crime novels of the year, for the annual Golden Dagger and Silver Dagger awards. Most of the other panel-members were professional literary critics, but Tim had thought it would be interesting to include among them an experienced Judge with knowledge of the actuality of the criminal milieu.

I had to read eight books which had previously been placed on a short list. Although I was not a habitual reader of crime novels I enjoyed them enormously. I thought they were all well-written, with credible characters and ingenious plots, but I had no great difficulty in picking the two I liked best.

The awards were to be presented at a dinner of the Crime-Writers Association by Lord Deedes - Bill Deedes as he was generally called - the former Conservative Minister and a past editor of the *Daily Telegraph*. The panel of Judges met beforehand in a private room to discuss the short-listed books and to decide on the two we intended to select. We sat round a large table while Tim Heald, acting as chairman, invited each of us in turn to state our opinions. I was pleasantly surprised to find that the other panel-members, the experts, had made the same choices as I had done.

The dinner was a very stimulating occasion for me as I was sitting on the top table between Margaret Drabble, the novelist, and Alison, Tim's attractive wife.

During the following year I attended a most interesting International PEN congress in Seoul. Our South Korean hosts entertained us admirably and had also arranged a post-congress tour to the enchanting Pacific island of Chezu, well known, we were told, as a resort for honeymooners.

While we were staying at a hotel in Chezu an Austrian girl, a member of the PEN party, asked me if I ought to do so much with my weak heart.

I told her that I did not suffer from a weak heart.

"I assumed you did," she said, "because when we go on sight-seeing expeditions you usually drop behind, and whenever we climb any steps or hills you seem to get so short of breath."

Until then I had been pretending to myself that my heart was functioning perfectly normally, and I had been trying to ignore my persistent lack of energy and my increasing breathlessness after the slightest exertion. Now I realized that I was not imagining my condition; other people were beginning to notice it too. I had been hoping that my aortic valve would recover on its own, or, at least, would not deteriorate any more, in spite of my cardiologist's pessimistic prognosis.

After the trip to Chezu we were taken back to our hotel in Seoul. I was not returning home immediately as Nancy Ing, the president of Taiwanese PEN, had arranged for some European writers to visit Taiwan for a week as guests of her government, and she had invited me to join the group.

Nancy, a distinguished journalist and translator, was a fascinating person of immense kindness and charm. Her father had been a close associate of Sun Yat Sen, the Chinese Nationalist leader. He had met his wife, a Virginian, while he had been at a university in the United States. Nancy had been educated at a French convent, a British school in Shanghai and a Chinese university. She was now married to a successful builder in Taipei.

Our group, which consisted of about 15 people, flew from Seoul to Taipai. Nancy had organized our programme very thoughtfully. There were, of course, the official receptions, lunches, and dinners and the media interviews. However, we also had time to visit many places of beauty and interest on the island, and we were shown something of its cultural activities. I would have enjoyed our visit far more if I had not been continually troubled by lack of energy and shortness of breath. I was always lagging behind the rest of the group, usually in the company of the president of French PEN, the poet René Tavernier. René was in a poor state of health and died soon afterwards.

Immediately on my return to London I saw my cardiologist and he arranged for me to have a series of X-rays and tests. When the results were through he asked me to come and see him again. He had never believed in equivocation or in the "bedside-manner" approach.

"Your aortic valve has now become useless to you," he told me. "If you don't get something done about it you'll develop heart-failure and that will be that. I advise an immediate operation."

He suggested the name of a surgeon who was very experienced in the replacement of aortic valves, but he said that it was such a big operation I should decide for myself who was going to carry it out.

I asked the advice of a friend of mine at the Garrick, a well-known pathologist, and he recommended a young consulting-surgeon at the Brompton Hospital. My cardiologist approved of the choice, all the necessary arrangements were soon made, and a date was fixed for the operation.

I had to go into the Brompton Hospital on a Sunday afternoon to be operated upon the following morning. I had sat at Knightsbridge Crown Court for the whole of the preceding week, finishing late on Friday when the jury in my court convicted a 21-year-old man of robbery with violence. Ironically, the defendant's counsel, pleading for him to be treated with leniency, said that he would never have committed the offence if he had not been so overcome with anxiety because he was about to enter hospital for a cartilage operation on one of his knees.

I spent most of Saturday tidying up my papers and making sure I had left clear instructions as to the whereabouts of such documents as my will, my share certificates, and the title deeds of my cottage. In the evening my sister Noreen, who was still living in the flat above mine, gave a fiftieth birthday party for her daughter Miranda. This helped me from thinking too much about the future.

Throughout the years since I had received my head wound I had been sustained by prayer in every illness and tribulation that had come my way. I was praying at this time both for my operation to prove successful and for me to be able to approach it with a peace of mind which would persist until the final phase when I was being wheeled along to the operating theatre.

When I went to bed after Noreen's party I wondered whether I would be in for a troubled night. So far, my mind had been unclouded by worry or fear, but I suspected that a sudden, bleak moment of realization would come upon me. However, I slept well and I woke up on Sunday morning feeling calm and untroubled. Early in the afternoon my niece, Fenella, Peter's daughter, and her husband Nick collected me in their car and drove me to the Brompton Hospital. I tried to obliterate from my memory the unhappiness I had endured there in the past but as I entered the reception hall the high grey walls seemed to close in on me and I felt a sense of captivity. I was shown into a dark, gloomy room in the private wing by a nurse who told me not to undress yet because I would presently be going down to the X-ray department.

In the evening I was visited by an Indian doctor. He came up to the side of my bed and said solemnly, "I have brought a form for you to sign consenting to the operation. Before you do so, I want you to think about it very carefully. You'll be agreeing to undergo a major operation to your heart. There's a possibility you won't survive it. You must be clear about this; you might die tomorrow."

"I gather that I'll die quite soon if I don't have the operation," I replied.

"I'm afraid that is absolutely true," he said. "But even so, you should still think very seriously about it before you sign. If you like, I'll bring back the form in about an hour."

"That will be unnecessary," I told him. "I'll sign it now."

Afterwards a young woman came round to see me who told me she was one of the anaesthetists who would be looking after me during the operation. She took my blood pressure, sounded my heart, and asked me various questions about my war wounds. Then she examined my mouth and commented that they would try not to damage the crowns on my teeth but that some of them might get broken unavoidably.

Before she left she said, "When you come round from the anaesthetic tomorrow you'll be on a life-support machine and there'll be a lot of gadgets in your mouth and over your face. Don't try to remove them - it's some people's first reaction on coming to, and we have to paralyse their limbs. We don't like doing it but there's no alternative."

After she had gone I thought about her warning and I wondered how much control I would have of my thoughts and my actions after a lengthy period of anaesthetised insensibility.

My prayer for mental tranquillity was granted. Even

when I woke up on the Monday morning and the preliminaries for the operation were commenced my mind was at peace.

I came round in the intensive care ward. Two young nurses, who were seated on either side of my bed, were bending over me. There was some large, troublesome object pressed hard into the back of my mouth and there were tubes up my nose. Presently I became aware of a blood-transfusion drip in my leg and of wires running out from my heavily bandaged chest to an instrument above my head. I felt weak, aching and exhausted.

The nurses saw that my eyes were open and at once became attentive, wiping my brow, adjusting my pillows, and assuring me that the appliance would soon be removed from my mouth. There followed a protracted, distressful period of impotence and chronic discomfort - but no definable pain.

At last a doctor walked up and looked at the instrument. "We'll try him on his own now," he said. The contraption was taken out of my mouth and I heard my heart commence to beat.

The next morning I was moved into a high-dependency ward which contained six beds and had at least one nurse continuously present. I remained there for three days and during this time my blood-drip and my catheter were removed. Then I was taken back to the room I had occupied before the operation. I was receiving no medication at that stage except heart-tablets and an occasional pain-killer, but a physiotherapist was visiting me regularly to give me breathing exercises and to take me for short walks along the corridors. After another week in hospital, Peter collected me in his car and drove me down to Chilham where I had arranged for someone to stay with me until I felt strong enough to look after myself.

I was soon leading a fairly normal life, and I no longer suffered from shortness of breath. I had convalesced for a couple of months before my new cardiologist considered that I was fit enough to resume my part-time sitting in court.

Almost immediately after my recovery Noreen was diagnosed as suffering from cancer of the colon. Despite an immediate operation the disease spread rapidly to her liver and her lungs. Her condition was then untreatable. She was very brave about it and although she had always dreaded the prospect of illness or of old age, she seemed to accept the imminence of death with a patient resignation. She died in a hospice at Taunton, where her daughter Miranda was living.

I was now the only one of the four of us who remained.

I had made up my mind that my acquisition of an artificial heart-valve would not be allowed to restrict the scope of my former activities. The International PEN congress that year was due to take place in Toronto and Montreal, barely six months after my operation. However, my cardiologist told me that it would be all right for me to attend provided I minimized the fatigue of the journey by flying to Canada and back more expensively by club class. I agreed to do this, but I found that the additional comfort on the flight from Heathrow was poor compensation for the loss of company of the rest of the English delegation who were all travelling in the tourist class. As I was still getting tired rather quickly I decided to return home as soon as the congress was over, instead of joining a party of my friends who were visiting Quebec.

I spent the final day of my trip to Canada with Pat Barker, as we were staying at the same hotel in Montreal and were both flying back to London the following morning, though we were travelling by different air lines. Pat, who wrote her novels and short stories as A.L. Barker, was small and deceptively demure in appearance. She was an extraordinarily interesting and most amusing companion with a shrewd perception of human nature. The time passed all too quickly.

The International Society of Judges were holding a meeting in West Berlin a few months after my return from Canada, and as usual I was invited to attend as one of the two English representatives. An old friend of mine, Sir Basil Kelly, a Lord Justice of Appeal, was to be the Northern Ireland member of the British delegation. I met Basil and his wife Pamela at Heathrow when their plane arrived from Belfast and we flew to Germany together.

We checked into the conference hotel in Berlin late in the afternoon, and the Kellys suggested that I should come to their room for a drink in about an hour's time before we went down to dinner.

The Judges in Northern Ireland had to be protected night and day from attack by terrorists and they could never leave their homes without a police escort. It must have been a great relief to them on their trips abroad to be freed from these intensive security precautions. However, the IRA were active in the West German Republic and had carried out several murders there a short time previously. As a consequence, Basil had been told that there would be an officer from the German Special Branch on continuous duty while he was at the hotel.

The Kellys had a small alcove leading off their bedroom, and we were sitting there having our pre-dinner drinks when someone knocked at the door. Basil went to see who it was. When he returned to the alcove he told us that a plumber had come to carry out a minor repair on the shower in their bathroom. I was slightly apprehensive about the man and as soon as he left I asked whether either at them had reported the defect. They both replied that they had known nothing about it - in fact, the shower had seemed to be working perfectly normally. They thought that my concern was fully justified, so Basil immediately rang the reception desk. He was informed that as far as was known the hotel plumber had not visited his room that evening and the matter was being reported to the police.

Presently a bunch of men came pounding down the corridor, led by Basil's special branch detective. The three of us were ushered out of the bedroom while a search was begun for a booby-trap or a time bomb. Ten minutes later Basil was told by the detective that it had been discovered that the caller had been the hotel plumber after all.

Basil and Pamela had remained imperturbable throughout the episode. Perhaps they had been living under the threat of terrorist violence for so long that they had become inured to false alarms: or perhaps it was just the indomitable courage of the Northern Irish people.

After the International Judges Association meeting had finished Basil and I crossed the border into Communist East Berlin and we spent a day in the desperately dreary, impoverished area of the city, where the numerous armed policemen reminded me of the photographs I had seen of pre-war Nazi storm troops.

I was finding, as many others have found, that after your retirement the days seem just as crowded as they were in the fullness of your working life. Although the urgency had lessened and the pressure abated, there was never sufficient time for all the things I wanted to do. It may well have been that my pauses for thought had lengthened and become more frequent, or that my attitude to life had become more leisurely; or it may merely have been the gradual process of deceleration, which presages the approach of your twilight years.

On average I was sitting in court as a temporary Judge for about one week in every three. Apart from that, I spent most of my mornings and afternoons writing. It was a desperately slow and labourious procedure as I had to break off repeatedly to check my spelling, and as often as not I was unable to visualise the structure and configuration of the simplest words, which caused me endless trouble in looking them up in a dictionary. A further problem arose from the fact that I used to write in longhand and my manuscripts had to be typed by someone who could read my ungainly scrawl. However, I managed to finish two more books during the early years of my retirement. The first was a history of the use of the military in aid of the civil power in Britain. It was published by Routledge both in a hardback and in a paperback edition. The second book, commissioned by Leo Cooper, was a study of the mutiny of the famous Irish regiment the Connaught Rangers, which had occurred in India in 1922.

To my great delight I was elected to serve on the General Committee of the Garrick. Our meetings took place in the late afternoon on the first Thursday of the month and were always both lively and interesting. We usually reached our decisions without much argument, but when matters were contentious the ensuing debates were conducted with eloquence, wisdom and wit. After a meeting we would adjourn to the bar, which was generally crowded by that time as Thursday evenings were very popular at the club.

I went on attending PEN international congresses in whatever part of the world they took place. During the year before I retired from part-time judicial sittings Josephine Pullein-Thompson, Francis King and I went to a literary conference organized by the Croatian Centre of PEN , at the height of the civil war which had followed the break-up of Yugoslavia. Originally it was to have been held in the picturesque port of Dubrovnik, but for reasons of safety the venue was altered to the island of Hvar, just off the Croatian coast. The participants, 200 or so authors, journalists and broadcasters, had assembled in Venice one afternoon and embarked on a specially chartered ship to cross the Adriatic Sea. Someone called it "The Ship of Fools" because we were going to pass within easy range of the Serbian guns. There was a spirit of adventure on board; the bars were packed all the evening and most of us retired to our cabins long after midnight. Peter, my brother-in-law, had been extremely doubtful if we would get through the United Nations naval blockade, but in fact we were not stopped at all. The next day we arrived at Hvar where a large crowd and a brass band were waiting for us on the quayside. We were greeted by cheering and martial music, as though we had run the gauntlet of enemy fire to reach the shelter of the island. At the conclusion of the conference we all spent two nights in Dubrovnik, which had recently been bombarded by Serbian artillery but was quiet for the whole of our stay.

Another memorable trip that year was a visit to Poland, newly freed from the yoke of Communism, as a guest of the Polish PEN Centre. Four of us from London were invited, the others being Ronald Harwood the playwright, who had just taken over as International President of PEN, his Russian wife Nathasha, and Josephine Pullein-Thompson, still the General Secretary of the English Centre. I had retained an immense admiration for the Polish people ever since the war years and I was eager to see their country.

The Polish and English PEN Centres had developed close ties of friendship. During the latter years of Communist oppression in Poland, the Government had regarded an independent democratic organization like PEN with suspicion and hostility. Two delegates had been allowed to attend at every international congress, but they had never known if on their return to Warsaw they would be arrested and charged with involvement in subversive activities. In 1983 the elected committee of the Polish Centre had been deposed by authorities and a puppet committee of Communist writers had been appointed in its place. At the international congress at Caracas in Venezuela a short while later the English and Austrian Centres had proposed a joint resolution condemning this action and declaring the nomination of the new committee to be invalid. After a short discussion the resolution was adopted with universal approval. The English delegates at Caracas who had helped to draft and to present it were Josephine Pullein-Thompson and myself.

The four of us flew to Warsaw and we were met at the airport by Artur Miedzyrzecki, the president of Polish PEN, and Anna Trzeciakowska, his vice-president, both of whom were the warmest of hosts from the start to the end of our visit. We were accommodated at a comfortable hotel and spent the next few days in sightseeing, interviews, and entertainment. Warsaw was still impregnated with memories of the thraldom and suffering its people had endured during the German occupation in the Second World War. Anna's husband had been severely wounded in the gallant attempt of the Polish Home Army to liberate Warsaw from its brutal oppression. They had fought a brave and hopeless fight against enormous odds before their Commander had sent his final tragic message to the Allies, "Our struggle is at its last agonizing stage. I shall be compelled to surrender."

We travelled by train from Warsaw to Cracow, the capital city of Poland until early in the seventeenth century. We spent several fascinating days there walking around the Old Town, with its ancient walls, its promenades and its impressive buildings.

After we returned home my esteem for the Polish nation was greater than ever.

I had been assessed as 100 per cent disabled since I was invalided out of the army, and I had not appeared before a war pensions medical board since the early 1950s. In fact, my disabilities did not alter until I reached the age of 70, when I noticed a deterioration in the functioning of my right leg and my limp became more evident. I attributed this to the neurological damage resulting from my head wound, and I regarded it as something that I would have to accept.

Early one Sunday morning, while I was alone at my cottage in Chilham, I had great trouble getting out of my bath, the left side of which was along a wall, so close that there was no exposed edge and nothing else to hold. Previously I had always heaved myself to my feet from a sitting position by grasping the top end of the bath behind my back with my left hand and taking the full weight of my body on my left arm. However, each time I tried to do this I slipped back again. Eventually, after about half an hour, I managed to struggle on to my knees and then to stand up. It was an unpleasant experience.

The next day I mentioned what had happened to a neighbour of mine, who had been a senior social worker before her marriage, and she advised me to consult the War Pensioners' Welfare Service. "This is just the sort of thing they're there to deal with," she said. "They'll arrange for an occupational therapist to look at your bathroom and to tell you exactly where you need to have handholds."

I knew that the War Pensioners' Welfare Service was a component of the Department of Social Security which had been set up in order to deal with the particular needs of the war-disabled. I wrote to their local office in South London and I was visited in my flat by a pleasant lady who introduced herself as the War Pensioner's Welfare Officer for the area. She told me that Chilham was outside her locality, but that she had referred my bathing trouble to the appropriate office in Kent. Her real purpose in coming to see me, she went on, was to find out if I had any other problems due to my disabilities. I replied that I could only think of the obvious difficulties of a one-armed person living alone - such routine matters as, for instance, the cutting of toenails or the sewing-on of buttons. She advised me to have my toenails cut in future by a good chiropodist. Since I had not been wounded in the feet, she added, I would have to pay the cost myself, but it would be fairly inexpensive. With regard to replacing buttons, she suggested that I should employ someone to come in regularly and do my sewing for me.

In due course I received a letter from South-East Kent Area Social Services. It began by saying that the nature of my problem had been explained to them by the War Pensioner's Welfare Service, and continued:

"All bath equipment in South East Kent is supplied by the Health Authority, and unfortunately, unless clients fit their criteria of suffering from incontinence, or a skin condition, clients have to purchase their own."

They enclosed several manufacturers' brochures advertising elaborate and costly bath seats which could be raised or lowered automatically by means of a hand-switch.

I decided that it would be simpler and far more economical to have a shower installed at my cottage.

In the spring of 1993, when I had just passed my seventy third birthday, I informed the Lord Chancellor's Department that I did not wish to continue any longer with my part-time judicial work. There were several reasons why I did this. Knightsbridge Crown Court had just moved from its building in the West End to a new location in Borough, south of the river, which was difficult for me to reach by public transport. Also, my worsening limp was causing me some embarrassment at the moments of entering or leaving a courtroom, when everyone present was standing and all eyes were on the Bench. A further cause for my decision to retire completely was that the media spotlight had been focused increasingly on the judiciary and there were incessant complaints about cases being tried by elderly Judges.

I had enjoyed my judicial career immensely and I could only hope that I had fulfilled my duties with a reasonable degree of competence. I had always realized that I was incredibly fortunate, because if the full extent of the brain-damage resulting from my head wound had been known in the first place it is most improbable that I would ever have been appointed to the Bench.

After my heart operation I had been told that my

artificial aortic valve would probably last for about eight years. By 1994 I had had it for five years, but I was determined to keep up all my interests and activities as long as it was possible to do so. In fact, 1994 proved to be rather an eventful year for me. In the early summer, to my surprise I received an invitation to the State Banquet at the Portsmouth Guildhall given in celebration of the 50th anniversary of the D-Day landings in Normandy. The Queen was present with the Duke of Edinburgh and various other members of the Royal Family, as well as the Heads of State of most of the nations which had contributed to the Allied war effort. It was a most impressive assembly of notabilities and must have been a considerable responsibility for those in charge of the security arrangements. And I had been elected Autumn Reader at the Middle Temple, an office which continued from the beginning of July until the end of December. The Reader's function was mostly honorary, but not entirely so. At every Call ceremony in Hall, and there were three of them during my Readership, he had to announce the full names of all the students who were being called to the Bar, and to present them separately to the Treasurer. A large number of our students came from Africa and the Far East, and the correct pronunciation of some of their names would have been difficult for a Westerner without any speech defect. I also had to give a reading in Hall after a term-time dinner on a subject of my own choice, and to make a speech about myself to my fellow-Benchers after presiding at the Reader's Feast.

And so it still went on.

People have sometimes asked me where I found the source of strength in confronting adversity. I have replied, "My principal strength has come from my Christian faith and from constant prayer."

Of one essential truth I feel certain. If grave misfortune befalls you in your earlier years, it need not be the end of your life - in many ways it can be a new beginning.

INDEX

AB refers to Anthony Babington